HEINRICH HEINE
Selected Works

HEINRICH HEINE

Selected Works

Translated and Edited by
HELEN M. MUSTARD

Poetry Translated by Max Knight

RANDOM HOUSE
New York

Library of Congress Cataloging in Publication Data

Heine, Heinrich, 1797–1856.
  Heinrich Heine: selected works.

  Includes bibliographical references.
  I. Mustard, Helen Meredith, ed. and tr.
II. Knight, Max, tr.
PT2316.A3M8 1973   831′.7   73–5095
ISBN 0–394–46052–9

Manufactured in the United States of America

FIRST EDITION

Contents

Introduction

More than a century has passed since Heine's death, but he still remains one of the most enigmatic figures among German writers. Very little is known about certain periods of his life, such as his student days in Bonn or his futile efforts to succeed in business; and his relationship with certain persons—for instance, with his cousin Amalie Heine, long assumed to be his truly great love and the inspiration of many of his poems, or, in later years, with his wife—seems to evade our grasp for lack of sufficient factual knowledge. Few poets wrote more about themselves, their feelings, thoughts, and experiences, either in letters to family and friends or in published works—much of his prose and poetry is openly presented as "autobiography"—yet precisely when Heine appears to reveal the most about himself, he actually gives us such a confusing mixture of fact and fantasy, of seriousness and jest, that he succeeds, whether or not this was his aim, in veiling his own real person in a mist of uncertainty. Thus the controversy has continued for a hundred years and more on matters ranging from the apparently trivial question as to the date of his birth to more fundamental questions. In how far was Heine's Jewish origin a problem for him in everyday life and in his own philosophy of life? What exactly was his political position? Did he really achieve a religious faith in his last years? It would be easy to add to these questions but

difficult to give an unequivocal answer to most, and one
of the striking, and fascinating, features of books or arti-
cles written about him is the sharp disagreement among
critics on basic issues. Such disagreement reveals some-
thing about Heine himself. It is not merely lack of perti-
nent facts that often makes it hard to understand him as
a person and a poet, but also the elusive complexity of
his own personality.

Heine was born in Düsseldorf in 1797[1] of Jewish par-
ents. Harry, the name he bore until his conversion to
Lutheranism in 1825, was the oldest of four children.
Charlotte, the second child, was only three years
younger, and except for an occasional rupture, Harry's
devotion to her remained steady throughout his life. His
two brothers, Gustav and Maximilian, being eight and
ten years younger, did not share in Heine's childhood
experiences as did his sister, and their careers as adults
differed sharply from that of their older brother, for they
both became very wealthy, Gustav as editor of a journal
in Vienna, and Max as a doctor in St. Petersburg.

Heine's parents did not rear their children in a strict
religious fashion. In his *Memoirs* Heine says that his fa-
ther was a very religious man, but it was his mother, not
the charming and unsuccessful dealer in textiles, who
apparently set the guidelines for Harry's education, and,
being liberal and enlightened and very ambitious for her
eldest son, she sent him to a Jesuit school, where he
received the customary humanistic training, somewhat
as Heine describes it playfully in the *Buch Le Grand.* He-
brew, of which his knowledge appears to have been

1. This is now the generally accepted date of his birth. It is to be hoped that
the lengthy, and often trivial, argument over the date has ended. In all fairness
to the many scholars who took part in this argument, it should be noted that
Heine did not make things easy for his biographers. From 1825 on, the year
in which he became a Protestant, he gave the year 1799 as his birth date, thus
providing another topic for scholarly speculation, namely, the purpose of the
falsification.

slight, he had learned earlier during a brief term in a small Jewish school.

After the early school years the problem of Harry's future occupation arose. He showed no special talent for anything in particular, and since funds were not plentiful, the decision was made to prepare him for business and finance, a field in which his wealthy uncle Salomon Heine of Hamburg might be willing to assist him. This experiment was a flat failure. He tried his hand as banker's assistant, then as a grocery clerk in Frankfurt, and finally went to his uncle in Hamburg, who, after giving him a year's training in his own firm, set him up in business for himself. The end of another six months saw the failure of Harry Heine & Co., and it became clear that he was not meant to be a businessman.

We know little about these years in the world of commerce, though they must have been torture for a young man of Heine's temperament, but we do know that they marked the beginning of one of the most crucial relationships with other people, the relationship with his uncle, whose way of life was completely incompatible with Heine's nature and on whom he was to be totally or partially dependent for many, many years. It was Uncle Salomon who provided the money to finance Heine's university studies, first at Bonn, then at Göttingen, and later in Berlin. His purpose was ostensibly to obtain a degree in law, but he neglected his law studies for others which interested him more, especially literature, and learned just enough about legal matters to pass without distinction the necessary examinations for the law degree.

During this first long stay in Hamburg Heine fell in love with his cousin Amalie, and she undoubtedly inspired some of his earliest poetry. Being penniless and without prospects, he could not have hoped, however, for marriage with a millionaire's daughter. On a later visit after Amalie's marriage he was apparently much taken with her younger sister Therese, but it is surely wrong, as earlier critics have consistently done, to interpret the many love poems Heine wrote in the '20's to his infatuation with these two girls; in fact, it seems a mistake to interpret them as directly autobiographical. The *Book of Songs* would have been written even if Amalie and Therese Heine had never existed.

In 1825, shortly before the last examination for the degree, Heine was baptized and became a member of the Lutheran church, a step for which, as he himself said, he was censured by friends and enemies alike. Heine did not take the step without due consideration, and he did not take it for religious reasons. He never displayed any enthusiasm for the Lutheran church, although he always cherished a great respect for Luther himself and for the contribution of the Reformation to German intellectual history. He became a Protestant purely for practical reasons, it being quite impossible for an unbaptized Jew to enter the legal profession or become a university professor in Germany at that time, and one can scarcely blame him for doing what many prominent and respectable Jews had already done. Such "conversions" were apparently accepted as a matter of course by both liberal Jews and Christians, and it is clear that Heine's millionaire uncle, though remaining a Jew himself, approved of his nephew's act.

Heine's letters to a close friend, Moses Moser, indicate that Heine himself had some qualms about the integrity of his action, even though he had no very strong roots in the Jewish faith, but the real mistake that he made was in assuming that baptism would open the way for a professorship at a university. This is only one instance among many which show how very unrealistic Heine often was in everyday affairs. He at first hoped for a professorship at the University of Berlin through the influence of his friend Karl August Varnhagen von Ense, a leading literary figure of the time, whose Jewish wife, Rahel, had so warmly welcomed the young student and poet to her *salon,* frequented by most of the famous men and women in Berlin. This hope was dashed, only to be replaced in 1828 by the even more preposterous hope of an appointment to a professorship at the University of Munich. If Heine's qualifications for a professor of literature in Protestant Berlin had been meager indeed—the possession of a law degree and the publication of a few poems and travel sketches and two bad plays—his qualifications for a similar appointment in Catholic Munich would seem to have been nonexistent. It is incredible that Heine could have supposed it possible for a Protestant Jew to obtain such a post, even with a friend at court and the reigning monarch favorably disposed toward him, as Heine fondly, but naively, believed, especially since Heine at the same time, with self-destructive behavior frequently characteristic of him, openly cultivated a very dubious person by the name of Wit von Dörring, who was disliked and distrusted by the very court from which Heine hoped for his financial salvation. Yet he not only hoped, he counted on it, and when, in the winter of 1828, on returning from a trip to Italy, he received the news that King Ludwig had refused to appoint him, it was a bitter blow, a blow which certainly accounts, in part at least, for the strongly anti-Catholic bias of *The Romantic School* and *Concerning the History of Religion and Philosophy in Germany,* written and published a few years later.

Heine had begun publishing poems as early as 1822, and his first volume of *Travel Sketches,* containing among other things *The Harz Journey* and *The North Sea,* appeared in 1826, but in 1827 the book that was to make Heine famous throughout the Western world, the *Book of Songs,* a carefully selected and arranged collection of his early poems, was published for the first time. This collection is now so well known, partly because of the poems themselves—Who does not know Lorelei?— partly because so many of the poems were set to music by famous composers, Schubert, Schumann, Brahms, and others, that many people assume the book made Heine famous overnight. Actually it sold quite slowly, and not until about a decade later was Heine's fame as a lyric poet well established even in Germany. His *Travel Sketches,* four volumes published between 1826 and 1831, were much better known.

Heine was now launched on his career as a writer, but he was far from being financially independent. He continued to ask and to receive, sometimes grudgingly, his Uncle Salomon's assistance, and was thus able to devote himself to writing and to visit Italy and England, as well as to spend several vacations on the island of Norderney, the inspiration for his cycle of sea poems and a prose essay.

In 1830, when reports of the July Revolution in France reached Germany, they were received enthusiastically by liberal Germans, and Heine, who likewise admired the determination of the French to achieve political liberty and equality, saw here an opportunity to report first-hand on conditions there and thus continue his series of *Travel Sketches,* which, though severely criticized in some quarters, had nonetheless been widely read. It was with this intention that he went to Paris in May, 1831. At that time he could have had no idea that this date was to be a turning point for him and that France was to be his home for the rest of his life. His political difficulties with German governments, especially with Prussia, which would have made return to Germany difficult if not impossible, had not yet begun. In later years Heine often spoke and wrote of himself as an exile; this was one of those dramatic poses which Heine cultivated and which were often used to great effect in his writings.

Paris received Heine with welcoming arms. He found there many Germans who were in a position to introduce him to French intellectual and artistic circles, men such as Mendelssohn, Meyerbeer, Alexander von Humboldt, and many others. He was well acquainted with French literature, had grown up in a part of Germany neighboring on France and had lived quite pleasantly under French occupation from 1806 to 1813, spoke the language fluently if not always idiomatically, and though at first he was a literary unknown, he was accepted with amazing rapidity by leading Frenchmen—and women— and was soon on intimate terms with persons like Balzac, George Sand, Alfred de Musset, and Berlioz, to mention only a few. This he undoubtedly owed not only to his German friends, but in large part to his own charm. He was, after all, a very personable, intelligent, witty, and gifted young man, intensely interested in French life and enthusiastic about Paris. Very soon his earlier works like *The Harz Journey* and *Buch Le Grand* appeared in French translation, and he was no longer an "unknown" but a very well-known personage in his own right.

The move to Paris also brought with it a change in the character of Heine's prose writings. Until this time his essays or sketches had largely been the outgrowth of personal experiences, such as the walking tour of the Harz described, not factually, but with imaginative exaggeration and fantasy, the *Buch Le Grand,* composed of one part autobiography, one part fiction, and one part a deep bow to Laurence Sterne, at that time Heine's idol as a writer, or the *English Fragments,* his reactions, chiefly negative, to England and the English. It would not be true to say that in Paris Heine's writing became more factual. He did write *Conditions in France* like the journalist which he actually was, giving a more or less accurate account of life in Paris under the citizen king. But facts were never as important to Heine as impressions and interpretations, and his essays on French painters, on music and musicians, and on French drama are just as remote from purely factual reality as the earlier works. Nor would it be true to say that Heine now wrote more objectively than in his first prose works. Heine never wrote objectively. He always wrote with a bias, for such was his nature.

The change, it seems to me, lies in the fact that Heine now formed for the first time a clear conception of his mission as a prose writer. As a lover of France, and of Germany too, despite the harsh criticisms which he fired at his native country from time to time, he desired quite seriously to serve as an interpreter of France to his fellow countrymen and as an interpreter of Germany to the French, at that time so lamentably ill-informed about German literature and intellectual life, in the hope of bettering the understanding between the two countries. This is the focus of most of his prose works after his arrival in Paris.

His first report to Germany on things French was the essay *French Painters,* followed very shortly by the series of articles called *Conditions in France.* Both appeared in German journals in 1831–1832. He then turned to the second part of his mission, producing between 1832 and 1835 his two major prose works, *The Romantic School* and *Concerning the History of Religion and Philosophy in Germany.* He wrote the first to amplify and correct the information on German literature given by Madame de Staël in her book on Germany, *De l'Allemagne,* published in France in 1814. Any reader will see that Heine does not write literary history with objective detachment. He attacks vigorously, and sometimes unjustly, those men whom he dislikes, and praises with enthusiasm those he admires, and he makes factual errors, some of which I have pointed out. Despite his obvious prejudices, he often shows a real gift for presenting in a paragraph or two the essence of a writer, and his undisguised partiality or dislike makes for lively reading. The book on religion and philosophy is also biased, but on the whole it is a more balanced account than the history of the Romantic School, possibly because it contains no figure who aroused such virulent antipathy in Heine as did August Wilhelm Schlegel. The memorable passages on Luther, Lessing, and Kant show Heine at his best and indicate clearly that, in spite of his many similarities to the Romanticists in motifs, in his love of fantasy, his interest in folklore, etc., he frankly avowed his prime allegiance to that other prominent strain in German intellectual life, the heritage of the age of Enlightenment.

The conclusion of this work has been and still is a controversial passage in Heine's writings. After the advent of Hitler it was generally interpreted as a prophetic insight into the intellectual and moral collapse of Germany, a collapse supposedly deriving directly from German philosophy, particularly Hegel. Before the 1930's such an interpretation was of course never thought of, though the passage was widely taken to be anti-German. In recent years a number of critics have questioned the validity of this interpretation. Some see in the description of the violence of the revolution yet to come in Germany a fear that the left-wing Hegelians might gain the upper hand, but at least one critic[2] sees it simply as one of Heine's typical, grotesquely witty extravaganzas, in which beneath the fun shines the hope of the ultimate triumph of what Heine viewed as the noblest current of German thought, that represented by Luther, Kant, and Fichte, namely, humanism. This view seems to me to be by far the most convincing.

Both works on Germany were much influenced by St.-

2. Ludwig Marcuse in his introduction to the reprint of John Snodgrass's translation, *Religion and Philosophy in Germany* (Boston, 1959), pp. xiii ff.

Simonism, which Heine became acquainted with in Paris and which admirably suited his mood during the first years there. He was already inclined to be anti-Catholic, due to his experience at Munich, and he found in St.-Simonism, or at least in what he chose to use of its philosophy, a rational foundation for the underlying thesis of both books. St.-Simon, the founder of the movement, had died before Heine went to Paris, but he knew at least one of the leading disciples, Barthélemy Prosper Enfantin, and read enough to be familiar with its tenets. Its aims were broadly socialist, including a sort of share-the-wealth economic system, a society in which traditional class distinctions were to be replaced by a division according to the abilities and contributions of its members, and a substitution of a pantheistic conception of God for traditional religious doctrines. Heine was not particularly interested in the social and political aspects of the movement; what appealed to him most was the so-called emancipation or rehabilitation of the flesh, and he used this emphasis on the value of the life of the senses in his attack on Christian asceticism, which he identifies with Catholicism. His exaggeration on both sides of the argument is so obvious that it needs no elaboration.

Another important change in Heine's life took place in 1834 when he met the girl who later became his wife. She was a Parisian grisette by the name of Crescentia Eugénie Mirat, not quite nineteen years old, almost illiterate, and according to some observers, not particularly attractive. Yet Heine fell madly in love with her at first sight, and despite some efforts to resist her charm, he soon succumbed and lived with her until 1841, when he married her at a Catholic ceremony according to her wish. Heine was always reticent about his relationships with women. We know almost nothing of his early love, if it was love, for his two cousins Amalie and Therese, and still less about any other affairs of the heart. About Mathilde, for this was the name Heine gave his wife, we have more factual information, from Heine's letters and from reports of friends and acquaintances, but the facts still do not explain what she must have meant to him. She remained scarcely literate, her extravagance knew no bounds, she did not fit with Heine's friends, French or German, she never had any idea that Heine was an important writer, and yet—. His devotion to her is obvious; the reasons for it are not. The love poems to and about her are not "romantic" lyric, but in their very homeliness they testify to the depth of this attachment. The poem on p. 444 beginning "I am not lured by Eden's fields" is a good example. "The heart hath reasons"—(may Pascal forgive me!)

The political situation in Germany affected the character of Heine's work to some extent, particularly after 1835, when he was listed in a decree of the Federal Diet of the German Federation as a member of the group of writers known as "Young Germany" and one of those whose works were banned. Heine's German publisher Campe in Hamburg, though perhaps less than generous with Heine in some ways, was extraordinarily clever about managing to avoid the censorship, and, as one might expect, the banned works were read all over Germany, even where sales were prohibited. Yet after the storm aroused by his history of German religion and philosophy, Heine felt it wiser to avoid controversial topics in his publications in the late '30's and was frank in admitting that he padded some volumes of his *Salon,* the general title he gave to the four volumes appearing after his move to Paris, with works of a deliberately light and often trivial nature. If a volume was over a certain length, it was not subject to censorship, so that the padding, while not adding to Heine's stature as a writer, served a useful purpose.

By the 1840's censorship had been somewhat relaxed, and in a resurgence of inspiration and energy Heine produced for the first time a considerable number of political lyrics and a satirical epic, *Germany, A Winter's Tale*, directed at Germany, especially Prussia, and a humorous epic poem, *Atta Troll, A Summer Night's Dream*, satirizing contemporary political poetry in Germany and the use of poetry as propaganda. He also wrote two more works on French life, *Concerning the French Stage*, published in France in 1838, but not appearing in Germany until 1840, and the first version of *Lutetia*, a series of articles on French politics and culture, with the emphasis on politics, written for the *Allgemeine Zeitung* in Augsburg from 1840 to 1843. In 1852, after his disappointment in the results of the Revolution of 1848, which seemed to him to have avoided facing the most serious and fundamental issues, Heine revised these articles, and they appeared in their altered form in two volumes in 1854.

In 1844 he also published his second large collection of lyrics, *New Poems*. The poems were not all new. Some had been written more than a decade earlier and resembled the lyrics in the *Book of Songs*, but new notes were to be found in the frankly sensual and often vulgar love poems to various unidentified women, in the group of political lyrics, and in the epic *Germany*, published here for the first time.

In the course of his life Heine wrote a substantial amount on politics, and yet he was never what one would call a political thinker. Because his attitude on specific issues shifted from time to time, he has often been accused of inconsistency, but this is to misunderstand Heine the person. He always preserved a measure of consistency, his belief in the best ideals of the eighteenth-century Enlightenment. Applied to politics, these included political freedom, and of course freedom of thought and speech, political justice for the individual, and political equality. He was not, however, an activist, and the attempts of German political emigrants to secure his participation in their meetings and intrigues irritated and repelled him. Though subscribing to the general principles of liberty and equality, he remained his whole life an "aristocrat," and he made no secret of his contempt for the "great unwashed." The account of his meeting with Wilhelm Weitling, apparently on one of his visits to Hamburg in the early '40's, as described by Heine in his *Confessions,* is a case in point. He speaks with repugnance of Weitling, a tailor's apprentice and Communist revolutionary, saying that what annoyed him most was Weitling's complete lack of respect for him, Heine. Weitling kept his cap on and remained seated while Heine stood! His belief in political equality did not include social or intellectual equality. To Heine the ideal form of government would probably have been a constitutional monarchy, and if he had not disliked England so much, he might well have held up its government as a model for other nations to follow.

Heine had never been robust. Even in his twenties he frequently complained of severe headaches, and as he grew older it became quite clear that he was not a well man. In the 1840's his health grew steadily worse, and in 1848 he collapsed completely and spent the remaining years until his death in 1856 in his "mattress tomb," as he called it, almost totally paralyzed and often in great pain. For a time he was still able to write, but only with difficulty; he had to hold up the eyelid of one eye with the one hand in order to see what he was reading or writing. His last works were dictated.

As if the strain of his progressive illness were not enough, he was overwhelmed with financial worries. His Uncle Salomon died in 1844, leaving Heine only a fixed sum, and his cousin Carl, the heir, stopped the yearly allowance which his uncle had provided the poet and had promised to continue to pay to him, and after his death the half of it to his widow. A long, nerve-racking, and rather unsavory family quarrel ensued. This conflict and the impossibility of living and meeting enormous medical expenses on his limited income from publications and the modest pension that the French government had granted him some years before, as well as the equal impossibility of providing for his wife after his death weighed on Heine's mind and mood. His wealthy brothers did lend him considerable sums occasionally, but what Heine needed was security of income, not occasional generosity. In the end, by threatening his cousin with the revelation of family skeletons in the *Memoirs* he intended to publish, Heine succeeded in obtaining his customary allowance in return for his promise to destroy the manuscript.[3]

Unbelievable as it may seem, Heine continued writing —or dictating to a secretary—what he had composed in his mind during sleepless nights. The major accomplishment was the completion of his third large collection of poetry, *Romancero,* poems written between 1844 and 1851, when the book was first published. It contains some of Heine's weakest poems, but also some of his very best. Six of the latter are included here, from "The Asra" through "Dame Care," pp. 435 ff. Heine also prepared for publication the revision of *Lutetia* mentioned above. His *Confessions,* published in German in 1854, may not be a major work, but it is of special interest because it is the only larger autobiographical work Heine left.

In the *Confessions,* as in other late writings and in letters to friends, Heine stated explicitly that he now believed in a personal God. This "confession," coming from a

3. It is still not certain who destroyed the manuscript nor when it was destroyed. At any rate, what was preserved and published posthumously is only a fragment of the work as planned and deals only with Heine's childhood years.

man who had so roundly condemned Catholicism, had remained, at best, lukewarm toward Protestantism, and had publicly proclaimed himself a pagan and a pantheist, for many years met only with skepticism or outright disbelief on the part of scholars, particularly because of the jesting tone in which Heine referred to his conversion. Many poems in the *Romancero* and others of later origin, some published posthumously, appear on the surface to be blasphemous. In more recent years, perhaps due to the desperate situation of our own times, which makes the need for religious faith seem more credible, most critics incline to believe that Heine meant what he said. Skepticism, even apparent blasphemy, is no proof of irreligiosity, and the jesting tone beneath which Heine concealed, or half concealed, the seriousness of the content, had always been typical of him. In the "Postscript to the *Romancero*" Heine writes that he has made his peace with his creator and been excommunicated by the higher clergy of atheism and continues, "Yes, I have returned to God like the prodigal son after having watched over the Hegelian sheep for a very long time. Was it misery that drove me back? Perhaps a less miserable reason. Homesickness for Heaven overwhelmed me and drove me on through forests and ravines, over the giddiest mountain paths of dialectics. On my way I found the god of the pantheists but he was of no use to me . . . If you want a God who can help—and this is of course the main thing—you also have to accept His being a person, His transcendence, and His holy attributes, infinite goodness, infinite wisdom, infinite justice, and so on. We then get immortality of the soul thrown in, so to speak, like the nice meat bone that the butcher gives free to the customers he is satisfied with." The mockery accompanies, but does not negate, the seriousness; Heine remained Heine to the last.

Heine's place in the world of letters is still a matter of

some dispute. At one time he was generally regarded as
the greatest German lyric poet after Goethe. Few critics,
I dare say, would now maintain this. He was a poet in an
age of transition, and as he himself saw clearly, he was
the last of the Romantics and the first poet of the modern
age. His early poems, full as they are of Romantic im-
agery and motifs, many written in the folksong form and
style so popular among the Romanticists, still do not fit
the Romantic pattern. They do not take themselves seri-
ously; they often carry Romantic qualities to an extreme,
only to destroy the mood by a sudden shift to irony or
prosiness at the close. Heine's conflict with his Romantic
heritage compelled him to destroy the Romantic sub-
stance even as he used it. In his later poetry he found a
new style; even in English translation one can feel this.[4]
In his use of vocabulary ordinarily regarded as unsuita-
ble for the lyric, a liberal sprinkling of foreign words
included, in his startling and effective use of dissonance,
whether in speech or in tone, in his seemingly prosaic
love poems, and in many other ways he anticipated poets
of a much later period.

Heine's prose works are less well known. Yet they
deserve to be more widely known, for their intrinsic in-
terest and for their contribution to German literary his-
tory. Heine was among the first modern German journal-
ists, and he was certainly the best known during his
lifetime, in other countries as well as in Germany. It was
he who elevated the German *feuilleton* to an art form. At
its best, Heine's prose style is brilliant, imaginative, and
witty; at its worst—and there are times when he lapses
into pedantry or verbosity—it is still better than the
prose of some of Germany's most respected authors, for
it always remains intelligible if not always first-rate. This
is all the more remarkable when one considers how few
good models Heine could have found in Germany for the

4. See "Which Way Now?" (p. 436) and the poems following.

essay style. Lessing was one, and it is surely significant that Heine admired Lessing more than any other German writer. He could have offered a model for clarity and forcefulness of expression, but not for the lightness and gaiety and wit and love of sheer nonsense which make Heine unique. These qualities were Heine's own, as natural to him as was writing itself. Apart from stylistic qualities, what strikes the reader of Heine's essays is the scope of subject matter. He did not write as a scholar or specialist, to be sure, but the range of topics he dealt with, no matter how superficially, is impressive. It would be difficult, I think, to find another journalist who was able to cope, and not always superficially, with literature, ancient and modern, religion, philosophy, folklore, contemporary politics, painting, theater, and music. And when he was completely beyond his depth, as he obviously was in writing about music, he could summon such a vast and interesting repertoire of diversionary tactics that one hardly notices on first reading that he has said nothing at all about the subject at hand.

Heine also stands out as the only German writer between Goethe and writers of the late nineteenth and early twentieth century such as Gerhart Hauptmann and Thomas Mann to achieve during his lifetime a reputation that went beyond the bounds of German-speaking countries. German literature from Goethe's death in 1832 to the end of the century remained provincial, and even today few, if any, names from those years would sound familiar to the average reader from a foreign country. Heine's name, however, is known to many, though they may know nothing that he wrote except by way of Schumann's *Dichterliebe*. Heine was a European as well as a German, in the tradition of Goethe and Schiller, and in addition he is, so far as I know, the only German writer ever to be whole-heartedly adopted as a citizen of France.

This anthology contains much more of Heine's prose

than of his poetry for two reasons: the prose is less familiar to English readers, and translations of many of his poems are easily accessible. Yet any anthology would seem incomplete without some of the poetry, and the poems included here, arranged in roughly chronological order, were selected with the hope of giving the reader at least a small sampling of the range of Heine's lyric. The prose works, or excerpts from larger works, are also varied and representative, but of course it is impossible to include in one volume all the prose that would be of interest. Some cuts were necessary in the works selected for this anthology, either because of limitations of space or to omit passages containing so many allusions to persons or events unfamiliar to us today that they would necessitate more footnotes than original text to make them intelligible. I have retained Heine's spelling of proper names and places, even inconsistencies, the paragraphing as given in the German edition, and also the punctuation as far as possible. Most of Heine's long sentences I left intact, but I did divide a few so as not to try the patience of the English reader too far.

There is still, even at this late date, no definitive critical edition of Heine's works. Two such editions are in the making, one in East Germany, the other in West Germany,' but they have not yet reached a stage where they would be helpful. I have used the two best existing editions, *Heinrich Heines sämtliche Werke*, edited by Ernst Elster (Leipzig and Vienna, 1887–1890), and *Heinrich Heines sämtliche Werke*, edited by Oskar Walzel (Leipzig, 1910–1915). I also consulted the East German edition edited by Hans Kaufmann, *Heinrich Heine. Werke und Briefe in zehn Bänden* (Berlin, 1961–1964), but found little in text or footnotes that goes beyond the information provided by Elster and Walzel. The notes in Elster's edition were very useful in the preparation of the footnotes in this translation, but since this anthology is intended for readers who do not know German and may also not be familiar with German history or literature, I have provided notes on many points which would be obvious to a German reader and are therefore not touched on in German editions. My sources for these notes are far too numerous to list.

The biographical sketch given here is of course only a sketch. There is as yet no definitive biography of Heine, even in German, and the best available for English readers is probably E. M. Butler's *Heinrich Heine* (Oxford, 1957). Anyone interested in further discussions of Heine and his works will find the following books valuable: Laura Hofrichter, *Heinrich Heine*, translated by Barker Fairley (Oxford, 1963) and William Rose, *Heinrich Heine: Two Studies of His Thought and Feeling: Heine's Political and Social Attitude; Heine's Jewish Feeling* (Oxford, 1956). Two other books in English are interesting, S. S. Prawer, *Heine the Tragic Satirist, A Study of the Later Poetry 1827–1856* (Cambridge, 1961) and Jeffrey L. Sammons, *Heinrich Heine, the Elusive Poet* (New Haven and London, 1969). Both books, however, pose a difficulty for the English reader; in the first, quotations from poetry are given in German without translation, and in the second, quotations from both poetry and prose are in German without translation.

I wish to express here my very special gratitude to Dr. Max Knight and Dr. Joseph Fabry for translating Heine's poems in *The Harz Journey* and those in the poetry section, as well as the poems which Heine quotes from other sources in *The Romantic School*. I am also indebted to other friends and colleagues for help on some points outside my competence, particularly to Professor Carl F. Bayerschmidt, Professor Emeritus of German, Columbia University, Professor Mary Heuser of the Department of

Art History at Wheaton College, Professor Daniel Pen-
ham of the French Department, Columbia University,
and Professor Ludwig Uhlig of the German Department,
University of Connecticut.

HELEN M. MUSTARD
Roxbury, Connecticut

PART I

Early Prose

The Harz Journey

Black their coats, of silk their stockings,
white their frilly cuffs, and smart,
smooth their talk and their embraces—
if they only had a heart!

If they had some heart, and loving,
loving, and a heart that glows—
ah, it kills me when I listen
to their lies of lovelorn woes.

I will climb the lofty mountains,
where the humble cabins stand,
where a man can breathe in freedom
and free air blows through the land.

I will climb the lofty mountains,
where dark fir trees tower high,
where the brooks rush, and the birds sing,
and the clouds sail proudly by.

Polished floors! And polished ladies!
Polished gentlemen! Adieu!
I will climb the lofty mountains,
laughing I'll look down on you.

The town of Göttingen, famous for its sausages and university, belongs to the King of Hanover and contains 999 dwellings, various churches, a maternity hospital, an observatory, a prison, a library, and a Ratskeller where the beer is very good. The brook flowing past is the Leine, and in summer it serves for bathing; the water is very cold and in some places so wide that Lüder[1] really had to take an enormous running start when he jumped across it. The town itself is very beautiful, and most pleasing of all when viewed with one's back to it. It must have existed for a very long time, for I remember when I matriculated there five years ago, only to be expelled soon afterward, it already had the same hoary, knowing appearance and was already completely supplied with nightwatchmen, beadles, dissertations, tea dances, laundresses, cyclopedias, roast pigeons, Guelfic orders, carriages for graduating doctoral candidates, pipe bowls, *Hofräte,*[2] councillors of justice, councillors for expulsion, bibliomaniacs, and other maniacs. Some even maintain that the town was built during the migration of the Germanic tribes, that every tribe left there an unbound sample of its members, and from these descended all the Vandals, Frisians, Swabians, Teutons, Saxons, Thuringians, and so on, who still roam in hordes down Weende Street in Göttingen today, distinguished only by the color of their caps and pipe tassels, are forever fighting among each other on the bloody battlefields of the Rasenmühle,[3] the Ritschenkrug,[3] and Bovden,[4] are still living according to the manners and customs of the age of the migrations, and are governed partly by their *duces,* who are called cocks of the roost, partly by their ancient law-book, which is called "Students' Code"

---

1. A student at Göttingen noted for his gymnastic prowess.
2. Plural of *Hofrat,* an honorary title with no English equivalent.
3. Favorite duelling places of the students.
4. Bovenden is a village not far from Göttingen.

and deserves a place among the *legibus barbarorum*.[5]

In general the inhabitants of Göttingen are divided into students, professors, philistines, and live stock, these four estates being, however, far from strictly differentiated. The live stock are the most important class. It would take too long to list here the names of all students and all full and less full professors; besides, I don't at this moment remember all the students' names, and among the professors there are many who as yet don't even have a name. The number of Göttingen philistines must be very large, like grains of sand, or better said, like sludge along the seashore; truly, when I saw them of a morning, planted before the portals of the academic court, with their dirty faces and immaculate accounts, I could scarcely comprehend how God could create such a huge pack of scoundrels.

More details about the town of Göttingen may easily be found in the description of the town by K. F. H. Marx.[6] Although I owe the most sacred obligations to the author, who was my physician and did me many kindnesses, I cannot recommend his work without reservation and must reproach him for not having contradicted firmly enough the mistaken opinion that the women of Göttingen have all-too-large feet. Indeed, I have occupied myself for a long time with a serious refutation of this opinion; therefore I studied comparative anatomy, took excerpts from the rarest books in the library, studied for hours the feet of the ladies passing by on Weende Street, and in the very scholarly treatise that will contain the results of these studies I shall speak 1) of feet in general, 2) of the feet of the ancients, 3) of elephants' feet, 4) of the feet of the women of Göttingen, 5) I shall

5. Laws of the barbarians.
6. Professor of medicine at the university. He had just published a book about Göttingen in 1824.

compile everything that has already been said about these feet in Ullrich's Garden,[7] 6) I shall consider these feet in their relation to one another and at this point shall enlarge upon calves, knees, etc., and finally, 7) if I can only get hold of paper large enough, I shall add some copper plates with facsimiles of the feet of Göttingen ladies.

It was still very early when I left Göttingen, and the learned—[8] was certainly still lying in bed and dreaming as usual that he was strolling in a beautiful garden in whose beds were growing nothing but little white slips of paper covered with quotes and shining delightfully in the sunlight and of which he picks several here and there and transplants them laboriously into a new bed while the nightingales rejoice his aged heart with their sweetest tones.

In front of the Weende gate I met two local schoolboys, and one was saying to the other, "I'm not going to have anything to do with Theodore any more. He's a no-good—yesterday he didn't even know the genitive of *mensa.*" However unimportant these words sound, yet I must repeat them. Indeed, I would like to have them inscribed right on the gate as town motto, for the youngsters chirp what the grown-ups whistle, and these words describe precisely the narrow, pedantic passion for note-taking of the highly learned Georgia Augusta.[9]

On the road a fresh morning breeze was blowing, and the birds sang merrily, and I too gradually began to feel fresh and merry. Such a revival was what I needed. I hadn't gotten away from the law stables for some time, Roman casuists had covered my spirit with a gray cob-

7. A pleasure resort in Göttingen.
8. The French edition, published in 1824, prints here the name of Eichhorn, a well-known professor at Göttingen, but Heine's note on his handwritten manuscript gives the name Blumenbach. This was Johann Friedrich Blumenbach, noted naturalist and anthropologist, also a professor at the university. He introduced the study of comparative anatomy in Germany.
9. The University of Göttingen.

web, my heart was as if pinched in between the iron paragraphs of self-centered legal systems, there was still a constant ringing in my ears like "Tribonian,[10] Justinian, Hermogenian,[11] and Simpleton," and I even took an affectionate pair of lovers sitting under a tree for an edition of the *corpus juris* with hands interlaced. Things began to get lively on the road. Milkmaids passed by, also donkey-drivers with their gray pupils. Beyond Weende I met Schäfer and Doris.[12] This is not the idyllic pair of whom Gessner[13] sings, but duly installed university beadles who have to watch out carefully to see that no students duel in Bovden and that no new ideas, which must still be quarantined for several decades before entering Göttingen, are smuggled in by speculative instructors.[14] Schäfer greeted me as if I were a colleague, for he is also a writer and has often mentioned me in his biennial publications,[15] and besides has often cited me and, on not finding me at home, was always so kind as to write the citation with chalk on the door of my room. Now and then a one-horse carriage rolled by, packed full with students going away for the holidays or even forever. In such a university town there is a constant coming and going. Every three years you find a new student generation there. It is an everlasting stream of people in which one semester-wave forces the other out, and only the old professors remain fixed within this general movement, immovably firm, like the pyramids of Egypt—except that in these university pyramids no wisdom is hidden.

10. A famous law teacher of the sixth century who, together with other legal scholars, established the Justinian codification of Roman law.

11. A Roman jurist of the time of Diocletian. The correct spelling of his name in English is Hermogenianus, but I have kept Heine's spelling for the sake of the whimsical end-rhymes in this enumeration.

12. Schäfer (meaning "shepherd") and Dohrs (Heine changes this to Doris) were university beadles.

13. A popular writer of idylls.

14. A *Privatdozent*, an unsalaried lecturer at a German university who receives only student fees as compensation.

15. These are the lists of students.

I saw two promising-looking youths ride out of the myrtle arbor near Rauschenwasser. A hussy who practices her horizontal handiwork there accompanied them to the road, clapped with practiced hand the lean shanks of the horses, laughed loudly when the one rider delivered a few courtesies with his whip on her broad behind, and then pushed on toward Bovden. The youths, however, raced along to Nörten, yodeling cleverly and singing very sweetly Rossini's song "Drink beer, darling, darling Liese." For a long time I still heard these tones in the distance, but the charming singers themselves I soon lost completely from sight since, in a quite horrifying fashion, they spurred and whipped on their horses, which by nature seemed to be sluggish like the Germans. Nowhere is the flaying of horses practiced more violently than in Göttingen, and often when I saw such a lame nag, dripping with sweat, being tortured for his bit of fodder by our Rauschenwasser knights or even being forced to drag a whole wagon full of students, I thought to myself, "O you poor beast, your forefathers must certainly have eaten forbidden oats in Eden." . . .

Beyond Nörten the sun stood high and brilliant in the sky. It had the best of intentions toward me and warmed my head so that all the unripe ideas in it attained full ripeness. The nice Sun Inn at Nordheim is also not to be despised. I stopped here and found the midday meal ready. All the dishes were tastefully prepared and pleased me better than the tasteless academic dishes, the unsalted, leathery codfish and warmed-over cabbage that were set before me in Göttingen. After I had appeased my stomach somewhat, I noticed in the same dining room a gentleman and two ladies who were about to depart. The gentleman was dressed all in green; he even wore green glasses that cast a gleam as of verdigris on his red copper nose, and he looked like King Nebuchadnezzar in his later years when, according to legend, he ate nothing but greens, like a beast in the forest. The green man desired me to recommend to him a hotel in Göttingen, and I advised him to ask the first student he met for the way to the Hotel de Brühbach. The one lady was his wife, a sizeable, extensive lady, her face a red square mile with dimples in the cheeks which looked like spittoons for amoretti, her long, fleshy, pendulous lower jaw appearing to be a poor continuation of her face, and a highstacked bosom that was walled in by stiff lace and jaggedly festooned frills as if by little towers and bastions, and resembled a fortress that certainly would resist an ass laden with gold just as little as those other fortresses of which Philip of Macedonia speaks. The other lady, his sister, constituted the exact antithesis of the one just described. If the former descended from Pharaoh's fat cows, the latter was descended from the lean ones. Her face only a mouth between two ears, her breast hopelessly desolate, like the Lüneburg Heath; the whole figure, with all the goodness boiled out, resembled free board for poor theological students. Both ladies asked me at the same moment whether respectable people stayed at the Hotel de Brühbach. I said "Yes" with a clear conscience, and as the charming cloverleaf drove away, I waved again from the window. The landlord of the Sun smiled slyly and no doubt knew very well that the prison in Göttingen is called Hotel de Brühbach by the students.

Beyond Nordheim the land already becomes hilly, and here and there beautiful knolls stand out. On the way I met mostly tradesmen going to the Braunschweig fair, also a swarm of women, each of whom was carrying on her back a large container almost as high as a house, covered with white linen. In these were all sorts of captive songbirds that constantly peeped and twittered as their bearers skipped gaily along, chattering with each other. To me it seemed silly indeed to see one bird carrying another to market.

I arrived in Osterode in pitchdark night. I had no

appetite for food and went straight to bed. I was tired as
a dog and slept like a god. In a dream I went back to
Göttingen, and to the library at that. I stood in a corner
of the Law Room, rummaged through old dissertations,
got absorbed in reading, and when I stopped, I noticed
to my surprise that it was night, and crystal chandeliers
hanging from the ceiling illuminated the room. The
nearby church clock was just striking twelve when the
room door opened slowly, and in stepped a proud gigan-
tic woman respectfully accompanied by the members
and disciples of the law faculty. The giant woman,
though already aged, nevertheless bore in her counte-
nance the traces of an austere beauty; every glance of
hers revealed the noble Titaness, the mighty Themis. In
one hand she casually held sword and scales, in the other
a roll of parchment, and two young *doctores juris* carried
the train of her faded gray gown. On her right the lank
Hofrat Rusticus, the Lycurgus of Hanover,[16] sprang gid-
dily back and forth, declaiming from his new draft of a
bill; on her left hobbled her *cavaliere servente*, the Privy
Counselor Cujacius,[17] constantly cracking legal jokes
and laughing at them himself so heartily that even the
grave goddess bent down to him several times with a
smile, tapped him on the shoulder with the huge roll of
parchment, and whispered affably, "Naughty little rascal
who lops off trees at the top!"[18] Each of the other gentle-
men now likewise approached with some remarks or a
smile, perhaps a freshly concocted little system or hy-

16. An allusion to a well-known contemporary professor of criminal law.
Lycurgus was one of the ten Attic orators of the Alexandrian canon.

17. Heine pays a compliment here to a law professor of his, Gustav Hugo,
by transforming him into Cujacius (actually Jacques de Cujas), a famous
French legal scholar of the sixteenth century.

18. A reference to the interpretation of a complicated but trivial law con-
cerning the cutting of trees, the question being whether trees on the border
of a field should be trimmed up to fifteen feet or whether the tops should be
cut off to keep them to a height of fifteen feet.

pothesis or some similar monstrosity from his own little mind. At this moment several more strange gentlemen entered through the opened door of the room, announcing themselves as the other great men of the illustrious order. Most of them were angular, hawk-eyed fellows who, with brash self-complacency, immediately plunged into defining and differentiating and disputing about every subheading of a pandect-title. New figures kept coming in, ancient legal scholars in outmoded gowns with white bagwigs and long forgotten faces, and much astonished that they, the very famous men of the past century, were not regarded as anything special; these now joined, in their fashion, in the general chattering and yelling and shrieking which, like the roar of the surf, more and more confused and louder and louder, roared about the noble goddess until she lost her patience and cried out suddenly with a tone of the most frightful giant pain, "Silence! Silence! I hear the voice of dear Prometheus. Mocking power and brute force[19] keep the innocent man chained to the martyr's rock, and all your chattering and wrangling cannot cool his wounds and break his fetters!" Thus the goddess called, and streams of tears gushed from her eyes; the entire assembly howled as though seized by mortal fear; the ceiling of the room creaked, the books tumbled down from their shelves; in vain old Münchhausen[20] stepped from his frame to demand order; the raging and screeching grew wilder and wilder—and I escaped from this oppressive madhouse noise to the History Room, to that shrine where the holy statues of the Belvedere Apollo and Venus of Medici stand side by side, and I fell at the feet of the goddess of beauty, at

19. In the French edition the phrase *de la sainte alliance* (of the Holy Alliance) makes clear the allusion to Napoleon.

20. Gerlach Adolf von Münchhausen (1688–1770), a statesman who played an important role in the founding and organizing of the University of Göttingen.

sight of her I forgot all the wild doings I had run from, my eyes drank in ecstatically the symmetry and eternal loveliness of her most blessed body, Grecian calm took possession of my soul, and over my head, like a heavenly benediction, Phoebus Apollo poured the sweetest tones of his lyre.

On awakening I still heard a pleasant tinkling. The herds were going to pasture, and their little bells were ringing. The lovely golden sun shone through the window and lighted up the paintings on the walls of the room. There were pictures of the Napoleonic War faithfully representing us all as heroes, also execution scenes from the period of the Revolution, Louis XVI on the guillotine and similar decapitations which you simply can't look at without thanking God that you are lying peacefully in bed, drinking good coffee, and still have your head sitting very comfortably on your shoulders.

After I had drunk coffee, dressed, read the inscriptions on the window panes, and settled my account at the inn, I left Osterode . . .

After having walked some distance, I caught up with a traveling journeyman who came from Braunschweig, . . . a nice little young man, so thin that the stars could shine through him as through Ossian's nebulous spirits, and in general a baroque mixture of whimsy and melancholy characteristic of the common folk. This was shown especially in the amusingly touching way in which he sang the wonderful folksong, "A beetle sat upon the fence; buzz, buzz!" This is the nice thing about us Germans; no one is so crazy but that he can find someone even crazier who understands him. Only a German can appreciate that song and nearly die with laughing and weeping when he hears it. I also noticed here how deeply Goethe's words have penetrated the life of the people. My thin companion likewise trilled to himself occasionally, "Sorrowful and joyful, our thoughts are free."[21] Such corruption of the text is quite usual among the common people. He also sang a song in which Lotte mourns at the grave of her Werther.[22] The tailor dissolved in sentimentality at the words,

> All alone I weep beside the rose bower,
> Where on us so oft the late moon gazed!
> Mournfully I stray beside the waters
> That once purled the promise of sweet joy.[23]

But soon after he became mischievous and told me, "We have a Prussian in the inn at Kassel who makes up just such songs himself. He can't sew a blessed stitch. If he has one groschen in his pocket, he is always thirsty enough to need two, and when he is drunk, he thinks the sky is a blue waistcoat and weeps like a gutter spout and sings a song with double poetry." I asked for an explanation of the latter expression, but my little tailor with his Ziegenhain[24] legs hopped back and forth calling out the whole time, "Double poetry is double poetry!" Finally I got out of him that he meant poems containing couplets, especially the eight-line stanza.—Meanwhile, because of our lively pace and the wind against us, the knight of the

21. A distortion of part of a popular German folksong. The first half is an inaccurate quotation from a love lyric in Goethe's *Egmont*, Act III; the last phrase is the ever-recurring motif in the folksong. The song actually did circulate in this version.

22. A reference to Goethe's first novel, *Die Leiden des jungen Werthers* (*The Sorrows of Young Werther*), 1774, in the tradition of the sentimental novel, then so popular in England and on the Continent. It was a "best-seller" not only in Germany but in all of Europe. Lotte is the heroine, at the beginning of the novel betrothed, and in the second half married. Werther's uncontrollable passion for her leads him in the end to commit suicide. The song referred to was not written by Goethe, but it did exist and was apparently well known.

23. My translation.

24. Walking sticks were made in Ziegenhain, formerly a village, now a part of the city of Jena. The fashionable canes in Heine's day were very slender; hence the description means "toothpick legs."

needle had become very tired. To be sure, he made some great efforts to continue and boasted, "Now I'll get a move on." But soon he was complaining that he had gotten blisters on his feet from walking and that the world was much too vast; and finally he let himself down gently by a tree trunk, moved his delicate little head like a melancholy lamb's tail, and exclaimed with a woebegone smile, "Poor devil that I am, I'm already bushed again!"

The hills were becoming even steeper here. The fir woods surged below like a green sea, and in the blue sky above sailed white clouds. The wildness of the region was tamed, as it were, by its uniformity and its simplicity. Like a good poet, nature does not love abrupt transitions. The clouds, though at times appearing in bizarre shapes, have a white or at least a soft tint corresponding harmoniously with the blue sky and the green earth, so that all the colors of a region melt into each other like soft music, and every view of the natural scene soothes the nerves and calms the spirit . . . Just like a great poet, nature knows how to produce the greatest effects with the slightest means—only one sun, trees, flowers, water, and love. To be sure, if the last is wanting in the heart of the observer, the whole view will probably seem poor, and the sun will then be only so and so many miles in diameter, and the trees will be good for kindling, and the flowers will be classified by their stamens, and the water will be wet . . .

The trip through the two best Klaustal mines, the "Dorothea" and the "Karolina," I found very interesting, and I must tell about it in detail.

Half an hour outside the town you reach two large, blackish buildings. Here you are immediately received by the miners. They wear dark, loose-fitting jackets, usually steel blue, that hang down over the stomach, trousers of a similar color, leather aprons tied on behind, and small

green felt hats, completely brimless, like a truncated
cone. The visitor is also fitted out with such clothes, but
without the apron behind, and a mine foreman, after
lighting his miner's lamp, guides him to a dark opening
that looks like a chimney sweep's hole, descends as far
as his chest, gives instructions about how to hold fast to
the ladders, and requests the visitor to follow without
fear. The business itself is not at all dangerous, though
you don't think so at first if you know nothing about
mines. It is a strange feeling to have to undress and put
on the dark prison garb. And then you're supposed to
climb down on all fours, and the dark hole is so dark, and
God knows how long the ladder may be. But you soon
see that there is not just a single ladder descending into
the black eternity but that there are several with fifteen
to twenty rungs, and that each leads to a narrow platform
on which you can stand and in which there is another
hole leading to another ladder. I descended the Karolina
first. It is the dirtiest and most unappetizing Karolina I
have ever known. The ladder rungs are wet as dung. And
you go down from one ladder to the next, the foreman
first, always assuring you that it is not at all dangerous,
you only have to hold fast to the rungs with your hands
and not look at your feet and not get dizzy and for hea-
ven's sake not step on the side plank where the whirring
bucket rope is now ascending and where two weeks ago
a careless person fell and unfortunately broke his neck.
Down below is a confused roaring and humming, you
constantly collide with beams and ropes that are in mo-
tion in order to haul up the buckets with broken ore or
the water that has seeped out. At times you also come to
hewn-out tunnels called galleries, where you see the ore
growing and where the solitary miner sits the whole day
laboriously knocking out the pieces of ore from the wall
with his hammer. I did not go down to the lowest depth
where, as some maintain, you can hear the people in

America shouting, "Hurrah Lafayette!"[25] Just between us, the level I descended to seemed to me quite deep enough:—constant roaring and buzzing, uncanny movement of machines, the murmuring of underground springs, water dripping down on all sides, earth vapors rising like smoke, the miner's lamp glimmering paler and paler into the lonely night. It was truly deafening; I found it hard to breathe, and I clung with difficulty to the slippery ladder rungs. I felt no trace of so-called anxiety, but oddly enough, down there in the depths I recalled that the year before, at about the same time, I had experienced a storm on the North Sea, and I felt now that it had actually been quite cozy and pleasant when the ship rocked back and forth, the winds let loose their trumpet blasts, and at intervals the lusty shouts of the sailors resounded and everything was freshly flooded with blessed open air. Yes, air!—Gasping for air I once more climbed several dozen ladders, and my foreman led me to the Dorothea mine through a very long, narrow tunnel cut into the mountain. Here it is airier and fresher, and the ladders are cleaner, but also longer and steeper than in the Karolina. Here I felt better, especially as I again perceived traces of living human beings. At the bottom moving lights appeared; miners with their miner's lamps were slowly ascending and greeted us with "Good luck!", while we on our part returned the greeting as they rose past us; and like a memory that is familiarly peaceful and yet at the same time tormentingly puzzling, the grave and patient faces of these young and old men, somewhat pale, and eerily illuminated by their mine lamps, met me with their pensively clear gaze. They had worked all day in their dark, lonely mine shafts and now yearned upward to the blessed light of day and to the eyes of wife and child.

25. At this time, in 1824, Lafayette was visiting America, where he was received with great enthusiasm.

My cicerone himself was a man of unquestionable honor and dog-like German loyalty. With profound satisfaction he showed me the gallery where the Duke of Cambridge,[26] on his visit to the mine, had dined with his entire retinue, and where the long wooden dining table still stands, as well as the large throne of ore on which the Duke had sat. This would remain a permanent memorial, said the good miner, and with enthusiasm he told how many festivities had taken place then, how the whole gallery had been decorated with lights, flowers, and foliage, how a young miner had played the zither and sung, how the nice fat jolly Duke had drunk to the last drop an exceedingly large number of toasts, how many of the miners—and most especially he himself—would gladly let themselves be killed for the nice fat Duke and the whole House of Hanover.—I am deeply touched whenever I see this emotion of the loyalty of a subject expressed in its simple naturalness. It is such a beautiful emotion! And it is such a genuinely German emotion! Other peoples may be cleverer and wittier and more amusing, but none is so loyal as the loyal German people. If I did not know that loyalty is as old as the world, I would believe that a German had invented it. German loyalty! It is no modern flowery phrase. At your courts, you German princes, one should sing, and sing again, the song of the faithful Eckart and the wicked Burgundian who had Eckart's dear children killed and yet still found him loyal.[27] You princes have the most loyal people, and you are mistaken if you think the sensible, loyal old dog has suddenly gone mad and is snapping at your venerable calves.

Like German loyalty the tiny miner's lamp, without

26. Son of the king of England, George III, who was also at this time regent of the kingdom of Hanover.

27. Heine's memory apparently played him false here, but his version, though inaccurate, serves the purpose intended.

much flickering, had now guided us quietly and surely through the labyrinth of shafts and galleries; we climbed out of the musty night of the mines, the sunlight was streaming—Good luck!

Most of the miners live in Klaustal and in the little mountain village of Zellerfeld adjoining it. I visited several of these sturdy folk, observed their meager household equipment, heard some of their songs, which they accompany very nicely on the zither, their favorite instrument, had them tell me old mining tales and also recite the prayers they are accustomed to say together before descending into the dark shaft, and I prayed many a good prayer with them. An old foreman even suggested that I ought to stay with them and become a miner . . .

The name Goslar sounds so pleasing, and so many ancient memories of emperors are connected with it that I expected an imposing, stately city. But so it goes when one sees celebrities at close range. I found a run-down, musty country town, with mostly narrow, crooked, labyrinthine streets, through the center of which flows a small stream, probably the Gose, and with pavement as rough as Berlin hexameters.[28] Only the ancient remains of the fortification, that is, vestiges of walls, towers, and battlements, lend the town a certain piquancy. One of these towers, called the "Zwinger," has such thick walls that entire rooms are hewn out within them.[29] The space in front of the town, where the far-famed shooting-match is held, is a beautiful, large meadow surrounded by high mountains. The marketplace is small; in the center is a fountain whose water overflows into a great metal basin. When there is a fire, it is struck several times and pro-

28. Heine had been a student in Berlin from 1821 to 1824 and is here making fun of its would-be literary lights. It is not clear from this reference just whom he had in mind.

29. It was a round tower, later turned into a restaurant, with walls eighteen feet thick.

duces a reverberating tone. Nothing is known of the origin of this basin. Some say the devil once placed it there on the marketplace during the night. At that time the people were still stupid, and the devil was also stupid, and they gave each other presents.

The town hall in Goslar is a guardroom painted white. The guild house next to it has a better appearance. At about an equal distance from the ground and from the roof stand the statues of German emperors, smoky black and partly gilded, holding in one hand the scepter, in the other the globe; they look like roasted university beadles. One of the emperors holds a sword instead of the scepter. I was not able to guess what this difference was supposed to mean; yet it certainly has some significance, for the Germans have the remarkable habit of reflecting about everything they do . . .

The churchyard in Goslar did not appeal to me very much. But all the more that lovely little head of curls that looked out with a smile from a rather high ground floor window on my arrival in the town. After dinner I looked again for the nice window, but now only a water glass with white Canterbury bells stood there. I climbed up, took the pretty flowers out of the glass, stuck them calmly in my cap, and paid slight attention to the gaping mouths, petrified noses, and popping eyes with which the people on the street, especially the old biddies, watched this petty thievery. When I passed the same house an hour later, the lovely girl was standing at the window, and when she noticed the Canterbury bells on my cap she blushed deep red and darted back. I had now seen the pretty face even more precisely; it was a sweet, transparent embodiment of summer evening breeze, moonlight, nightingale song, and scent of roses.—Later, when it had become quite dark, she stepped out of the door. I went toward her—I went closer—she retreats slowly into the dark entrance hall—I take her by the hand and say, "I am a lover of beautiful flowers and kisses, and

what is not given me voluntarily I steal"—and I kissed
her quickly—and as she is about to flee, I whisper sooth-
ingly, "Tomorrow I am leaving and I'll probably never
return"—and I feel the secret response of the sweet lips
and the little hands—and laughing I hasten away. Yes, I
have to laugh when I reflect that I unconsciously uttered
that magic spell with which, more frequently than with
their mustachioed charm, our redcoats and bluecoats
conquer the hearts of the ladies, "I am leaving tomorrow
and I'll probably never return." . . .

During the night that I spent in Goslar something very
strange happened to me. I still cannot think back on it
without fear. I am not fearful by nature, but I am almost
as afraid of ghosts as *Der österreichische Beobachter*.[30] What
is fear? Does it originate in the mind or in feeling? I
debated this question so often with Dr. Saul Ascher[31]
whenever we met by chance in the Café Royal, where for
a long time I took my noon meal. He always maintained
that we fear something because we recognize it as fright-
ening by the process of reasoning. Only reason has
power, he said, not feelings. While I ate well and drank
well, he constantly demonstrated to me the advantages
of reason. Toward the end of his demonstration he used
to look at his watch and always closed with the words,
"Reason is the highest principle!" . . .

But back to Goslar. "The highest principle is reason!"
I said soothingly to myself as I got into bed. But it didn't
help. I had just read in Varnhagen von Ense's *German
Tales*,[32] which I had brought along from Klaustal, that

30. A well-known Vienna newspaper of the time, the official organ of the
conservative Austrian government, hence opposed to everything progressive
or unusual.

31. A Jewish friend of Heine's in Berlin.

32. A wealthy and cultivated Jew who, with his equally cultivated wife Rahel,
had been very friendly to Heine in Berlin. Their home was a literary and
artistic center, and Heine met there many celebrities in the world of letters.
Varnhagen was not an important writer, despite Heine's praise.

terrifying story of the son whose own father intended to murder him, and who is warned by the ghost of his dead mother. The wonderful narration of this story was so affecting that during the reading an inner horror chilled me through and through. Also ghost stories arouse a more awesome emotion if you read them on a journey and especially at night, in a town, in a house, in a room, where you have never been before. "How many horrible things may already have happened in the very spot where you are lying?" you think involuntarily. Besides, the moon was now shining into the room so ambiguously, all kinds of unbidden shadows moved along the wall, and when I sat up in bed to look in that direction, I saw—

There is nothing more uncanny than accidentally to see your own face in the mirror by moonlight. At the same moment a ponderous, yawning clock struck, and indeed so long and so slowly that after the twelfth stroke I thought surely that in the meanwhile a full twelve hours had elapsed and the clock would have to begin all over again to strike twelve. Between the next to the last and the last stroke another clock struck, very rapidly, almost shrewishly shrill, and perhaps annoyed at the slowness of its good neighbor. When both iron tongues fell silent and the deep stillness of death reigned in the entire house, I suddenly seemed to hear something shuffling and clumping in the corridor outside my room like the uncertain gait of an old man. Finally my door opened, and slowly the deceased Doctor Saul Ascher walked in. Cold chills ran through the very marrow of my bones, I shook like aspen leaves, scarcely daring to look at the ghost. He looked as usual, the same transcendental-gray frock coat, the same abstract legs, and the same mathematical face, except that the latter was a bit sallower than usual, and his lips, which ordinarily formed two angles of 22 1/2 degrees, were tightly pressed together, and the eye sockets had a larger radius. Tottering and, as always, supporting himself on his Spanish cane, he approached me and in his customary drawling dialect he said cordially, "Don't be frightened, and don't think I am a ghost. It is a delusion of your imagination if you think you are seeing me as a ghost. What is a ghost? Give me a definition. Deduce for me the conditions of the possibility of a ghost. What rational connection would such a phenomenon have with reason? Reason, I say reason—" And now the ghost proceeded to an analysis of reason, cited Kant's *Critique of Pure Reason,* Part 2, Division 1, Book 2, Section 3, the distinction between phenomena and noumena, then constructed the problematic belief in ghosts, piled one syllogism on the other, and concluded with the logical proof that there are absolutely no ghosts. Meantime cold sweat ran down my back, my teeth chattered like castanets, in mortal terror I nodded unconditional agreement at every argument with which the ghostly Doctor proved the absurdity of all fear of ghosts, and he demonstrated so zealously that once he absent-mindedly pulled a handful of worms out of his watch pocket instead of his gold watch and, noticing his error, stuck them back again with comically nervous haste. "Reason is the highest—" then the clock struck one, and the ghost vanished.

The next morning I went on from Goslar . . . Once more nice, lovely Sunday weather. I climbed hills and mountains, observed how the sun tried to disperse the fog, walked joyously through the shivering forests, and about my dreamy head rang the little Canterbury bells of Goslar. The mountains stood in their white night-robes, the firs shook the sleep out of their limbs, the fresh morning breeze curled their hanging green locks, the birds said their morning prayers, the meadow valley sparkled like cloth of gold studded with diamonds, and the shepherd strode across it with his tinkling herd. I suppose I had actually lost my way. One is always taking side paths and footpaths, thinking to reach one's destination sooner. As in life in general, so it goes with us in the Harz mountains. But there are always kind souls who put us on the right path again; they like doing it and also experience a special pleasure whenever they can point out to us, with self-complacent expression and benevolently loud voice, what enormous detours we made, into what abysses and swamps we could have fallen and how fortunate it is to meet just at the right time people who know the road as they do. I met such a monitor not far from the Harzburg.[33] He was a well-nourished citizen of Goslar with a shiny, bloated, stupidly cunning face; he looked as though he had invented the foot-and-mouth disease. We walked a stretch together, and he told me all sorts of ghost stories that might have sounded nice if they hadn't all ended with there being no real ghost after all—the white figure was a poacher, and the whimpering voices came from a wild sow's newly born piglets, and the noises in the attic came from the house cat. Only when a person is sick, he added, does he think he sees ghosts; as for his humble self, he was rarely sick, he suffered only occasionally from skin diseases, and then he always cured himself with saliva secreted on an empty stomach. He also called my attention to the purposefulness and utility of nature. The trees are green because green is good for the eyes. I agreed with him, adding that God had created cattle because meat broths strengthen a person, that He had created asses so that they could serve people for comparisons, and that He had created man himself so that he should eat meat broths and not be an ass. My companion was delighted to have found a kindred spirit, his countenance beamed ever more happily, and at our parting he was moved.

33. Not the town of Harzburg, but the remains of a fortress on a mountain near the town.

As long as he walked beside me, nature was robbed of its magic, so to speak, but as soon as he was gone, the trees began to speak again, and the sunbeams rang, and the meadow flowers danced, and the blue heavens embraced the green earth. Yes, I know better—God created man so that he might admire the splendor of the world. Any author, no matter how great, wishes his work to be praised. And in the Bible, God's memoirs, it is stated expressly that He created man for His own glory and honor . . .

Again I walked uphill and downhill, and before me floated the lovely sun, illuminating ever new beauties. The spirit of the mountains was clearly favoring me; he knew very well that such a poet-person as I can relate many nice things, and on this morning he let me see his Harz as certainly not everyone has seen it. But the Harz also saw me as only few have seen me; in my eyelashes glittered pearls as precious as those in the grass of the valley. The morning dew of love moistened my cheeks, the rustling firs understood me, their branches opened wide, moving up and down like deaf-mutes who show their joy with their hands, and in the distance sounded wonderfully mysterious tones like the pealing of the bells of a lost forest chapel. These are the herd bells, they say, which in the Harz are tuned so sweetly, clearly, and purely . . .

Golden sunbeams pierced the thick green of the firs most charmingly. The tree roots formed a natural stairway. Everywhere undulating mossy banks; for the stones are overgrown a foot deep with the most beautiful kinds of moss, like bright green velvet cushions. Sweet coolness and the dreamy murmur of springs. Here and there you can see the water trickling silvery bright from under the stones and rippling over the bare roots and fibers of the trees. If you bend down closer to this activity, you can overhear, so to speak, the secret cultural history of the plants and the quiet heartbeat of the mountain. In some spots the water gushes out more vigorously from the stones and roots and forms small cascades. It is nice sitting here. There is such a wonderful murmuring and rustling, the birds sing fragmentary songs of yearning, the trees whisper as with a thousand girls' tongues, and as if with a thousand girls' eyes the unusual mountain flowers gaze at us and stretch out to us their strangely broad, curiously notched leaves, the merry sunbeams flash playfully back and forth, the pensive little plants tell each other green fairy tales, everything is as though enchanted, becoming more and more mysterious, an ancient dream comes to life, the beloved appears—alas that she vanishes again so quickly!

The higher one ascends the mountain, the shorter and more dwarfed do the firs become; they seem to shrink more and more until only huckleberry and raspberry bushes and mountain plants remain. It also grows perceptibly colder. The strange groups of granite blocks are even more clearly visible here and are often of astonishing size. They may well be the balls that the evil spirits throw to each other in the Walpurgis Night when the witches come riding up on broomsticks and manure forks and the fantastic, infamous orgy begins, as the credulous nursemaid tells it, and as it can be seen in the illustrations for *Faust* by Master Retzsch . . .[34]

In fact, if one climbs the upper half of the Brocken, one cannot help thinking of the delightful stories about the Blocksberg[35] and especially of the great mystic German national tragedy of Dr. Faust.[36] I felt the entire time as if the cloven foot were climbing up beside me and as if someone were panting facetiously. And I believe that

34. A well-known painter and engraver of that time. Among his works are twenty-six engravings for Goethe's *Faust.*

35. Another name for the Brocken.

36. Heine is not thinking here of Goethe's *Faust,* which is not a tragedy, but of the medieval legends about Faust and possibly of his own plans to attempt a *Faust* of his own.

even Mephisto must gasp for breath when he climbs his
favorite mountain; it is a most exhausting path, and I was
glad when I at last caught sight of the long yearned for
Brocken House . . .[37]

Entering it aroused in me a somewhat unusual fairy-
tale-like sensation. After long, lonely clambering about
through firs and cliffs, one is suddenly transported into
a house in the clouds; towns, mountains, and forests lay
below, and up above one finds an oddly composed com-
pany of strangers by whom, as is natural in such places,
one is received almost like an expected comrade, half
curiously and half indifferently. I found the house full of
guests, and as becomes a wise man, I was already think-
ing of the night, of the discomfort of a straw bed; with
a faint voice I immediately asked for tea, and the Brocken
landlord was sensible enough to see that a sick person
like me had to have a decent bed for the night. This he
provided for me in a narrow little room where a young
merchant, a long emetic in a brown overcoat, had already
established himself. In the public room I found nothing
but life and commotion. Students from various universi-
ties. Some have just arrived and are refreshing them-
selves, others are preparing for departure, lacing up
their knapsacks, writing their names in the guest book,
receiving Brocken bouquets from the maids; there is
pinching of cheeks, singing, jumping, yodeling, there are
questions and answers, good weather, good luck on your
way, here's to your health, adieu. Some of the departing
guests are a little tipsy and experience double pleasure
in the lovely view, since a drunk man sees everything
double.

After I had revived myself a bit, I climbed the observa-
tion tower and found there a short gentleman with two
ladies, one young and one elderly. The young lady was

37. A hotel on top of the mountain.

very beautiful. A splendid figure, on her curly head a helmet-like black satin hat with whose white plumes the breezes played, her slender limbs so tightly enveloped in a black silk cloak that their fine form was visible, and her great, bold eyes looking calmly down into the great, bold world.

When I was still a boy, I thought of nothing but tales of magic and marvels and took every beautiful lady with ostrich feathers on her head for a queen of the elves, and if I saw that the train of her dress was damp, I took her for a water nymph. Now I think differently, since I know from natural history that those symbolic feathers come from the stupidest bird and that the train of a lady's dress can get damp in a very natural way. If, with those boyish eyes, I had seen on the Brocken the lovely young lady just mentioned, in the posture described, I would certainly have thought, "That is the fairy of the mountain, and she has just uttered the magic spell that makes everything down below appear so wonderful." Yes, when one first looks down from the Brocken, everything seems ever so wonderful, all facets of our nature receive fresh impressions, and these, usually varied, even contradictory, combine in our soul into one immense, still confused, uncomprehended emotion. If we succeed in grasping this emotion in its essence, then we recognize the character of the mountain. This character is wholly German, in its defects as well as in its merits. The Brocken is a German. With German thoroughness it shows us, clearly and distinctly, in the form of a gigantic panorama, the many hundred cities, towns, and villages, most of which lie to the north, and round about all the mountains, forests, rivers, plains, in an infinite expanse. For this very reason, however, everything looks like a sharply delineated, clearly illuminated local map; nowhere do really beautiful landscapes delight the eye; just as it always happens that we German compilers, because of the honest precision with which we want to present absolutely everything, never think of presenting the particular in a pleasing fashion. The mountain also has such a German placidity, something so reasonable and tolerant about it, simply because it can survey things so clearly and at such a remote distance. And when such a mountain opens its giant eyes, it may well see something more than we dwarfs with our stupid little eyes when we climb about on it. Many maintain, to be sure, that the Brocken is very philistine, and Claudius[38] sang, "The Blocksberg is the big tall Mr. Philistine." But that is an error. Because of its bald head, which it covers at times with a white cloud cap, it does give itself a tinge of philistinism, but, as with some other great Germans, this is done out of pure irony. It is even notorious that the Brocken has its wild, fantastic times, for example, the first night of May. Then it jubilantly throws its cloud cap into the air and goes crazy, just like the rest of us, in a truly German romantic fashion.

I tried at once to engage the beautiful lady in conversation, for one enjoys the beauties of nature all the more if one can talk about them right on the spot. She was not witty, but attentively thoughtful. Really well-bred manners. I do not mean the usual stiff, negative breeding that knows exactly what must be avoided, but that rarer, unconstrained, positive breeding that tells us exactly what we are permitted to do and, with complete lack of affectation, gives us the greatest social ease. To my own astonishment I developed much geographical information, gave the curious beauty all the names of the towns that lay before us, looked for and showed them to her on my map which, with a genuine professorial air, I spread out on the stone table in the center of the tower platform. Some towns I could not find, perhaps because I looked

38. Matthias Claudius, a German poet of the eighteenth century.

more with my fingers than with my eyes, which mean-
while explored the lovely lady's face and found there
more beautiful regions than "Schierke" and "Elend."[39]
This face was one of those that never charm, seldom
delight, and always please. I love such faces because they
smile my tempest-tossed heart into calm.

I could not guess what connection the short gentleman
accompanying the ladies had with them. He was a pecu-
liar, thin figure. A small head, sparsely covered with gray
hair that extended across his narrow forehead right to
his greenish, dragon-fly eyes, his round nose sticking far
out, mouth and chin, on the other hand, timidly retreat-
ing toward his ears. This miniature face seemed to be
made of a soft, yellowish clay such as sculptors mold
their first models from; and when his thin lips closed
tightly, several thousand fine, semicircular wrinkles were
drawn across his cheeks. The little man said not a word,
and only occasionally, when the older lady whispered
some friendly remark to him, did he smile like a pug-dog
with a cold.

The older lady was the mother of the younger, and she
too had the most refined manners. Her eyes revealed a
morbidly sentimental melancholy, while her mouth
showed an austere piety, although it seemed to me as if
it had once been very beautiful and had laughed often
and received—and given—many kisses. Her face resem-
bled a *codex palimpsestus*[40] on which, under the fresh black
transcription by a monk of the text of a church-father,
the half-obliterated verses of an ancient Greek love poet
peered through. Both ladies had been in Italy this year

---

39. Villages on the southeast slope of the Brocken. Heine probably men-
tions these two because a scene in Goethe's *Faust* takes place near them, but
he may also be punning. "Schierke" resembles the word "Schurke," meaning
"scoundrel," and "Elend" means "misery."

40. A parchment on which an earlier manuscript has been scratched off or
painted over so that it could be used again for a different text.

with their companion and told me all sorts of nice things about Rome, Florence, and Venice. The mother talked a great deal about the Raphael paintings in Saint Peter's; the daughter said more about the opera in the Fenice Theater.

As we talked, it began to grow dusk. The air became even colder, the sun sank lower, and the tower platform filled with students, traveling journeymen, and a few respectable bourgeois together with their wives and daughters, all of them wanting to see the sunset. It is a sublime sight which atunes the soul to prayer. Everyone stood perhaps a quarter of an hour in earnest silence and watched as the beautiful ball of fire gradually sank out of sight in the west; faces were lighted up by the sunset glow, hands were folded involuntarily; it was as if we were standing, a silent congregation, in the nave of a giant cathedral while the priest elevated the Host, and down from the organ pealed Palestrina's immortal choral work.

As I stood thus, absorbed in my devotions, I heard someone beside me exclaim, "How beautiful nature is, generally speaking!" These words came from the sentimental breast of my roommate, the young merchant. They put me once more into my everyday mood, and I was now able to make quite a number of nice remarks to the ladies about the sunset and to lead them calmly to their room as if nothing had happened. They even permitted me to talk to them for another hour. Like the earth itself, our conversation turned around the sun. The mother declared that the sun sinking into the mist had looked like a blush-red rose which the gallant heavens had thrown down into the outspread white bridal veil of its beloved earth. The daughter smiled and said that the too frequent sight of such natural phenomena weakened their effect. The mother corrected this erroneous opinion with a passage from Goethe's travel letters[41] and asked me if I had read *Werther*. I think we also talked about Angora cats, Etruscan vases, Turkish shawls, maccaroni, and Lord Byron, from whose poems the elder lady recited some sunset passages, murmuring and sighing quite prettily. I recommended to the younger lady, who did not understand English and wanted to become familiar with these poems, the translations by my beautiful and brilliant countrywoman Baroness Elise von Hohenhausen, at which opportunity I did not fail, as is my custom with young ladies, to rail against Byron's lack of religion, uncharitableness, pessimism, and Heaven knows what else.

Afterwards I went for a walk on the Brocken, for it never gets completely dark there. The fog was not thick, and I gazed at the outlines of the two hills called the Witches' Altar and the Devil's Pulpit. I shot off my pistols, but there was no echo. Suddenly, however, I hear familiar voices and feel myself embraced and kissed. It was my compatriots, who had left Göttingen four days later than I and were greatly astonished to find me again quite alone on the Blocksberg. Then there was telling of tales, exclamations of surprise, arranging future meetings, laughing and reminiscing, and in spirit we were once more in our learned Siberia, where the culture is so great that the bears are tied up in the inns[42] and the sables say "Good evening" to the hunters.[43]

The evening meal was being served in the large hall. A long table with two rows of hungry students. At first the usual university talk: duels, duels, and more duels.

41. The passage referred to is in Goethe's *Briefe aus der Schweiz (Letters from Switzerland)*, October 3, 1779.
42. Heine is punning. This expression is slang for "debts are contracted in the inns."
43. Slang for "young ladies say 'Good evening' to the students."

The company consisted mainly of Halle students, and so Halle became the chief topic of conversation . . .

A young *Burschenschafter*[44] who had recently been in Berlin to clear himself of a charge of treason talked a great deal about this city, but very one-sidedly. He had visited Wisotzki[45] and the theater and judged both incorrectly . . . He spoke of the expenditures for costumes, scandals about actors and actresses, etc. The young man did not know that, since in Berlin it is the appearance of things that really counts most, as the common expression *man so duhn*[46] indicates quite sufficiently, this illusory reality has to flourish all the more on the stage and that the management must therefore be concerned most of all with "the color of the beard in which a role is played," with the authenticity of the costumes that are designed by attested historians and are made by scientifically trained tailors. And this is necessary. For if Mary Stuart should by chance wear a skirt belonging to the age of Queen Anne, the banker Christian Gumpel would quite rightly complain that because of this he had lost all illusion of reality; and if perchance Lord Burleigh had put on by mistake Henry IV's trousers, the wife of Kriegsrat[47] von Steinzopf, née Lilientau,[48] would not forget this anachronism the whole evening. Such meticulousness in the preservation of illusion on the part of the general management extends not merely to skirts and trousers, but also to the persons enveloped in them. Hence in the future, Othello is to be played by a real

44. A member of one of the *Burschenschaften*, student societies that had been suppressed in Prussia shortly before this time because they were hotbeds of liberal political agitation. The police considered such students dangerous characters.

45. A restaurant owner in Berlin.

46. Low German dialect meaning "just act that way" or "just act as if."

47. Head clerk in the War Office.

48. Fictitious names, probably chosen for the comical effect of the literal meanings in this context. The first means "stone queue," the second "dew on the lilies."

Moor whom Professor Lichtenstein[49] has already ordered from Africa for this purpose; in *The Stranger*[50] Eulalia will be played from now on by a really wanton hussy, Peter by a really stupid youth, and the stranger by a Privy Cuckold, all three of which need not be ordered from Africa . . .

At our table the conversation became louder and louder, and more and more familiar, wine replaced beer, the punch bowls steamed, there was drinking, toasts in pledge of friendship, and singing . . . And outside there was a roaring as if the old mountain were singing with us, and some unsteady friends even declared that it was joyfully shaking its bald head, thus causing our room to move back and forth. Bottles became emptier and heads fuller. Someone bellowed, another sang falsetto, a third recited from *Guilt*,[51] a fourth spoke Latin, a fifth gave a sermon on moderation, and a sixth stood up on his chair and lectured: "Gentlemen! The earth is a round cylinder,[52] human beings are single pins on it, apparently distributed at random; but the cylinder turns, the pins strike here and there and produce sounds, some often, others rarely, the result is a wonderful, complicated music, and this music is called world history. Hence we shall speak first about music, then about the world, and finally about history; the last, however, we shall divide into the positive and Spanish flies—" And so it continued with sense and nonsense . . .

During the confused turmoil, when the plates learned

49. Professor of zoology in Berlin and founder of the Berlin Zoological Garden.

50. The title given this very popular play by August von Kotzebue in the English translation. The German title *Menschenhass und Reue* means literally *Misanthropy and Repentance.* It had its premiere in 1789, was performed in Germany countless times, and was translated into most other modern languages.

51. A tragedy of fate by Adolf Müllner, one of the most popular examples of this genre so much admired in Heine's day and also one of the bloodiest.

52. The reference is to a Swiss music box.

to dance and the glasses to fly, two youths were sitting
opposite me, handsome and pale as marble statues, the
one more like Adonis, the other resembling Apollo.[53]
The light rosy tinge that the wine cast upon their cheeks
was scarcely noticeable. They gazed at each other with
infinite love as if one could read the eyes of the other,
and these eyes shone as if some drops of light had fallen
into them from that bowl full of glowing love which a
devout angel up above transports from one star to an-
other. They spoke softly, their voices trembling with
yearning, and it was sad tales they told, from which
sounded the tones of a strange anguish. "Now Lore is
dead, too," said the one and sighed, and after a pause he
told of a girl from Halle who was in love with a student,
and, when the latter left Halle, spoke with no one, ate
little, wept day and night, and kept watching the canary
her lover had once given her. "The bird died, and soon
afterward Lore died too." So the story ended, and both
youths fell silent again and sighed as if their hearts would
break. Finally the other said, "My soul is sad! Come out
with me into the dark night. I want to breathe in the
breath of the clouds and the rays of the moon. Compan-
ion of my melancholy, I love you, your words sound like
the whisper of reeds, like flowing streams, they echo in
my breast, but my soul is sad!"

The two youths now rose, one flung his arm around
the neck of the other, and they left the uproarious room.
I followed them and saw them enter a dark chamber,
where the one opened, instead of the window, a large
clothes closet, and both stepped in front of it with arms
outstretched longingly and spoke by turns. "O breezes

53. The episode of the two youths is a satire on the vogue of exaggerated
sentimentality, and most of their rhetorical speeches are a parody on Ossian
and his German imitators. Goethe had used his own translation of excerpts
from Ossian at a crucial point in his sentimental novel, *The Sorrows of Young
Werther*.

of the darkening night," exclaimed the first, "how refreshingly you cool my cheeks! How sweetly you play with my fluttering locks! I stand on the mountain's beclouded peak, beneath me lie the sleeping cities of men, and the blue waters sparkle. Hark! down below in the valley the firs are rustling! There above the hills, in misty forms, pass the spirits of our forefathers. Oh, could I only race with you, on my cloud-steed, through the stormy night, across the rolling sea, and up to the stars! But alas, I am laden with sorrow, and my soul is sad!" The other youth had likewise stretched out his arms yearningly to the clothes closet, tears gushed from his eyes, and with mournful voice he addressed a pair of yellow leather trousers, which he took to be the moon, "You are beautiful, daughter of Heaven! Charming is the serenity of your countenance! You move in loveliness. The stars follow your blue paths in the east. At sight of you the clouds rejoice, and their dark contours brighten. Who in Heaven is like unto you, daughter of the night? The stars are put to shame in your presence and turn aside their green sparkling eyes. Where, when in the morning your countenance pales, do you flee from your course? Do you have your mansion, as I do? Do you dwell in the shadow of sadness? Have your sisters fallen from Heaven? They, who joyfully roamed with you through the night, do they no longer exist? Yes, they have fallen, o lovely light, and you hide yourself often to mourn them. But the night will come when you, you too will have passed away and abandoned your blue paths there above. Then the stars, whom once your presence put to shame, will lift their green heads and rejoice. But now you are clothed in your radiant splendor and look down from the gates of Heaven. Tear away the clouds, o winds, that the daughter of night may shine forth and the shaggy mountains may gleam, and the ocean roll its foaming waves in light!"

A familiar, not very slender friend, who had drunk more than he had eaten, although this evening, as usual, he had also consumed a helping of beef from which six lieutenants of the guard and one innocent child would have been replete, now came running up, in all too good a mood, that is, just like a pig, pushed the two elegiac friends somewhat roughly into the closet, stumbled noisily to the house door, and carried on outside like a demon out of hell. The tumult in the room became more and more confused and muffled. The two youths in the closet moaned and whimpered that they were lying shattered at the foot of the mountain; the choice red wine streamed from their throats, they flooded each other by turns, and the one said to the other, "Farewell! I feel that I am bleeding to death. Why do you wake me, air of spring? You woo me and say, 'I am bedewing you with dewdrops from Heaven.' Yet the time of my wilting is near, and near is the storm that will scatter my leaves. Tomorrow the wanderer will come, he who saw me in my beauty will come, his eye will seek me round about in the field and will not find me.—" But the familiar bass voice outside the door drowned out everything else, complaining blasphemously, with curses and huzzas, that in all of dark Weende Street not a single lantern was burning, and you couldn't even see whose window panes you had smashed . . .

The Brocken landlord extricated me from this tumult by waking me to see the sunrise.[54] On the tower I found several people already waiting, rubbing their freezing hands; others, sleep still in their eyes, were staggering up. At last the quiet congregation of the evening before stood assembled once more, and silently we watched as the small crimson sphere ascended at the horizon, a wintry pale illumination fanned out, the mountains swam in

54. The reference is to a dream, here omitted.

a surging sea of white with only their peaks visible, so that one felt as if he were standing on a small hill in the center of a flooded plain where only here and there a dry clod appeared . . .

Meanwhile my longing for breakfast was likewise strong, and after making a few polite remarks to the ladies, I hurried down to drink coffee in the warm room . . .

Alas, the coffee was even to blame that I had forgotten my beautiful lady, and now she was standing outside the door, with mother and escort, about to get into the coach. I had scarcely time to hurry up to her and assure her that it was cold. She seemed annoyed that I had not come sooner, but I soon smoothed the ill-humored wrinkles on her beautiful brow by presenting her an unusual flower that I had picked the day before from a steep rock wall at the risk of breaking my neck. The mother desired to know the name of the flower, as if she found it improper for her daughter to pin a strange, unfamiliar flower on her breast—for the flower did indeed receive this enviable position, something it would certainly never have dreamed of yesterday on its lonely heights. The taciturn companion now suddenly opened his mouth, counted the stamens, and said rather dryly, "It belongs to the eighth family."

It always irritates me when I see that even God's dear flowers have been divided into classes, just as we have been, and according to similarity in externals, namely, the difference in the stamens. If a classification has to be made, then one should follow Theophrastus'[55] proposal to classify flowers according to their spirit, that is, according to their scent. As far as I am concerned, I have my own system in natural science, and classify everything

55. A Greek philosopher, pupil of Plato and Aristotle. In one of his works on plants he dealt with their taste and their odor.

accordingly: into what can be eaten and what can't . . .

The students now also made preparations for departure. Knapsacks were tied, bills, which proved to be reasonable beyond all expectation, were settled; the susceptible maids, traces of happy love on their faces, brought the Brocken bouquets, as is the custom, helped to fasten them to our caps, were rewarded for this with kisses or groschen, and so we all descended the mountain, some . . . taking the path to Schierke, and the others, about twenty persons, including my countrymen and myself, led by a guide, went down through the so-called "snow-holes"[56] to Ilsenburg.

We went full-tilt. Halle students march faster than the Austrian militia.[57] Before I knew it, the bald part of the mountain with the piles of boulders scattered over it lay behind us, and we passed through a fir forest such as I had seen the day before. The sun was already pouring down its most festive rays, lighting up the lads clad in a comical motley of colors who pressed so cheerfully through the thicket, now vanishing from view, now appearing again, at swampy places running over the tree trunks laid across, climbing precipitous slopes by the intertwining roots, shouting out the most delightful tunes, and receiving just as merry an answer from the twittering forest birds, from the rustling firs, from the invisibly rippling springs, and from the ringing echoes. When happy youth and lovely nature meet, they rejoice together.

The lower we descended, the sweeter was the murmur of the underground waters, only here and there, beneath stones and underbrush, did they flash out and seemed secretly to be listening to see whether they dared venture forth, and at last one tiny wave sprang out resolutely.

56. These are narrow gorges on the north side of the Brocken, protected from the sun enough so that snow and ice are often found there until August.

57. Proverbial for its slowness on the march.

Now the usual phenomenon appears: a bold one makes the beginning, and the great throng of timid ones is suddenly, to its own astonishment, inspired with courage and hastens to join the first. Many other springs now hopped hastily out of hiding, united with the one that had leaped out first, and soon they formed together a sizeable little brook that rushes down the mountain valley in countless waterfalls and curious meanderings. This is the Ilse, the lovely, sweet Ilse. It passes through the blessed Ilse valley, on both sides of which the mountains gradually rise higher, and these are for the most part covered right to the foot with beeches, oaks, and common deciduous shrubs, no longer with firs and other conifers. For the former predominate in the Lower Harz, as the east side of the Brocken is called, in contrast to the west side, which is called the Upper Harz and is actually much higher and therefore much more suitable for the thriving of conifers.

It is indescribable with what joyousness, naivete, and charm the Ilse plunges down over the fantastically shaped boulders it finds in its course, so that the water hisses up wildly here or overflows in foam, and in another spot gushes in unbroken arches from all sorts of crevices between the stones as if out of frenzied watering cans, and below trips along again over the small stones like a happy girl. Yes, the legend is true, the Ilse is a princess who runs down the mountain laughing and blooming. How her white robe of foam flashes in the sunlight! How the silver ribbons she wears on her breast flutter in the breeze! How her diamonds sparkle and blaze! The tall beeches stand there like solemn fathers who, smiling to themselves, watch the mischievousness of the lovely child; the white birches move like delighted aunts, and yet at the same time anxious about her daring leaps; the proud oak tree looks on like an ill-tempered uncle who has to foot the bills; the birds in the air carol out their applause; the flowers on the bank whisper affectionately, "Oh, take us with you, take us with you, dear sister,"—but the merry maiden leaps along impetuously, and suddenly she seizes the dreaming poet, and a flower-rain of sounding rays and radiant tones pours down on me, and I lose consciousness from sheer splendor, and I can hear only the flute-sweet voice:

> I am the princess Ilse,
> I dwell at Ilsenstein;
> let us be blessed together,
> come to the castle mine.

> There I will bathe your temples
> with waters clear and bright,
> till you forget your suffering,
> you sick and hapless wight.

> With my white arms around you,
> cradled on my white breast,
> you shall be happily dreaming
> of legends as you rest.

> I'll play with you and kiss you
> as I once kissed and played
> with my beloved Heinrich
> ere he to rest was laid.

> The dead stay dead forever,
> only the living live,
> my laughing heart is trembling,
> I've love and life to give.

> And when my heart is trembling,
> my crystal halls ring out,
> with knights and ladies dancing,
> while joyous vassals shout.

The silken trains are rustling,
the spurs a-jingle, heigh-ho!
The dwarfs sound blaring trumpets,
they fiddle, and drum, and blow.

My arms shall warmly hold you
as once they held my king;
I covered the ears of Heinrich
when the trumpets began to ring.[58]

It is an infinitely blissful feeling when the physical world blends with our inner world, and green trees, thoughts, birdsong, sadness, the blue of the sky, memory, and fragrance of herbs intertwine in sweet arabesques. Women know this feeling best, and this may be the reason why such a charmingly sceptical smile hovers about their lips when we boast with pedantic pride of our logical accomplishments, how we have divided everything so neatly into objective and subjective, how we have furnished our heads with a thousand drawers, in one of which is reason, in the next intelligence, in the third wit, in the fourth vulgarity, and in the fifth nothing at all, namely, the idea.

Wandering on as in a dream, I almost failed to notice that we had left the depths of the Ilse valley and were again climbing uphill. It was very steep and strenuous going, and many of us got out of breath. But like our late-lamented cousin who lies buried in Mölln,[59] we thought in anticipation of the descent and were all the merrier. Finally we arrived at the Ilse Stone.

58. The reference is supposedly to Emperor Henry the Fowler, the founder of Goslar, and one of the many German emperors who loved the Harz region.

59. A reference to Till Eulenspiegel, who lived in the fourteenth century and is supposed to have been buried at Mölln, near Lübeck, where his gravestone bears the image of an owl *(Eule)* looking into a mirror *(Spiegel)*. He became the roguish hero of a chapbook of the sixteenth century, a collection of anecdotes. The one referred to here is that when Till was climbing a mountain, he was always cheerful, since he knew he would soon enjoy the easy descent.

This is an enormous granite cliff rising boldly far out of the depths. High forest-covered mountains surround it on three sides, but the fourth, the north side, is open, and here one can see Ilsenburg below and the Ilse flowing far down into the lowlands. On the tower-like peak of the cliff stands a large iron cross, and in a pinch there is still room for four human feet.

Just as nature has adorned the Ilse Stone with the fantastic charms of its position and shape, so legend has also shed its rosy glow upon it. Gottschalk[60] reports: "It is said that an enchanted castle stood here, in which the rich and beautiful Princess Ilse lived, and that she bathed every morning in the Ilse; and anyone so fortunate as to hit upon the right time is led by her into the cliff, where her castle is, and royally rewarded." Others tell a nice story about the love between Miss Ilse and the knight of Westenberg . . . Still others tell the story differently. It is said to have been the Old Saxon Emperor Heinrich[61] who enjoyed the most imperial hours with Ilse, the beautiful nymph, in her enchanted cliff castle. A modern writer, Mr. Niemann, Esq.,[62] who has written a guide book to the Harz, in which he has given, with admirable industry and precise figures, the height of the mountains, variations of the magnetic needle, debts of the towns, and the like, maintains however: "What is told about the beautiful Princess Ilse belongs to the realm of fable." So say all people to whom such a princess has never appeared, but we who have been especially favored by fair ladies know better. Even Emperor Heinrich

60. Author of *Ein Taschenbuch für Reisende in den Harz (A Handbook for Travelers to the Harz)*, published in 1806, from which Heine seems to have obtained considerable information.

61. Henry the Fowler, mentioned above. See note 58.

62. Ludwig Ferdinand Niemann wrote a guide book to the Harz in 1824. The title given him here is used sarcastically to indicate the commonplace character of the author, who, as Heine describes the book, had no feeling for the beauty of the region.

knew better. Not for nothing were the Old Saxon emperors so very attached to their native Harz. Just leaf through the attractive *Lüneburg Chronicle,* in which the good old gentlemen are portrayed in curiously naive woodcuts, well-armored, high on their well-accoutered battle chargers, the holy imperial crown on their precious heads, scepter and sword in firm hands; and in their dear, mustachioed faces one can read distinctly that often they longed for the sweet hearts of their Harz princesses and the familiar rustling of the Harz forests when they were sojourning abroad, perhaps even in Italy, overflowing with lemons and poison, a land to which they and their successors were so often lured by the desire to be called Roman Emperors, a truly German lust for titles which brought about the downfall of emperors and empire.

I, however, advise anyone who stands on the peak of the Ilse Stone to think neither of emperor and empire nor of the beautiful Ilse, but simply of his own feet. For as I stood there, lost in thought, I suddenly heard the subterranean music of the magic castle and I saw the mountains round about stand on their heads, the red tile roofs in Ilsenburg began to dance, the green trees flew around in the blue air so that everything began to swim before my eyes and, seized by a fit of dizziness, I would certainly have plunged into the abyss if I had not, in my mortal distress, clung firmly to the iron cross. Surely no one will blame me for doing this in such precarious circumstances.[63]

63. Heine was no doubt thinking of the step he took the following year, 1825, when he became a member of the German Lutheran Church. The flippant tone of the reference is characteristic of Heine and is one of the qualities that make him, to this day, an enigmatic person.

At this point the original *Harz Journey* ended. Two years later Heine added approximately four pages, but these contribute nothing to the interest of the work, nor do they alter its fragmentary nature.

Buch Le Grand [1]

CHAPTER I

She was lovable, and he loved her; but he was not lovable, and she did not love him.
(FROM AN OLD PLAY)

Madame, do you know the old play? It is a very extraordinary work, only somewhat too melancholy. I once played the leading role in it, and all the ladies wept; only one did not, not a single tear did she weep, and this was just the point of the play, the real catastrophe.—

Oh, this single tear! It still torments me in my thoughts; when Satan tries to destroy my soul, he whispers in my ear a song about this unwept tear, an ominous song with an even more ominous melody—alas, only in Hell does one hear this melody!-----

You can well imagine, Madame, what life in Heaven is like, particularly as you are married. There one amuses oneself superbly, one has all kinds of entertainment, one lives in sheer delight and *plaisir* exactly as God does in France. You dine from morning till night, and the cuisine is as good as Jagor's,[2] roast geese fly around with little

1. Le Grand may have been a real person, a drum-major quartered in Heine's home during the occupation of Düsseldorf by the French. The name comes from the French term for Napoleon's army, *la Grande Armée*.

2. In Berlin.

bowls of gravy in their beaks and feel flattered when you consume them, tarts shiny with butter grow wild like sunflowers, everywhere brooks with bouillon and champagne, everywhere trees on which napkins flutter, and you dine and wipe your mouth and dine again without ruining your stomach; you sing psalms, or dally and flirt with the sweet little amorous angels, or you take a walk on the green Halleluja meadow, and the white flowing garments fit very comfortably, and nothing disturbs the feeling of bliss, no pain, no discomfort—why, even when someone accidentally trods on another's corns and exclaims, *"Excusez,"* the latter smiles as if transfigured and assures him, "Your step, Brother, does not hurt, but *au contraire,* my heart merely feels the Heavenly ecstasy to be all the sweeter for it."

But of Hell, Madame, you have absolutely no idea. You know perhaps among all the devils only the most insignificant, the laddie Beelzebub, Amor, the agreeable croupier of Hell. Hell itself you know only from *Don Giovanni,* and for this deceiver of women, who sets a bad example, it never seems to you hot enough, even though our most esteemed theater managers shoot off as great a display of flames, fireworks, powder, and rosin as any good Christian can ask for in Hell.

But things are far worse in Hell than our theater managers know—otherwise they wouldn't put on so many bad plays—in Hell it is quite hellishly hot, and when I was there once during the dog days, I found it unendurable. You have no idea of Hell, Madame. We get few official reports from there. That the poor souls down there are forced to read the whole day all the bad sermons that are printed up here—this is slander. It is not that bad in Hell; Satan will never concoct such subtle tortures. On the other hand, Dante's description is a little too moderate, altogether much too poetic. To me Hell seemed like a big middle-class kitchen with an end-lessly long stove on which stood three rows of iron pots, and in these sat the damned and were roasted. In one row sat the Christian sinners, and—you wouldn't believe it—their number was not so very small, and the devils stirred up the fire under them with particular zeal. In the next row sat the Jews, who screamed constantly and sometimes were teased by the devils, and it did look too funny when a fat, puffing pawnbroker complained about the too great heat and a little devil poured some pails of cold water over his head so that he could see that baptism is a real, refreshing blessing. In the third row sat the heathens, who, like the Jews, cannot partake of eternal bliss and must burn forever. I heard one of them call out indignantly from his pot as a thickset devil was putting fresh coals under him, "Spare me, I was Socrates, the wisest of mortals. I taught truth and justice and sacrificed my life for virtue." But the stupid, thickset devil went about his business unconcernedly and snarled, "Nonsense, all heathens have to burn, and we can't make any exceptions just for one person."—I assure you, Madame, the heat was frightful, and there was a shrieking, sighing, groaning, croaking, whining, squealing—and through all these horrible sounds there penetrated audibly that ominous melody of the song about the unwept tear.

CHAPTER II

She was lovable, and he loved her; but he was not
lovable, and she did not love him.
(OLD PLAY)

Madame, the old play is a tragedy, though the hero is not murdered nor does he kill himself. The heroine's eyes

are beautiful, very beautiful—Madame, don't you smell
the fragrance of violets?—very beautiful, and yet so
keenly sharpened that they pierced my heart like glass
daggers and certainly peeped out my back—but I did not
die of these assassin eyes. The heroine's voice is beauti-
ful too—Madame, didn't you just hear a nightingale
singing?—a beautiful, silken voice, a sweet web of the
sunniest tones, and my soul was caught in it and was
tortured and strangled. I myself—it is the Count of the
Ganges who is now speaking, and the story takes place
in Venice—I myself had had enough of such tortures,
and as early as the first act I thought of putting an end
to the play and shooting off the fool's cap and bells along
with my head, and I went to a fancy-goods store on the
via Burstah,[3] where I found displayed a box with a pair
of beautiful pistols. I still remember them very well; next
to them were many gay toys of mother-of-pearl and gold,
iron hearts on gilded chains, porcelain cups with amor-
ous mottos, snuffboxes with pretty pictures, for example,
the magnificent story of Susanna, Leda's swan song, the
rape of the Sabines, Lucretia, that fat personification of
virtue with the bared bosom into which she subsequently
thrusts her dagger, the deceased Bethmann,[4] *la belle fer-
ronnière*,[5] all of them alluring faces—but I bought the
pistols anyway, without much haggling, and then I
bought powder and shot, and then I went to Signor
Greed's tavern and ordered oysters and a glass of Rhine
wine.—

I could not eat, much less drink. Hot drops fell into my
glass, and in the glass I saw my beloved homeland, the
sacred, blue Ganges, the eternally radiant Himalayas, the

3. A street in Hamburg.

4. Friederike Bethmann (1760-1814), one of the best actresses of her time.

5. An allusion to a portrait with this title believed to be by Leonardo da
Vinci. A *ferronnière* was a headband which originally formed the velvet rim of
a hair net, but was later made of gold and ornamented with jewels.

giant forests of banyan trees on whose broad, arbored paths clever elephants and white pilgrims strolled peacefully, strange, dreamy flowers gazed at me in secret warning, exotic golden birds rejoiced wildly, glittering sunbeams and sounds of sweet nonsense from laughing monkeys teased me charmingly. From remote pagodas sounded devout prayers of priests, and in between rang the meltingly lamenting voice of the Sultana of Delhi. She raced stormily back and forth in her carpeted boudoir, she tore her silver veil, she knocked down the black slave-girl with her fan of peacock feathers, she wept, she raged, she shrieked. I could not understand her though; Signor Greed's tavern is 3000 miles away from the harem at Delhi, and besides the beautiful Sultana had been dead for 3000 years—and I hastily drank the wine, the clear, joyous wine, and yet my soul became ever gloomier and sadder—I was condemned to death-----

When I ascended the tavern steps again, I heard the execution bell ringing. A throng of people surged past; I, however, stationed myself at the corner of the *strada* San Giovanni[6] . . . and as I stood there, a condemned man, doomed to death, I suddenly caught sight of *her!*

She was wearing her blue silk dress and the rose-red hat, and her eyes looked at me so gently, so victorious over death, so life-giving—Madame, you know well from Roman history that when the vestal virgins in ancient Rome met on their road a criminal who was being led to his execution, they had the right to pardon him, and the poor rogue remained alive.— With a single glance she saved me from death, and I stood before her like a new man, as if blinded by the sunny radiance of her beauty, and she went her way—and let me live.

6. The *Johannisstrasse* (St. John's Street) in Hamburg.

CHAPTER III

And she let me live, and I am alive, and that is the main thing.

Let others enjoy the good fortune of having their sweethearts decorate their graves with wreaths of flowers and water them with tears of fidelity—O, women! hate me, laugh at me, jilt me, but let me live. Life is just too amusingly sweet, and the world is so charmingly confused; it is the dream of an intoxicated god who has stolen away *à la française* from the carousing assembly of the gods and lain down to sleep on a lonely star and does not know himself that he also creates everything he dreams—and the dream images take shape, often madly lurid, but often harmoniously sensible. The Iliad, Plato, the battle of Marathon, Moses, the Venus of Medici, the Strassburg cathedral, the French Revolution, Hegel, steamships, etc., are excellent individual ideas in this creative divine dream. But it won't be long before the god will awaken and rub his sleepy eyes and smile—and our world will have vanished into nothing, indeed, it will never have existed.

No matter. I am alive. Even if I am only a phantom in a dream, this is better than the cold, black, empty nothingness of death. Life is the greatest of blessings, and the worst evil is death . . .

And I am alive! Nature's great pulse beat throbs in my breast too, and when I rejoice, a thousand-fold echo answers me. I hear a thousand nightingales. Spring sent them to waken the earth from its dawn slumber, and the earth trembles with delight; its flowers are the hymns it sings to the sun in its enthusiasm. The sun moves far too slowly; I would like to whip its fiery steeds so that they would race along faster.—But when it sinks down hissing into the sea, and the immense night ascends with its large, yearning eyes, oh, only then does real ecstasy thrill through me, like flattering maidens the evening breezes touch my stormy heart, and the stars beckon, and I rise and hover above the paltry earth and the paltry thoughts of men.

CHAPTER IV

But the day will come when the fire in my veins will be quenched, in my breast winter will dwell, its white flakes will flutter sparsely about my head, and its mists will veil my eyes. My friends lie in weathered graves, I alone have remained behind like a lonely stalk forgotten by the reaper, a new generation has blossomed forth with new desires and new ideas; with astonishment I hear new names and new songs. The old names are forgotten, and I myself am forgotten, still honored, perhaps, by a few, scorned by many, and loved by none! And the rosy-cheeked lads run up to me, pressing the old harp into my trembling hand, and say laughing, "You have been silent a long time, you lazy greybeard, sing to us again about the dreams of your youth."

Then I seize the harp, and old joys and sorrows awaken. The mists melt away, tears bloom again from my dead eyes, once more there is spring in my heart, sweet tones of melancholy quiver in the harp strings, I see again the blue river and the marble palaces, and the beautiful faces of women and girls—and I sing a song of the flowers by the Brenta.[7]

It will be my last song. The stars will gaze on me as in

7. A river in northeast Italy. It flows through Venezia into the lagoons of Venice.

the nights of my youth. The amorous moonlight kisses my cheeks again, the spirit choirs of dead nightingales flute from the distance, drunk with sleep my eyes close, my soul fades away like the tones of my harp—the flowers by the Brenta send forth their fragrance.

A tree will shade my gravestone. I would have liked a palm, but it does not thrive in the north. It will probably be a linden, and on summer evenings lovers will sit there and talk; the siskin rocking in the branches listens and keeps silent, and my linden rustles with sympathy above the heads of the happy lovers, so happy that they don't even have time to read what is written on the white tombstone. But when later the lover has lost his girl, he will return to the familiar linden and sigh and weep and look long and often at the tombstone and read the inscription on it:—He loved the flowers by the Brenta.

CHAPTER V

Madame, I lied to you. I am not the Count of the Ganges. I have never in my life seen that sacred river, never the lotos flowers that are mirrored in its pious waves. I never lay dreaming under Indian palms, I never lay praying before the diamond God in Juggernaut,[8] who might very possibly have helped me . . .

No, I was not born in India; I saw the light of the world on the banks of that beautiful river where Folly grows on the green hills, and in the autumn is picked, pressed, poured into casks, and sent abroad.—It is really true that yesterday at table I heard someone make a foolish remark which in the year 1811 was lodged in a grape that

8. A famous Indian place of pilgrimage where especially Krishna, but also other gods, were worshipped.

I myself saw growing then on the Johannisberg.—Much folly, however, is also consumed in the country itself, and the people there are as everywhere:—they are born, they eat, drink, sleep, laugh, cry, slander others, are anxiously concerned about the propagation of their species, try to appear what they are not and to do what they are incapable of, don't shave until they have a beard, and often have a beard before they have common sense, and even after that they get drunk again on white and red folly.

Mon Dieu! If I only had enough faith to move mountains—the Johannisberg would be just the mountain I would have follow me everywhere. But since my faith is not that strong, my imagination must help me, and it will transport me to the beautiful Rhine.

Oh, that is a lovely land, full of charm and sunshine. In the blue river are mirrored the hilly banks with their fortress ruins and woodlands and ancient towns.— There, on summer evenings, the townspeople sit in front of their houses, drinking from large mugs and chatting cosily about how the grapes, thank God, are flourishing, and how the courts must by all means be public, and how Marie Antoinette was simply guillotined unceremoniously, and how the state tobacco administration has raised the price of tobacco, and how all men are equal . . .

I never bothered about such conversations and preferred sitting with the girls at the bay window, laughing at their laughter, letting myself be pelted in the face with roses, and pretending to be angry until they told me their secrets or some other important concern. Lovely Gertrude was mad with joy when I sat down beside her; she was like a flaming rose, and once when she threw her arms about my neck, I thought she would burn up in my arms and disappear. Lovely Katharine dissolved in sweet-voiced tenderness when she spoke to me, and her eyes were of a pure, intense blue such as I have never yet seen in human beings or animals and only rarely in flowers. You enjoyed looking into them; you could imagine so many sweet things. But beautiful Hedwig loved me; for when I approached her, she bowed her head so that her black locks fell over her blushing face and her sparkling eyes shone like stars from a dark sky. Her bashful lips spoke no word, and I too could say nothing. I coughed, and she trembled. Sometimes she had her sister ask me not to climb the cliffs so fast and not to swim in the Rhine if I were heated from running or drinking. Once I overheard her reverent prayer before the little statue of Mary which stood in a niche in the hallway, decorated with gold spangles and encircled by the glitter of a burning lamp; I distinctly heard her ask the Blessed Virgin to forbid him to climb, drink, or swim. I would certainly have fallen in love with the beautiful girl if she had cared nothing about me; and I didn't care about her because I knew that she loved me—Madame, if anyone wants to be loved by me, she will have to treat me *en canaille.* [9]

Lovely Johanna was the cousin of the three sisters, and I liked to sit beside her. She knew the most delightful legends, and when she pointed with her white hand from the window toward the hills where everything she told had happened, I felt downright bewitched. The old knights emerged distinctly from the fortress ruins and hacked each other's iron garments to pieces; the Lorelei again stood on the mountain top and sang into the depths her sweet and disastrous song; and the Rhine murmured so sensibly, soothingly, and yet at the same time with teasing eeriness—and the lovely Johanna looked at me so strangely, so mysteriously, with such enigmatic familiarity, as if she herself were a part of the fairy tales of which she had just been speaking. She was

9. Like the scum of the earth.

a pale, slender girl, sick unto death, and pensive. Her eyes were clear as truth itself, her lips devoutly arched, in the features of her countenance lay a great story, but it was a sacred story—perhaps a love story? I do not know, nor did I ever have the courage to ask her. If I looked at her for a long time, I became calm and serene, and felt as if a peaceful Sabbath reigned in my heart, with angels holding devotionals there.

In such good hours I told her stories of my childhood, and she always listened seriously; and strange to say, if I could no longer recall the names, she reminded me of them. Then when I asked her in surprise how she knew them, she answered smiling that she had heard them from the birds that nested in the tiled eaves above her window. And she even tried to make me believe that these were the same birds I had bought as a boy with my pocket-money from the hard-hearted farm boys and had then let fly away to freedom. I believe, however, that she knew everything because she was so pale and actually died soon after. She also knew when she would die and wanted me to leave Andernach the day before. On parting she gave me both hands—they were sweet, white hands and pure as the Host—and she said, "You are very good, and if you become wicked, think once more of little, dead Veronica."

Did the talkative birds reveal this name to her too? I had so often racked my brains in hours of yearning memories without being able to remember that dear name.

Now that I have it again, my earliest childhood opens its blossoms again in my mind, and I am a child again, playing with other children on the Castle Square in Düsseldorf on the Rhine.

CHAPTER VI

Yes, Madame, I was born there, and I note this expressly in case after my death, seven cities—Schilda, Krähwinkel, Polkwitz, Bockum, Dülken, Göttingen, and Schöppenstedt—quarrel over the honor of being my home town.[10] Düsseldorf is a city on the Rhine, 16,000 people live there, and in addition many hundred thousands lie buried there. And among these are many of whom my mother says it would be better if they were still alive, for example, my grandfather and my uncle, the old Mr. v. Geldern and the young Mr. v. Geldern, who were both such famous doctors and cured so many people of death and yet had to die themselves . . .

The town of Düsseldorf is very beautiful, and if you think of it when you are far away, and happen to have been born there, you have a strange feeling. I was born there, and I feel as if I had to go home immediately. And when I say "go home," I mean Bolker Street and the house where I was born. This house will some day be very famous, and I have sent word to the old woman who owns it for Heaven's sake not to sell it. She would now get scarcely as much for the whole house as the tips alone will amount to which the green-veiled, elegant English women will one day give the maid when she shows them the room where I first saw the light of the world and the chicken house where father usually locked me in when I had been nibbling grapes on the sly, and also the brown door on which mother taught me to write the letters of

10. The reference is to the legend that seven cities claimed to be the birthplace of Homer. With the exception of Göttingen, on which Heine always liked to vent his spite, these towns are all insignificant, and probably all are meant to represent the stereotype of provincial stupidity. Schilda, for instance, was immortalized in a sixteenth-century chapbook, a collection of anecdotes about the stupidity of its inhabitants, such as building a town hall with no windows and then trying to carry light inside in pails and bags.

the alphabet with chalk.—Ah me! Madame, if I become
a famous writer, it will have cost my poor mother plenty
of trouble . . .

At that time rulers were not so beset with cares as now,
and their crowns had grown fast to their heads, and at
night they just pulled their night caps over them and
slept peacefully. And the nations slept peacefully at their
feet, and when they awoke in the morning, they said,
"Good morning, father,"—and the rulers answered,
"Good morning, dear children."

But suddenly things changed. One morning when we
woke up in Düsseldorf and were about to say "Good
morning, father," father had gone away, and in the
whole city there was nothing but a dull anxiety, a fune-
real air pervaded everything, and people crept silently to
the market place to read the long paper placard on the
door of the town hall. The weather was gloomy, and yet
the thin tailor, Kilian, stood in his Nanking jacket, which
he usually wore only in the house, and his blue woolen
stockings hung down, so that his bare legs peeped out
mournfully, and his thin lips trembled as he mumbled to
himself the words on the placard. An old disabled vet-
eran from the Palatinate read somewhat louder, and at
many a word a bright tear trickled down into his honest
white moustache. I stood beside him and cried with him
and asked him why we were crying. And he answered,
"The Elector expresses his gratitude." And then he read
on, and at the words "for the proven loyalty of his sub-
jects" "and releases you from your obligations," he wept
even more bitterly.—To see such an old man in a faded
uniform and with a scarred soldier's face suddenly burst
into tears is a strange sight. As we were reading, the
electoral escutcheon was taken down from the town hall.
A frightening desolateness hung over everything, and it
seemed as if we were expecting an eclipse of the sun. The
town councillors walked slowly about, with an air of hav-

ing been dismissed. Even the all-powerful constable looked as if he had no more orders to give and stood there so calmly and unconcernedly, even though crazy Alouisius was again standing on one leg, cackling out the names of the French generals with foolish grimaces, while drunken, misshapen Gumpertz was rolling around in the gutter singing, "*Ça ira, ça ira.*"[11]

I, however, went home and cried and lamented, "The Elector expresses his gratitude." My mother had a hard time with me; I knew what I knew, and would not let myself be talked out of it. I went to bed crying, and during the night I dreamed the world was coming to an end; the pretty flower gardens and green meadows were taken up and rolled together like carpets from the floor; the constable climbed a tall ladder and took the sun down from the sky; the tailor Kilian stood watching and talking to himself, "I have to go home and put my best clothes on, for I am dead and am to be buried today." And it became darker and darker; up above a few stars shone dimly, and even these fell down like yellow leaves in the autumn. The people gradually vanished; I, poor child, wandered anxiously about, finally stopped in front of the willow hedge of a run-down farm, and saw there a man digging in the ground with a spade and beside him an ugly, malicious-looking woman holding in her apron something resembling a decapitated human head, and that was the moon, and she laid it with extravagant care in the open pit.—And behind me stood the disabled veteran from the Palatinate sobbing and spelling out, "The Elector expresses his gratitude."

When I awoke, the sun was shining through the window again as usual, on the street a drum was beating, and when I entered our living room and said "Good morning" to my father, who was sitting in his white dressing

11. French popular song of the Revolution.

gown, I heard the agile hairdresser, while doing his hair, telling him in every tiny detail that today allegiance would be sworn to the new Grand Duke Joachim[12] at the town hall and that he was from one of the best families, had married Emperor Napoleon's sister, was really very refined, wore his beautiful black hair in curls, would make his entrance into the town any minute, and would surely find favor with all the women. Meanwhile the drumming outside continued, and I went out in front of the house and watched the French troops marching in, this happy nation of glorious renown that marched through the world with flourish of trumpets and beating of drums, the serio-comic faces of the grenadiers, the bearskin caps, the tricolored cockades, the glittering bayonets, the light-infantrymen full of gaiety and *point d'honneur,* and the almightily tall, silver-embroidered drum-major, who could throw his baton with the gilded head up to the second story of a house and his eyes as high as the third—where beautiful girls were sitting at the windows. I was glad we were to have troops quartered on us—my mother wasn't—and I hurried to the market place. There things looked completely different; it was as if the world had been freshly painted, a new coat-of-arms hung on the town hall, the iron railing on its balcony was draped with embroidered velvet, French grenadiers stood guard, the old town councillors had put on new faces and were wearing their Sunday jackets and looked at each other in French and said *bon jour,* ladies peered from all the windows, inquisitive townsmen and spruce soldiers filled the square, and some other boys and I climbed up on the Elector's big horse and from there looked down on the motley throng in the market place . . .

12. Joachim Murat, husband of Napoleon's sister Caroline, was given this title by Napoleon. Murat played an important role during Napoleon's campaigns.

Big Kurz told us there would be no school today because of the oath of allegiance. We had to wait a long time for the ceremony to begin. At last the balcony of the town hall filled with gay-colored gentlemen, banners, and trumpets, and the lord mayor in his famous red coat made a speech that stretched in length like rubber elastic or a knitted night cap into which a stone has been thrown — only not the philosopher's stone—and I could hear some phrases quite distinctly, for example, that they wanted to make us happy—and at the last word the trumpets were blown, the banners waved, the drums beaten, and there were shouts of *Vivat;* and while I myself shouted *Vivat,* I held fast to the old Elector. This was necessary, for I actually got dizzy, I even thought the people were standing on their heads because the world turns, the Elector's head with his bagwig nodded and whispered, "Hold fast to me"—and only the cannonade that now started on the ramparts brought me back to earth, and I slowly climbed down again from the Elector's horse.

On my way home I once more saw crazy Alouisius dancing on one leg and screeching out the names of the French generals, and deformed, drunken Gumpertz rolling in the gutter and roaring *"Ça ira, ça ira,"* and I said to my mother, "They want to make us happy, and so there is no school today."

CHAPTER VII

The next day the world was again completely in order, and there was school as usual, and there was memorizing as usual—the Roman kings, dates, *nomina* ending in *im, verba irregularia,* Greek, Hebrew, geography, German,

mental arithmetic—God! my head still gets dizzy from
it—everything had to be memorized . . . I had trouble in
school with the many dates! With actual arithmetic it was
even worse. I understood subtraction best, and for that
there is a very practical rule: "Four can't be subtracted
from three, so I have to borrow one"—but I advise
everyone in such cases always to borrow a few groschen
more, for you can never know.—

As for Latin, Madame, you have absolutely no idea
how complicated it is. The Romans would certainly not
have had time enough left to conquer the world if they
had first had to learn Latin. These lucky people already
knew in their cradles which *nomina* have *im* in the accusa-
tive. But I had to memorize them by the sweat of my
brow; still it is good that I know them. Supposing, for
example, on the 20th of July, 1825, when I debated in
Latin in public in the main auditorium at Göttingen—
Madame, it was worth listening to—I had said *sinapem*
instead of *sinapim*, the first-year students present would
perhaps have noticed it, and that would have been for me
an everlasting disgrace . . .

About Greek I don't care to speak at all or I'll get too
angry. The monks in the Middle Ages were not so en-
tirely wrong when they maintained that Greek was an
invention of the devil. God knows the suffering I en-
dured from it. In Hebrew things went better since I al-
ways had a special liking for the Jews, although, even to
this hour, they crucify my good name. But I still couldn't
get as far in Hebrew as my pocket watch, which was on
very intimate terms with pawnbrokers and for this reason
took on many a Jewish custom—for example, on Satur-
days it didn't run—and learned the holy language and
also later studied the grammar, so that to my astonish-
ment I often heard it during sleepless nights ticking con-
tinuously to itself: "*katal, katalta, katalti—kittel, kittalta,*

kittalti——pokat, pokadeti—pokat, pokadeti—pikat—pik—pik. ''[13]—

I understood the German language much better, and *it* is after all not exactly child's play. For we poor Germans, who are already plagued enough with quartering of foreign troops, military duties, poll taxes, and a thousand different kinds of fees, have saddled ourselves with Adelung[14] into the bargain and torture each other with the accusative and the dative . . .

While writing steadily and at the same time thinking of many things, I have unintentionally got onto the subject of old school stories, and I seize this opportunity to show you, Madame, that it was not my fault if I learned so little about geography that later I couldn't find my way about in the world. You see, at that time the French had moved all the boundaries. Every day the countries were colored differently; those formerly blue now suddenly turned green, many even became blood-red; the exact populations given in our textbooks got so mixed-up that nobody could make head or tail of them; the products of the countries also changed, chicory and beets now grew where formerly there were only hares and country squires running after them. Even the character of the peoples changed; the Germans became docile, the French stopped flattering, the English no longer threw their money out of the window, and the Venetians were not cunning enough. There were many promotions among the rulers; old kings received new uniforms, new kingdoms were baked and sold like hotcakes, many potentates, however, were chased out of house and home and had to try to earn their living in some other way, and

13. *Katal,* etc., are forms of the perfect tense of the Hebrew verb meaning "to kill," the model verb used in many Hebrew grammars; *pokat, pokadeti, pikat* are corresponding forms of the verb meaning "to seek."

14. A German grammarian whose dictionary and books on German grammar and syntax were regarded as the standard works in the field.

some therefore learned a trade when young and made sealing-wax, for example, or—Madame, this sentence is finished at last, I was about to run out of breath—in brief, at such times you can't get very far in geography.

One has an easier time with natural history, not so many changes can occur there, and we have accurate copper engravings of monkeys, kangaroos, zebras, rhinoceros, etc. Because such pictures stuck in my mind it later happened very often that many people looked to me right away like old friends.

I did well in mythology too. I enjoyed tremendously the rabble of gods that ruled the world in cheerful nudity. I don't think there was ever a schoolboy in ancient Rome who memorized the chief articles of his catechism, for example, Venus' love affairs, more thoroughly than I. To be honest, since we had to memorize the ancient gods anyway, we should have kept them too, and perhaps we are not much better off with our neo-Roman trinitarianism or even with our Jewish mono-idolatry. Perhaps this mythology was after all not so immoral as it has been called; for instance, it is a very decent idea of Homer's to give his much-beloved Venus a husband.

I did best of all in the French class of the Abbé d'Aulnoi,[15] a French emigrant who had written a lot of grammars and wore a red wig and jumped around skillfully when he recited his *Art poétique*[16] and his *Histoire allemande*[17]. . .

Parbleu Madame! I became very proficient in French! I understand not only patois, but even aristocratic nursery French. Not long ago, at a fashionable party, I understood almost half the conversation of two German countesses, each of whom was over sixty-four years old and possessed that many ancestors. What is more, at the Café

15. Heine also refers to him in his *Memoirs,* but writes the name "Daunoi." The abbot was apparently an uninspiring teacher.
16. *Art of Versification.*
17. *German History.*

Royal in Berlin I once heard Monsieur Hans Michel Martens[18] speak French and understood every word even though it made no sense. You have to know the spirit of the language, and this you learn best by beating the drum. *Parbleu!* how much I owe the French drummer who was quartered at our house so long and looked like a devil, while at heart he was good as an angel and drummed so very splendidly.

His figure was small and lithe, and he had a dreadful black moustache, beneath which his red lips protruded defiantly as his fiery eyes darted back and forth.

Little boy that I was, I stuck to him like a burr and helped him polish his buttons until they shone like mirrors and whiten his vest with chalk—for Monsieur Le Grand enjoyed admiration—and I also followed him to guard duty, to inspection, and on parade, where there was nothing but the gleam of arms and gaiety—*les jours de fête sont passés!*[19] Monsieur Le Grand knew only a little broken German, only the most important expressions—bread, kiss, honor—yet on the drum he could make himself understood very well. For instance, if I did not know what the word *liberté* meant, he drummed the Marseillaise—and I understood him. If I did not know the meaning of the word *égalité*, he drummed the march "*Ça ira, ça ira---les aristocrates à la lanterne!*"[20]—and I understood him. If I did not understand *bêtise*,[21] he drummed the Dessau March,[22] which we Germans, as even Goethe reports, drummed in Champagne—and I understood him. Once he wanted to explain to me the word *l'Al-*

18. Heine probably meant Karl von Martens, nephew of a well-known diplomat.

19. The festive days are past.

20. "It will go on, it will go on--- Hang the aristocrats!"

21. Stupidity.

22. A military march song named after Prince Leopold of Anhalt-Dessau, who took part in the War of the Spanish Succession and assisted in the battle of Turin in 1706 which resulted in the permanent exclusion of the French from Italy. Leopold was welcomed by this march upon his entrance into Turin.

lemagne,[23] and he drummed that all too simple primitive melody that one often hears played on market days for dancing dogs, namely, Dum—Dum—Dum—[24] I was annoyed, but still I understood him.

He also taught me modern history in a similar fashion. To be sure, I did not understand the words he spoke, but since he drummed constantly as he talked, I knew what he meant. Actually, this is the best method of instruction. You really understand the story of the storming of the Bastille, of the Tuileries, and so on, if you know how they beat the drums on those occasions. In our textbooks you read only: "Their Excellencies the Barons and Counts and their devoted consorts were beheaded—their Highnesses the Dukes and Princes and their most devoted consorts were beheaded—His Majesty the King and his most exceedingly devoted consort were beheaded—" but only when you hear the red guillotine march[25] drummed, do you understand all this rightly, and you learn the why and the how. Madame, it is a very curious march. It chilled me to the marrow of my bones when I first heard it, and I was glad to forget it.—One does forget such things as one gets older. A young man has so much other knowledge to keep in his head nowadays —whist, Boston,[26] genealogical tables, decrees of the Diet of the German Federation, dramaturgy, liturgy, the carving of meat—and really, despite all jogging of my memory, for a long time I could not recall that stirring melody. But just think, Madame, not long ago I was sitting at table with a whole menagery of counts, princes, princesses, chamberlains, wives of court marshals, court cupbearers, chief ladies-in-waiting, keepers of the court silver, ladies of the chase, and whatever else these ele-

23. Germany.

24. Heine makes here a pun that is also obvious in English, *dum* for the sound of the drum, with its other meaning *dumm* (dumb) implied.

25. The Marseillaise.

26. Like whist, a game of cards.

gant domestics may be called, and their subordinate
domestics ran behind their chairs and shoved the loaded
plates in front of their mouths—I, however, who had
been passed by and overlooked, sat idle without the
slightest activity of my jaws, and I kneaded little balls of
bread and drummed with my fingers out of boredom,
and to my horror I was suddenly drumming the red,
long-forgotten guillotine march.

"And what happened?" Madame, these people don't
let themselves be inconvenienced while eating and don't
know that other people, when they have nothing to eat,
suddenly begin to beat their drums and to play very
curious marches, supposedly long since forgotten.

Now whether drumming is an inborn talent or whether
I developed it at an early age, suffice it to say, it's in my
very limbs, in my hands and feet, and often expresses
itself involuntarily. Involuntarily. In Berlin I once at-
tended a lecture by Geheimrat Schmalz,[27] a man who
saved the state by his book on the danger of black coats
and red coats—[28] . . . I was attending his lectures on the
rights of the peoples, and it was a boring summer after-
noon, and I was sitting on the bench and hearing less and
less—my head had gone to sleep—but suddenly I was
awakened by the sound of my own feet, which had re-
mained awake and had probably heard that just the op-
posite of the rights of the peoples was being expounded
and that the demand for constitutional government was
being condemned; and my feet, which could see through
the doings of the world with their little corns[29] better
than the Geheimrat with his big Juno-eyes, these poor,
mute feet, unable to express in words their humble opin-

27. *Geheimrat* means literally "member of the privy council." It is a rather
common honorary title. Schmalz, a writer on law and politics and a judge of
appeal, had been a professor at the University of Berlin since 1810.

28. A reference to Schmalz' denunciation of various patriotic student organ-
izations as revolutionary and radical.

29. A pun impossible to translate into English. The German word for
"corns," *Hühneraugen*, means literally "hens' eyes."

ion, tried to make themselves understood by drumming on the floor, and they drummed so hard that I very nearly got into trouble because of it.

Cursed, thoughtless feet! They once played me a similar trick when I was attending a lecture in Göttingen by Professor Saalfeld[30] and he leaped back and forth on the rostrum with clumsy agility and worked himself into a passion the better to abuse the Emperor Napoleon roundly—no, poor feet, I can't blame you for drumming then; in fact, I wouldn't have blamed you if in your mute naivete you had expressed yourselves more clearly with a kick. How can I, a pupil of Le Grand, hear the Emperor abused? The Emperor! the Emperor! the great Emperor![31]

When I think of the great Emperor, my memory summons a vision all summer-green and golden. A long avenue of flowering lindens rises up before me, on their leafy branches perch singing nightingales; the waterfall roars; flowers in circular beds dreamily move their lovely heads—I stood there in curious communion with them; painted tulips greeted me condescendingly in their beggar's pride; neurotic lilies nodded with melancholy tenderness; ravishingly red roses smiled at me even from afar; the dame's violets sighed . . . I am speaking of the palace garden at Düsseldorf where I often lay on the lawn, listening reverently as Monsieur Le Grand told me about the great Emperor's military exploits, at the same time beating the marches that were drummed during these actions, so that I saw and heard everything vividly. I saw the march over the Simplon[32]—the Emperor leading the way and the brave grenadiers climbing behind

30. Professor of philosophy in Göttingen and author of numerous historical writings including a biography of Napoleon, published 1815 to 1817.

31. Like many Germans, Heine, too, greatly admired Napoleon.

32. An Alpine pass crossed by the Simplon Road, built by Napoleon in 1800-1806.

him, while startled birds set up their screeching, and glaciers thundered in the distance—I saw the Emperor clasping the standard on the bridge of Lodi[33]—I saw the Emperor in his gray cloak at Marengo—I saw the Emperor on horseback in the battle of the Pyramids—nothing but powder smoke and Mamalukes—I saw the Emperor at the battle of Austerlitz—whew! how the bullets whistled over the slippery ice field—I saw, I heard the battle of Jena—dum, dum, dum—I saw, I heard the battle of Eylau, of Wagram-----no, I could scarcely bear it! Monsieur Le Grand beat his drum till my own ear drum nearly cracked.

CHAPTER VIII

But who can describe my feelings when my own eyes were blessed by the sight of him himself, him himself, hosanna! the Emperor!

It was right there in the avenue of the palace garden in Düsseldorf. As I pressed through the gaping crowd, I thought of the exploits and battles that Monsieur Le Grand had drummed for me; my heart beat the call to arms—and yet at the same time I thought of the police regulation that one couldn't ride down the avenue without paying a fine of five taler. And the Emperor with his retinue rode right down the avenue; the shuddering trees bent forward as he rode past; the sunbeams quivered, timidly curious, through the green foliage; and in the blue sky above, clearly visible, swam a golden star. The Emperor was wearing his plain green uniform and his small, historic hat. He rode a little white horse that

33. A city in northern Italy where Napoleon defeated the Austrians in May, 1796.

stepped with such calm pride, such assurance, such dis-
tinction—if I had been the Crown Prince of Prussia then,
I would have envied this tiny steed. The Emperor sat
carelessly, almost slouching, his one hand holding the
reins high, the other patting the horse's neck good-
naturedly.—It was a gleaming marble hand, a mighty
hand, one of the two hands that had subdued the many-
headed monster of anarchy and settled the disputes be-
tween one nation and another—and it patted the horse's
neck good-naturedly. Even his face had the color that we
find in marble Greek and Roman busts; its features were
also nobly proportioned like those of the ancients, and
on this face stood written: "Thou shalt have no other
gods before me." A smile that warmed and soothed ev-
ery heart hovered about his lips—and yet one knew these
lips needed only to whistle—*et la Prusse n'existait plus*[34]—
these lips needed only to whistle—and the whole clergy
was done for—these lips needed only to whistle—and
the entire Holy Roman Empire danced. And these lips
smiled, and even his eyes smiled.—They were eyes clear
as the sky; they could read the hearts of men; they per-
ceived quickly and simultaneously all earthly things,
whereas we others see them only one by one and even
then merely their tinted shadows. His brow was not so
clear; on it brooded the spirits of future battles, and
occasionally a quiver passed across this brow, and this
was his creative thoughts, the great seven-league-boot
thoughts with which the Emperor's spirit stalked invisi-
bly over the world—and I think any one of these
thoughts would have provided a German writer abun-
dant material to write about for the whole of his life.

The Emperor rode calmly down the avenue; no police-
man opposed him; behind him rode his retinue, proudly
seated on snorting steeds laden with golden, bejeweled

34. And Prussia no longer existed.

trappings. The drums rolled, the trumpets sounded, beside me crazy Alouisius whirled round and round, screeching out the names of his generals; not far away drunken Gumpertz bellowed, and the people cried with a thousand voices: "Long live the Emperor!"

CHAPTER IX

The Emperor is dead. On a barren island in the Indian Ocean is his lonely grave, and he, for whom this world was too small, rests peacefully beneath a little mound where five weeping willows let their green hair stream down sadly, and a devout little brook ripples past with mournful plaint. There is no inscription on his tomb, but Clio, with her just stylus, wrote on it invisible words that will ring like spirit-voices though the millennia.

Britannia! the ocean belongs to you. But the ocean does not contain water sufficient to wash you clean of the disgrace which this great mortal bequeathed you when he died. Not your blustering Sir Hudson,[35] no, you yourself were the Sicilian jailer hired by the plotting kings to revenge in secret on the man of the people what the people had once publicly done to one of your company. —And he was your guest and had seated himself at your hearth— . . .

35. Sir Hudson Lowe (1769-1844), an English general, from 1815 to 1821 governor of St. Helena and Napoleon's custodian. He gained a bad reputation for treating Napoleon without the proper respect, and in 1830 he published a self-vindication in two volumes, *Mémorial relatif à la captivité de Napoléon à Ste.-Hélène.*

CHAPTER X

It was a clear, frosty autumn day when a young man, apparently a student, walked slowly down the avenue of the palace garden at Düsseldorf, sometimes, as if in childish delight, kicking up the rustling leaves that covered the ground, sometimes, however, looking up sadly at the bare trees, on which only a few yellow leaves still hung . . .

In earlier days the young man had looked up at these very same trees with quite different thoughts. He was a boy then and was looking for birds' nests or for ladybugs, which delighted him greatly when they buzzed along merrily and rejoiced at the beautiful world and were content with a juicy green leaflet holding a small drop of dew, with a warm sunbeam, and with the sweet fragrance of herbs. Then the boy's heart was just as happy as the fluttering insects. But now his heart had grown older, the little sunbeams in it had vanished, all the flowers in it had died, even its beautiful dream of love had faded, in his wretched heart there was nothing but ill-humor and sorrow, and, to tell the most painful part —it was my heart . . .

I was not tired, but still I felt the desire to sit again on the wooden bench on which I had once carved the name of my girl. I could scarcely find it; so many new names had been scratched across it . . .

As I was sitting on the old bench in the palace garden, dreaming of days gone by, I heard behind me a confusion of voices lamenting the fate of the poor Frenchmen who, dragged to Siberia as prisoners in the Russian War, had been detained there for several years, despite the peace, and were only now returning home. When I looked up, I actually saw these orphans of glory; naked

misery peered through the tears in their ragged uni-
forms; in their weather-beaten faces were sunken,
mournful eyes; and although maimed, exhausted, most
of them limping, they nevertheless kept in step after a
fashion, and oddly enough a drummer with a drum tot-
tered in the lead. And with an inward shudder I was
overwhelmed by the recollection of the tale about the
soldiers who fell in battle during the day and at night rise
again from the battlefield and, with the drummer at the
head, march back to their native town . . .

Indeed the poor French drummer appeared to have
climbed, half decomposed, from the grave. He was only
a tiny shadow in a dirty, ragged gray overcoat, with a
dead yellow face and a large moustache that hung down
sadly over his pale lips; his eyes were like burned-out
tinder in which only a few sparks still glowed, and yet by
just one of these sparks I recognized Monsieur Le
Grand.

He recognized me too and pulled me down on to the
lawn, and there we sat once more as we used to when he
taught me French and modern history on the drum. It
was still the familiar old drum, and I could not get over
my astonishment at his having protected it from Russian
greed. He beat the drum again as of old, but without
speaking. Though his lips were uncannily compressed,
his eyes spoke all the more, and they lighted up trium-
phantly as he drummed the old marches. The poplars
beside us trembled when he let the red guillotine march
rumble out again. He drummed the old wars of libera-
tion as before, the old battles, and the Emperor's ex-
ploits, and it seemed as if the drum itself were a living
thing that rejoiced at being able to express its inner
ecstasy. I heard once more the thunder of cannons, the
whistle of bullets, the noise of battle; I saw once more the
guard regiment steadfast unto death, I saw once more
the waving banners, I saw once more the Emperor on

horseback. But gradually a note of sadness crept into these deliriously joyous rolls, from the drum issued sounds in which the wildest jubilation and the most agonizing sorrow were uncannily blended; it seemed to be at once a triumphal march and a death march; Le Grand's eyes opened wide like a ghost's, and I saw in them nothing but a vast white field of ice covered with corpses—it was the battle of Moscow.

I would never have thought that the hard old drum could produce such painful sounds as Monsieur Le Grand was now able to entice out of it. They were drummed tears, and they sounded fainter and fainter, and deep sighs, like a melancholy echo, burst from Le Grand's breast. He grew weaker and weaker and more and more ghostlike, his withered hands shook from cold, he sat as in a dream, beating only the air with his drumsticks and listening as if to voices far away, and finally he looked at me with a deep, abyss-deep, pleading look—I understood him—and then his head sank down upon the drum.

Monsieur Le Grand never drummed again in this life. Nor did his drum ever produce another sound; it would never serve any enemy of liberty by beating a servile retreat. I had understood very well Le Grand's last, pleading look and immediately drew my sword from my cane and pierced the drum.

CHAPTER XI

Du sublime au ridicule il n'y a qu'un pas, Madame![36]

But life is so desperately serious at bottom that it could not be endured without this combination of the pathetic and the comic. Our poets know this. Aristophanes shows

36. It is only a step from the sublime to the ridiculous, Madame!

us the ghastliest picture of human madness only in the laughing mirror of wit, Goethe dares to express the great anguish of a thinker who comprehends his own nothingness only in the doggerel of a puppet play,[37] and Shakespeare puts the deadliest lament about the wretchedness of the world into the mouth of a fool, at the same time taking pains to shake the fool's cap and bells.

They all learned this from the great primeval poet who, as we see every day, knows how to attain the highest humor in his thousand-act tragedy of life:—after the exit of the heroes, the clowns and harlequins enter with their fools' clubs and wooden swords. After the bloody scenes of revolution and imperial battles, the fat Bourbons come waddling on again with their stale old jokes and nice Legitimist *bonmots,* and the old aristocracy trips on gracefully with its starved smile, and behind it a procession of pious cowls with torches, crosses, and church banners. Comical touches usually slip into even the most exalted pathos of this world tragedy; the despairing Republican who thrust the knife into his heart perhaps smelled the blade first to see that no herring had been cut with it, and after all, on this great world stage things proceed exactly as they do on our trashy stage; even on it there are drunken heroes, kings who forget their lines, scenery that gets stuck, resounding prompters' voices, danseuses who get their effects with the poetry of their hips, costumes that stand out as the most important part of the play.—And meanwhile, up in Heaven, in the first row, sit the sweet little angels peering down through their lorgnettes at us actors here below, and the dear Lord sits solemnly in His enormous box, bored perhaps, or calculating that this theater can't last much longer because one actor gets too much pay and another too little and all of them play their parts much too poorly . . .

37. A reference to Goethe's *Faust.*

CHAPTER XII

The German censors – – – – – – – – – – – – – – –
– –
– – – – – – – – – – – – – – – blockheads   – –
– –
– –

CHAPTER XVI

When I arrived in Godesberg, I seated myself once more at the feet of my beautiful friend—and her brown dachshund lay down beside me—and both of us looked up into her eyes.

Almighty God! In those eyes lay all the splendor of earth and a whole heaven besides. I could have died of bliss as I gazed into them, and if I had died at that moment, my soul would have flown directly into those eyes. Oh, I cannot describe those eyes! . . . The features of her face were noble and Grecian, the lips boldly arched, expressing sadness, bliss, and childlike capriciousness, and when she spoke, the words came in low tones, almost with a sigh, and yet were flung out with impatient speed—and when she spoke and the words fell from her beautiful mouth like a warm, serene rain of flowers—oh! then an afterglow descended on my soul, memories of childhood passed through it in melodious harmonies, above all, however, there sounded within me, like tiny bells, the voice of little Veronica—and I seized my friend's lovely hand and pressed it to my eyes until the ringing in my soul was past—and then I jumped up and laughed, and the dachshund barked, . . . and I sat down again, and again seized the lovely hand and kissed it and talked about little Veronica.

CHAPTER XVII

. . . Madame, you can scarcely imagine how pretty little Veronica looked as she lay in her tiny coffin. The burning candles standing round about cast their gleam on the pale, smiling face and on the red silk roses and rustling gold spangles with which her head and white shroud were adorned. The devout Ursula had led me into the quiet room at night, and when I saw the little corpse laid out with the candles and flowers on the table, I thought at first it was a pretty waxen image of a saint; but I soon recognized the dear countenance and asked laughing why little Veronica was so quiet, and Ursula said, "Death does this."

And when she said, "Death does this"—But I don't want to tell this story today; it would be too long; I would first have to talk about the lame magpie that limped around on the Castle Square and was three hundred years old, and I could become really melancholy.—I suddenly feel inclined to tell a different story; and it is a merry one and very appropriate here, for it is actually the story I intended to tell in this book.

CHAPTER XVIII

In the heart of the knight all was darkness and pain. The dagger thrusts of calumny had struck their mark, and as he walked along across St. Mark's Square, he felt as though his heart would break and he would bleed to death. His feet wavered from fatigue—the noble quarry had been hunted the whole day, and it was a hot summer day—sweat was on his brow, and when he stepped into his gondola, he sighed deeply. With mind blank he sat in the dark cabin of the gondola, the gentle waves rocked him idly and bore him along the familiar way to the Brenta—and on getting out in front of the familiar palace, he was told Signora Laura was in the garden.

She stood leaning against the statue of Laocoön, beside the red rose-tree, at the end of the terrace, not far from the weeping willows that bend down mournfully over the passing stream. She stood there smiling, a tender image of love, surrounded by the fragrance of roses. He, however, awakened as from a black dream and was suddenly as if transformed into tenderness and yearning. "Signora Laura!" he said, "I am wretched and oppressed by hate and misery and lies"—and then he hesitated and stammered,—"but I love you"—and then joyful tears rushed into his eyes, and with moist eyes and burning lips he cried out, "Be mine, my dear one, and love me."

A dark veil of mystery hangs over this hour; no mortal knows what Signora Laura answered, and if you ask her good angel in Heaven about it, he covers his face and sighs and is silent.

For a long time the knight remained standing alone by the statue of Laocoön. Like it, his countenance was white and distorted by pain; without thinking he picked the petals from all the roses on the rose-tree, even crushing the young buds.—The tree never blossomed again. In the distance a mad nightingale lamented, the weeping willows whispered anxiously, the cool waves of the Brenta murmured dully, night rose up with her moon and her stars—one beautiful star, the most beautiful of all, fell down from the sky.

CHAPTER XIX

Vous pleurez, Madame?[38]

Oh, may the eyes that now shed such lovely tears brighten the world with their glow for a long time to come, and may a warm, loving hand one day close them in the hour of death! . . . Oh, may God then reward you for the tears that have flowed for me—for I am myself the knight for whom you have wept, I am myself that erring knight of love, the knight of the fallen star.

Vous pleurez, Madame?

Oh, I know these tears! Why pretend any longer? You, Madame, are yourself the beautiful woman who wept so sweetly in Godesberg when I told the sad tale of my life. —Lovely tears rolled over your lovely cheeks like pearls over roses; the dachshund was silent, the evening bells of Königswinter died away, the Rhine murmured more softly, night covered the earth with its black cloak, and I sat at your feet, Madame, and gazed up into the starry sky. At first I thought your eyes were also two stars.—But how can one confuse such beautiful eyes with stars? These cold lights of the sky cannot weep over the misery of a man who is so wretched that he can no longer weep.

And I had special reasons for not failing to recognize these eyes—in these eyes dwelt the spirit of little Veronica.

I have calculated, Madame, that you were born on the

38. You are weeping, Madame?

very day that little Veronica died. Johanna in Andernach had prophesied to me that I would find little Veronica again in Godesberg—and I recognized you immediately— . . . After the devout Ursula said to me, "Death does this," I walked about, alone and serious, in the great picture-gallery. I did not like the pictures as well as before; they suddenly seemed faded; only one had retained its color and its radiance.—You know, Madame, which picture I mean:—

It is the Sultan and the Sultana of Delhi.

Do you remember, Madame, how we used to stand for hours in front of it, and the devout Ursula smirked so strangely when people were struck by the fact that the faces in that picture showed so much similarity to ours? Madame, I think that picture was a very good likeness of you, and it is incredible how the painter portrayed you even to the clothing you wore then. They say he was mad and dreamed your portrait. Or did his spirit perhaps dwell in that huge, sacred monkey that waited on you like a groom?—In that case he certainly must have remembered the silvery gray veil which he once spilled red wine on and ruined.—I was glad when you discarded it; it was not particularly becoming to you, just as in general European dress is much more becoming to women than Indian dress. Of course beautiful women are beautiful in any costume . . .

For men, however, Indian dress is far more becoming than European. Oh, my rose-red, lotos-flowered pantaloons from Delhi! If I had worn you when I was standing before Signora Laura, pleading for love, the preceding chapter would have read differently! But alas, at that time I was wearing straw-yellow pantaloons woven by a prosaic Chinaman from Nanking—my ruin was woven into them—and I became wretched.

It often happens that a young man sits in a small German *café*, peacefully drinking his cup of coffee, and meanwhile in vast, distant China his ruin grows and flowers and is spun and woven there, and in spite of the high Chinese Wall it is able to find its way to the young man, who thinks it is a pair of Nanking trousers and unsuspectingly puts them on and becomes wretched.—And, Madame, in the small heart of a man a considerable amount of misery can be concealed, so well concealed that the poor man himself does not feel it for days on end and is in good spirits and dances and whistles merrily and trills—lalarallala, lalarallala, lalaral—la—la—la.

CHAPTER XX

She was lovable, and he loved her; but he was not lovable, and she did not love him.
(OLD PLAY)

And because of this stupid affair you wanted to shoot yourself? Madame, when a person wants to shoot himself, he always has adequate reasons. You can rely on that. But whether he himself knows these reasons, that is the question. Till the last moment we play a role even to ourselves. We disguise our misery, and while we are dying of a wound in the heart, we complain of toothache.

Madame, surely you know a remedy for toothache?

But I had toothache in my heart. This is an extremely serious malady, and filling with lead and the toothpowder invented by Barthold Schwarz[39] help a great deal.

Misery gnawed and gnawed in my heart like a worm—the poor Chinaman is not to blame; I was born with it.

39. A German Franciscan monk and alchemist of the fourteenth century. He was formerly credited, especially in Germany, with the invention of gunpowder.

It was already with me in my cradle, and when my mother rocked me, she rocked it too, and when she sang me to sleep, it fell asleep with me, and it awakened as soon as I opened my eyes again. As I grew older, the misery grew too and finally became very large and burst my—

Let's talk about other things . . ., about masquerades, about pleasure and nuptial joys—lalarallala, lalarallala, lalaral—la—la—la.—

PART II

*Heine
as Interpreter
of France
to Germany*

Conditions in France

Vive la France! quand même—[1]

ARTICLE I

Paris, December 28, 1831

The hereditary peers have now given their *last speeches* and were clever enough to declare themselves dead so as not to be killed by the people. The reason for this action was urged on them very particularly by Casimir Périer.[2] From this quarter there is therefore no longer any excuse for mutinies. Meanwhile, the situation of the poor people of Paris is, they say, so hopeless that at the slightest provocation from outside a rebellion more menacing than usual can occur. Nevertheless, I do not believe that we are as close to such outbreaks as people now maintain. Not that I consider the government to be much too powerful or the opposition parties much too powerless —on the contrary, the government shows its weakness at every opportunity; this happened especially at the time of the Lyons riots. And as for the opposition parties, they are embittered enough and, what is more, might find the most foolhardy support among thousands who are dying of poverty;—but it is now cold, foggy winter weather.

1. Nevertheless—long live France!
2. A French statesman prominent in the July Monarchy of Louis Philippe. When the Lafitte ministry fell in 1831, he headed the new ministry.

"They won't come this evening because it's raining," said Pétion,[3] after opening the window and calmly closing it again, whereas his friends, the Girondists, were expecting an attack by the people, who were being incited to revolt by the Mountain Party.[4] In histories of the Revolution this anecdote is told to illustrate Pétion's phlegm. But ever since I have studied the nature of the revolts of the Paris people with my own eyes, I realize how very much these words were misunderstood. For good revolts you need really fine weather, comfortable sunshine, a pleasantly warm day, and so they always turned out best in June, July, or August. It mustn't rain either, for the Parisians fear nothing more than rain, and it scares away the hundreds of thousands of men, women, and children who, dressed up and merry, are usually going to visit the battlefields[5] and by their numbers increase the courage of the agitators. The air must not be misty either, otherwise you can't read the big posters that the government puts up on the street corners; and yet this reading cannot help but draw masses of people together at certain places where they can best press, shove, and become riotously excited. When he was Minister of the Interior, Guizot,[6] an almost German

3. Jérôme Pétion de Villeneuve, French revolutionist. A leader of the Jacobins, he was a member of the National Assembly. In November, 1791, he was elected mayor of Paris, and by his inaction aided the insurrection of June 20, 1792. Elected to the Convention, he went over to the Girondists. When they fell, he was proscribed (May, 1793) but escaped and died in mysterious circumstances while in hiding.

4. So called from their seats in the Legislative Assembly, which were the highest on the left side of the hall. These were the leaders of the Jacobins and the Cordeliers, all advocates of a united, indivisible republic.

5. Probably a reference to places in the city where important events of the French Revolution took place.

6. François Guizot, French statesman and historian, for a time a professor at the University of Paris. He became one of the leading exponents of the July Monarchy and served in the ministry on several occasions. He was Minister of the Interior from August to November, 1830.

pedant, tried to display on these posters all his philoso-
phical and historical knowledge, and there are those who
maintain that just because the throngs of people were
not able to get through the reading so easily and thus the
crowds on the street corners became all the larger, the
revolt grew so threatening that the poor doctrinaire, a
victim of his own scholarliness, had to give up his office.
The most important thing, however, is perhaps that in
cold weather no newspapers can be read in the Palais
Royal, even though it is here that the most zealous politi-
cians assemble beneath the lovely trees, read the news-
papers aloud, debate in furious groups, and spread their
ideas in all directions.

It has now become clear how unjust people were to the
earlier Orléans, Philippe Égalité, when they accused him
of directing most of the popular revolutions because it
had then been discovered that the Palais Royal, where he
was living, was the center of them. This year the Palais
Royal still proved to be such a center. It was still the
headquarters of the dissidents, and yet its present owner
certainly had not summoned and paid such people. The
spirit of the Revolution had no intention of abandoning
the Palais Royal even though its owner had become king,
and he was therefore forced to give up his old residence.[7]
There was talk about special apprehensions which had
caused that change of residence, particularly talk about
the fear of a French Gunpowder Plot. To be sure, since
the ground floor of part of the palace, whose second
floor was occupied by the King, is rented for shops, it
would have been easy to take the powder kegs there and
to blow up His Majesty with the greatest of ease. Others
declared it was not proper for Louis Philippe to reign
upstairs with Mr. Chevet selling his sausages downstairs.

7. Louis Philippe left the Palais Royal for the Tuileries toward the end of
1831.

The latter business, however, is after all just as honorable, and a citizen king would not have needed to move out simply for that reason, especially Louis Philippe, who just the previous year had made fun of all feudal and imperial tradition and historical pageantry and had said to some young Republicans that the golden crown was too cold in winter and too hot in summer, a scepter was too blunt to use as a weapon and too short to use as a support, and a round felt hat and a good umbrella were much more useful in present times.

I don't know whether Louis Philippe can still remember these remarks, for it has been a long time since he roamed the streets of Paris for the last time with his round hat and umbrella and played with subtle naivete the role of an upright, simple head of a household. At that time he shook the hand of every grocer and workman, and wore for this purpose, so they say, a special, dirty glove which he took off again and exchanged for a cleaner kid glove whenever he ascended once more to his higher sphere, to his ancient aristocracy, banker-ministers,[8] intriguers, and amaranth-red lackeys. When I last saw him, he was strolling up and down between the little gold towers, marble vases, and flowers on the roof of the Galerie Orléans. He was wearing a black jacket, and across his broad face roved a serenity at which we feel almost horror when we consider the man's precarious situation. They say, though, that his feelings were not as serene as his face.

It is certainly reprehensible that the King's face is selected as the object of most gibes, and that he is displayed in all the cartoon shops as the butt of mockery. If the courts try to put a stop to such an outrage, this usually only increases the trouble. Thus we saw recently how out of a case of this kind another developed in which

8. Lafitte and Périer were both bankers.

the King was compromised all the more. Philippon, the editor of a comic journal, defended himself as follows: if you wanted to find a similarity with the King's face in a certain caricature, you would also find it, if you only wanted to, in any portrait you choose, no matter how dissimilar, so that ultimately no one was safe from the accusation of offence against the sovereign. To prove his premise, he drew on a piece of paper several caricatures of faces, the first of which strikingly resembled the King; the second, however, resembled the first, only lacking the all too noticeable similarity to the King; in the same manner the third again resembled the second, and the fourth the third face, but in such a way that the fourth face looked just like a pear and yet presented a faint, but all the more amusing similarity with the features of the beloved monarch. Now since Philippon was nevertheless condemned by the jury, he printed his defense speech in his journal, and among the documents he published a lithograph of the sheet with the four caricatures of faces. Because of this lithograph, known as "the pear," the ingenious artist was accused once more, and the most delightful complications are expected from this case. I do not think Louis Philippe is an ignoble man. He certainly does not have evil intentions and merely has the defect of failing to recognize the principle that governs his own individual life. He can be ruined by this. "For," as Sallust says profoundly, "governments can maintain themselves only by the same means by which they originated." Thus, for example, a government which was founded by violence can maintain itself only by violence, not by cunning, and vice versa. Louis Philippe has forgotten that his government arose through the principle of the sovereignty of the people, and in the most wretched delusion he would now like to try to maintain it by means of a quasi-legitimacy, by an alliance with absolute princes, and by a continuation of the Restoration period. This is the reason why the spirits of the Revolution are now angry at him and feud with him in all sorts of ways. This feud is at any rate more justifiable than the feud against the previous government, which was not indebted to the people for anything and opposed them with open hostility right from the start. Louis Philippe, who owed the people and the July cobblestones his crown, is an ungrateful man whose defection is all the more irritating since one realizes more and more every day that one has been grossly deceived. Yes, every day visible retrogression occurs, and just as the cobblestones, which were used as weapons in the July days and have been lying piled up in various places ever since, are now being quietly put back in place so that no external trace of the Revolution may remain, so the people are now being pounded back into their former position like cobblestones into the ground and are being trod on the same as ever.

I forgot to mention above that among the reasons attributed to the King when he left the Palais Royal and moved into the Tuileries was the rumor that he had accepted the crown only as a matter of form, that in his heart he had remained loyal to his legitimate lord, Charles X, that he was preparing for Charles' return, and therefore was not going to move into the Tuileries. The Carlists had hatched this rumor, and it was absurd enough to have an effect on the people. Well, this rumor has been contradicted by the deed. Égalité's son has finally entered as victor by the triumphal arch of the Carrousel and now goes walking through the historic chambers of the Tuileries with his serene face and with hat and umbrella. They say the Queen was very much opposed to living in this "house of misfortune." People claim to know that the King could not sleep so well as usual the first night there and was plagued by all kinds of visions; for example, he saw Marie Antoinette running around, breathing fire and fury, as earlier on the tenth of August;[9] then he heard the malicious laughter of that little red man who sometimes even laughed audibly behind Napoleon's back just when the latter was issuing his proudest commands in the presence chamber;[10] finally, however, Saint Denis appeared to him and, in the name of Louis XVI, challenged him to a duel with guillotines. As everyone knows, Saint Denis is the patron saint of the kings of France, and proverbially a saint who is portrayed carrying his own head in his hands.[11]

More ominous than all the ghosts that may lurk within the palace are the follies that are revealed in its bulwarks. I am speaking of the famous *fossés des Tuileries*.[12] For a long time these were a favorite topic of conversation in the *salons* as well as on the street corners, and they still belong to the realm of the bitterest and most hostile discussion. When the high board fences that concealed those bulwarks from the eyes of the public were still standing in front of the façade of the Tuileries facing the park, you heard the most absurd theories about them. Most people thought the King wanted to fortify the castle on the park side, where before, on the tenth of August, the people were able to penetrate so easily. They even said the Pont Royal was demolished for this reason. Others thought the King merely wanted to erect a long wall to conceal, for his own sake, the view toward the Place de la Concorde, not out of childish fear, but from delicacy of feeling, for his father died on the Place de Grève, but the Place de la Concorde was the place of

9. On August 10, 1792, the Tuileries were attacked, and consequently the King and his family sought refuge with the National Assembly.

10. In Caput (Chapter) VI of his *Germany. A Winter's Tale* Heine mentions the little red man who appeared to Napoleon before any important event.

11. Legend tells that after being beheaded Saint Denis carried his head in his hands for some distance. He is usually portrayed thus in paintings.

12. These ditches were almost concealed by flowers and designed to protect the royal residence on the side next to the public park.

execution for the older line. When those mysterious board fences in front of the palace were torn down again, neither fortifications nor ramparts, neither entrenchments nor bastions, were to be seen, but sheer stupidity and flowers. Crazy about building as he is, the King had had the idea of separating off from the larger public park a small park for himself and his family in front of the palace, this separation had been carried out only by an ordinary ditch and a wire grating several feet high, and in the beds that had been dug there were already flowers, just as innocent as the King's park idea itself.

Casimir Périer is said to have been very annoyed about this innocent idea, which was carried out without his knowledge. In any case it is the cause of the justified displeasure of the public at the disfiguring of the entire park, a masterpiece of Le Nôtre's,[13] which is so very impressive just by virtue of its magnificent ensemble. It is exactly as if one were to delete some scenes from a tragedy by Racine. English parks and Romantic dramas can always be shortened without injury, often even to their advantage; but Racine's poetic parks with their sublimely boring unities, solemn marble characters, measured exits, and generally rigid structure, cannot be changed in the least without destroying their symmetry and thus their real beauty, just as little as can Le Nôtre's green tragedy, which begins so grandly with the broad Tuileries exposition and ends so grandly with the majestic terrace where one views the catastrophe of the Concorde Square.[14] Besides, this untimely park structure is harmful to the King for other reasons as well. In the first

13. André Le Nôtre (1613–1700), a French landscape architect who planned the parks and gardens at the Tuileries, Versailles, St.-Cloud, Fontainebleau, and elsewhere.

14. In keeping with the parallel drawn between Le Nôtre and Racine, Heine is here using technical terms, exposition and catastrophe, usually associated with the structure of the classical tragedy.

place, he gets talked about all the more because of it, and this is certainly not particularly advantageous for him; secondly, because of it a lot of idle onlookers, who sneer critically, who perhaps try to forget their hunger in their curiosity, yet in any case have long, idle hands, are constantly gathering close to his own person. You hear bitterly sharp remarks and vulgar jokes that remind you of the nineties. At the one entrance side of the new park stands a metal cast of *The Knife Grinder*,[15] the original of which can be seen in the Tribuna[16] in Florence and about the significance of which there are various opinions. Here, however, in the Tuileries Park, I heard some modern interpretations of the meaning of this statue at which many antiquarians would smile pityingly and many aristocrats secretly tremble.

This park structure is certainly a colossal piece of folly and exposes the King to the most spiteful accusations. It can even be interpreted as a symbolic action. Louis Philippe digs a ditch between himself and the people; he separates himself from them even visually. Or has he interpreted the nature of the constitutional monarchy so faint-heartedly and conceived of it so narrowly that he thinks if he leaves the larger part of the park to the people, he can occupy the smaller part all the more exclusively as his private park? No, the absolute monarchy with its magnificently egotistical Louis XIV, who, instead

15. One of a group of figures illustrating the punishment of Marsyas, the Phrygian satyr who challenged Apollo to a contest in playing the lyre. Apollo consented under the condition that the victor might do as he pleased with the loser. Marsyas lost, and Apollo flayed him for his presumption. In this group from the Hellenistic period, one figure is that of Marsyas hanging from a tree, about to be flayed. At his feet crouches a Scythian sharpening his knife, the statue Heine mentions, clearly a threatening figure.

16. A room in the Uffizi Gallery containing many famous paintings and pieces of sculpture. It is not certain whether the figure Heine mentions is a copy (the only one) or the original. Margarete Bieber thinks it may be the original, as Heine obviously thought. (See *The Sculpture of the Hellenistic Age*, N.Y., 1955, pp. 110 ff.)

of *L'état c'est moi*, could also say *Les tuileries c'est moi*, would then seem much more splendid than the constitutional sovereignty of the people with its Louis Philippe I, who fearfully circumscribes his little private park and lays claim to a pitiful *chacun chez soi*.[17] They say that all the construction will be complete in the spring. Then the new monarchy, which is now still so far from complete and so plaster-fresh, will also look somewhat more finished. Its present appearance is most extraordinary. Indeed, if you look at the Tuileries from the park side and see all that digging and re-digging, the moving of the statues, the planting of the leafless trees, the old stone rubble, the new building materials, and all the repairs, during which there is so much hammering, shrieking, laughing, and commotion, you think you have before you a symbol of the new, unfinished monarchy itself.

ARTICLE IX

Paris, June 16, 1832

. . . When I spoke above about the republicanism of the French, I had in mind, as I mentioned before, rather the instinctive tendency of the people than their avowed will. The fifth and sixth of June[18] have shown how unfavorable to the republicans the avowed will of the people is just now. I have already given sufficiently sorrowful reports of these memorable days so that I may be excused

17. Place of his own.

18. During the ceremonies at the burial service for General Lamarque on June 5, 1832, a revolt against the government began, but was suppressed without difficulty by the following day.

from a detailed discussion of them. In addition, the documents concerning them are not yet complete, and perhaps the court-martial hearings will give us more information about those days than we have been able to obtain as yet. We still do not know the real beginnings of the battle, much less the number of participants. The Philipists are interested in presenting the affair as a conspiracy prepared long in advance and in exaggerating the number of their enemies. By so doing they justify the present despotic measures of the government and thus gain the glory of a great military exploit. The opposition, on the other hand, asserts that not the slightest preparation had been made for that riot, that the Republicans had been without any leader at all and their numbers very small. This seems to be the truth. At any rate, it is nevertheless a great misfortune for the opposition that while it was assembled *in corpore*[19] and stood in battle array, as it were, that unsuccessful attempt at a revolution took place. If, however, the opposition has lost respect because of this, the government has lost still more respect by the rash declaration of an *état de siège.*[20] It is as if the government wanted to show that, if necessary, it could make an even more spectacular fool of itself than the opposition. I really believe that the days of June 5 and 6 can be viewed as a mere incident which was not especially prepared. The funeral procession for Lamarque was intended only to be a great review of the opposition troops. But the gathering of so many valiant and belligerent people suddenly became so irresistibly enthusiastic, the Holy Ghost descended upon them at the wrong time, they began to prophesy at the wrong time, and the sight of the red flag is said to have confused their minds like a magic spell.

19. In a body.
20. State of siege.

There is something mystical about this red banner with the black fringe, on which were written in black the words *"la liberté ou la mort!,"*[21] and which, like a banner of consecration unto death, rose above all the heads on the Pont d'Austerlitz. Several people who saw the mysterious standard-bearer himself say he was a tall, thin person with a long, corpselike face, staring eyes, and firmly closed mouth, above which a black, Old Spanish moustache protruded with its points far out on either side, an uncanny figure who sat motionless as a ghost on a huge black nag while round about the battle raged in all its violence.

The rumors about Lafayette that are connected with this banner are now denied very nervously by his friends. They say he did not festoon with a garland either the red banner or the red cap. The poor general sits at home and weeps about the grievous outcome of that ceremony, at which, as at most of the popular insurrections since the beginning of the Revolution, he once again played a role —carried along in a more and more peculiar fashion by the general agitation and with the good intention of keeping the people from too great excesses by his own presence. He is like the private tutor who followed his pupil into the brothels so that he wouldn't get drunk there and went with him into the tavern so that at least he wouldn't gamble there, and even accompanied him to the gambling casinos in order to preserve him from duels;—but if it came to a real duel, the old fellow served as his second.

Even though one could foresee that some disturbances would take place at the burial of Lamarque, where a host of dissatisfied citizens were assembled, yet no one believed there would be an outbreak of a real insurrection. Perhaps it was the thought that they were all so

21. Liberty or death.

nicely gathered together which caused some Republicans to improvise an insurrection. The moment was not at all badly chosen to produce general enthusiasm and even to inflame the faint-hearted. It was a moment which at all events powerfully aroused the spirit and banished from it the ordinary work-a-day mood and all petty cares and scruples. This funeral procession could not but make a great impression even on the tranquil observer, both because of the number of mourners, over a hundred thousand, and because of the mysteriously courageous spirit expressed in their looks and bearing. The effect was impressive and yet also frightening, particularly the sight of youths from all the universities in Paris, of the *amis du peuple*,[22] and of so many other Republicans from all classes who, filling the air with terrifying exultation, passed by like bacchants of liberty, in their hands leafy staves which they swung as their thyrsi, green willow wreaths around their small hats, their dress fraternally simple, their eyes as though intoxicated with a passion for action, necks and cheeks flaming red,—alas, on many a face I also observed the melancholy shadow of impending death, such as can very easily be prophesied for young heroes. Anyone who saw these youths in their high-spirited ecstasy of liberty certainly felt that many of them would not live long. It was also a disturbing omen that the chariot of victory which these bacchantic lads followed with shouts of rejoicing bore not a living, but a dead conqueror.

Poor Lamarque! How much blood your funeral service cost! And it was not impressed or hired gladiators who were massacred in order to elevate mere funeral pomp by means of sports. It was enthusiastic youth in its flower that gave its blood for the most sacred feelings, for the

22. "Society of the Friends of the People," one of the opposition parties active after the July Revolution.

most magnanimous dream of their souls. It was the best blood of France that flowed in the Rue Saint-Martin, and I do not think there was any braver fighting at Thermopylae than at the entrance to the narrow little streets of Saint-Mery[23] and Aubry des Bouchers, where, at the end, a handful of some sixty Republicans defended themselves against 60,000 army regulars and National Guards and twice drove them back. Napoleon's old soldiers, who are as good experts in military exploits as we are, let's say, in Christian dogmatics, the reconciliation of extremes, or the artistic achievements of an actress, declare that the battle in the Rue Saint-Martin is one of the greatest heroic deeds of modern history. The Republicans performed miracles of bravery, and the few who remained alive asked for no quarter. All the investigations which I conscientiously made, as my position requires, confirm this. Most of them were killed with bayonets by the National Guards. When all resistance was futile, some Republicans approached their enemies with chests bared and let themselves be shot. When the corner house of the Rue Saint-Mery was captured, a student from the École d'Alfort[24] climbed onto the roof with the banner, called out his *"Vive la République,"* and fell to the ground, pierced with bullets. Soldiers entered a house whose second floor was still held by the Republicans and tore down the stairs; the Republicans, however, not wishing to fall into their enemies' hands alive, killed themselves, and only a room full of corpses was conquered. I was told this story in the church of Saint-Mery, and I had to lean against the statue of St. Sebastian so as not to collapse from heartfelt emotion, and I wept like a boy.

23. The correct spelling, here and below, is "Merry."
24. A school for veterinarians in Alfort, on the outskirts of Paris.

Nothing definite has as yet been ascertained about the number of those who fought in the Rue Saint-Martin. I believe that at the beginning about two hundred Republicans had assembled there, but finally the number, as indicated above, had shrunk during the day of June 6 to sixty. Not a single man among them bore a well-known name or would have been familiar earlier as a distinguished champion of Republicanism. This is another sign that, if not many heroes' names now ring out very loudly in France, a lack of heroes is by no means to blame for it. In general the epoch seems to be past when the deeds of individuals stand out; the nations, the parties, the masses themselves are the heroes of modern times. Modern tragedy differs from ancient tragedy in that now the choruses act and play the real chief roles, whereas the gods, heroes, and tyrants who used to be the acting characters now sink to representatives of the will of the party and of popular action and are put on stage to babble their reflections as royal orators, as master of ceremonies at banquets, deputies to the diet, prime ministers, tribunes, etc. The Round Table of the great Louis Philippe, the whole opposition with its *comptes rendus*,[25] with its delegates, Messers Odilon-Barrot, Lafitte, and Arago,[26] —how passive and petty these commonplace renowned people seem, these so-called notables, if one compares them with the heroes of the Rue Saint-Martin, whose names no one knows, who died, as it were, anonymously.

The modest death of these great unknowns has the power not only of inspiring in us a melancholy sympathy,

25. Statements of accounts.

26. After the June insurrection these three men went to Louis Philippe as representatives of the opposition to ask for amnesty for the prisoners and to persuade him that only a more liberal policy would assure peace within France.

but also of raising our spirits as testimony that many thousands of people whom we do not even know are ready to sacrifice their lives for the sacred cause of humanity. The despots, however, must be seized with secret terror at the thought that such an unknown host of men with a passion for death constantly surrounds them like the masked servants of a holy vehme.[27] They fear France, as well they may, the crimson earth of liberty.

It is an error if one by any chance believes that the heroes of the Rue Saint-Martin were from the lower classes or perhaps, as the expression goes, from the rabble; no, most of them were students, splendid youths from the École d'Alfort, artists, journalists, in general men with aspirations, among them some workers as well, who wore very fine hearts beneath their rough jackets. At the cloisters of Saint-Mery only young people appear to have fought; at other places old people fought too. Among the prisoners whom I saw led through the city there were even aged men, and I was particularly struck by the bearing of an old man who was taken to prison together with some students from the École polytechnique. The latter walked with bowed heads, somber and in disarray, their spirits as torn as their clothing; but the old man walked along, shabbily dressed, to be sure, and in antiquated fashion, but neatly, in a threadbare, straw-yellow dress-coat and ditto vest and trousers, cut according to the latest style of 1793, with a large three-cornered hat on his powdered old head, and his face as carefree, almost as joyous as if he were going to a wedding. An old woman ran along behind him, in her hand an umbrella that she seemed to be bringing him, and in every wrinkle of her face a mortal terror such as we feel when we are

27. A tribunal exercising criminal jurisdiction which operated throughout the German kingdom in the Middle Ages. Secret assemblies and secrecy as to the proceedings of the court were not uncommon.

told that one of our loved ones is to be court-martialed and shot within twenty-four hours. I can never forget the face of that old man. On the eighth of June I also saw in the morgue an old man who was covered with wounds and, as a National Guardsman standing beside me assured me, had also been very much compromised as a Republican. He lay on a slab in the morgue. This is, you know, a building where the corpses found on the street or in the Seine are brought and displayed, and where you therefore usually look for relatives who are missing.

On the day mentioned above, June 8, so many people went to the morgue that they had to stand in line as in front of the Grand Opera when *Robert le Diable*[28] is given. I had to wait almost a whole hour before I could get in and had plenty to time to observe in detail this gloomy building, which more closely resembles a big heap of stones. I don't know the significance of a yellow wooden disk with blue background like a huge Brazilian cockade hanging in front of the entrance. The house number is 21, *vingt-un*. Inside it was sad to watch how anxiously a number of people looked at the dead bodies laid out there, always afraid of finding the one they sought. There were two terrible scenes of recognition. A little boy caught sight of his dead brother and stopped speechless, as though rooted to the spot. A young girl found there her dead lover, and, screaming, fell into a faint. Since I knew her, I had the sad task of taking the inconsolable girl home. She worked in a millinery in my neighborhood, where eight young ladies work, all of them Republicans. Their sweethearts are all young Republicans. In this house I am always the only Royalist.

28. *Robert the Devil*, written by Meyerbeer and first produced in 1831. It was a tremendous success.

French Painters

Exhibition of Paintings in Paris, 1831

The gallery is now closed after the paintings had been on exhibit since the beginning of May. Most people looked at them only casually; their minds were occupied elsewhere and full of anxiety about the political situation.[1] As for me, visiting the capital for the first time and preoccupied with countless new impressions, I was even less able than others to stroll through the galleries of the Louvre with the necessary peace of mind. There they were, side by side, about three thousand of them, the pretty pictures, the poor children of art, to whom the busy populace tossed only the alms of an indifferent glance . . .

The Catholic Church, once a mother also to the other arts, is now poverty-stricken and herself helpless. Every present-day painter paints for himself and at his own risk. The mood of the moment, the whim of the wealthy or of his own aimless heart provide him the material, his palette provides him the most brilliant colors, and the canvas is patient. In addition, a misunderstood romanticism now rages among French painters, and, following its main principle, each one strives to paint differently

1. France was still in a rather unsettled state as a consequence of the July Revolution of 1830. For some of Heine's comments on conditions at that time see the preceding section, *Conditions in France.*

from the others or, as the current expression goes, to let his own individuality stand out.

Since the French possess a great deal of healthy common sense, they have always judged failure accurately, easily recognized the truly individual, and easily discovered the genuine pearls in a motley ocean of pictures. The painters whose works were most discussed and praised as the best were A. Scheffer, H. Vernet, Delacroix, Decamps, Lessore, Schnetz, Delaroche, and Robert. I can therefore limit myself to reviewing public opinion. It is not very different from my own. I shall avoid as much as possible a judgment of technical merits or defects. Such things are of little use with paintings that do not remain on exhibit in public galleries, and are even less useful to the Germans receiving this report, who have not seen them at all. Only indications about the subject matter and the significance of the paintings will probably be welcomed by them. As a conscientious reporter I shall first call attention to the paintings of

A. SCHEFFER[2]

During the first month of the exhibition this painter's *Faust* and his *Gretchen* attracted the most attention since the best works by Delacroix and Robert were exhibited only later. Besides, anyone who has never seen a work by Scheffer is immediately struck by his style, which expresses itself particularly in his use of color. His enemies claim that he paints only with snuff and green soap. I do not know in how far they are unjust to him. His brown shadows are frequently very affected and fail to give the

2. In his early works Ary Scheffer (1795–1858) often took his themes from the works of Goethe, Schiller, Bürger, Uhland, and other German writers.

intended lighting effect in Rembrandt's manner. His faces usually have that unfortunate color that could often make us disgusted with our own face when we caught sight of it, exhausted and peevish, in those green mirrors that one always finds in old inns where the coach stops of a morning. But if you examine Scheffer's pictures more closely and longer, you become reconciled to his manner, you find the treatment of the whole very poetic, and you see that out of the gloomy colors a bright spirit bursts forth like sunbeams out of clouds of fog. This kind of painting, sullenly brushed and rubbed, these deathly tired colors with mysteriously vague outlines, are actually very effective in the pictures of Faust and Gretchen. Both are life-size, half-length portraits. Faust is seated in a medieval red armchair beside a table covered with books bound in parchment, the table serving as support for his left arm, on which his bare head rests. He has his right arm against his hip, with the palm turned outward. Clothing soap-greenish blue. The face almost profile and dun-colored like snuff; its features austerely noble. Despite the sickly color, the hollow cheeks, the withered lips, the marked ravages, this face nonetheless bears traces of its former beauty, and as the eyes cast their sweetly melancholy light over it, it looks like a beautiful ruin illuminated by the moon. Yes, this man is a beautiful human ruin, in the wrinkles above these weathered eyebrows brood learned owls of fable, and behind this forehead lurk evil spirits; at midnight the graves of dead wishes open there, pale phantoms throng out, and through the desolate brain-cells, as if with fettered feet, creeps Gretchen's ghost. This is just the merit of the painter that he has painted for us only the head of a man and that the mere sight of it communicates to us the feelings and thoughts stirring in his brain and heart. In the background, scarcely visible and painted all green, repulsively green, you also see the head of Mephisto-

pheles, the evil spirit, the father of the lie, the god of the
flies, the god of green soap.

Gretchen is a companion piece of equal value. She is
also sitting in a dull red armchair, the motionless spin-
ning wheel with full distaff at her side. In her hand she
holds an open prayer book which she is not reading and
from which a little picture of the Blessed Virgin in bright
colors, now faded, looks forth consolingly. She holds her
head bowed, so that the greater part of her face, also
almost profile, is strangely shadowed. It is as if Faust's
gloomy soul cast its shadow over the countenance of the
quiet girl. The two pictures hung close to each other, and
it was all the more noticeable that in the picture of Faust
the whole lighting effect had been devoted to the face,
whereas in Gretchen's picture the face is less il-
luminated, but its outlines all the more. Due to this the
figure gained an indescribably magical quality. Gretch-
en's bodice is a luscious green, a little black cap covers
the crown of her head, but just barely, and from both
sides her smooth, golden yellow hair billows out all the
more brilliantly. Her face forms a movingly noble oval,
and its features possess a beauty that would like to con-
ceal itself out of modesty. She is modesty itself with her
sweet blue eyes. A quiet tear crosses her lovely cheek, a
mute pearl of sorrow. She is, to be sure, Wolfgang Goe-
the's Gretchen, but she has read all of Schiller, and she
is much more sentimental than naive[3] and much more
ponderously idealistic than lightly graceful. Perhaps she
is too faithful and too serious to be graceful, for grace
consists in movement. And she has something as de-
pendable about her, as stable, as real as a louis d'or in
cash which one still has in his pocket. In short, she is a
German girl, and if you look deep into the melancholy
violets, you think of Germany, of fragrant lindens, of

3. An allusion to Friedrich Schiller's essay, *Naive and Sentimental Poetry*.

Hölty's poems,[4] of the stone Roland in front of the town hall,[5] of the old assistant headmaster, of his rosy niece, of the forester's house with the antlers, of bad tobacco and good companions, of grandmother's graveyard stories, of trusty night watchmen, of friendship, of first love, and all sorts of other silly things.—Truly, Scheffer's Gretchen cannot be described. She has more heart than face. She is a painted soul. Whenever I passed by her, I always said involuntarily, "dear child." . . .

4. Ludwig Hölty (1748–1776) had a modest but genuine gift for poetry. Heine may be thinking of the delicate love poems or of Hölty's liking for the theme of the sweetness of spring.

5. There is a famous statue of Roland in front of the town hall in Bremen.

Concerning
the French Stage

Confidential Letters to August Lewald[1]

FIRST LETTER

. . . The French writer of comedy seldom deals with the public activities of the people as his main subject matter; he usually uses only single aspects of it. On this soil he picks here and there a few flowers of folly with which to wreathe the mirror from whose ironically polished facets the domestic activities of the French smile at us. The comedy writer finds a greater yield in the contrasts between many an ancient institution and present-day customs and between many present-day customs of the people and their private ideas; and, finally, very especially fruitful for him are the contrasts that appear so delightfully when the noble enthusiasm which flames up so easily in the French and also dies out easily collides with the positivist, industrial tendencies of the times. We stand here on ground where the great despot, the Revolution, has exercised its tyranny for fifty years, tearing down this, sparing that, but everywhere shaking the

1. Lewald (1792–1871) was an actor for some years, in 1834 he founded the journal *Europa* in Stuttgart, and from 1849 to 1862 he was director of the court theater there and later in Munich. Heine became acquainted with him in Hamburg, and the two became close friends.

foundations of social life. And this rage for equality which could not elevate the low, but could only level off the elevations; this dispute between the present and the past jeering at each other, the quarrel of a madman with a ghost; this overthrow of all authorities, spiritual as well as material; this stumbling over their last vestiges; and this stupidity in awesome hours of destiny when the necessity for an authority is perceptible and when the destroyer takes fright at his own work and begins to sing out of fear and finally bursts into a loud laugh—This is terrible, yes, even horrifying, but for comedy it is very good!

Yet a German feels somewhat uneasy here. By the immortal gods! We should thank our Lord and Saviour every day that we don't have comedy as the French do, that in Germany no flowers grow that can blossom only from a mountain of debris, a heap of rubble like French society. The French writer of comedies sometimes seems to me like a monkey sitting on the ruins of a devastated city and making faces and bursting out in sneering laughter when from the shattered Gothic arches of the cathedral the head of a real fox peers out, when in the former boudoir of the King's mistress a real sow has her litter, or when the ravens gravely hold council on the spires of the guild hall or the hyena even grubs up the old bones in the royal burial vault.

I have already mentioned that the main themes of French comedy are not taken from public conditions of the people but from domestic conditions, and here the relationship between man and wife is the most fruitful theme. Just as in all relationships in life, all bonds in the French family have also been loosened and all authority broken down. It is easy to understand that the respect of son and daughter for their father has been destroyed if you consider the corrosive power of that criticism which emerged from materialistic philosophy. This lack of reverence is expressed far more harshly in the relation between man and woman, in marital as well as in extra-marital unions, which here take on a character that makes them particularly suitable for comedy. This is the original locale of all those wars between the sexes which are familiar to us in Germany only from bad translations or adaptations and which a German in the role of a Polybius can hardly portray, and certainly never in the role of a Caesar.[2] To be sure, like man and woman in general, both spouses wage war in all countries, but everywhere except in France the fair sex lacks freedom of action, and the war must be carried on more subtly; it cannot achieve external, dramatic form. Anywhere else the woman can hardly get as far as a little mutiny, at most an insurrection. But here the two marital powers oppose each other with equal military forces and wage the most horrifying domestic battles. Given the monotony of German life, you are very much amused in a German theater at the sight of these campaigns by both sexes where one tries to outwit the other by strategic devices, hidden ambush, nocturnal attack, equivocal truce, or even by permanent peace treaties. But if you are here in France in the very arenas where such battles are fought, not merely for show but also in actuality, and if you have a German heart in your breast, your enjoyment of the best French comedy diminishes. And alas, I haven't laughed for a long time at Arnal[3] when he plays the cuckold with his most delightful artlessness. And I no longer laugh at Jenny Vertpré[4] when, as a great lady, displaying the utmost grace, she toys with the flowers of adultery. And I

2. Polybius (202–122 B.C.), a Greek historian who accompanied Scipio to Africa and described the conquest and destruction of Carthage. Caesar described his own military victories.

3. Étienne Arnal (1794–1872), French comedian who played for a long time at the vaudeville theater in Paris.

4. French actress (1797–1865) who first became famous during Napoleon's reign.

don't laugh any longer at Mademoiselle Déjazet[5] either, who, as you know, understands so well how to play the role of a grisette, with a classic lewdness. How many defeats of virtue were necessary before this woman was able to achieve such triumphs in art! She is perhaps the best actress in France. How superbly she plays the poor milliner who, through the generosity of a rich lover, suddenly finds herself surrounded by all the luxury of a great lady, or the little laundress who for the first time lends an ear to the amorous speeches of a *carabin* (in German *studiosus medicinae*) and permits him to take her to the *bal champêtre*[6] at the Grande Chaumière.[7] —Ah, this is all very nice and amusing, and the people laugh, but I, when I think to myself where such comedy ends in the real world, namely, in the gutters of prostitution, in the hospitals of St.-Lazare, on the tables of the dissecting room where the *carabin* not infrequently sees his former love-mate cut up for his edification—Then the laughter sticks in my throat and if I were not afraid of seeming a fool in the eyes of the most cultivated public in the world, I would not be able to hold back my tears . . .

SIXTH LETTER

. . . The best French writers of tragedy are still Alexander Dumas and Victor Hugo. The latter I name last because his effect on the theater is not so great and successful, although in literary importance he surpasses all his contemporaries this side of the Rhine. I certainly do not mean to deny his talent for the dramatic form, as do

5. Pauline Virginie Déjazet (1797–1875), a celebrated actress who played at the *Théâtre du Palais Royal* from 1834 to 1844.

6. Country ball.

7. An amusement place in Paris.

many who, with perfidious intent, constantly praise his greatness in the lyric. He is a poet and commands poetry in any form. His plays are just as praiseworthy as his odes. But in the theater the rhetorical is more effective than the poetic, and the reproaches cast at the poet when a play fails would more justly strike the majority of the audience, which is less receptive to simple natural tones, profound characterisations, and psychological subtleties than to pompous phrases, the crude neighing of passion, and playing to the gallery . . .

Victor Hugo is really not yet honored here in France according to his full worth. German criticism and German impartiality are able to measure his merits by a better standard and to appreciate them with more open praise. Here not only wretched carping but also political factiousness are obstacles to giving him recognition. The Carlists consider him an apostate who knew how to retune his lyre, while it was still vibrating with the last chords of the anointment song for Charles X, to a hymn to the July Revolution.[8] The Republicans distrust his zeal for the popular cause and suspect in every phrase a hidden preference for aristocracy and Catholicism. Even the invisible Church of the St.-Simonists,[9] which is everywhere and nowhere like the Christian Church before Constantine—it too rejects him, for it regards art as a priesthood and requires every work of a poet, painter, sculptor, or musician to bear witness to his higher consecration, to proclaim his holy mission, to aim at benefiting and improving the human race. Victor Hugo's masterpieces do not tolerate any such moral standard; indeed, they sin against all those magnanimous, but erroneous demands of the new Church. I call them erroneous because, as you know, I am in favor of the autonomy of art.

8. The Revolution of 1830.
9. See below, p. 306, note 43.

It should serve neither religion nor politics as maid servant; like the world itself, it is its own ultimate purpose. Here we encounter the same biased reproaches that Goethe had to endure from pious Germans, and like him Victor Hugo also has to hear the inappropriate accusation that he feels no enthusiasm for the ideal, that he lacks moral fiber, that he is a cold-hearted egoist, etc. In addition, there is a false criticism which declares his finest and most laudable characteristic, his talent for the artistic portrayal of what is perceptible to the senses, to be a defect, and they say that his creations lack heartfelt poetry, *la poësie intime;* that outline and color are for him the main thing; that he provides literature that is easy to understand because of external qualities; that he is inclined toward the material; in short, they criticize in him the very most commendable quality, his feeling for vividness.

And such injustice is done him not by the old classicists, who fought him with Aristotelian weapons and have long since been defeated, but by his former companions-in-arms, a group within the French Romantic School which has fallen out entirely with its literary gonfaloniers. Almost all his former friends have deserted him and, to be truthful, deserted him due to his own fault, offended by that egoism which is very advantageous in creating masterpieces but is a great disadvantage in social intercourse. Even Saint-Beuve could not get along with him any longer; even Saint-Beuve, he who was once the most faithful shield-bearer of his fame, criticizes him now. As in Africa, when the King of Dafur[10] rides out in public, a panegyrist runs along in front of him, continually calling out in his loudest voice, "Look at the buffalo there, the descendant of a buffalo, the steer of steers, all others are oxen, and only he is the true

10. Darfur.

buffalo," so Saint-Beuve formerly ran along in front of Victor Hugo whenever the latter appeared before the public with a new work, blew his trumpet, and praised extravagantly the buffalo of poetry. This time is past; Saint-Beuve now extols the ordinary calves and distinguished cows of French literature, the voices of Hugo's friends criticize or are silent, and the greatest poet of France can no longer find in his native land the recognition due him.

Yes, Victor Hugo is the greatest poet of France and, something that means a great deal, even in Germany he could occupy a place among first-rate poets. He has imagination and feeling and in addition a lack of tact such as is never found in the French but only in us Germans. His spirit is lacking in harmony, and he is full of extravagances in bad taste like Grabbe[11] and Jean Paul.[12] He lacks the fine moderation that we admire in classical writers. Despite her magnificence, his muse is afflicted with a certain German clumsiness. I would like to say the same thing about his muse as is said about beautiful English women, "She has two left hands."

Alexander Dumas is not so great a poet as Victor Hugo, but he possesses qualities with which he can accomplish far more in the theater than the latter. He commands that direct expression of passion which the French call *verve*,[13] and besides, he is more French than Hugo—he sympathizes with all the virtues and weaknesses, the daily stresses and anxieties of his fellow countrymen; he is enthusiastic, passionate, theatrical, generous, frivolous, boastful, a genuine son of France, the Gascon[14] of Europe. He speaks with his heart to the

11. Christian Dietrich Grabbe (1801–1836), a gifted dramatist, but unbalanced and disorganized in his own life and in his writing.

12. Pseudonym for Johann Paul Richter (1763–1825), a German novelist noted for his eccentricity in style and form.

13. The word has the same meaning in English.

14. The people of Gascony have the reputation of being braggarts.

hearts of others and is understood and applauded. His head is an inn where good ideas sometimes stop but do not stay longer than overnight; very often it is empty. No one has a talent for the dramatic like Dumas. The theater is his true profession. He is a born playwright, and by rights all dramatic subjects belong to him, whether he finds them in real life or in Schiller, Shakespeare, and Calderón. He draws fresh effects out of them, he recasts the old coins so that they once more gain a pleasant current value, and we ought even to thank him for his thefts from the past, since with them he enriches the present. An unfair criticism, an article that appeared under grievous circumstances in the *Journal des Débats,* did a great deal of harm to our poor poet among the large, ignorant masses by pointing out, for many scenes in his plays, the most striking parallel passages in foreign tragedies. But nothing is more absurd than this reproach of plagiarism; there is no sixth commandment[15] in art; the poet may help himself anywhere where he finds material for his works and may even appropriate whole columns with chiseled capitals if only the temple he supports with them is magnificent. Goethe understood this very well, and before him even Shakespeare. Nothing is more absurd than the demand that a poet should create all his material from within himself, this being originality. I remember a fable in which a spider talks with a bee and reproaches it for collecting from a thousand flowers the material with which to make its structure of wax and the honey in it. "I, however," the spider adds triumphantly, "I draw my whole artful web in original threads out of myself."

As I just mentioned, the article against Dumas in the *Journal des Débats* appeared under grievous circumstances; it was written by one of the fanatical young parti-

15. "Thou shalt not steal" is the eighth commandment.

sans who blindly obey Victor Hugo's commands, and was printed in a paper whose directors were very intimate friends of Hugo's. He was noble enough not to deny his knowing about the publication of the article, and he thought he had dealt his old friend Dumas, as is customary in literary circles, the opportune deathblow at the right moment. As a matter of fact, after that, black mourning-crape hung over Dumas' reputation, and many people maintained that if you drew away the crape you would see nothing at all behind it. But since the performance of a play like *Edmund Kean*[16] Dumas' reputation has reappeared, gleaming, from behind its dark veil, and he proved anew his great dramatic talent.

This play, which the German theater has surely also appropriated, is conceived and executed with such liveliness as I have never yet seen; it has a unity, a novelty in techniques that seem to emerge spontaneously, a plot whose complications develop quite naturally, one out of the other, a feeling that comes from the heart and speaks to the heart—in short, it is a masterpiece. Though Dumas makes small mistakes in externals of costume and locale, nonetheless a deeply moving genuineness prevails in the picture as a whole. He transported me once more in spirit back to Old England, and I thought I saw once more in the flesh the late Kean himself, whom I had seen there so often. To be sure, the actor playing the role of Kean also contributed to this illusion, even though his outward appearance, the imposing figure of Frédéric Lemaître,[17] was so very different from the short, stocky figure of the late Kean. The latter did have, however, in his personality and in his acting something that I also find in Frédéric Lemaître. There is a wonderful affinity between them. Kean was one of those exceptional per-

16. *Kean ou désordre et génie (Kean, or Insanity and Genius)*, published in 1836.
17. One of the leading actors in Paris.

sons who bring to life by unexpected bodily movements, an inconceivable tone of voice, and an even more inconceivable look in his eyes not so much universal simple emotions, but far, far more the unusual, the bizarre, the extraordinary things that can transpire within a human heart. It is the same with Frédéric Lemaître; he is also one of those terrifying jesters at the sight of whom Thalia turns pale from horror and Melpomene smiles in ecstasy. Kean was one of those persons whose character defies all the frictions of civilization, who are made, I won't say of better stuff than we others are, but of entirely different stuff, unpolished eccentrics with a one-sided talent, but in this one-sidedness they are extraordinary, surpassing everything else that exists, filled with that devilishly divine power, limitless, unfathomable, unconscious, which we call the demonic. This demonic quality is found to a greater or lesser extent in all great men of action or of words. Kean was by no means a versatile actor; to be sure, he could play various kinds of roles, but in these roles he always played himself. In so doing, however, he always gave us a moving reality, and though ten years have passed since then, I still see him standing before me as Shylock, as Othello, Richard, Macbeth, and his acting unlocked for me the full understanding of many obscure passages in these plays of Shakespeare's. There were modulations in his voice which revealed a whole life of terror; there were lights in his eyes that illuminated inwardly all the blackness of a Titanic spirit; there were sudden movements of his hand, his foot, his head that said more than a four-volume commentary by Franz Horn.[18]

18. A writer long since forgotten, who wrote a five-volume work on Shakespeare's plays, published 1823–1831.

NINTH LETTER

. . . Nothing is more inadequate than theorizing in music; there are laws, to be sure, mathematically determined laws, but these laws are not the music, only its prerequisites, just as the technique of drawing and the theory of color or even brush and palette are not painting, but only necessary means. The essence of music is revelation, it is impossible to explain it, and true musical criticism is an empirical science . . .

You notice, dear friend, that I shall not annoy you with any conventional phrases regarding opera. Yet in discussing the French theater I cannot leave it entirely without mention. Nor do you need to fear from me any comparison between Rossini and Meyerbeer in the usual fashion. I limit myself to loving both, and I love neither at the expense of the other. If I perhaps find the former more congenial than the latter, this is only a personal feeling and in no way an acknowledgement of greater value. Perhaps it is the very imperfections that seem so akin to many corresponding imperfections in me. I am inclined by nature to a certain *dolce far niente,* and I like to rest on flowery swards and watch the peaceful processions of the clouds and take delight in their illumination, but as luck would have it, I was very often awakened from this comfortable reverie by Fate's hard nudges in the ribs, I was forced to take part in the sorrows and struggles of the times, and my participation was then honest, and I fought as well as the bravest.—But I don't know how to express myself—my feelings still retained a certain separateness from the feelings of the others. I knew how they felt, but I felt quite differently, and no matter how vigorously I wheeled my battlesteed around and charged the enemies so mercilessly with my sword, the fever or the love or the fear of battle never seized me. I often felt uneasy about my inner calm, I noticed that my thoughts dwelt elsewhere as I fought in the thickest throng of the party war, and I sometimes felt like Ogier the Dane, who fought in a dream against the Saracens.[19] Rossini is naturally more to the taste of such a person than Meyerbeer, and yet at certain times he will surely admire the latter's music enthusiastically, though not surrendering to it completely. The individual joys and sorrows of mankind rock most comfortably on the waves of Rossini's music; love and hate, affection and longing, jealousy and pouting—all this is here the isolated feeling of an individual. Thus the predominance of melody, always the direct expression of an isolated emotion, is characteristic for Rossini's music. In Meyerbeer, on the other hand, we find the supremacy of harmony; in the flood of massed harmonies the melodies die away, yes, they are drowned, just as the particular feelings of the individual are submerged in the collective feeling of a whole people, and our soul likes to plunge into these harmonic streams when it is seized with the sorrows and joys of the whole human race and espouses the cause of the great problems of society. Meyerbeer's music is more social than individual; the grateful present, which rediscovers in his music its inner and outer struggles, its divided mind and its contest of wills, its misery and its hope, extolls its own passion and enthusiasm as it applauds the great master. Rossini's music was more appropriate for the time of the Restoration when, after great struggles and disappointments, the stupefied people's perception of their considerable collective interests had to retreat into the background and the feelings of

19. Heine is alluding to a tale in the *Chansons de geste* as told by Dobeneck, the source Heine so often used. Morgan le Fay promised Ogier the Dane her love. Under her protection he won a battle against the Saracens, after which she took him back with her to Avalon.

individuality were again able to enter into their legitimate rights. Rossini would never have attained his great popularity during the Revolution and the Empire. Robespierre would perhaps have accused him of unpatriotic, politically moderate melodies, and Napoleon would certainly not have appointed him director of the band with his great army, where he needed collective enthusiasm . . . The Restoration was Rossini's time of triumph, and even the stars in the heavens, which were then having a holiday and no longer troubling themselves about the fate of the nations, listened to him with delight. Meanwhile the July Revolution created a great stir in the heavens and on the earth; stars and people, angels and kings, even the dear Lord Himself, were snatched out of their state of peace; they have their hands full again, they must put a new age in order, they have neither time nor sufficient peace of mind to revel in the melodies of individual emotion, and only when the huge choruses of *Robert the Devil* or even of *The Huguenots* roar in harmony, rejoice in harmony, sob in harmony, do their hearts give ear and sob, rejoice, and roar in enthusiastic accord.

This is perhaps the ultimate reason for the incredible, colossal acclamation that Meyerbeer's two great operas enjoy throughout the entire world. He is the man of his age, and the age, which always knows how to choose its people, has tumultuously raised him on its shield, proclaiming his sovereignty and making with him its joyous entry. It is not exactly a comfortable position to be carried in triumph this way; misfortune or the clumsiness of a single shield bearer can cause a critical shakiness, if not severe injury; the wreaths of flowers that fly at your head can sometimes hurt rather than invigorate you, perhaps even dirty you if they come from dirty hands, and the overload of laurels can certainly squeeze a lot of cold sweat out of you . . .

Meyerbeer is now writing a new opera which I am

looking forward to with great curiosity. The development of this genius is to me a most remarkable spectacle. I follow with interest the phases of his musical as well as of his personal life and have observed the reciprocal influences between him and his European audiences. It has now been ten years since I first met him in Berlin, between the university and the guardroom, between knowledge and the drum, and he seemed to feel very uneasy in this position. I remember I met him in the company of Dr. Marx,[20] who at that time belonged to a certain musical regency which, during the minority of a certain young genius, regarded as the legitimate successor to Mozart's throne,[21] constantly extolled Sebastian Bach. The enthusiasm for Sebastian Bach was intended not merely to fill out this interregnum, but also to destroy the reputation of Rossini, whom the regency feared most and hence hated most. Meyerbeer was then considered to be an imitator of Rossini, and Dr. Marx treated him with a certain condescension, with the affable air of a superior authority, which I have to laugh at heartily now. Rossiniism was at that time Meyerbeer's great crime; he was still very remote from the honor of being persecuted for his own sake. He also wisely refrained from any pretensions, and when I told him with what enthusiasm I had recently watched a performance of his *Crusader*[22] in Italy, he smiled with a droll melancholy and said, "You will compromise yourself if you praise me, a poor Italian, here in Berlin, the capital of Sebastian Bach!"

At that time Meyerbeer had indeed become completely an imitator of the Italians. His irritation at the damply cold, colorless Berlin style with its purely rational wit had early caused a natural reaction in him; he

20. Adolf Bernhard Marx, a musicologist.
21. Felix Mendelssohn.
22. *Il crociato in Egitto (The Crusader in Egypt)*.

fled to Italy, lived happily, gave himself up completely to his private emotions, and composed there those delightful operas in which Rossiniism is intensified with the sweetest exaggeration; the gold is gilded again and the flower perfumed with even stronger scents. This was Meyerbeer's happiest time. He wrote in the joyous ecstasy of Italian voluptuousness, and in life as in art he plucked the gayest flowers.

But this sort of thing could not satisfy a German temperament for long. A certain nostalgia for the solemnity of his fatherland awakened in him. While lying under Italian myrtles, the memory of the mysterious awesomeness of German oak woods stole over him; while southern zephyrs caressed him, he thought of the gloomy chorales of the north wind. Perhaps the same thing happened to him as to Madame de Sévigné[23] who, when she was living beside an orangery and was constantly surrounded by nothing but the fragrance of orange blossoms, finally began to yearn for the bad smell of a healthy manure cart.—In short, another reaction occurred, and Signor Giacomo suddenly became a German again and rejoined Germany, not the old, rotten, decrepit Germany of narrow-minded Philistinism, but the young generous Germany, open to the world, the new generation, which has made all the problems of humanity its own and which bears these great human problems inscribed, if not always on its banner, yet all the more indelibly in its heart.

Soon after the July Revolution Meyerbeer appeared before the public with a work that originated in his mind during the birth-pangs of that revolution, *Robert the Devil*, the hero who does not know exactly what he wants, who is continually in conflict with himself, a faithful image of

23. A French writer of the seventeenth century. Her letters, especially those to her daughter, Countess of Grignan, are famous.

the moral vacillation of that time, a time that moved with such agonizing restlessness between virtue and vice, exhausted itself in exertions and frustrations, and did not always have enough strength to withstand the temptations of Satan! I am not at all fond of this opera, this masterpiece of indecision, I say indecision not just in regard to the content but also the execution, for the composer did not yet trust his genius, did not yet dare to surrender to its absolute will, and tremblingly served the masses instead of ruling them unafraid. Meyerbeer was at that time called a timid genius. He lacked the triumphant faith in himself; he displayed fear of public opinion; the slightest criticism frightened him; he flattered every whim of the public and shook hands left and right with the greatest eagerness as if he acknowledged the sovereignty of the people even in music and were establishing his government on majority vote in contrast to Rossini, who ruled by the grace of God with absolute power in the kingdom of music. This anxiety has not yet left him. He is still concerned about public opinion, but fortunately the success of *Robert the Devil* had the effect that he is not troubled by this worry when he is working, that he composes with far more assurance, that he permits the great will of his spirit to show in his works. And in this expanded freedom of mind he wrote *The Huguenots*, in which all doubts have disappeared, the inner conflict has ceased, and the outer conflict has begun, and whose colossal structure amazes us. Only with this work did Meyerbeer win his everlasting citizenship in the eternal city of spirits, in the heavenly Jerusalem of art. In *The Huguenots* he at last reveals himself without timidity; with intrepid strokes he sketched here his own thought and dared to express in unrestrained tones everything that moved his heart.

What distinguishes this work particularly is the balance between fervor and artistic perfection, or, to express myself better, the equal height which passion and art attain in it. The man and the artist competed here, and when the former rang the tocsin for the wildest passions, the latter knew how to transfigure the crude tones of nature into thrilling, sweetest euphony. While the great masses are moved by the inner force, by the passion of *The Huguenots,* the connoisseur admires the skill manifested in the form. This work is a Gothic cathedral whose soaring pillars striving toward the heavens and whose colossal dome seem to have been erected by the bold hand of a giant, whereas the countless delicately fine festoons, rose windows, and arabesques spreading out over them like a lace veil of stone bear witness to the indefatigable patience of a dwarf. Giant in the conception and shaping of the whole, dwarf in the painstaking execution of the details, the architect of *The Huguenots* is just as incomprehensible to us as the composers of the ancient cathedrals. When I stood not long ago with a friend in front of the cathedral of Amiens, and my friend looked with terror and compassion at this monument of cliff-storming, gigantic strength and of the patience of a dwarf tirelessly carving away and finally asked me how it happened that we no longer created such buildings today, I answered, "Dear Alphonse, in those old days people had convictions. We moderns have only opinions, and something more than a mere opinion is necessary to construct a Gothic cathedral like this."

This is the thing. Meyerbeer is a man of conviction, not actually in reference to social questions of the day, although even in this respect Meyerbeer's attitudes are more firmly established than those of other artists. Meyerbeer, whom the princes of this earth shower with every conceivable honor and who is also so susceptible to these distinctions, nevertheless has a heart that glows for the most sacred interests of mankind, and he frankly confesses his worship of the heroes of the Revolution. It is fortunate for him that many Nordic officials don't understand music, or they would see in *The Huguenots* something more than merely a party struggle between Protestants and Catholics. But nevertheless his convictions are not really of a political, even less of a religious nature. Meyerbeer's real religion is the religion of Mozart, Gluck, Beethoven; it is music. He believes only in it, and only in this faith does he find his salvation and live with a conviction similar in depth, ardor, and persistence to the convictions of earlier centuries . . .

The Huguenots is far more a work of conviction than *Robert the Devil*, in content as well as form . . . Meyerbeer has attained his greatest success in the instrumentation. The treatment of the choruses, which express themselves here like individuals and have been freed of all operatic tradition, is marvelous. There has certainly been no grander spectacle in the realm of music since *Don Giovanni* than the fourth act of *The Huguenots*, where, following the gruesomely moving scene of the consecration of the swords, of consecrated lust for murder, another duet is placed which surpasses even the effect of the first, a colossal venture one would scarcely expect from the timid genius, but the success of which arouses our delight as much as our astonishment. As for me, I think Meyerbeer solved this problem not by artistic means but by natural means, having that splendid duet express a sequence of emotions which perhaps never, or at least never so faithfully, appeared in opera before, for which, however, the most passionate sympathy flames up in the people of today. As for me, I confess that never, in hearing any piece of music, did my heart pound so tumultuously as in hearing the fourth act of *The Huguenots*, but that I prefer to avoid this act and its excitements and listen with far greater pleasure to the second act. This is an idyll similar in charm and grace to Shakespeare's romantic comedies, perhaps even more similar to Tasso's *Aminta*. In fact, among the roses of joy a gentle melancholy lies hidden, reminiscent of the court poet of Ferrara. It is more the yearning for happiness than happiness itself; it is not hearty laughter, but a smile of the heart, a heart that is secretly ill and can only dream of health. How does it happen that an artist from whom all life's troubles have been fanned away from his cradle on, who, born in the lap of wealth, pampered by the whole family, which readily, even enthusiastically, pandered to all his inclinations, was far more qualified for happiness than any other mortal artist—how does it happen that he has still experienced those dire sorrows that sigh and sob at us from his music? For a musician cannot express so powerfully, so movingly, what he does not feel himself. It is strange that the artist whose material needs are satisfied is plagued all the more by moral torments! But it is fortunate for the public, which owes its most ideal joys to the sorrows of the artist . . .

People have accused *The Huguenots* even more than *Robert the Devil* of a lack of melody. This reproach is based on an error. "They can't see the woods for the trees." In *The Huguenots* melody is subordinated to harmony, and even in a comparison with Rossini's music, in which the reverse relationship occurs, I have pointed out that it is this predominance of harmony that gives Meyerbeer's music the character of a humanly motivated, socially modern music. It certainly does not lack melodies, but these melodies are not allowed a prominence that would be disturbingly abrupt, I might say, egotistical; they merely serve the whole; they are disciplined, instead of, as with the Italians, asserting themselves in isolation, I might almost say illegally, about like their famous bandits . . .

The supremacy of harmony in Meyerbeer's works is perhaps an inevitable result of his broad education encompassing the realm of thought and of physical phenomena. A fortune was spent on his education, and his mind was receptive; he was initiated at an early age into all branches of knowledge and in this is different from most musicians, whose dazzling ignorance is to some extent excusable since they usually lacked the means and the time to acquire any great knowledge outside of their own field. What Meyerbeer learned became second nature, and the school of the world provided him the fullest development. He belongs to the small number of Germans whom even France had to acknowledge as models of urbanity. Such a high level of education was perhaps necessary in order to collect the material needed for the creation of *The Huguenots* and to shape it with a sure sense of purpose. But it is a question whether, having gained in breadth of conception and clarity of perspective, he has not lost other qualities. Education destroys in an artist that sharp accentuation, that abrupt shading, that originality of ideas, that immediacy of feeling which we admire so very much in crudely limited, uneducated persons.

In general, education is always bought dearly, and little Blanca is right. This daughter of Meyerbeer's, perhaps eight years old, envies the idleness of the little boys and girls she sees playing in the street and recently expressed her opinion as follows: "What bad luck that I have educated parents! I have to memorize all sorts of things and sit still and be good from morning till night while the uneducated children down there can run around happily and have fun all day long!"

TENTH LETTER

. . . I do not need to talk to you about Liszt's talent; his fame is European. He is unquestionably the artist who finds the most unequivocal enthusiasts in Paris, but also the most fervent opponents. It is significant that no one can speak of him with indifference. Without some positive substance you can arouse neither favorable nor hostile passions in this world. Fire is needed to enflame people, to hatred as well as to love. The thing that best bears witness in Liszt's favor is the complete respect with which even his opponents acknowledge his personal merit. He is a man of eccentric, but noble character, unselfish and without guile. His intellectual tendencies are most remarkable; he has a strong proclivity for speculation, and the investigations of the various groups that occupy themselves with the solution of the great problem encompassing heaven and earth interest him even more than the concerns of his art. For a long time he was enthusiastic about the beautiful philosophy of Saint-Simon;[24] later the spiritualistic, or rather, nebulous ideas of Ballanche[25] befogged him; now he raves about the Republican-Catholic doctrines of a Lamennais,[26] who has planted the Jacobin cap on the Cross.— Heaven knows in what intellectual stables he will find his next hobby horse. But this inexhaustible thirst for enlightenment and divinity still remains commendable; it testifies to his feeling for the sacred, the religious. Obviously such a restless person who feels it necessary to take an interest in all the needs of mankind and likes to stick his nose into all the pots where the good Lord is cooking the future—obviously Franz Liszt cannot be a calm pianist for peaceful citizens and good-natured lazybones. When he sits at the piano and has smoothed back his hair from his forehead several times and begins to improvise,

24. Originator of a movement in France aiming at social, economic, and religious reforms. See also p. 306, note 43.

25. Pierre Simon Ballanche, a philosopher of history who tended toward a mystical type of socialism.

26. Félicité Robert de Lamennais (1782–1854), Roman Catholic apologist and liberal, who believed the Church could thrive only under a democratic form of government.

he not infrequently rages all too madly over the ivory keys, and a jungle of lofty ideas resounds, with the sweetest flowers spreading their fragrance at intervals, so that you are at the same time frightened and enraptured—but more frightened than otherwise . . .

It would be unfair not to mention on this occasion a pianist who, next to Liszt, is admired most. This is Chopin, who is striking not just by his technical perfection as virtuoso, but who also produces superior works as composer. He is a man of the first rank. Chopin is the darling of those elite who seek in music the highest delights of the spirit. His fame is of an aristocratic nature; it is perfumed with the eulogies of good society; it is as refined as his own person.

Chopin was born in Poland of French parents and received part of his education in Germany. This influence of three nationalities makes his personality a highly remarkable phenomenon, for he has appropriated the best characteristics that distinguish the three nations. Poland gave him its sense of gallantry and its historical suffering, France gave him its airy charm and its grace, and Germany gave him romantic melancholy.—Nature, however, gave him a delicate, slender, somewhat frail figure, the most noble of hearts, and genius. Yes, one must concede to Chopin genius in the full meaning of the word. He is not merely a virtuoso, he is also a poet, he can make the poetry that exists in his soul come alive for us, he is a tone poet, and nothing resembles the pleasure he gives us when he sits at the piano and improvises. He is then not a Pole, nor a Frenchman, nor a German; he reveals a far loftier origin; you notice then that he comes from the land of Mozart, Raphael, and Goethe; his true fatherland is the dream world of poetry . . .

PART III

Heine as Interpreter of Germany to France

The Romantic School

BOOK ONE

Mme. de Staël's book *De l'Allemagne*[1] is the only comprehensive information the French have received concerning the intellectual life of Germany. And yet a long time has passed since this book appeared, and meanwhile an entirely new type of literature has developed in Germany. Is it only a literature of transition? Has it already reached its prime? Is it already in a state of decline? Opinions are divided about these questions. Most people think that with Goethe's death[2] a new literary period began in Germany, that the old Germany went to its grave with him, that the aristocratic period of literature came to an end and the democratic period began, or, as a French journalist expressed it recently, "the spirit of man as an individual has ceased to exist, the spirit of collective man has begun."

For my part, I cannot pass judgment in such a categorical fashion on the future evolutions of the German mind. Many years ago, however, I predicted the end of the "Goethean Period of Art," the term I first used to designate this period. It was easy enough to prophesy. I was

1. *Concerning Germany.* Since the author was *persona non grata* in France, the work appeared first in London in 1813, but it was published in France the following year.

2. 1832.

very familiar with the ways and means of those malcontents who wanted to put an end to the Goethean realm of art, and some even claim to have seen me myself taking part in the mutinies of those days against Goethe. Now that Goethe is dead, a strange sadness overwhelms me.

In announcing these pages as a kind of continuation of Mme. de Staël's *De l'Allemagne,* and while praising the information that can be derived from this work, I must nevertheless recommend a certain caution in using it and characterize it as altogether a coterie book. Mme. de Staël, of glorious memory, established here, in the form of a book, a kind of salon, in which she received German writers and gave them an opportunity to make themselves known to the French civilized world, but in the din of voices of every sort which cry out from the pages of this book, the most distinctly audible is always the clear falsetto of Mr. A. W. Schlegel.[3] In the passages where she is completely herself, where this woman of great sensitivity speaks out directly with all her glowing heart, with the full pyrotechnical display of her intellectual rockets and brilliant eccentricities, the book is good and admirable. The instant she obeys suggestions from without; the instant she does homage to a school whose character is completely alien and incomprehensible to her; the instant she encourages, by praising this school, certain ultramontane tendencies which are in direct contradiction to her Protestant enlightenment, her book is wretched and unbearable. Besides, she exhibits conscious as well as unconscious biases, and in eulogizing intellectual life and idealism in Germany, her real inten-

3. August Wilhelm Schlegel (1767–1845) and his brother Friedrich were the leading theoretical writers in German literary Romanticism. Both were critics and interpreters rather than poets. In 1804 Madame de Staël engaged A. W. Schlegel as traveling companion and tutor to her son. He later acted as her adviser in writing *De l'Allemagne.*

tion is to criticize the realism of the French at that time, the material splendor of the period of the Empire. In this respect her book *De l'Allemagne* resembles Tacitus' *Germania*,[4] for in his apologia of the Germans he also perhaps intended to write an indirect satire on his own countrymen.

When I mentioned above a school to which Mme. de Staël did homage and whose tendencies she encouraged, I meant the Romantic School. In the following pages it will become clear that in Germany this was something entirely different from what is designated by this name in France and that its tendencies were quite different from those of the French Romanticists.

But what was the Romantic School in Germany?

It was nothing other than the revival of the poetry of the Middle Ages as manifested in the songs, sculpture, and architecture, in the art and life of that time. This poetry, however, had had its origin in Christianity; it was a passion flower rising from the blood of Christ. I do not know whether the melancholy flower that we call passion flower in Germany also bears this name in France and whether that mystical origin is likewise attributed to it by folk legend. It is a strange flower of unpleasing color, in whose chalice can be seen depicted the instruments of torture used at the Crucifixion of Christ, namely, hammer, tongs, nails, etc., a flower that is by no means ugly, only eery, indeed, the sight of which even arouses in us an uncanny pleasure like the convulsively sweet sensations which result even from suffering itself. In this respect the flower would be the most fitting symbol for Christianity, whose most gruesome attraction consists in this very ecstasy of suffering.

4. In *Germania*, written at the end of the first century, Tacitus praised the virtue of the Germanic tribes in contrast to the effeminate luxury and moral degeneration apparent among the Romans.

Although in France the name Christianity means only Roman Catholicism, I must nonetheless emphasize as preface to my remarks that I am speaking only of Roman Catholicism. I am speaking of the religion whose earliest dogmas contain a condemnation of the flesh, and which not merely grants the spirit superiority over the flesh but also deliberately mortifies the flesh in order to glorify the spirit. I am speaking of the religion whose unnatural mission actually introduced sin and hypocrisy into the world, since just because of the condemnation of the flesh the most innocent pleasures of the senses became a sin and just because of the impossibility of our being wholly spirit hypocrisy inevitably developed. I am speaking of the religion which also, due to the doctrine of the evil of earthly possessions and the doctrine that imposed a dog-like humility and an angelic patience, became the most reliable support of despotism. People have now recognized the nature of this religion, they will no longer let themselves be fooled by promissory notes on Heaven, they know that material things also have their good side and are not totally evil, and they now vindicate the pleasures of the earth, of this beautiful garden of God, our inalienable heritage. Just because we now comprehend so completely all the consequences of that absolute spiritualism, we can also believe that the Catholic Christian philosophy of life is doomed. For every epoch is a sphinx that plunges into the abyss as soon as its riddle has been solved.

We by no means deny, however, the good brought about in Europe by the Catholic Christian philosophy of life. It was necessary as a wholesome reaction against the dreadful and colossal materialism which had developed in the Roman Empire and was threatening to destroy all the spiritual grandeur of mankind. As the licentious memoirs of the century just past constitute, so to speak, the *pièces justificatives*[5] of the French Revolution, as the terrorism of a *Comité du salut public*[6] seems to us necessary medicine after reading the confessions of the fashionable world in France since the Regency, so we also recognize the salutariness of ascetic spiritualism if we have read, say, Petronius[7] or Apuleius,[8] books which can be considered *pièces justificatives* of Christianity. The flesh had become so insolent in this Roman world that it needed the Christian discipline to mortify it. After the banquet of a Trimalchio a fasting cure like Christianity was needed.

Or is it possible that just as grey-haired libertines inflame their flagging flesh with whippings to renewed capacity for enjoyment, aging Rome wanted to let itself be scourged in monkish fashion in order to discover subtle pleasures in the torture itself and ecstasy in suffering?

Disastrous overstimulation! It robbed the Roman body politic of its last energies. Rome did not perish because of the division into two kingdoms. On the Bosporus as well as on the Tiber, Rome was swallowed up by the same Jewish spiritualism, and here as well as there, Roman history became a slow ebbing away, an agony that lasted for centuries. Can it be that assassinated Judea, in presenting the Romans its spiritualism as a gift, meant to take revenge on the victorious enemy as did once the dying centaur who so craftily succeeded in passing on to Jupi-

5. Supporting documents.

6. Committee of Public Safety, established in 1793, whose members exercised dictatorial power.

7. Roman satirist who died c. 66 A.D. His best-known work, or rather, fragment, *Trimalchio's Dinner*, is the description of a freedman's vulgar display of his newly acquired wealth.

8. A Latin writer of the second century, whose *Golden Ass* is one of the few surviving examples of the Latin novel. Among other things, it deals with the bizarre effects of sensual indulgence.

ter's son the fatal garment poisoned with his own blood?[9] It is a fact that Rome, the Hercules of nations, was so effectively devoured by the Jewish poison that helmet and armor dropped from its withering limbs, and its imperial battle cry sank to the praying whimper of priests and the trilling of eunuchs.

But what debilitates an old man strengthens a young one. This spiritualism had a salutary effect on the super-healthy peoples of the north; their all too full-blooded barbaric bodies were spiritualized by Christianity. European civilization began. This is a praiseworthy, venerable aspect of Christianity. In this regard the Catholic Church earned its greatest claims to our respect and admiration. By means of great and ingenious institutions she was able to tame the bestiality of the northern barbarians and to overpower brute matter.

The art works of the Middle Ages show the mastery of matter by the spirit, and often this is actually their whole mission. The epics of this period could easily be classified according to the degree of such mastery.

One cannot speak here of lyric or dramatic works, for the latter did not exist, and the former are pretty much alike in any age, like the songs of the nightingales every spring.

The epic poetry of the Middle Ages was divided into sacred and profane, but both categories were completely Christian in character, for though the sacred poetry celebrated exclusively the Jewish people, who were consid-

9. When the centaur Nessus tried to rape Hercules' wife, Deianira, Hercules killed him. As he lay dying, Nessus advised Deianira to make from his blood a magic salve which would keep Hercules true to her. Soon after, upon Hercules' return from a successful campaign, he ordered his wife to provide him with a white garment in which he could offer the gods a sacrifice as tribute for the victory. Deianira, seeing the beautiful prisoner, Iola, brought back by her husband, rubbed the garment with the magic salve, to discover only too late that it was a fatal poison which would have killed Hercules if the gods had not rescued him from the funeral pyre and taken him to Olympus.

ered the only sacred people, and their history, recognized as the only sacred history, the heroes of the Old Testament and the New, the legends of saints, in short, the Church, yet in the profane poetry the whole life of the times was reflected with all its Christian views and aspirations. The flower of sacred poetry in the German Middle Ages is perhaps *Barlaam and Josaphat*,[10] a work in which the doctrine of denial, of temperance, of renunciation, of contempt for all worldly glory was consistently expressed. After it I would consider the *Eulogy of St. Anno*[11] the best of the sacred literature. But this latter work extends far into the secular realm. In general it differs from the former as, let us say, a Byzantine picture of a saint differs from an ancient German picture. We also see in *Barlaam and Josaphat,* as in those Byzantine paintings, the utmost simplicity with no accessories such as perspective, and the tall, thin, statuesque bodies with their solemn, idealized faces stand out in sharp outline as if against a soft gold background. In the *Eulogy of St. Anno* the accessories almost become the main point, and despite the grandiose design every detail is most minutely executed, and one doesn't know whether to admire in the work the conception of a giant or the patience of a dwarf. Otfried's poem on the Gospels,[12] usually praised as the chief work of the sacred literature, is not nearly so good as the two works mentioned.

In the profane literature we find, as I indicated above,

10. Written c. 1220–1230 by Rudolf von Ems. It is one of the many versions found in western literature of an old Buddhistic legend which tells how the Indian prince, Josaphat, becomes a convert to the Christian asceticism of the hermit Barlaam.

11. A biography of Anno II, Archbishop of Cologne, written by a monastic poet at the end of the eleventh century or early in the twelfth. It begins with the Creation, continues with the Fall, the Redemption, the spread of Christianity, and at last arrives at the founding of Cologne and the celebration of Anno's life and work.

12. The so-called *Harmony of the Gospels (Evangelienharmonie),* written c. 865. It alternates between narrative and exegesis.

first the epic cycle of the Nibelungen[13] and the *Book of Heroes;*[14] in these the whole pre-Christian way of thinking and feeling still prevails; crude energy has not yet been refined into chivalry; the unyielding warriors of the north still stand like statues of stone, and the gentle light and moral spirit of Christianity have not yet penetrated their iron armor. But dawn is gradually breaking over the ancient Germanic forests, the old sacred oaks are felled, and thus a clear arena is formed, where the Christian battles with the heathen. This we find in the cycle of sagas about Charlemagne, in which it is the crusades with their religious tendencies that are actually portrayed.[15] Now, however, from the vitality spiritualized by Christianity developed the most characteristic phenomenon of the Middle Ages, chivalry, which was ultimately refined into a religious chivalry. The former, secular chivalry, we find most charmingly idealized in the cycle of legends about King Arthur, which are full of the sweetest gallantry, the most refined courtesy, and the most adventuresome knight-errantry. From the delightfully extravagant arabesques and fantastic, flowery tapestries of these works we are greeted by excellent

13. The *Nibelungenlied* was the work of an unknown poet, probably during the first decade of the thirteenth century. It is an heroic epic in which Siegfried's courtship of Kriemhild at the court of Worms, his marriage to her, and his early death at the hands of the treacherous Hagen occupy the first part. In the second part, located chiefly in Austria, Kriemhild, who has married Etzel (the historical Attila), plots, and carries out a bloody and successful revenge on Hagen. The narrative, background, and tone are relatively untouched by Christian chivalry.

14. A collection of epic poems dealing with various Germanic heroic legends printed toward the close of the fifteenth century. In many of them Dietrich of Bern (Theoderic the Great) plays a role, as he does at the close of the *Nibelungenlied*.

15. The legends about Charlemagne are more important for French literature than for German. The *Song of Roland (Chanson de Roland)* is well known. There is also a German *Song of Roland* by a priest Konrad, written c. 1140. The French epic was Konrad's source, but the German version emphasizes Christianity and Christian ideals rather than *la douce France*.

Iwain,[16] peerless Lanzelot of the Lake,[17] and brave, gallant, honest, but somewhat boring Wigalois.[18] In addition to this cycle of legends and closely related to it and interwoven with it, we find the cycle about the Holy Grail, in which religious chivalry is idealized, and here we encounter three of the most magnificent works of the Middle Ages, *Titurel, Parcival,* and *Lohengrin.*[19] Here we stand personally face to face with Romantic poetry, as it were, we look deep into its eyes, full of suffering, and before we know it, it entangles us in its scholastic web and draws us down into the mad depths of medieval mysticism. Lastly, however, we also meet with works from that time which do not necessarily pay homage to Christian spiritualism, indeed, works in which this spiritualism is even criticized, in which the poet casts off the fetters of abstract Christian virtues and plunges joyously into the epicurean world of glorified sensuality. And it is not exactly the worst poet who has bequeathed to us the most important work with this tendency, *Tristan and Isolde.* Yes, I must confess that Gottfried von Strassburg,[20] the author of this most beautiful work of the Middle Ages, is perhaps also its greatest poet, even surpassing all the excellence of Wolfram von Eschilbach,[21] whom we admire so much in *Parcival* and in the frag-

16. Heine's spelling. Iwein is the hero of an epic, written c. 1200, by Hartman von Aue, one of the most important Middle High German poets.

17. *Lanzelot* was written by Ulrich von Zazikhoven toward the end of the twelfth century.

18. Written by Wirnt von Gravenberg c. 1205.

19. Wolfram von Eschenbach wrote *Parzival* in the first decade of the thirteenth century. *Titurel,* Wolfram's last work, c. 1219, was not completed, and only two short fragments have been preserved. Both *Parzival* and *Titurel* belong to Arthurian romance. *Lohengrin* is a much later work, whose author is unknown. It is a continuation of Wolfram's *Parzival,* dealing with the adventures of Parzival's son.

20. By far the best version of this famous romance, though Gottfried left it unfinished. It dates from about 1210.

21. Heine's spelling.

ments of *Titurel.* Perhaps it is now permissible to praise
and acclaim Master Gottfried unreservedly. At his time
the work was certainly considered irreligious, and similar
writings, including even *Lanzelot,* were thought danger-
ous. And perilous incidents actually did occur. Francesca
da Polenta and her handsome friend had to pay dearly
for having one day read together from such a book. To
be sure, the greater danger lay in the fact that they sud-
denly stopped reading.[22]

The poetry in all these medieval works possesses a
definite character which distinguishes it from the poetry
of the Greeks and Romans. To mark this difference we
call the former romantic and the latter classical litera-
ture. These terms are, however, only vague labels, and
up to now have led to the most unedifying confusion,
which was worse confounded when ancient poetry was
called "plastic" instead of "classical." This was above all
the origin of such misconceptions as that artists should
always treat their material, whether Christian or pagan,
in plastic fashion, should present it in clear outlines—in
short, that plastic organization should be the chief con-
cern in modern Romantic art, as it was in ancient art.
And in fact, are not the figures in Dante's *Divine Comedy*
or in Raphael's paintings just as plastic as the figures in
Virgil or those on the walls of Herculaneum? The differ-
ence is that the plastic figures in ancient art are com-
pletely identical with what is to be represented, with the
idea which the artist intended to present. For example,
the wanderings of Ulysses mean nothing other than the
wanderings of a man who was the son of Laertes and
husband of Penelope and whose name was Ulysses. Fur-

22. An allusion to the famous passage at the end of the fifth canto of Dante's
Inferno, where Francesca da Rimini, wife of Guido da Polenta, tells the poet
about the day when she and her lover, Paolo, on reading a certain passage in
the romance of Lancelot and Guinevere, confessed their love for the first time
and read no more that day.

ther, Bacchus, whom we see in the Louvre, is nothing but the charming son of Semele with bold sadness in his eyes and a holy voluptuousness in his soft, arched lips. In romantic art it is different; the wanderings of a knight have an added esoteric meaning; they indicate perhaps the wanderings of life in general; the vanquished dragon is sin; the almond tree that from afar wafts its fragrance so comfortingly toward the hero is the Trinity, God-Father and God-Son, and God-Holy Ghost, who at the same time constitute a unity, just as shell, husk, and kernel are one and the same almond. When Homer describes a hero's armor, it is simply an excellent suit of armor and nothing more, worth so and so many oxen; but when a medieval monk describes in his poem the Madonna's skirts, you can be sure that with these skirts he means a like number of different virtues, that a special significance is concealed beneath the holy coverings of Mary's immaculate virginity, for, quite logically, she is also celebrated in poetry as the almond blossom, since her son is the almond kernel. Such is the nature of medieval poetry, which we call romantic.

Classical art had only to represent the finite, and its figures could be identical with the idea of the artist. Romantic art had to represent, or rather, suggest, the infinite and purely spiritual relationships and had recourse to a system of traditional symbols, or rather, to parables, just as Christ himself tried to make clear his ideas about things of the spirit by using all kinds of nice parables. Hence the mystical, enigmatic, marvelous, and extravagant elements in the art works of the Middle Ages. Fantasy makes her most atrocious efforts to represent pure spirit by means of sense images and invents the most colossal extravaganzas, piling Pelion on Ossa, *Parcival* on *Titurel,* in order to reach Heaven.

Among the peoples whose literature likewise strove to represent the infinite and consequently produced monstrous abortions of imagination, for example, in Scandinavia and India,[23] we find works that we also consider romantic and are accustomed to call romantic.

We cannot say much about medieval music. The documents are lacking. Only very late, in the sixteenth century, did the masterworks of Catholic church music originate, which, as representative of their style, cannot be esteemed highly enough, since they are the purest expression of Christian spirituality. The vocal arts, spiritual by their very nature, were able to thrive fairly well under Christianity, but this religion was less advantageous for the plastic arts. Since the latter were also supposed to represent the victory of spirit over matter and yet had to use this very material as their means of representation, they were forced to solve, so to speak, an unnatural problem. Hence those repulsive subjects in sculpture and painting: pictures of martyrs, crucifixions, dying saints, destruction of the flesh. Such tasks were themselves a martyrdom of sculpture, and whenever I look at these distorted works, in which Christian abstinence and passionless spirituality are supposed to be represented by means of crooked, pious heads, long, thin arms, skinny legs, and uneasily awkward garments, I am seized with an inexpressible pity for the artists of that time. The painters probably had it somewhat better, since the medium of their representation, color, in its intangibility, in its many-hued shadings, was not in such crass opposition to spirituality as the sculptors' material; nevertheless, the painters also had to load their groaning canvas with the most repulsive suffering figures. Indeed, if one looks at many collections of paintings and sees nothing pictured but gory scenes, floggings, and executions, one would think the old masters had painted these pictures for an executioner's gallery.

23. Heine is thinking of the *Edda*, the *Ramayana*, the *Mahabharata*, etc.

But human genius can transfigure even unnaturalness, many painters succeeded in solving the unnatural problem beautifully and sublimely, and particularly the Italians were able to pay homage to beauty somewhat at the expense of spirituality and to rise to that purity of conception which reached its peak in so many portrayals of the Madonna. In any case, with regard to the Madonna, the Catholic clergy always made some concessions to sensualism. This image of unsullied beauty, transfigured by maternal love and suffering, enjoyed the privilege of being celebrated by poets and painters and adorned with every sensuous charm. For this image was a magnet able to attract the great masses to the bosom of Christianity. Madonna Mary was, as it were, the lovely *dame du comptoir*[24] of the Catholic Church, who attracted its customers, especially the barbarians of the north, with her heavenly smile and held them fast.

Architecture in the Middle Ages bore the same character as the other arts; as a rule all manifestations of life harmonized marvelously with each other in those times. In architecture there is the same parabolic tendency as in literature. When we enter an ancient cathedral today, we scarcely sense the esoteric meaning of its symbolism in stone. Only the total impression directly penetrates our minds. We feel here the elevation of the spirit and the trampling of the flesh. The interior of the cathedral itself is a hollow cross, and we stroll there within the very instrument of martyrdom; the stained glass windows cast their red and green lights upon us like drops of blood and pus; funeral dirges moan all about us; beneath our feet tombstones and putrefaction, and like the colossal pillars our spirit strives upward, painfully tearing itself from the body, which sinks to the earth like a weary garment. If you look at them from outside, these Gothic

24. According to the edition by O. Walzel, Heine means a *Büfettdame*, i.e., a waitress or barmaid.

cathedrals, these enormous edifices, fashioned so airily, so finely, so delicately, so transparently that they might be taken for carvings, or Brabant lace made of marble, you feel more than ever the power of that age, which could master even stone so that it seems to be almost uncannily permeated with spirit, so that even this hardest of all substances expresses Christian spirituality.

But the arts are merely the mirror of life, and as Catholicism was extinguished in life, it also faded and died away in the arts. At the time of the Reformation Catholic literature gradually disappeared in Europe, and in its place we find Greek literature, long since dead, coming to life again. To be sure, it was only an artificial spring, a product of the gardener and not of the sun, and the trees and flowers stood in small pots, and a glass sky protected them from cold and the north wind.

Not every event in world history is the direct consequence of another, but all events are mutually interconnected. Love of Hellenism and the mania for imitating it did not become common with us merely because of the Greek scholars who emigrated to Germany after the conquest of Constantinople; in art as in life there arose a simultaneous "Protestantism." Leo X, the splendid Medici, was as zealous a Protestant as Luther;[25] just as in Wittenberg they protested in Latin prose, so in Rome they protested in stone, in color, and in ottava rima. Michelangelo's powerful marble figures, the laughing faces of Giulio Romano's[26] nymphs, and the exuberant gaiety in the verses of Master Ludovico[27]—aren't these a protesting antithesis to traditionally dismal, languishing Catholicism? The painters in Italy perhaps carried on a much more effective polemic against clericalism than

25. Pope Leo X (1475–1521) was Giovanni de Medici, son of Lorenzo de Medici, well-known patron of the arts and sciences.

26. Romano (c. 1492–1546) was a painter and architect, a pupil of Raphael's.

27. Lodovico Ariosto (1474–1533), Italian epic and lyric poet.

the Saxon theologians. The voluptuous flesh in Titian's paintings—all of this is Protestantism. The loins of his Venus are much more fundamental theses than those the German monk posted on the church door in Wittenberg. —The men of that time seemed to feel themselves suddenly liberated from the constraint of a thousand years; especially the artists breathed freely again when relieved of the nightmare of Christianity; they plunged enthusiastically into the sea of Grecian gaiety, and from its foam the goddesses of beauty rose up to meet them. Once more painters painted the ambrosian joys of Olympus; once more sculptors, with the same ecstasy as of old, chiseled the ancient heroes out of the block of marble; once more poets celebrated in song the house of Atreus and of Laius; the period of neoclassical poetry began.

Just as modern life developed to its greatest perfection in France under Louis XIV, so neoclassical poetry likewise achieved here in France a consummate perfection, indeed, a kind of independent originality. Through the political influence of the great monarch this neoclassical literature spread through the rest of Europe. In Italy, where it had already established itself,[28] it took on a French complexion; with the Angevins the heroes of French tragedy also went to Spain;[29] they went to England with Madame Henriette;[30] and we Germans, of course, built our clumsy temples to the powdered Olympus of Versailles. Their most famous highpriest was Gottsched,[31] that big periwig whom our be-

28. Actually the literature of the Renaissance began in Italy and from there spread to the other European countries. Heine seldom hesitated to sacrifice historical accuracy to his desire to pay a compliment.

29. Philip V (1701–1746), the first Bourbon on the Spanish throne, was the grandson of Louis XIV. He had previously held the title of a Duke of Anjou.

30. Henriette Marie (1609–1669), the daughter of Henry IV of France and the sister of Louis XIII, was married in 1625 to Charles Stuart, later King Charles I.

31. Johann Christoph Gottsched (1700–1766) attempted to reform German poetry and drama by imitation of French models.

loved Goethe described so perfectly in his memoirs.[32]

Lessing was the literary Arminius[33] who liberated our theater from this foreign domination. He showed us the vacuity, the absurdity, the bad taste of those imitations of the French theater, which itself seemed to be an imitation of the Greek. He became the founder of modern German national literature, not simply through his criticism, but also through his own creative writings. This man pursued every branch of knowledge, every aspect of life, with enthusiasm and impartiality. Art, theology, the study of antiquity, literature, dramatic criticism, history —he pursued all these with the same zeal and for the same purpose. All his works are animated by that great social idea, that progressive humanism, that religion of reason whose John the Baptist he was and whose Messiah we are still awaiting. He never ceased to preach this religion, though unfortunately often completely alone and in the wilderness. And besides he lacked the art of turning stones into bread; he spent the greatest part of his life in poverty and hardship; this is a curse that weighs upon nearly all great minds in Germany and will perhaps be eliminated only by political liberation. Lessing was also more politically motivated than anyone suspected, a characteristic that we do not find at all among his contemporaries. Only now do we see what he meant by the description of petty despotism in *Emilia Galotti*.[34] In his own time he was regarded merely as a champion of intel-

32. In *Poetry and Truth (Dichtung und Wahrheit)*, Book VII.

33. Arminius, a German national hero because he was the leader of the armies that vanquished the Romans under Varus in the crucial battle of the Teutoburger Wald in 9 A.D.

34. The action takes place in Italy, but the unscrupulous immorality and tyranny of the court could apply as well to some courts in the Germany of Lessing's time. The Prince's attempt to seduce the virtuous heroine Emilia was unsuccessful, but was pursued with such persistence that in the course of the play Emilia's fiancé is killed, she herself is taken prisoner by the Prince's villainous confidant, and finally feels forced to goad her father into killing her in order to preserve her virtue.

lectual freedom and an opponent of clerical intolerance, for his theological writings were better understood. The fragments, *Concerning the Education of the Human Race,* translated into French by Eugène Rodrigue, may possibly give the French some idea of the comprehensive scope of Lessing's mind. The two critical writings that had the greatest influence on art are his *Hamburg Dramaturgy* and his *Laocoön, or An Essay on the Limits of Painting and Poetry.* His best plays are *Emilia Galotti, Minna von Barnhelm,* and *Nathan the Wise.*

Gotthold Ephraim Lessing was born in Kamenz in Lausitz on January 22, 1729, and died in Brunswick February 15, 1781. He was no one-sided man, but while fighting with his polemic to destroy outworn traditions, was himself creating at the same time something new and better. "He resembled," says a German writer, "those devout Jews who, during the second building of the temple, being often disturbed by attacks from their enemies, then fought against them with one hand and continued building the house of God with the other hand." This is not the place for me to say more about Lessing, but I cannot refrain from remarking that in the whole history of literature he is the writer I love best. I want to mention here another writer whose efforts were made in the same spirit and for the same purpose and who may be called Lessing's immediate successor. To be sure, an evaluation of him does not belong here either. Actually he occupies a very solitary place in literary history, and his relationship to his time and his contemporaries cannot yet be judged definitively. He is Johann Gottfried Herder, who was born in Morungen in East Prussia in 1744 and died in Weimar in Saxony in the year 1803.

The history of literature is the great morgue where everyone looks for the dead whom he loves or to whom he is related. When among so many insignificant corpses I catch sight of Lessing or Herder, with their noble hu-

man faces, my heart pounds. How could I pass by with-
out lightly kissing your pale lips!

Yet though Lessing resolutely put an end to the imita-
tion of French pseudo-Hellenism, nonetheless, merely
by calling attention to the real art works of Greek an-
tiquity, he himself to some extent furthered a new kind
of silly imitations. By fighting against religious supersti-
tion he even encouraged the pedantic mania for Ration-
alism that flaunted itself in Berlin and possessed in the
late Nicolai its main mouthpiece and in the *Allgemeine
deutsche Bibliothek*[35] its arsenal. During those years the
most wretched mediocrity began to play havoc more dis-
gustingly than ever, and triviality and inanity swelled up
like the frog in the fable.

It is a great mistake to think that Goethe, who at that
time had already appeared on the scene, was then gener-
ally recognized. His *Götz von Berlichingen* and his *Werther*[36]
had been received with enthusiasm, but so had the works
of the most commonplace dabblers, and Goethe was
given only a tiny niche in the temple of literature. As I
said, the public had received only *Götz* and *Werther* with
enthusiasm, more on account of the subject matter than
because of their artistic merits, which almost no one was
capable of appreciating in these masterpieces. *Götz* was
a dramatized novel of chivalry, a genre very popular at
that time. In *Werther* people saw only the adaptation of
a true story, that of young Jerusalem, a young man who
shot himself for love and thus created a tremendous
sensation in that time of dead calm; they read his touch-
ing letters with tears in their eyes; they noted discern-
ingly that the manner in which Werther was removed
from a social gathering of the aristocracy increased his

35. Christoph Friedrich Nicolai (1733–1811), an active and influential
champion of Rationalism, was the editor of the journal mentioned here, pub-
lished from 1765 to 1800.

36. The first play and the first novel of Goethe's to attract attention.

disgust with life;[37] the question of suicide caused more discussion of the book; some idiots hit on the idea of likewise shooting themselves at this opportune moment; thanks to its contents the book was a striking sensation. But August Lafontaine's[38] novels were read just as enthusiastically, and since he never stopped writing, he was more famous than Wolfgang Goethe. Wieland[39] was the great poet then, with whom perhaps only Mr. Ode-Writer Ramler[40] in Berlin could compete in the realm of poetry. Wieland was worshipped idolatrously, more than Goethe ever was. The theater was dominated by Iffland[41] with his sentimental middle-class plays and Kotzebue[42] with his tritely witty farces.

Such was the literature against which a school arose in Germany during the last years of the past century. We call it the Romantic School, and Messers August Wilhelm and Friedrich Schlegel presented themselves to us as its directors. Jena, where the two brothers and many other kindred spirits sometimes resided, was the center from which the new doctrine of esthetics spread.[43] I say

37. On this occasion Werther, who belonged to the middle class, forgetting the class distinctions with which he was quite familiar, stayed on after an afternoon call at the home of a friend, a Count, and finally had to be asked to leave as the party of aristocrats gathered for an evening of sociability.

38. A writer of sentimental novels, once popular, now completely forgotten.

39. Christoph Martin Wieland (1733–1813), poet and novelist. He also translated seventeen of Shakespeare's plays.

40. Karl Wilhelm Ramler (1725–1788) was a poet and translator, devoid of originality, but much read in his day.

41. August Wilhelm Iffland (1759–1814), dramatist, very popular actor, and from 1811 to 1814 director of the royal theater in Berlin.

42. August von Kotzebue (1761–1819), prolific writer of shallow plays that were very popular on the stage.

43. A. W. Schlegel lived in Jena from 1796 to 1801 and became a professor at the University of Jena in 1798. His brother was a *Privatdozent* at the university from 1799 to 1801. Ludwig Tieck, Novalis, and Clemens Brentano were also there during part of these years, as well as the philosophers Fichte and Schelling.

"doctrine" because this school began with a critical examination of the art works of the past and with a recipe for the art works of the future. In both these pursuits the Schlegel school did great service to esthetic criticism. In evaluating art works already in existence, either their defects and weaknesses were demonstrated or their merits and beauties analyzed. In their polemic, in the exposure of artistic defects and weaknesses, the Schlegels were faithful imitators of old Lessing; they seized possession of his great battle sword; but Mr. August Wilhelm Schlegel's arm was much too delicate and feeble and his brother Friedrich's eyes much too beclouded with mysticism for the former to be able to hit the mark as powerfully and the latter as accurately as Lessing. In appreciative criticism, however, where the beauties of a work of art are illustrated, where the important thing was a fine sensitivity for the characteristics of a work, and where these had to be made comprehensible, the Schlegels were far superior to old Lessing. But what shall I say about their prescriptions for producing masterpieces! Here the Schlegels displayed an impotence that we also find in Lessing. Vigorous though he was in negative criticism, even he was weak in affirmative criticism; rarely was he able to establish a basic principle, still more rarely a correct one. He lacked the firm grounding of a philosophy, of a philosophical system. The same is true of the Schlegels to a far more hopeless degree. A lot of nonsense is talked about the influence of Fichte's idealistic philosophy and Schelling's nature philosophy on the Romantic School, even to the extent of maintaining that it had its origin in these philosophies. But I find, at most, the influence of a few fragments of Fichte's and Schelling's ideas, and no influence whatsoever of a philosophy. Mr. Schelling, who was then teaching in Jena, did, however, exercise a strong personal influence on the Romantic School; he is a bit of a poet—a fact not known in

France—and they say he is still uncertain as to whether
he should publish his collected philosophical doctrines
in poetic or even metrical form. This uncertainty is char-
acteristic of the man.

Though the Schlegels could specify no fixed theory for
the masterpieces that they commissioned from the poets
of their school, they compensated for this lack by
strongly recommending the best art works of the past as
models and by making them accessible to their pupils.
These were principally the Catholic-Christian works of
the Middle Ages. The translation of Shakespeare, who
stands on the border-line of this art and already smiles
upon our modern age with Protestant clarity, was in-
tended solely for polemical purposes, a discussion of
which would occupy too much space here.[44] Besides, this
translation was undertaken by Mr. A. W. Schlegel at a
time when enthusiasm had not yet transported him and
his followers completely back to the Middle Ages. Later,
when this occurred, Calderón was translated[45] and
praised far more highly than Shakespeare, for in Cal-
derón the literature of the Middle Ages was found in its
purest form, certainly in the two main components, chiv-
alry and monasticism. The pious comedies of the Castil-
ian priest and poet, whose poetic blossoms are sprinkled
with holy water and perfumed with churchly incense,
were now imitated with all their sacred solemnity, with
all their sacerdotal pomp, with all their sanctified absurd-
ity. And in Germany there sprang up those confusedly
devout, crazily profound writings in which the characters
fell mystically in love, as in *Devotion to the Cross,* or fought

44. In an essay on Shakespeare's female characters Heine presented his
theory that the translation of Shakespeare was meant to depreciate Schiller as
a dramatist.

45. Schlegel translated five of Calderón's plays. They appeared in Berlin,
1803–1809, under the title of *Spanish Theater.*

in honor of the Blessed Virgin, as in *The Steadfast Prince;*[46] and Zacharias Werner[47] went as far as anyone could without being locked up in an insane asylum by order of the authorities.

Our literature, said the Schlegels, is old, our Muse is an old woman with a spinning wheel, our Cupid is not a fair-haired boy, but a shriveled-up dwarf with grey locks, our emotions have withered, our imagination has dried up, and we must renew our strength, we must seek again the choked-up springs of simple, artless, medieval poetry, and the fountain of youth will gush forth. The arid, parched nation did not need to be told this twice; especially the poor thirsty souls who lived on the sands of Brandenburg wanted to become verdant and youthful once more, and they rushed to the miraculous springs to swill and lap and gulp with extravagant greediness. But they fared as did the elderly lady's-maid about whom the following story is told. She had noticed that her mistress possessed a magic elixir that restored youth; when her mistress was absent, she took from her dressing table the little flask containing the elixir, but instead of drinking only a few drops, she took such a big, long swallow that, due to the greatly intensified magic power of the rejuvenation potion, she became not merely young again, but turned into a tiny little child. And this is exactly what happened to our admirable Mr. Tieck,[48] one of the best poets of the School. He had gulped down so many of the medieval chapbooks and poems that he became almost a child again and retrogressed to that babbling simplicity which Mme. de Staël found so very diffi-

46. Calderón's *La devoción de la Cruz* and *El príncipe constante.*

47. A talented, but unbalanced person whose life ranged from the extreme of debauchery to the devout Catholicism of his later years. Most of his plays dealt with religious subjects, and his dramatic technique was often bizarre and crudely melodramatic.

48. Ludwig Tieck (1773–1853), poet, dramatist, novelist, writer of *novelle*, critic, and translator.

cult to admire. She admitted herself that it seemed
strange to her for a character in a play to make his first
appearance with a monologue that begins, "I am valiant
Boniface, and have come to tell you," etc.[49]

In his novel *Sternbald's Travels*[50] and in *Heartfelt Senti-
ments of an Art-Loving Friar,* edited by him and written by
a certain Wackenroder,[51] Mr. Ludwig Tieck had pre-
sented the naive, crude beginnings of art as models even
for sculptors and painters. The piety and the childlike
quality of these works, which are revealed by the very
awkwardness of their technique, were recommended for
imitation. Raphael was completely ignored, and little was
heard even about his teacher, Perugino,[52] who, to be
sure, was ranked higher and in whom were discovered
vestiges of the virtues so devoutly admired in all their
abundance in the immortal masterpieces of Fra Giovanni
Angelico da Fiesole. If you want to get an idea of the
taste of these art enthusiasts, you must go to the Louvre,
where the best paintings of those masters, then un-
reservedly revered, still hang; and if you want to get an
idea of the great multitude of poets who were then imi-
tating in every conceivable kind of verse the writings of
the Middle Ages, you have to go to the insane asylum at
Charenton.[53]

But in my opinion the pictures in the first hall of the

49. A very free, in fact, inaccurate, rendering of the opening words of
Tieck's dramatic fairy tale *The Life and Death of Saint Genevieve.* St. Boniface
speaks a prologue and an epilogue to the play.

50. *Franz Sternbald's Travels,* published in 1798.

51. Wilhelm Heinrich Wackenroder, 1773–1798. His principal writings are
the essays Heine mentions here, one of the earliest of Romantic writings in
Germany, with the characteristic emotional approach to art and the passionate
seriousness with which art, here particularly painting and music, became a
religion. Heine exaggerates in what follows. Wackenroder admired Raphael
greatly.

52. Pietro Vannucci, called Perugino (c. 1445–c.1523), head of the Um-
brian school of painters.

53. Near Paris.

Louvre are much too charming to give a true notion of
the taste of the day. One must, in addition, imagine these
old Italian pictures translated into old German. For the
works of the old German painters were considered far
more simple and childlike than those of the old Italians,
and therefore more worthy of imitation. The Germans
are able, so it was said, by virtue of their temperament
(a word for which the French language has no equiva-
lent),[54] to comprehend Christianity more profoundly
than other nations, and Friedrich Schlegel and his friend
Mr. Joseph Görres[55] rummaged through the old towns
on the Rhine for remains of old German paintings and
sculpture, which were worshipped in blind faith like holy
relics.

I have just compared the German Parnassus of that
time with Charenton, but I think that here, too, I have
said much too little. French madness is far from being so
mad as German madness, for in the latter, as Polonius
would say,[56] there is method. The Germans cultivated
that madness with unequalled pedantry, with horrifying
conscientiousness, with a thoroughness which a superfi-
cial French madman cannot even conceive of.

Political conditions in Germany were still especially
favorable for the medieval-Christian movement. "Misery

54. Nor does the English. The word *Gemüt* means many things. One word
connoting "mind, soul, heart, spirit" would be needed to convey the total
meaning of the German word.

55. German author (1776–1848), interested in medieval literature and ac-
tive as a journalist and political writer. He was a devout Catholic. In this work
and in the *History of Religion and Philosophy* Heine uses the title "Mr." in
referring to certain persons but omits it when writing of others. Here, for
instance, the title is used with Görres' name, but not with Friedrich Schlegel's.
I have retained in my translation Heine's use of the title because I believe it
was deliberate. He uses the title when referring to men he disliked, for exam-
ple, A.W. Schlegel and Joseph Schelling, but usually omitted it when discuss-
ing writers whom he liked or toward whom he felt no antipathy; hence the title
seems to add a note of sarcasm or disdain, or at the least, a touch of irony.

56. *Hamlet*, II, 2. "Though this be madness, there is method in it."

teaches us to pray," runs the proverb, and indeed, never was the misery greater in Germany, hence the nation was never more susceptible to prayer, religion, and Christianity than then. No people retains more devotion for its rulers than the Germans, and it was the pitiful sight of their conquered sovereigns, whom they saw groveling at Napoleon's feet, that distressed the Germans beyond endurance, far more than the sorry state to which the country had been reduced by war and foreign domination. The whole nation resembled those faithful old servants of great families who feel all the humiliations which their gracious masters must endure even more deeply than the latter themselves and who shed in private their most sorrowful tears when, for example, the family silver has to be sold and who even secretly use their pitiful savings so that no middle-class tallow lights will be placed on the master's table instead of aristocratic wax candles, scenes we view with suitable emotion in old plays. The general distress found consolation in religion, and there arose a pietistic resignation to the will of God, from whom alone help was expected. And in fact, against Napoleon no one else *could* help but the good Lord Himself. People could no longer count on the secular forces and had to turn their eyes trustfully toward Heaven.

We would have endured Napoleon with equanimity. But our rulers, while hoping to be liberated from him by God, at the same time indulged in the idea that the collective forces of their peoples might also be of great help. With this intention an attempt was made to arouse public spirit among the Germans, and even the most exalted personages began to talk of German nationality, of a common German fatherland, of the unification of the Christian, Germanic tribes, of the unity of Germany. We were ordered to be patriotic, and we became patriots, for we do everything our rulers order us to. One must not think of this patriotism, however, as the same

emotion which bears this name here in France. A French-
man's patriotism means that his heart is warmed, and
with this warmth it stretches and expands so that his love
no longer embraces merely his closest relatives, but all
of France, the whole of the civilized world. A German's
patriotism means that his heart contracts and shrinks like
leather in the cold, and a German then hates everything
foreign, no longer wants to become a citizen of the
world, a European, but only a provincial German. So
now we saw the perfect boorishness which Mr. Jahn[57]
developed into a system; there began the mean, coarse,
uncultured opposition to the most magnificent and ven-
erable convictions that Germany has produced, namely,
to the humanism, to the universal brotherhood of man,
to the cosmopolitanism which our great minds, Lessing,
Herder, Schiller, Goethe, Jean Paul,[58] which all educated
Germans have always believed in.

What happened soon afterward in Germany is all too
familiar to you. When God, the snow, and the Cossacks
had destroyed Napoleon's best forces, we Germans re-
ceived the royal command to free ourselves from the
foreign yoke, and we flared up in manly indignation at
the servitude endured all too long, and we were inspired
by the good melodies and bad verse of Körner's[59] songs,
and we fought and won our freedom, for we do every-
thing we are ordered to do by our rulers.

The period of preparation for this struggle was natu-

57. Ludwig Jahn, one of the founders of the student union known as the
Burschenschaft in 1815. It was open to all students, regardless of class distinc-
tions, and attempted to combine ethics and patriotism in its goal of personal
and political reform. This was the beginning of other, widespread student
movements throughout Germany.

58. Pseudonym for Johann Paul Richter (1763–1825), a German novelist.

59. Theodor Körner, a poet who died in battle in 1813 at the age of
twenty-two. His patriotic poems written during the Wars of Liberation were
very popular, and his early death on the battlefield helped to keep his memory
alive.

rally the most favorable soil for a school that was hostile to the French spirit and extolled everything characteristically German in art and life. At that time the Romantic School went hand in hand with the aims of the governments and the secret societies, and Mr. A. W. Schlegel conspired against Racine with the same objective as that of Prime Minister Stein when he conspired against Napoleon. The School swam with the current of the time, the current that was flowing back to its source. When at last German patriotism and German nationality were completely victorious, the national-Germanic-Christian-Romantic School, the "neo-German-religious-patriotic art"[60] also triumphed conclusively. Napoleon, the great Classicist, as classic as Alexander and Caesar, fell, and Messers August Wilhelm and Friedrich Schlegel, the inconsequential Romanticists, just as romantic as Tom Thumb and Puss in Boots,[61] rose up as conquerors.

But here too the reaction which follows in the wake of every exaggeration was not slow to appear. As spiritual Christianity was a reaction against the brutal domination of imperial Roman materialism; as the renewed love for the serene joyousness of Greek art and science should be viewed as a reaction against the degeneration of Christian spirituality into idiotic asceticism; as the revival of medieval romanticism can also be regarded as a reaction against the pedantic imitation of ancient classical art, so we now see a reaction against the reintroduction of that Catholic, feudalistic turn of mind, that chivalry and clericalism, which had been preached in paintings and in words, and under the strangest circumstances. For when

60. Under this title Goethe's friend Heinrich Meyer published an essay in 1817 in Goethe's journal *Über Kunst und Altertum*. Meyer, and implicitly Goethe also, here rejected the Romantic movement in Germany.

61. A reference to two "fairy-tale" plays by Ludwig Tieck. Heine chose these two plays because the subject matter was familiar to the French from Charles Perrault's fairy tales.

the old artists of the Middle Ages, the recommended models, were so highly praised and admired, their merit could be explained only by the fact that these men believed in the subject that they represented; that in their artless simplicity they could achieve greater things than the later masters who were vastly superior in technique, but lacked faith; that faith had worked miracles in them. And indeed, how could one explain the splendors of a Fra Angelico da Fiesole or Brother Otfried's poem[62] otherwise? Hence the artists who took art seriously and wished to imitate the magnificent distortion of these miraculous paintings and the godly awkwardness of these miraculous poems, in short, the inexplicable mystical quality of the ancient works, decided to go to the very same Hippocrene from which the old masters had drawn their miraculous inspiration; they pilgrimaged to Rome, where, with the milk of his jenny ass, the representative of Christ would restore to health tubercular German art; in a word, they betook themselves to the bosom of the Roman Catholic Apostolic Church, the only true faith. For several members of the Romantic School there was no need of any formal conversion, they being Catholic by birth, for example, Mr. Görres and Mr. Clemens Brentano, and they merely renounced the freethinking views they had previously held. Others, however, had been born and reared within the bosom of the Protestant Church, for example, Friedrich Schlegel, Mr. Ludwig Tieck, Novalis, Werner, Schütz, Carové, Adam Müller,[63] etc., and their conversion to Catholicism required a public record. I have mentioned here only writers; the number of painters who renounced the Protestant faith in droves was far larger.

62. See above, p. 135, note 12.

63. Neither Tieck nor Novalis ever became a Catholic. Carové attempted in his writings to introduce a uniform religion including both Catholics and Protestants.

When these young people were seen standing in line, so to speak, in front of the Roman Catholic Church and crowding back into the old prison of the mind from which their forefathers had freed themselves so vigorously, people in Germany shook their heads very doubtfully. But when it was discovered that the propaganda of priests and *Junkers,* who had formed a conspiracy against the religious and political freedom of Europe, had a hand in the matter, and that it was really Jesuitism that succeeded in luring German youth to their destruction with the sweet tones of Romanticism as the mythical pied piper had once lured the children of Hamlin, great indignation and flaming wrath broke out among the friends of freedom of thought and of Protestantism in Germany.

I have mentioned freedom of thought and Protestantism together, but I hope that no one will accuse me of bias in favor of the latter, even though I belong to the Protestant Church in Germany. I have mentioned freedom of thought and Protestantism together without any bias whatsoever; it is a fact that in Germany a friendly relationship exists between the two. In any case they are related to each other like mother and daughter. Although the Protestant Church is accused of much disastrous bigotry, one claim to immortal fame must be granted it: by permitting freedom of inquiry in the Christian faith and by liberating the minds of men from the yoke of authority, it enabled freedom of inquiry in general to take root in Germany and made it possible for science to develop independently. German philosophy, though it now puts itself on an equal basis with the Protestant Church or even above it, is nonetheless only its daughter; as such it always owes the mother a forbearing reverence, and affinity of interests required them to become allies when both were threatened by the common enemy, Jesuitism. All friends of freedom of thought and of the Protestant Church, the sceptics as well as the orthodox, rose up simultaneously against the restorers of Catholicism; and of course the liberals, who were not really concerned about the interests of philosophy or of the Protestant Church, but about the interests of middle-class freedom, likewise joined this opposition group. In Germany, however, the liberals had also always been, up to this time, academic philosophers and theologians, and it was always the same idea of freedom for which they fought, whether they were treating a purely political or a philosophical or a theological subject. This is shown very clearly in the life of the man who was undermining the Romantic School in Germany from its very beginning and contributed the most to overthrowing it. He is Johann Heinrich Voss.

He is completely unknown in France, and yet there are few men to whom the German people are more indebted for their intellectual development. After Lessing he is perhaps the greatest middle-class writer in German literature. At any rate, he was a great man and deserves a discussion that is not all too scanty.

The biography of the man is almost that of nearly every German writer of the old school. He was born in Mecklenburg in 1751 of poor parents, studied theology, neglected it after becoming acquainted with literature and the Greeks, applied himself seriously to both subjects, taught to keep from starving, became a schoolteacher in Otterndorf in the district of Hadeln, translated the classics, and lived poor, frugal, and industrious to the age of seventy-five. He had a distinguished reputation among poets of the old school, but the modern Romantic poets constantly plucked at his laurel wreath and sneered profusely at decent, old-fashioned Voss, who, in unsophisticated language, even in Low German, had celebrated in verse the petty bourgeois life on the Lower Elbe, who did not select medieval knights and madonnas as heroes of his works, but a simple, Protestant pastor and his virtuous family, and who was so thoroughly wholesome and middle-class and natural, whereas they, the modern troubadours, were so somnambulistically sickly, so chivalrously refined, and so brilliantly unnatural. How odious he must have been to Friedrich Schlegel, the ecstatic bard of the lasciviously romantic *Lucinde*,[64] this pedantic Voss with his chaste "Luise" and his venerable old "Pastor of Grünau"![65] Mr. August Wilhelm Schlegel, who never had such honorable intentions about lasciviousness and Catholicism as his brother, was able to get along much better with old Voss, and there existed between them merely a rivalry as translators, which, incidentally, was of great benefit to the German language. Even before the rise of the new school Voss had translated Homer; now he also translated, with incredible industry, the other pagan poets of antiquity, while Mr. A. W. Schlegel translated the Christian poets of the Romantic-Catholic age. The works of both were occasioned by an indirectly polemic purpose; Voss wanted to promote classical literature and ideas with his translations, whereas Mr. A. W. Schlegel wanted to make the Christian, Romantic poets accessible to the public in good translations for imitation and edification . . . At last Voss, not to be outdone, decided that he too would translate Shakespeare, whom Mr. Schlegel had translated into German so excellently during his first period, but old Voss suffered for this and his publisher even more, since the translation was an utter failure. Where Mr. Schlegel perhaps translates too smoothly and his verses are sometimes like whipped cream, so that you don't know, when you take them into your mouth, whether to eat them or drink them, Voss is hard as stone, and you risk breaking your jaw by reading his verses

64. An erotic novel published in 1799 in which Schlegel earnestly, but inartistically, crusades against the "double standard."

65. Main characters in *Luise*, a popular epic idyll by Voss.

aloud. But precisely what distinguished Voss so sharply was the energy with which he struggled against all difficulties, and he struggled not only with the German language, but also with that Jesuitical, aristocratic monster which was then rearing its misshapen head from the forest-like darkness of German literature, and Voss dealt it a mighty wound.

Mr. Wolfgang Menzel,[66] who is known as one of the most bitter opponents of Voss, calls him a Low Saxon peasant. Despite the abusive intention, this designation is very suitable. Voss was, in fact, a Low Saxon peasant, just as Luther was; he was completely lacking in chivalry, knightly courtesy, and grace; he was a true descendant of that sturdily vigorous, strongly masculine German stock to whom Christianity had to be preached with fire and sword, who submitted to this religion only after losing three battles, who have still retained much of the Nordic pagan obstinacy, and in their material and spiritual struggles show themselves to be as courageous and unyielding as their old gods. Indeed, when I look at Johann Heinrich Voss, his polemics and his whole character, I feel as if I were seeing old one-eyed Odin himself, who left his Asenburg to become a schoolteacher in Otterndorf in the district of Hadeln and who drilled Latin declensions and Christian catechism into the blond Holsteiners and in his free time translated the Greek poets into German, borrowing Thor's hammer to pound the verses into shape . . .

Meantime Voss' polemic had a powerful impact on the public and turned public opinion against the increasing

66. Menzel, journalist and writer, was an extreme nationalist and an opponent of political liberalism. It was his attacks against the young writers who came to be known as "Young Germany" that were the chief occasion for the decree of 1835 prohibiting the publication of politically suspect writers and works. Heine himself suffered from the restrictions and in turn attacked Menzel more than once.

partiality for the Middle Ages. This polemic had aroused Germany; a large portion of the public declared itself unreservedly for Voss; a larger portion declared itself only for his cause. A war of pamphlets ensued, and the old man's last days were not a little embittered by these quarrels. He was dealing with the worst of opponents, with the clergy, who attacked him under all disguises. Not only the crypto-Catholics, but also the Pietists, the Quietists, the Lutheran mystics, in short, all the supernatural sects of the Protestant Church, which hold such very different opinions, nonetheless united with equally intense hatred for the Rationalist, Johann Heinrich Voss. In Germany one designates with this name those who recognize the rights of reason even in religion, in contrast to the supernaturalists, who in religious matters more or less renounced any recognition of reason. The latter, in their hatred of the poor rationalists, are like the insane in an insane asylum, who, though seized by the most antithetical lunacies, still get along fairly well with one another but are full of the most violent bitterness toward the person whom they regard as their common enemy, none other than the psychiatrist who is trying to restore their reason.

If the Romantic School was wrecked by the revelation to the general public of Catholic intrigues, it suffered at the same time a catastrophic protest within its own temple, and that from the lips of one of the gods whom they themselves had enshrined there. It was Wolfgang Goethe who stepped down from his pedestal and pronounced judgment on the Messers Schlegel, the very high priests who had enveloped him in such thick clouds of incense. His voice destroyed the entire phantasma; the ghosts of the Middle Ages fled; the owls crept back into the dark castle ruins; the ravens fluttered back to their old church towers; Friedrich Schlegel went to Vienna, where he attended mass every day and ate roast chicken;

Mr. August Wilhelm Schlegel withdrew into Brahma's pagoda.[67]

Frankly speaking, Goethe played at that time a very ambiguous role, and it is impossible to praise him unreservedly. To be sure, the Schlegels never acted quite honestly with him. It may only have been because, in their polemic against the old school, they felt bound to set up a living poet as model and found no one more suitable than Goethe, also because they expected some literary assistance from him, that they built him an altar, burned incense to him, and bade the people to kneel before him. Then, too, he was their near neighbor. An avenue of lovely trees, with plums growing on them, connects Jena with Weimar; these plums taste very good when you are thirsty from the summer heat. The Schlegels traveled this road very often, and in Weimar they had many a conversation with Privy Councillor von Goethe, who was always a consummate diplomat and listened quietly to the Schlegels, smiled approvingly, sometimes gave them something to eat, did them other favors as well, and so on. They had also approached Schiller, but he was an honest man and would have nothing to do with them. The correspondence between him and Goethe, published three years ago,[68] throws considerable light on the relations of both poets to the Schlegels. Goethe dismissed them with a superior smile; Schiller was annoyed at their impertinent scandal-mongering, at their habit of attracting attention by means of scandals, and he called them "show-offs."[69]

No matter how superior Goethe acted, he nonetheless owed the greatest part of his fame to the Schlegels. They introduced and promoted the study of his works. The

67. From 1818 on, when he became professor at the University of Bonn, A. W. Schlegel pursued his studies of Sanskrit.

68. 1828–29.

69. Schiller used the word *Laffen* only in reference to Friedrich Schlegel.

disdainful, insulting manner in which he finally rejected these two men smacks very much of ingratitude. Perhaps Goethe, perceptive as he was, was angered because the Schlegels tried to use him only as a means to achieve their aims; perhaps these aims threatened to compromise him, the minister of state of a Protestant government; perhaps it was the ancient pagan divine wrath that awoke in him when he saw the covert Catholic machinations:—for just as Voss resembled the inflexible, one-eyed Odin, so Goethe resembled the mighty Jupiter in his figure and in his thinking. To be sure, Voss had to bang hard with Thor's hammer; Goethe had only to shake his head with its ambrosian locks indignantly, and the Schlegels trembled and slunk away. A public sample of this protest by Goethe appeared in the second number of a journal edited by him, *Kunst und Altertum,* and it bore the title "Concerning Christian Patriotic Modern German Art." This article was, as it were, Goethe's 18th Brumaire[70] in German literature, for by so rudely driving the Schlegels out of the temple, by attracting many of their most enthusiastic disciples to himself, and receiving the acclamations of the public, to which the Schlegels' Directory had long since been an abomination, he established his absolute monarchy in German literature. From this moment on nothing more was heard of the Messers Schlegel; only now and then were they mentioned, as one now speaks occasionally of Barras or Gohier;[71] people no longer talked about Romanticism and classical literature, but about Goethe, and then Goethe all over again. Meanwhile, to be sure, several poets appeared on the scene who were not greatly inferior to Goethe in

70. On November 9 (18th Brumaire) Napoleon, with the help of some members of the Directory, carried out a *coup d'état* against the government of the Directory and established the government of the Consulate.

71. Paul Jean François Nicolas, Count of Barras (1755–1829), and Louis Jérôme Gohier (1746–1830), members of the French Directory.

power and imagination, but out of courtesy they recognized him as their sovereign, surrounded him admiringly, kissed his hand, and knelt before him. These grandees of Parnassus were distinguished from the great masses, however, by being allowed to keep their laurel wreaths on their heads even in Goethe's presence. Occasionally they opposed him, but they became angry when any lesser person considered himself justified in criticizing Goethe. However angry aristocrats are at their sovereign, they still become annoyed if the rabble also revolts against him. And during the last two decades the intellectual aristocrats in Germany had very just grounds for being angry at Goethe. As I myself stated publicly at that time, with plenty of bitterness, Goethe resembles the Louis XI who oppressed the nobility and exalted the *tiers état*.[72]

It was disgusting that Goethe was afraid of any writer with originality and praised and eulogized all the insignificant nobodies. He carried such praise so far that at last it was considered a testimonial of mediocrity to have been praised by Goethe.

I shall discuss later the new poets who appeared during Goethe's reign as Emperor. They are still saplings whose trunks are only now showing their size since the fall of the centennial oak whose branches towered far above them and overshadowed them.

As I have already said, there was no lack of an opposition declaiming bitterly aginst Goethe, that mighty tree. People of the most conflicting opinions united in this opposition. The traditionalists, the orthodox party, were annoyed at finding in the trunk of the great tree no niche with a saint's image and at discovering that the naked dryads of paganism were actually carrying on their witchery in it, and, like Saint Boniface, they would have liked

72. Third Estate.

to take the consecrated axe and fell this ancient magic oak. The moderns, the followers of liberalism, on the other hand, were annoyed that this tree could not be used as a liberty tree, least of all as a barricade. Indeed the tree was too tall; you couldn't hang a red cap on its top and dance the carmagnole beneath it.[73] The general public, however, revered the tree just because it was so magnificent in its independence, because it filled the whole world so sweetly with its fragrance, because its branches towered so splendidly right up into the heavens that the stars seemed to be merely the golden fruits of the grand and wondrous tree.

The opposition to Goethe really began with the appearance of the so-called spurious *Wanderjahre*, which were published by the firm of Gottfried Basse in Quedlinburg in 1821, hence shortly after the decline of the Schlegels, under the title *Wilhelm Meisters Wanderjahre*.[74] Goethe had already announced, under this very title, a sequel to *Wilhelm Meister's Apprenticeship*, and oddly enough this sequel appeared at the same time as its literary double, in which not only Goethe's style was imitated, but also the hero of Goethe's original novel figured as one of the characters. This parody gave evidence not so much of great intellectual powers as of great discretion, and since the author managed for some time to preserve his anonymity, and people tried in vain to guess his identity, the interest of the public was artfully heightened still more. It came out at last that the author was a hitherto unknown country parson by the name of "Pustkuchen,"[75] which in French means *omelette*

73. A popular song and dance at the time of the first French Revolution.

74. The translation of *Wanderjahre* as *Years of Travel* is a distortion of the meaning, hence the retention of the German title.

75. Johann Friedrich Wilhelm Pustkuchen-Glanzow (1793–1834), a Lutheran minister and writer, produced several parodistic sequels to Goethe's first novel about Wilhelm Meister.

soufflée, a name which also characterized his entire person. The book was nothing but the old Pietistic sour dough, puffed out with the help of esthetic techniques. Goethe was reproached by the writer for having no moral purpose in his writings, for not being able to create noble characters, but only vulgar ones, whereas Schiller had represented characters most noble in their ideals and was thus a greater poet.

This last statement, that Schiller was greater than Goethe, was the particular controversial point the book raised. A mania developed for comparing the works of the two poets, and opinions were divided. The Schiller faction boasted of the moral grandeur of a Max Piccolomini, of a Thekla,[76] of a Marquis Posa,[77] and of others among Schiller's dramatic heroes, whereas they declared Goethe's characters, a Philine,[78] a Käthchen,[79] a Klärchen,[80] and other such lovely creatures to be immoral hussies. The Goethe faction remarked with a smile that these heroines could hardly be defended as moral, nor Goethe's heroes either, but that the promotion of morality, which was being demanded of Goethe's works, was by no means the purpose of art; in art there were no purposes, just as in the universe itself, where only man had read into it the concepts of ends and means; art, like the world, existed for its own sake, and just as the world forever remains the same, despite the constant change of man's views in his judgment of it, so art too must remain independent of the transient opinions of mankind; hence art must remain particularly independent of morality, which is constantly changing on earth as often as a new religion arises and supplants the old religion. In fact,

76. Characters in Schiller's tetralogy *Wallenstein.*
77. A character in *Don Carlos.*
78. A character in *Wilhelm Meister's Apprenticeship.*
79. Heine must mean Gretchen in Goethe's *Faust.*
80. In Goethe's *Egmont.*

since a new religion always appears in the world in the course of a few centuries and, passing over into life and manners, establishes itself as a new morality, every age would charge the art works of the past with moral heresy if these were judged by the standard of current morality ... A religion, for instance, that found God only in matter, and hence regarded only the flesh as divine, would perforce, in passing over into life and manners, produce a code of morals according to which only those art works were praiseworthy which glorify the flesh, and the Christian art works, which represent only the vanity of the flesh, would be rejected as immoral. Indeed, art works that in one country can be regarded as moral, can be considered immoral in another country where a different religion has merged into the national manners and customs; for example, our plastic arts arouse disgust in a strictly orthodox Moslem, while many arts which are considered completely innocent in the harems of the Orient are to the Christian an abomination. Since in India the position of a Bajadere is not condemned by the moral code, *Vasantaséná,*[81] a play whose heroine is a prostitute, is not considered immoral at all, but if one ventured to produce this play in the *Théâtre Français,* the whole orchestra floor would howl about immorality, the same audience that watches every day with pleasure the plays of intrigue, whose heroines are young widows who marry happily in the end instead of burning with their deceased husbands, as Indian morality requires.

By proceeding from such a point of view the Goetheans regard art as an independent second world which they rank so highly that all activities of human beings, their religion, and their morality, course along below it, changing and changeable. I cannot, however, subscribe

---

81. Not the title of the play, but an important character in an Indian play entitled *Mricchakatika (The Clay Cart)* by Sudrakā.

unconditionally to this point of view; because of it the Goetheans allowed themselves to be misled into proclaiming the supremacy of art and turning away from the demands of that original real world which, after all, must take precedence.

Schiller attached himself to this original world much more firmly than Goethe, and we must praise him for this. The spirit of his age took strong hold of him, Friedrich Schiller, he wrestled with it, was conquered by it, followed it to battle, bore its banner, and it was the same banner under which those on the other side of the Rhine fought so enthusiastically and for which we are still ready to shed our best blood. Schiller wrote for the great ideas of the Revolution; he destroyed the Bastilles of the intellectual and spiritual world; he helped to build the temple of liberty, that very great temple which is to embrace all nations like a single community of brothers; he was a cosmopolitan. He began with the hatred for the past which we see in *The Robbers*,[82] where he resembles a young Titan who has run away from school, gotten drunk, and smashes Jupiter's windows. He ended with that love for the future which bursts into blossom like a forest of flowers as early as *Don Carlos,* and he himself is the Marquis Posa who is both prophet and soldier, who also fights for what he prophesies and under his Spanish cloak bears the noblest heart that ever loved and suffered in Germany.

A poet, the small imitator of the Creator, also resembles the good Lord in that he creates his characters after his own image. Hence if Karl Moor[83] and Marquis Posa are Schiller to the life, Goethe resembles his Werther, his Wilhelm Meister, and his Faust, and in them one can study the various phases of his genius. Schiller threw

82. Schiller's first play.
83. The hero of *The Robbers*.

himself heart and soul into history, became enthusiastic about the social progress of mankind, and wrote about world history; Goethe tended to become absorbed in the emotions of the individual, or in art, or in nature. It was inevitable that in the end Goethe, the pantheist, occupied himself with natural history as his chief study and gave us the results of his investigations not merely in literary, but also in scientific works. His indifferentism was likewise the result of his pantheistic philosophy of life.

Unfortunately it is true—we must admit it—that pantheism has not rarely turned people into indifferentists. They thought if everything is God, it does not matter what we concern ourselves with, whether with clouds or with antique gems, whether with folksongs or with the bones of apes, whether with human beings or with actors. But herein lies the fallacy; everything is not God, but God is everything. God does not manifest Himself in like manner in all things; on the contrary, He manifests Himself in various degrees in the various things, and each bears within it the urge to attain a higher degree of divinity; and this is the great law of progress in nature. The recognition of this law, most profoundly revealed by the Saint-Simonists, transforms pantheism into a philosophy of life which certainly does not lead to indifferentism but to forging ahead by means of the most passionate self-sacrifice. No, God does not manifest Himself equally in all things as Wolfgang Goethe believed, an opinion which made of him an indifferentist occupied only with the toys of art, anatomy, the theory of colors, botany, and observations of clouds, instead of with the loftiest concerns of mankind. God manifests Himself in things to a greater or lesser degree; He exists in this continual manifestation; God is to be found in movement, in action, in time; His sacred breath wafts through the pages of history, and history is the real book of God.

Friedrich Schiller sensed this and became a "prophet in retrospect,"[84] and he wrote *The Defection of the Netherlands, The Thirty-Years' War,* and *The Maid of Orleans* and *Tell.*[85]

To be sure, Goethe also celebrated some great histories of emancipation, but he celebrated them as an artist. Since he irritatedly rejected Christian fervor, which was odious to him, and did not understand or did not want to understand the philosophical fervor of our time simply for fear of being wrenched away from his placid self-composure, he treated fervor in general as completely historical, as something given, as material to be dealt with; in his hands spirit turned to matter, and he gave it beautiful, pleasing form. Thus he became the greatest artist in our literature, and everything he wrote became a perfectly rounded work of art.

The master's example governed the disciples, and there began in Germany that literary period which I once characterized as the "Age of Art" and whose harmful influence on the political development of the German people I demonstrated. I did not deny, however, in so doing, the intrinsic merit of Goethe's masterpieces. They adorn our dear fatherland as beautiful statues adorn a garden, but they are, after all, statues. You can fall in love with them, but they are sterile; Goethe's works do not beget deeds as do Schiller's. A deed is the child of the word, and Goethe's beautiful words are childless. This is the curse on everything that has originated in art alone. The statue that Pygmalion made was a beautiful woman, even the artist fell in love with her, she came to life from his kisses, but as far as we know she never had children. I believe Mr. Charles Nodier[86] once said something simi-

84. From Friedrich Schlegel's *Atheneum* fragment no. 80: *Der Historiker ist ein rückwärts gekehrter Prophet* (The historian is a prophet in retrospect).

85. Schiller's play *Wilhelm Tell.*

86. A prolific French writer (1780–1844) who imitated Goethe's *Werther* in several novels and even tried his hand at a *Faust.*

lar in this connection, and I was reminded of it yesterday when, wandering through the lower halls of the Louvre, I looked at the ancient statues of the gods. There they stood with their blank white eyes, a secret melancholy in their marble smiles, perhaps a sad recollection of Egypt, the land of the dead, from which they came, or painful longing for life, from which they have now been crowded out by other deities, or even sorrow at their lifeless immortality. Strange!—these antiquities reminded me of Goethe's works, which are just as perfect, just as magnificent, just as serene, and also seem to feel with melancholy that their rigidity and coldness separate them from the stir and warmth of modern life, that they cannot suffer and rejoice with us, that they are not human, but unfortunate half-breeds of divinity and stone.

These few hints will explain the animosity of the various groups in Germany who have been clamoring against Goethe. The Orthodox were indignant at the great pagan, as Goethe is commonly called in Germany; they feared his influence on the people, whom he imbued with his philosophy of life by pleasant writings, even by the most unpretentious little lyric; they saw in him the most dangerous enemy of the Cross, which, as he said, was as repulsive to him as bedbugs, garlic, and tobacco. For this is the approximate wording of the epigram that Goethe dared to utter right in Germany, in the country where these vermin, garlic, tobacco, and the Cross, rule everywhere in Holy Alliance. It was not this aspect of Goethe, however, which displeased us, the men of action.[87] As I have already said, we condemned the sterility of his writing, the sphere of art which he fostered in Germany, which had a quietive effect on German youth, and which frustrated the political regeneration of

87. Heine is not referring to any special political action. He is thinking of the liberals among his, the younger generation, who were not organized into a party but who shared with each other certain liberal ideas.

our fatherland. Thus the indifferent pantheist was attacked from the most opposite quarters. The extreme Right and the extreme Left (to borrow the French phrase) joined forces against him, and while the black-coated priests attacked him with the Crucifix, the raging sansculottes charged him at the same time with their pikes. Mr. Wolfgang Menzel, who led the battle against Goethe with a display of wit worthy of a better cause, did not exhibit so one-sidedly in his polemic the spiritual Christian or the dissatisfied patriot, but based his attacks in part on the last dicta of Friedrich Schlegel, who after his fall, from the depths of his Catholic cathedral, cried out his lament over Goethe, over the Goethe "whose poetry had no central focus." Mr. Menzel went even further and proved that Goethe was not a genius but merely a man of talent, he eulogized Schiller as contrast, and so on. This happened some time before the July Revolution. Mr. Menzel was then the greatest admirer of the Middle Ages, both of the art works and of the institutions of the period; he reviled Johann Heinrich Voss with unceasing fury and praised Mr. Joseph Görres[88] with incredible enthusiasm. His hatred of Goethe was thus genuine, and he wrote against him from conviction and not, as many thought, in order to gain notoriety. I myself was at that time an opponent of Goethe, but I was displeased by the harshness with which Mr. Menzel criticized him, and I deplored this lack of reverence. My comment was that Goethe was still the king of our literature, and that if the critics knifed him, they should at least not be found wanting in the courtesy like that shown by

88. Joseph von Görres (1776–1848), a Catholic writer and journalist. In the beginning he supported the French Revolution, but later turned against it and became a liberal nationalist with an intense dislike for Napoleon. From 1814–1816 he edited *Der Rheinische Merkur*, the most influential paper in Germany as long as he was editor. In later years he took up the cause of ultramontanism, and his liberal views and activities of the earlier years were neglected or forgotten.

the executioner who had to behead Charles I and, before performing his office, knelt down before the king and requested his royal pardon . . .

Nothing is sillier than the disparagement of Goethe in favor of Schiller, towards whom the critics' intentions were by no means honorable and whom they praised all along in order to degrade Goethe. Or did people really not know that those much praised, much idealized characters, those altar-pieces of virtue and morality, which Schiller undertook, were far easier to create than the sinful, provincial, imperfect beings which Goethe lets us see in his works? Don't they know that mediocre painters usually daub life-sized saints' pictures on the canvas, but that only a great master can paint a Spanish beggar lad delousing himself, a Dutch peasant vomiting or having a tooth pulled, and ugly old women as we see them in small Dutch miniatures, true to life and technically perfect? It is far easier to portray grand and terrible subjects in art than tiny, trivial things. Egyptian magicians were able to imitate many of Moses' feats, for instance, the snakes, the blood, even the frogs, but when he produced seemingly far easier magic things, namely, vermin, they admitted their powerlessness, and they could not copy the tiny vermin, and they said, "This is the finger of God." Go ahead and scold about the vulgarities in *Faust*, about the scenes on the Brocken,[89] in Auerbach's tavern, scold about the dissoluteness in *Meister*[90]— you still can't imitate any of it. This is the finger of Goethe! But you don't want to imitate it anyway and I hear you declare with disgust, "We are not wizards, we are good Christians." That you are not wizards I already know.

Goethe's greatest merit is precisely the perfection of everything he creates. There are no passages that are

89. A mountain in the Harz, where the Walpurgisnacht scene in *Faust* takes place.

90. The novel *Wilhelm Meister's Apprenticeship.*

powerful while others are weak; no portion is portrayed in detail while another was merely sketched; there is no bungling, no conventional padding, no predilection for details. He treats every character in his novels and plays, wherever he appears, as if he were the protagonist. So it is also in Homer and in Shakespeare. There are actually no secondary characters in the works of any great poet; every character is the leading figure in its province. Such poets are like absolute monarchs, who attribute no individual value to human beings but who themselves, at their own discretion, award them their highest value. When a French ambassador once mentioned to Emperor Paul of Russia that an important person in his kingdom was interested in a certain matter, the Emperor interrupted him sternly with the remarkable words, "In this kingdom there is no person of importance except him with whom I am speaking at the moment, and he is important only so long as I speak with him." An absolute poet, who has also received his power by God's grace, likewise regards as the most important that person in his spirit-world whom he allows to speak at the moment, about whom he is just writing, and out of such artistic despotism arises that wonderful perfection of the most minor figures in the works of Homer, Shakespeare, and Goethe.

I may have spoken somewhat harshly about Goethe's opponents, but I could say even harsher things about his apologists. In their zeal most of them have uttered still greater nonsense . . . Lectures on Goethe were given at various German universities, and of all his works it was chiefly *Faust* with which the public concerned itself. Sequels and commentaries were often written, and it became the secular Bible of the Germans.

I would not be a German if, at the mention of *Faust*, I did not express some explanatory ideas about it. From the greatest thinker to the most insignificant waiter, from the philosopher down to the doctor of philosophy, everyone exercises his ingenuity on this book. But it is actually just as comprehensive as the Bible, and like the Bible it includes Heaven and earth and humanity and human exegesis. The subject matter is the main reason why *Faust* is so popular. It is proof of Goethe's unconscious profundity, of his genius, which was always able to seize on the most familiar theme and the right one, that he sought out this subject matter in folk legends. I can safely assume that the content of *Faust* is well known, for the book has recently become famous even in France. But I do not know whether the old folk tale itself is known here, whether in this country too a dingy volume of blotting-paper, poorly printed, and decorated with crude woodcuts, is sold at the annual fairs, a book in which can be read the full story of how the arch-sorcerer Johannes Faustus, a learned doctor who had studied all branches of knowledge, finally cast aside his books and made a pact with the devil by which he could enjoy all the sensuous pleasures of earth, but then had to surrender his soul to destruction in Hell.[91] In the Middle Ages the common people always attributed any great intellectual power, wherever they saw it, to a pact with the devil, and Albertus Magnus, Raimund Lullus, Theophrastus Paracelsus, Agrippa von Nettesheim, even Roger Bacon in England, were regarded as magicians, necromancers, and exorcists. But far stranger things are told about Doctor Faustus, who demanded of the devil not merely the knowledge of phenomena but also the most substantial pleasures, and this is the very same Faust who invented printing[92] and who lived at the time when people were

91. This type of version of the Faust legend was preceded by earlier versions, the first printed in 1587. Another appeared at the end of the sixteenth century, was re-edited in the following century, and this in turn was re-worked and published early in the eighteenth century and formed the basis for the popular version to which Heine refers.

92. A reference to the assumption, for a time widely accepted as a fact, that Faust and Gutenberg's partner Fust were one and the same person. This theory has long since been disproved.

beginning to preach against the rigid authority of the Church and to do independent research, so that with Faust the medieval age of faith ends and the modern critical age of science begins. It is indeed significant that the Reformation began precisely at the time when, according to popular belief, Faust lived, and that he himself should have invented the art which procured for science the victory over faith, namely, printing, an art which, however, also deprived us of the Catholic peace of mind and plunged us into doubts and revolutions—someone other than myself might say "and finally delivered us into the power of the devil." But no, knowledge, the perception of phenomena by means of reason, science, gives us in the end the pleasures which faith, Catholic Christianity, has for so long cheated us of. We realize that human beings are called to equality, not only in Heaven, but also on earth; political brotherhood, preached to us by philosophy, is more salutary for us than purely spiritual brotherhood, which Christianity has helped us to obtain; and knowledge becomes word, and word becomes deed, and we can still enjoy bliss on earth during our own lifetime. If in addition we then partake of heavenly bliss after death, as Christianity so firmly promises us, we will be very pleased . . .

Less well-known here in France than *Faust* is Goethe's *Westöstlicher Divan,* a later work which Madame de Staël did not know yet[93] and which we must here mention particularly. It contains, in bright lyrics and pithy gnomic poems, the Oriental manner of thought and feeling; and there is a fragrance and a glow in the book like a harem full of amorous odalisks with black, rouged, gazelle-like

93. It was first published in 1819, six years after Mme. de Staël's book on Germany. The chief literary inspiration for this book of poetry was the Persian poet Hafis, whose work Goethe became acquainted with, in translation, in 1813. There is no good English translation of the title; it means a collection of poems combining Occidental and Oriental characteristics.

eyes and passionate white arms . . . Here Goethe put the most intoxicating enjoyment of life into verse so light, so gay, so aery, so ethereal that one is amazed that such a thing was possible in the German language. In addition, he also gives in prose the most delightful commentaries on customs and activities in the Orient, on the patriarchal life of the Arabs; and while doing so, Goethe is always smiling serenely and is as innocent as a child and as full of wisdom as an old man. The prose is as transparent as the green sea on a bright summer afternoon with no wind, when one can look down quite clearly into the depths where sunken cities with their forgotten splendors become visible; but sometimes the prose is also as magical, as prescient as the sky at twilight, and Goethe's great thoughts then stand out, pure and golden as the stars. The magic of this book defies description; it is a *salaam* sent by the Occident to the Orient, and there are strange flowers in it: sensuous red roses, hortensias like the naked white bosoms of young girls, droll snapdragons, purple foxgloves like long fingers, twisted crocus noses, and in the center, snugly protected, modest German violets. After he had expressed in *Faust* his discontent with abstract intellectuality and his longing for real pleasures, Goethe threw himself heart and soul, as it were, into the arms of sensualism by writing the *Westöstlicher Divan.*

Hence it is very significant that this work appeared soon after *Faust.*[94] It was Goethe's last phase and was of great influence on literature. Our lyricists now celebrated the Orient in song.—It may also be worth mentioning that while celebrating Persia and Arabia so joyously, Goethe expressed the most decided repugnance for India. He disliked in this country the grotesque, the

94. Heine is referring to the publication of *Faust, Part I,* in 1808. *Part II* did not appear in entirety until 1832.

disorder, the lack of clarity, and this antipathy may have arisen because he suspected Catholic wile in the Sanskrit studies of the Schlegels and their friends. For these gentlemen regarded Hindustan as the cradle of the Catholic world order; they saw there the model for their hierarchy; they found there their trinity, their incarnation, their penance, their atonement, their mortification of the flesh, and all their other beloved manias. Goethe's antipathy toward India irritated these people not a little, and Mr. August Wilhelm Schlegel called him with glassy anger "a pagan converted to Mohammedanism."

Among the writings about Goethe which have appeared this year, a posthumous work by Johannes Falk, *A Portrait of Goethe Drawn from Close Personal Association*,[95] deserves very laudatory mention. Besides a detailed discussion of *Faust* (which could not be omitted!), the author has given us in this book the most excellent accounts of Goethe, showing him to us in all his relationships, completely true to life, completely objective, with all his virtues and defects. Here we see Goethe in relation to his mother, whose temperament is so wonderfully reflected in her son; we see him as natural scientist, observing a caterpillar that has spun itself a cocoon and will burst out as a butterfly; we see him in connection with the great Herder, who was seriously angry at the indifference with which Goethe ignored the emergence of mankind itself from its cocoon; we see him sitting among fair-haired ladies-in-waiting at the court of the Grand Duke of Weimar, improvising gaily like Apollo among King Admetus' sheep; we see him again as, with the haughtiness of a Dalai Lama, he refused to recognize Kotzebue; we see how the latter, in order to disparage Goethe, arranged a public celebration in Schiller's

95. Published in 1832. Heine had translated part of the book for the French reading public.

honor;[96]—everywhere, however, we see him wise, handsome, lovable, a charmingly refreshing figure, resembling the immortal gods.

As a matter of fact, one found in Goethe the complete harmony between personality and genius that one expects in extraordinary persons. His outward appearance was just as distinctive as the words that lived in his writings; even his figure was harmonious, clear, joyous, nobly proportioned, and you could study Greek art in him just as in a classical statue. This majestic form was never contorted by groveling Christian humility; the features of this countenance were not disfigured by Christian contrition; these eyes were not downcast with a Christian sense of sin, not over-pious and canting, not swimming with emotion:—no, his eyes were as calm as a god's. For it is a universal characteristic of the gods that their gaze is steady and their eyes do not twitch back and forth uncertainly . . . Goethe's eyes remained just as godly in his old age as in his youth. To be sure, time could cover his head with snow but could not bend it. He always held it proud and high, and when he spoke he became taller and taller, and when he stretched out his hand it was as if with his finger he could prescribe to the stars in the sky the course they should travel. Some claim to have noticed a cold expression of egoism about his mouth, but even this expression is characteristic of the immortal gods and especially so of the father of the gods, the great Jupiter, to whom I have already compared Goethe. I assure you, when I visited him in Weimar[97] and stood face to face with him, I involuntarily glanced to the side, thinking to see beside him the eagle with lightning in his

96. Goethe and Schiller joined forces to prevent this celebration.

97. Heine saw Goethe only once, in the autumn of 1824 after his tour of the Harz mountains. Needless to say, the account given here bears no resemblance to what actually took place at the meeting.

beak. I was about to address him in Greek, but noticing that he understood German, I told him in German that the plums along the road between Jena and Weimar tasted very good. During so many long winter nights I had thought about how many lofty and profound things I would say to Goethe if I ever saw him. And when at last I saw him, I told him that Saxon plums tasted very good. And Goethe smiled. He smiled with the very lips with which he had once kissed the beautiful Leda, Europa, Danaë, Semele, and so many other princesses or even ordinary nymphs--

Les dieux s'en vont.[98] Goethe is dead. He died on March 22 of last year, the momentous year when our earth lost its greatest names. It is as if in this year Death suddenly became an aristocrat, as if he wanted to distinguish particularly the notables of this earth by sending them to the grave at the same time. It is even possible that he wanted to establish a peerage in the other world, in Hades, and in that case his *fournée*[99] was very well chosen. Or, on the contrary, did Death try last year to favor democracy by destroying with the great names their authority as well and promoting intellectual equality? Was respect or insolence the reason why Death spared the kings in the past year? He had absentmindedly raised his scythe against the King of Spain,[100] but changed his mind in time and let him live. Last year not a single king died. *Les dieux s'en vont;*—but we keep the kings.

98. The gods are dying.
99. Group of people.
100. King Ferdinand VII became seriously ill in 1832 but did not die until the following year.

BOOK TWO

I

With the conscientiousness which I have strictly pre-
scribed for myself, I must mention here that several
Frenchmen have complained that my criticism of the
Schlegels, especially Mr. August Wilhelm, has been
much too harsh. I believe, however, that such a com-
plaint would not occur if people here were better ac-
quainted with the history of German literature. Many
Frenchmen know Mr. A. W. Schlegel only from the book
by Madame de Staël, his noble patroness. Most of them
know only his name, and this name rings in their memory
like something venerably famous, such as, for example,
the name Osiris, about whom they also know only that
he is a peculiar freak of a god who was worshipped in
Egypt. About the other points of similarity between Mr.
A. W. Schlegel and Osiris they know absolutely nothing.

Since I was once a student of the elder Schlegel at the
university, one might think I owed him a certain forbear-
ance. But did Mr. A. W. Schlegel spare old Bürger,[101] his
literary father? No, and he acted according to custom
and tradition. For in literature, as in the forests of the
North American Indians, fathers are killed by their sons
as soon as they have become old and feeble.

I have already remarked in the preceding section that
Friedrich Schlegel was more important than Mr. August
Wilhelm, and indeed the latter lived only on his bro-
ther's ideas and understood only the art of developing

101. When Schlegel studied at Göttingen in 1786–88, he was aided and
encouraged in his own career by Gottfried August Bürger, then a professor
at the university and also a poet of some contemporary renown. He was known
chiefly for his ballads, of which "Lenore" became by far the most famous. It
was not Schlegel's critique of Bürger's work which gave Bürger the *coup de grâce*
as a writer but Schiller's scathing article published in 1791.

these ideas. Fr. Schlegel was a man of profound mind. He recognized all the glories of the past, and he felt all the sufferings of the present. But he did not understand the sacredness of these sufferings and the necessity of them for the future salvation of the world. He saw the sun going down and gazed sadly at the spot of its setting and lamented the nocturnal darkness that he saw approaching; and he did not notice that a new dawn was gleaming from the opposite direction. Fr. Schlegel once called the historian "a prophet in retrospect." This expression is the best description of him himself. He hated the present, the future frightened him, and his inspired, prophetic gaze penetrated only into the past, which he loved.

Poor Fr. Schlegel, he did not see in the sufferings of our time the sufferings of rebirth but the agony of dying, and from fear of death he fled to the tottering ruins of the Catholic Church. After all, it was the most suitable refuge for a man of his temperament. He had enjoyed considerable cheerful gaiety in his life, but he considered this sinful, a sin which required subsequent expiation, and the author of *Lucinde* had of necessity to become a Catholic.

Lucinde is a novel, and except for his poems and an adaptation of a Spanish play, *Alarkos*,[102] it is the only original work Fr. Schlegel left behind. In its day there was no lack of eulogists of the novel. The present Right Reverend Mr. Schleiermacher[103] published enthusiastic letters about *Lucinde.* There was not even any lack of critics who praised this work and prophesied confidently that it would one day be considered the best book in German literature. The authorities should have arrested these people, just as in Russia the prophets who prophesy a public catastrophe are locked up until their

102. *Lucinde* appeared in 1799, *Alarkos* in 1802.

103. Friedrich Schleiermacher (1768–1834), the most important Protestant theologian of German Romanticism.

prophecy has been fulfilled. No, the gods have preserved our literature from such a misfortune. Schlegel's novel was soon generally condemned because of its dissolute inanity and is now forgotten. Lucinde is the name of the heroine, a sensual, witty woman or, rather, a mixture of sensuality and wit. Her worst fault is simply that she is not a woman but an unpleasant combination of two abstractions, wit and sensuality. May the Blessed Virgin forgive the author for having written this book; the Muses will never forgive him.

A similar novel called *Florentin* is mistakenly attributed to the late Schlegel. They say this book is by his wife, a daughter of the famous Moses Mendelssohn, whom he took away from her first husband and who went over with him to the Roman Catholic Church.

I believe that Fr. Schlegel was serious about Catholicism. I do not believe this of many of his friends. In such matters it is very difficult to ascertain the truth. Religion and hypocrisy are twin sisters, and the two look so alike that sometimes they cannot be distinguished. The same figure, clothing, and speech. Except that the second of the two sisters drawls out the words somewhat more melodiously and repeats the little word "love" more often.—I am speaking of Germany; in France the one sister has died, and we see the other still in deepest mourning.

After the appearance of Madame de Staël's *De l'Allemagne* Fr. Schlegel presented the public with two more large works, which are perhaps his best and in any case deserve very laudatory mention. They are his *Wisdom and Language of India*[104] and his *Lectures on the History of Literature*.[105] With the former book he not only introduced the study of Sanskrit into Germany but also founded it. He

104. *Concerning the Language and Wisdom of India,* published in 1808.

105. Published in 1815. Heine does not use the exact title which, translated, was *History of Ancient and Modern Literature.* The content consists of lectures given in Vienna in 1812.

became for Germany what William Jones[106] was for England. He had learned Sanskrit with great ingenuity, and the few fragments which he gives in this book are skillfully translated. With his profound powers of intuition he recognized perfectly the significance of the Indian epic meter, the *sloka*,[107] which flows along as broad as the clear and sacred river, the Ganges . . . Fr. Schlegel's work on India has certainly been translated into French, and I can spare myself further praise. My only criticism is the ulterior motive behind the book. It was written in the interests of Catholicism. These people had rediscovered in the Indian poems not merely the mysteries of Catholicism, but the whole Catholic hierarchy as well and its struggles with secular authority. In the *Mahabharata* and in the *Ramayana* they saw, as it were, an elephantine Middle Ages. As a matter of fact, when in the latter epic King Wiswamitra quarrels with the priest Wasischta, this quarrel concerns the same interests about which the Emperor quarreled with the Pope, although here in Europe the point in dispute was called investiture and there in India it was called the cow Sabala.[108]

The same fault can be found with Schlegel's lectures on literature. Friedrich Schlegel surveys the entire literature from an elevated point of view, but this elevated point of view is nonetheless always the belfry of a Catholic church. And with everything Schlegel says you hear these bells ringing; sometimes you even hear the croaking of the church ravens that flutter around him. To me the whole book is redolent of the incense of high mass, and I seem to detect nothing but tonsured ideas peeking

106. Sir William Jones (1746–1794) was the actual founder of Sanskrit studies, beginning with a translation of *Sakuntala* in 1789.

107. This meter consists of two lines with sixteen syllables in each and a caesura in the middle of each line.

108. Sabala was a sacred cow which could endow its possessor with all the wealth in the world. King Wiswamitra tried to obtain the cow from Wasischta, its owner, finally resorting to force when all other efforts failed, but Sabala came to the aid of Wasischta and the king was defeated.

out of its most beautiful passages. Yet in spite of these defects I know of no better book in this field. Only by combining Herder's works of a similar kind could one get a better survey of the literature of all peoples. For Herder did not sit in judgment on the various nations like a literary grand inquisitor, condemning or absolving them according to the degree of their faith. No, Herder viewed all mankind as a mighty harp in the hand of the great master, each nation seemed to him one string of this giant harp tuned to its special note, and he understood the universal harmony of the harp's various tones.

Fr. Schlegel died in the summer of 1829, as a result of gastronomical intemperance, it was said. He was fifty-seven years old. His death caused one of the most repulsive literary scandals. His friends, the party of the clergy, whose headquarters were in Munich, were annoyed at the discourteous manner in which the liberal press had discussed the death, so they defamed and abused and insulted the German liberals. Yet they could not say of any of them "that he had seduced the wife of an intimate friend and for a long time afterward lived from the alms of the wronged husband."

Now, since it is expected of me, I must speak of the elder brother, Mr. A. W. Schlegel. If I tried to talk about him in Germany, people there would look at me in surprise.

Who in Paris still talks about giraffes?[109]

Mr. A. W. Schlegel was born in Hanover on September 5, 1767. I do not have this information from him. I was never so ungallant as to ask him about his age. I found this date, if I am not mistaken, in Spindler's *Encyclopedia of German Women Writers.*[110] Hence Mr. A. W. Schlegel is

109. Giraffes made their first appearance in Western Europe in 1827, having been sent as presents by Egyptian royalty. In his *Memoirs* Heine mentions them as among his first impressions in Paris.

110. In Heine's text the name of the author and the title of the work are wrong. The book was *German Women Writers of the Nineteenth Century* by K. W. O. A. Schindel, published 1822–1825.

now sixty-four years old. Mr. Alexander v. Humboldt and other natural scientists maintain that he is older. Champollion[111] was also of this opinion. If I am to speak of his literary merits, I must praise him again primarily as translator. In this field his achievements were unquestionably extraordinary. His translation of Shakespeare into German is masterly, incomparable. With the possible exception of Mr. Gries[112] and Count Platen,[113] Mr. A. W. Schlegel is certainly the greatest versifier in Germany. In all his other work he is only second- if not third-rate. In esthetic criticism he lacks, as I have said, the foundation of a philosophy, and other contemporaries far surpass him, particularly Solger.[114] In the study of medieval German Mr. Jakob Grimm towers sublimely above him; with his work on German grammar Grimm freed us from the superficiality with which, following the example of the Schlegels, old German literary texts had been edited. Mr. Schlegel could perhaps have achieved something in the study of medieval German if he had not leaped over into Sanskrit. But medieval German had become unfashionable, and with Sanskrit you could create a new sensation. Here too he remained, to a certain extent, a dilettante, the stimulus for his ideas he owed to his brother Friedrich, and the scientific aspects, the actual facts, in his works on Sanskrit were, as everyone knows, the work of Mr. Lassen,[115] his learned collaborator. Mr. Franz Bopp[116] in Berlin is the real Sanskrit scholar in Germany; he is the leader in his specialty. Mr.

111. Jean François Champollion-Figeac (1791–1832), founder of Egyptian archaeology.

112. Johann Dietrich Gries (1775–1842) translated Tasso's *Jerusalem Delivered,* Calderón's plays, etc.

113. August, Graf von Platen-Hallermünde (1796–1835), a facile writer of verse in the strictest forms.

114. Karl Solger (1780–1819), a noted esthetician.

115. Christian Lassen (1800–1876), a Norwegian, an important Sanskrit scholar, published with A. W. Schlegel *Hitopadesa,* a collection of fables. This is primarily Lassen's work.

116. A professor in Berlin and the founder of comparative philology.

Schlegel once tried to cling to the reputation of Nie-buhr,[117] whom he attacked, but if we compare Schlegel with this great scholar or with a Johannes v. Müller, a Heeren, a Schlosser,[118] and similar historians, we can only shrug our shoulders. But how far has he gotten as a poet? This is difficult to determine.

The violinist Solomons, who gave lessons to the King of England, George III, once said to his illustrious pupil, "Violin players are divided into three classes. To the first class belong those who can't play at all, to the second belong those who play very badly, and to the third class belong those who play well. Your Majesty has already moved up to the second class."

Now does Mr. A. W. Schlegel belong to the first class or to the second class? Some say he isn't a poet at all; others say he is a very bad poet. This much I know, he is no Paganini.

Mr. A. W. Schlegel actually achieved fame only by the unparalleled effrontery with which he attacked the contemporary literary authorities. He tore the laurel wreaths from their old powdered wigs and in so doing raised clouds of dust. His fame is an illegitimate daughter of scandal.

. . . After recovering from the astonishment aroused in us by every act of insolence, we realize fully the intrinsic barrenness of Schlegel's so-called criticism. For example, when he tried to disparage the poet Bürger, he compared his ballads with the old English ballads that Percy[119] collected, and demonstrated that the latter were written in a much simpler, naiver, more ancient, and

117. Barthold Georg Niebuhr, a German historian. His chief work was his three-volume history of Rome, published between 1811 and 1832.

118. All three were well-known historians who had published distinguished works.

119. Thomas Percy, Bishop of Dromore, an English man of letters who published *Reliques of Ancient English Poetry* in 1765, thus making available a wealth of ballads and medieval romance and influencing the literary development in both England and Germany.

consequently more poetic style. Mr. Schlegel under-
stood quite well the spirit of the past, especially of the
Middle Ages, and thus he succeeded in pointing out this
spirit in the art works of the past and in demonstrating
their beauties from this point of view. But he does not
understand anything of the present; at most he glimpses
only something of the physiognomy, a few external fea-
tures of the present, and these are usually the less beauti-
ful traits. Not understanding the spirit animating the
present, he sees in all our modern life only a prosaic
caricature. As a rule, only a great poet can appreciate the
poetry of his own age; the poetry of a past time is re-
vealed to us far more easily, and the perception of it is
easier to impart. Hence Mr. Schlegel succeeded in exalt-
ing, for the great mass of people, the works in which the
past lies entombed at the expense of the works in which
our modern present lives and breathes. But death is not
more poetic than life. The old English poems that Percy
collected express the spirit of their age, and Bürger's
poems express the spirit of ours. This spirit Mr. Schlegel
did not understand . . .

What increased Mr. Schlegel's fame still further was
the sensation he later made here in France when he also
attacked the literary authorities of the French. With
proud joy we saw our pugnacious countryman prove to
the French that their entire classical literature was worth-
less, that Molière was a buffoon and not a poet, that
Racine was no good either, whereas we Germans should
be regarded as the kings of Parnassus. His refrain was
always that the French were the most prosaic nation in
the world and that no poetry existed in France. The man
said this at a time when before his very eyes many a
choragus of the Convention, that great tragedy of Titans,
was still walking about alive, at a time when Napoleon
was improvising a good epic every day, when Paris
thronged with heroes, kings, and gods.—Mr. Schlegel,

democratic and Protestant element which was so very repulsive to the chivalric and Olympian-Catholic Aristophanes.

Perhaps, however, I am doing Mr. A. W. Schlegel an undeserved honor by attributing to him definite sympathies and antipathies. It is possible that he had none at all. In his youth he was a Hellenist and only later became a Romanticist. He became the choragus of the new school, it was named after him and his brother, and he himself was perhaps the very one who was least serious about the Schlegel School. He supported it with his talents, he worked his way into it with his studies, he took pleasure in it as long as it prospered, but when the School came to a bad end, he again worked his way into a new field with his studies.

Although the School now went to pieces, Mr. Schlegel's efforts still bore good fruit for our literature. In particular, he had shown how to treat scholarly subjects in elegant language. Previously few German scholars had dared to write a scholarly book in a clear and attractive style. The average scholar wrote a confused, pedantic German that reeked of tallow candles and tobacco. Mr. Schlegel was one of the few Germans who do not smoke, a virture he owed to the society of Madame de Staël. In general, he owes to this lady the outward polish which he was able to show to great advantage in Germany. In this respect the death of the excellent Madame de Staël was a great loss for this German scholar, who found in her salon so much opportunity to become acquainted with the newest fashions and, as her companion in all the main cities of Europe, was able to view the fashionable world and to adopt the most fashionable worldly manners. Such instructive relationships had become for him so very much a necessity for a happy life that after the death of his noble patroness he was not averse to offering the famous Catalani[121] his companionship on her travels.

As I have said, the furtherance of elegance is one of Mr. Schlegel's main merits, and through him more civilization entered the lives of German poets. Goethe had already set the most influential example of how one can be a German poet and still preserve outward dignity. In earlier times German poets despised all conventional forms, and the name "German poet" or even the name "poetic genius" acquired a most unsavory connotation. Formerly a German poet was a man who wore a shabby, tattered coat, fabricated baptismal and wedding poems for a taler apiece, enjoyed in lieu of good society, which rejected him, drinks that were all the better, perhaps even lay drunk in the gutter of an evening, kissed tenderly by Luna's affectionate beams. Grown old, these poets generally plunged still more deeply into their misery; it was, to be sure, a misery without cares, or whose only care consisted in where to get the most liquor for the least money.

This is what I too had imagined a German poet to be. How pleasantly surprised I was, therefore, in 1819 when, as a very young man, I attended the University of Bonn and there had the honor of seeing the poet A. W. Schlegel, the poetic genius, face to face. With the exception of Napoleon he was the first great man I had seen, and I shall never forget this sublime sight. I still feel today the thrill of awe that filled my soul as I stood in front of his rostrum and heard him speak. In those days I wore a rough white coat, a red cap over my long blond hair, and no gloves. Mr. A. W. Schlegel, however, wore kid gloves and still dressed completely in the latest Paris fashion; he was still highly perfumed with good society and *eau de mille fleurs.*[122] He was grace and elegance personified, and

121. Angelica Catalani, a well-known Italian singer.

122. "Toilet water from a thousand flowers," a fictional scent, of course, used ironically.

when he spoke about the Lord High Chancellor of England, he added "my friend," and beside him stood his servant in the most baronial Schlegel family livery and trimmed the wax candles that were burning in silver candelabras standing on the desk beside a glass of sugar water in front of the man prodigy. A servant in livery! Wax candles! Silver candelabras! My friend the Lord High Chancellor of England! Kid gloves! Sugar water! What unheard-of things at a German professor's lecture! This splendor dazzled us young people not a little, and especially me, and I wrote three odes to Mr. Schlegel, each beginning with the words "O thou who" etc. But only in poetry would I have dared to address such a distinguished man with "thou." His outward appearance did indeed give him a certain distinction. On his puny little head only a few silver hairs still shone, and his body was so thin, so emaciated, so transparent, that he appeared to be all spirit and looked almost like a symbol of spirituality.

Despite this he was at that time married, and he, the chief of the Romanticists, married the daughter of Parish Councillor Paulus in Heidelberg,[123] the chief of the German Rationalists. It was a symbolic marriage. Romanticism was wedded, so to speak, to Rationalism, but the marriage bore no fruit. On the contrary, because of it the split between Romanticism and Rationalism became even wider, and the very morning after the wedding night Rationalism ran back home and would have nothing more to do with Romanticism. For Rationalism, being always sensible, did not want to be merely symbolically wedded, and as soon as it discovered the wooden worthlessness of Romantic art, it ran away. I know I am speaking obscurely and will try to express myself as clearly as possible:

Typhon, wicked Typhon, hated Osiris (who, as you

123. Heinrich Paulus, professor of theology in Heidelberg.

know, is an Egyptian god), and when he got him in his power, he tore him to pieces. Isis, poor Isis, Osiris' wife, laboriously collected the pieces, patched them together, and succeeded in repairing her mutilated husband completely. Completely? Alas, no, one important piece was missing, which the poor goddess could not find, poor Isis! She had to content herself with a replacement made of wood, but wood is only wood, poor Isis! Thus there arose in Egypt a scandalous myth and in Heidelberg a mystical scandal.

After this Mr. A. W. Schlegel disappeared from sight entirely. He was forgotten. Displeasure at being forgotten finally drove him once more, after many years of absence, to Berlin, the former capital of his literary glory, and there he again gave some lectures on esthetics. But meanwhile he had learned nothing new, and he now addressed an audience that had received from Hegel a philosophy of art, a science of esthetics. He was ridiculed and disdained. He fared as does an old actress who, after an absence of twenty years, once more sets foot on the scene of her previous success and wonders why people laugh instead of applauding. The man had changed shockingly, and he delighted Berlin for four whole weeks with his display of absurdities. He had become a vain old fop who let himself be made a fool of everywhere . . .

Here in Paris I had the misfortune to see Mr. A. W. Schlegel again in person. I really had no conception as yet of the change until I was convinced of it with my own eyes. It was a year ago, shortly after my arrival in the capital. I was just on my way to visit the house where Molière had lived, for I honor great poets and seek out everywhere with religious piety the traces of their life on earth. This is a form of worship. On my way, not far from that consecrated house, I caught sight of a creature whose features, webbed with wrinkles, showed a similarity with the former A. W. Schlegel. I thought I was seeing his spirit. But it was only his body. His spirit is dead, and his body still walks the earth like a ghost and in the meantime has become quite fat. Flesh had formed again on the thin, spiritual legs; one could even see a belly, and above it hung a great many ribands and orders. The little grey head, formerly so delicate, wore a golden-yellow wig. He was dressed in the latest fashion of the year in which Madame de Staël died. And he was smiling with the old-fashioned sweetness of an aged lady with a lump of sugar in her mouth and tripped along as youthfully as a coquettish child. Truly, a strange rejuvenation had taken place in him; he had experienced, as it were, a facetious second edition of his youth; he seemed to have come into full bloom again, and I even suspect that the redness of his cheeks was not rouge but a healthy irony of nature.

It seemed to me at this moment as if I saw the late Molière standing at the window and smiling down at me, pointing at that apparition both melancholy and gay. Suddenly all its absurdity became completely obvious to me; I understood the whole profundity and fullness of the jest contained it it; I understood completely the comedy-like character of this incredibly ridiculous personage who unfortunately has found no great comic writer to use him suitably for the stage. Molière alone would have been the man to adapt such a figure to the French theater; he alone had the necessary talent. Mr. A. W. Schlegel sensed this very early, and he hated Molière for the same reason that Napoleon hated Tacitus. Just as Napoleon Bonaparte, the French Caesar, probably felt that the republican historian would not have portrayed him in rosy colors, Mr. A. W. Schlegel, the German Osiris, had long sensed that if Molière were still alive, he would never have escaped the great writer of comedy. And Napoleon said of Tacitus that he was the slanderer of Tiberius, and Mr. August Wilhelm Schlegel said of Molière that he was no poet, but only a buffoon.

Mr. A. W. Schlegel left Paris a short time later, after

having been decorated with the order of the Legion of Honor by His Majesty Louis Philippe I, King of the French. The *Moniteur* has delayed as yet in reporting properly on this event, but Thalia, the muse of Comedy, hastily jotted it down in her notebook of jests.

II

After the Schlegels, Mr. Ludwig Tieck was one of the most active writers of the Romantic School. He battled and wrote for it. He was a poet, a name that neither of the two Schlegels deserves. He was a true son of Phoebus Apollo, and like his ever-youthful father he carried not only a lyre, but also a bow with a quiver full of ringing arrows. Like the Delphic god, he was drunk with lyric ecstasy and critical brutality. When, like the latter, he had mercilessly flayed some literary Marsyas,[124] he would gaily pluck with bloody fingers the golden strings of his lyre and sing a joyous love song.

The poetic controversy that Mr. Tieck carried on in dramatic form against the opponents of the School[125] is one of the most extraordinary phenomena of our literature. These are satiric dramas usually compared with Aristophanes' comedies. But they differ from the latter almost as a Sophoclean tragedy differs from a Shakespearean. Ancient comedy had the uniform structure, the strict course of action, and the exquisitely polished metrical language of ancient tragedy, of which it may be considered a parody, but Mr. Tieck's dramatic satires are

124. A Phrygian satyr of Greek mythology. He found the flute which Athena had invented but had discarded and became such a skillful player that he challenged Apollo to a contest. Apollo accepted on the condition that the victor might do as he pleased with the loser. The Muses, acting as judges, awarded the victory to Apollo's lyre-playing, and Apollo promptly flayed Marsyas for his presumption.

125. For example, in *Puss in Boots* and *Prince Zerbino*.

just as daring in structure, as full of English irregularity, as capricious in their prosody, as Shakespeare's tragedies. Was this form an original invention of Mr. Tieck's? No, it already existed among the common folk, particularly in Italy. Anyone who knows Italian can get a fairly accurate idea of these plays of Tieck's if he dreams some German moonlight into Gozzi's motley, bizarre fairy-tale comedies, which are as fantastic as Venice.[126] Tieck even borrowed most of his characters from this merry child of the lagoons. Following Tieck's example many German poets likewise appropriated this form, and we got comedies whose comic effect is produced not by an amusing character or by a funny plot, but by transporting us directly into a comic world, into a world where animals speak and act like human beings and where chance and caprice have taken the place of the natural order of things. We also find this in Aristophanes. Except that the latter chose this form in order to reveal to us his most profound views about the world, as for instance in *The Birds,* where the craziest actions of people are portrayed in the most farcical antics, their passion for building the most magnificent castles in empty air, their defiance of the immortal gods, and their fancied triumphal joy. It is just for this reason that Aristophanes is so great, because his philosophy of life was so great, because it was greater, indeed more tragic, than that of the tragic writers themselves, because his comedies were truly "bantering tragedies." For example, Paisteteros[127] is not represented at the end of the work in his ridiculous nullity, as a modern poet would represent him, but, on the contrary, he wins the lovely Basilea, who is gifted with magic

126. Carlo Gozzi (1720–1806), Italian dramatist from Venice, who tried to revive the dying *commedia dell' arte* and founded the fable play or fairy-tale play in Italy.

127. In the English translation originally published by The Athenian Society, London, 1912, the name is spelled Pisthetaerus.

powers, ascends to his city in the air with his divine spouse, the gods are compelled to yield to his will, Folly celebrates its marriage with Power, and the play ends with nuptial songs of rejoicing. Is there anything more terribly tragic for a sensible person than this fool's victory and triumph! Our German Aristophaneses, however, have never had such high aspirations; they abstained from any exalted philosophy of life; with great modesty they held their tongues about the two most important conditions of man, the political and the religious; they ventured to treat only the theme that Aristophanes discussed in *The Frogs;* as the main subject of their dramatic satires they chose the theater itself and satirized the defects of our theater more or less entertainingly.

But one must also consider the lack of political freedom in Germany. Our would-be wits have to refrain from any sarcasm in regard to actual rulers and thus want to take substitute revenge for this restriction on the theater kings and stage princes. We Germans, who possessed almost no serious political newspapers, were always doubly blessed with a host of esthetic journals containing nothing but worthless fairy tales and theatrical reviews, so that anyone who saw them was almost compelled to think that the whole German nation consisted simply of babbling nursemaids and theater critics. This would have been unfair to us, however. How little such wretched scribbling satisfied us was demonstrated after the July Revolution when it looked as though a free word could also be uttered in our dear fatherland. Suddenly journals sprang up which reviewed the good or bad acting of real kings, and many of them, who forgot their lines, were booed in their own capitals. Our literary Scheherazades, who used to lull the public, the coarse sultan, to sleep with their little *novelle,* were now forced into silence, and the actors saw with astonishment how empty the orchestra was, no matter how divinely they played, and that even the reserved seat of the formidable town critic very often remained unoccupied. Previously the good stage heroes had always complained that they and only they had to serve as public topic of conversation and that even their domestic virtues were disclosed in the newspapers. How frightened they were when it looked as though there might be no talk about them at all any more!

In point of fact, when the Revolution broke out in Germany, this was the end of the theater and theater criticism, and the alarmed writers of *novelle,* actors, and theater critics feared quite rightly "that art was dying." But our fatherland was successfully saved from this horrible fate by the wisdom and energy of the Frankfurt Diet of the German Confederation. It is to be hoped that no revolution will break out in Germany; we are protected from the guillotine and all the terrors of freedom of the press; even the chambers of deputies, whose competition had done so much harm to the theaters despite concessions granted these long before, are being abolished, and art has been saved. Everything possible is now being done in Germany for art, especially in Prussia. The museums are ablaze with artful delight in color, the orchestras roar, the danseuses leap their loveliest *entrechats,* the public is enchanted with the Arabian Nights of *novelle,* and theater criticism flourishes once more . . .

We now have peace in Germany, theater criticism and *novelle* are again the main thing, and since Mr. Tieck excells in both, he is shown due admiration by all friends of art. He is in fact the best *novella* writer in Germany. Not all of his narrative works, however, are of the same genre or of the same value. As with painters, several styles can be perceived in Mr. Tieck. His earliest style still belongs entirely to the old school. At that time he wrote only at the suggestion of or on commission from a book-dealer who was none other than the late Nicolai himself,[128] the most obstinate champion of Enlightenment and humanism, the great enemy of superstition, mysticism, and Romanticism. Nicolai was a bad writer, a prosaic old fogy, and he often made himself extremely ridiculous by his habit of smelling a Jesuit everywhere. But we of the younger generation must admit that old Nicolai was a thoroughly honest man, a genuine friend of the German nation, who, out of love for the sacred cause of truth, did not shrink from even the worst form of martyrdom, becoming ridiculous. As I was told in Berlin, Mr. Tieck at one time lived in his house, one floor above him, and modern times were already trampling over the head of the old.

The works that Mr. Tieck wrote in his earliest style, chiefly stories and big long novels of which *William Lovell*[129] is the best, are very insignificant, with a complete lack of poetic quality. It is as if his rich poetic nature had been miserly in its youth and had saved all its intellectual wealth for a later time. Or did Mr. Tieck himself not know the riches of his own breast, and did the Schlegels first have to discover them with a divining rod? As soon as Mr. Tieck came in contact with the Schlegels, all the treasures of his imagination, his spirit, and his wit were disclosed. Diamonds sparkled there, the clearest pearls welled up, and above all the carbuncle flashed there, the precious stone of fable about which the Romantic poets spoke and sang so much. This rich breast was the real treasure chamber on which the Schlegels drew for the military expenses of their literary campaigns. Mr. Tieck had to write for the School the satiric comedies already mentioned and at the same time prepare according to the new esthetic recipes a quantity of poetic works of

128. See above, p. 146, and note 35 on that page.
129. Published 1795–1796.

every kind. This is Mr. Ludwig Tieck's second style. The dramatic works in this style most worthy of recommendation are *Emperor Octavian, Saint Genevieve,* and *Fortunatus,*[130] three plays adapted from the chapbooks bearing the same titles. The poet clothed these old legends, still preserved by the German people, in luxurious modern garments. But, to be honest, I love them more in their old, naive, and simple form. Beautiful as Tieck's *Genevieve* is, I much prefer the old chapbook very poorly printed in Cologne on the Rhine with its bad woodcuts in which, however, one gets a very moving sight of the poor naked Countess Palatinate, with only her long hair to cover her nakedness, holding her babe Schmerzenreich to the teats of a compassionate hind.

The *novelle* that Mr. Tieck wrote in his second style are far more worthwhile than the plays. They were also usually adapted from old folk legends. *Blond Eckbert* and *The Runic Mountain*[131] are the best. A mysterious inwardness, a strange sympathy with nature, especially with the plant and mineral kingdom, dominate these writings. The reader feels as if he were in an enchanted forest; he hears the subterranean springs murmuring melodiously; at times he fancies he hears his own name in the whispering of the trees; broad-leaved climbers often entangle his feet alarmingly; strange magical flowers gaze at him with their bright, longing eyes; invisible lips kiss his cheeks with teasing tenderness; tall mushrooms like golden bells rise up, chiming, at the base of the trees; great silent birds rock in the branches and nod down at him with their wise, long beaks; everything is breathing, listening, quivering with expectation—then suddenly the mellow

130. The first, a comedy, appeared in 1804, *The Life and Death of Saint Genevieve,* a tragedy, was written in 1800, and the third, a fairy-tale play, was written in 1815–1816.

131. The first was written in 1796, the second in 1802.

French horn sounds, and a beautiful woman, with waving feathers in her cap and her falcon on her fist, gallops past on a white palfrey. And this beautiful lady is as beautiful, as fair-haired, as violet-eyed, as smiling and also as serious, as real and yet as ironic, as chaste and also as passionate, as the imagination of our excellent Ludwig Tieck. Yes, his imagination is a charming lady of noble birth hunting mythical beasts in an enchanted forest, perhaps even the rare unicorn, which permits itself to be captured only by a pure virgin.

But then a remarkable change took place in Mr. Tieck, and this was revealed in his third style. Having been silent for a long time after the fall of the Schlegels, he again made a public appearance, and in a manner one would least have expected from him. The former enthusiast, who out of fanatical ardor had betaken himself into the bosom of the Catholic Church,[132] who had fought so vigorously against Enlightenment and Protestantism, who reveled in the Middle Ages, only the feudal Middle Ages, who loved art only as a naive outpouring of the heart—this man now appeared as an opponent of enthusiasm, as a portrayer of the most modern middle-class life, as an artist who demanded the clearest self-awareness in art, in short, as a man of reason. It is thus that we see him in a series of more recent *novelle,* several of which have also become known in France. The study of Goethe is apparent in them; indeed, Tieck appears in his third style as a true disciple of Goethe. The same artistic clarity, serenity, calm, and irony. If the Schlegel School had earlier been unsuccessful in drawing Goethe over to it, we now see how this School, represented by Mr. Tieck, went over to Goethe. This is reminiscent of a Mohammedan tale. The prophet had said to the mountain, "Mountain, come to me." But the mountain did not

132. Tieck did not become a Catholic.

go. And behold, the greater miracle occurred; the prophet went to the mountain.

Mr. Tieck was born in Berlin on May 31, 1773. Some years ago he settled in Dresden,[133] where he occupied himself chiefly with the theater, and he, who in his earlier writings had constantly made fun of *Hofräte*[134] as stock figures of absurdity, himself became a royal Saxon *Hofrat*. The good Lord is still a greater ironist than Mr. Tieck.

A strange disparity between this writer's intellect and his imagination now made its appearance. The former, Tieck's intellect, is a respectable, prosaic philistine who subscribes to utilitarianism and will have nothing to do with enthusiasm; the latter, however, Tieck's imagination, is still the noble lady with the waving feathers in her cap and the falcon on her fist. These two lead a curious wedded life, and it is sometimes sad to see how the unfortunate lady of high degree has to help her pedantic middle-class husband in his affairs or even in his cheese store. But sometimes, at night, when her spouse is snoring peacefully with his cotton nightcap on his head, the noble lady arises from the confining conjugal bed, mounts her white steed, and once more gallops as joyously as before in the enchanted forest of romance.

I cannot refrain from remarking that in his latest *novelle* Tieck's intellect has become even more ungracious, while at the same time his imagination has lost more and more of her romantic character and on cool nights even remains with yawning enjoyment in the nuptial bed and almost lovingly nestles close to her prosy spouse.

Mr. Tieck, however, is still a great poet. For he can create characters, and from his heart flow words that move our own hearts. But a timorous manner, a certain

133. He lived in Dresden from 1818 to 1841.
134. Plural of *Hofrat*, an honorary title with no English equivalent.

indefiniteness, uncertainty, and weakness are noticeable in him not only now, but were noticeable from the very beginning. This lack of decisive vigor is all too clearly evident in everything he did and wrote. Certainly no independence is revealed in any of his writings. His first style shows him to be nothing at all; his second shows him to be a faithful squire of the Schlegels; his third style shows him to be an imitator of Goethe. His theater reviews, which he collected under the title *Dramaturgical Notes,* are still the most original work he has produced. But they are theater reviews . . .

Besides Goethe it is Cervantes whom Mr. Tieck imitated most often. The humorous irony—I could also say the ironic humor—of these two modern poets diffuses its fragrance through the *novelle* in Mr. Tieck's third style. Irony and humor are so closely blended that they seem to be one and the same. We talk a good deal about this humorous irony, the Goethean school of art praises it as a special excellence of their master, and it now plays a large role in German literature. But it is only a sign of our lack of political freedom, and as Cervantes had to take refuge in humorous irony at the time of the Inquisition in order to intimate his ideas without leaving a weak spot exposed for the serfs of the Holy Office to seize upon, so Goethe also used to say in a tone of humorous irony what he, as minister of state and courtier, did not dare to say outright. Goethe never suppressed the truth; when he could not show it naked, he clothed it in humor and irony. Especially writers who languish under censorship and all kinds of restrictions on freedom of thought and yet can never disavow their heartfelt opinion have to resort to the ironic and humorous manner. It is the only solution left for honesty, and in this disguise such honesty is revealed most movingly . . .

In addition, I must praise two other works of Mr. Tieck's by which he has earned the special gratitude of

the German public. They are his translation of a number
of English plays from the pre-Shakespearean period and
his translation of *Don Quixote*. The latter is extraor-
dinarily successful; no one has understood so well and
reproduced so faithfully as our excellent Tieck the
ridiculous dignity of the ingenuous hidalgo of La Man-
cha.

It is quite amusing that it was precisely the Romantic
School that provided us with the best translation of a
book in which its own folly is exposed so very delight-
fully. For this School was deluded by the same madness
that also inspired the noble man of La Mancha to all his
follies. It too wished to restore medieval chivalry; it too
wanted to revive a dead past. Or did Miguel de Cervantes
Saavedra, in his absurd epic, intend to make fun of other
knights as well, that is, all human beings who fight and
suffer for some idea? Did he really intend to parody in
his tall, haggard knight enthusiasm for ideals in general
and in the knight's rotund squire realistic common
sense? At any rate, the latter plays the more ridiculous
role, for realistic common sense, with all its traditional
sayings meant to benefit society, must nonetheless trot
along on his tranquil donkey behind enthusiasm; despite
his better insight he and his donkey must share all the
calamities that so often befall the noble knight; in fact,
enthusiasm for ideals is so tremendously alluring that
realistic common sense, together with its donkeys, is al-
ways forced to follow it involuntarily.

Or did the profound Spaniard intend to deride human
nature even more astutely? Did he perhaps allegorize the
human mind in the figure of Don Quixote and the human
body in the figure of Sancho Panza, and the whole work
would then be nothing but a great mystery play in which
the question of mind and matter is discussed in all its
most shocking reality? This much I see in the book: that
poor, matter-of-fact Sancho has to suffer greatly for the

spiritual Don Quixoteisms; that he often gets the most
ignoble beatings for the noblest intentions of his master;
and that he is always more sensible than his pompous
master, for he knows that beatings leave a very bad taste
but that the sausages in an olla-podrida taste very good.
Truly, the body seems to have more judgment than the
mind, and a human being often thinks much more accu-
rately with his back or stomach than with his head.

III

Among the lunacies of the Romantic School in Ger-
many the ceaseless praise and eulogy of Jakob Böhme
deserve special mention. This name was, so to speak, the
shibboleth of these people. Whenever they uttered the
name Jakob Böhme, their faces assumed their most pro-
found expression. Was this in earnest or was it a joke?

Jakob Böhme was a shoemaker who first saw the light
of this world in Görlitz in Oberlausitz and left a great
many theosophical writings. They are in German and
hence were all the more accessible to our Romanticists.
I cannot judge very exactly whether this strange shoe-
maker was as distinguished a philosopher as many Ger-
man mystics maintain, since I have not read him at all.
I am convinced, however, that he did not make as good
boots as Mr. Sakoski. Shoemakers play quite a role in our
literature, and Hans Sachs, a shoemaker who was born
in Nürnberg in 1454 and spent his life there,[135] was
lauded by the Romantic School as one of our best poets.
I have read him, and I must confess that I doubt whether
Mr. Sakoski ever wrote as good verses as our admirable
old Hans Sachs.

I have already touched on Mr. Schelling's influence on

135. Hans Sachs (1494–1576) was a very prolific writer known chiefly for
his poems and his Shrovetide plays and farces.

the Romantic School. Since I shall discuss him separately later, I can spare myself a detailed criticism here. In any case this man deserves our utmost attention. For in his early years, due to him, a great revolution took place in the German intellectual world, and in his later years he changed so much that uninformed people make the greatest mistakes by confusing the early Schelling with the present Schelling. The early Schelling was a bold Protestant who protested against Fichtean idealism. This idealism was a strange system which would necessarily seem especially odd to a Frenchman. For while in France a philosophy was coming into fashion which clothed the spirit in flesh and blood, so to speak, which recognized the spirit only as a modification of matter, in short, while in France materialism had prevailed, there arose in Germany a philosophy which, quite in contrast, admitted only the spirit as reality, declared all matter only a modification of the spirit, and even denied the existence of matter. It seemed almost as if, across the Rhine, the spirit sought revenge for the insult done it on this side. When the spirit was denied existence here in France, it emigrated, as it were, to Germany and there denied the existence of matter . . . But this philosophy, which actually forms the highest peak of spiritualism, was just as little able to maintain itself as the crass materialism of the French. Mr. Schelling was the man who came forward with the doctrine that matter or, as he called it, nature, exists not merely in our spirit but also in reality, that our perception of phenomena is identical with the phenomena themselves. This is Schelling's theory of identity or, as it is also called, nature philosophy.

This happened at the beginning of the century. Mr. Schelling was then a great man. Meanwhile, however, Hegel appeared on the philosophical scene; Mr. Schelling, who in later years wrote almost nothing, was eclipsed, indeed forgotten, and retained only a literary-historical significance. Hegelian philosophy became dominant, Hegel became the sovereign in the realm of intellect, and poor Schelling, a fallen, mediatized philosopher, wandered mournfully about among the other mediatized gentlemen in Munich.[136] I once saw him there and could almost have wept tears at the pitiful sight. And what he said was the most pitiful thing of all; it was an envious railing at Hegel, who had supplanted him. As one shoemaker talks about another whom he accuses of having stolen his leather and made boots of it, so I heard Mr. Schelling, when I once saw him by chance, talk about Hegel, about Hegel, who "had taken his ideas"; and "it is my ideas that he took," and again "my ideas"—this was the poor man's constant refrain. I assure you, if the shoemaker Jakob Böhme once talked like a philosopher, the philosopher Schelling now talks like a shoemaker.

Nothing is more absurd than ownership claimed for ideas. Hegel did, to be sure, use many of Schelling's ideas for his philosophy, but Mr. Schelling would never have known what to do with these ideas anyway. He always just philosophized, but was never able to produce a philosophy. And besides, one could certainly maintain that Mr. Schelling borrowed more from Spinoza than Hegel borrowed from Schelling. If Spinoza is some day liberated from his rigid, antiquated Cartesian, mathematical form and made accessible to a large public, we shall perhaps see that he, more than any other, might complain about the theft of ideas. All our present-day philosophers, possibly without knowing it, look through glasses that Baruch Spinoza ground.[137]

Envy and jealousy have caused the fall of angels, and

136. Schelling lived in Munich from 1808 to 1820, then went to Erlangen, and in 1827 was appointed professor of philosophy at the University of Munich.

137. A reference to the fact that Spinoza earned his living as an optician.

it is unfortunately only too certain that annoyance at Hegel's ever-increasing importance led poor Mr. Schelling to where we find him now, namely in the snares of Catholic propaganda, which has its headquarters in Munich. Mr. Schelling betrayed philosophy to the Catholic religion. All witnesses agree in this, and one could foresee long ago that it was inevitable. From the mouths of several powerful authorities in Munich I had so often heard the words, "Religion and science must be allies." This phrase was as innocent as a flower, and behind it lurked the serpent. Now I know what you wanted. Mr. Schelling must now serve the purpose of justifying the Catholic religion with all his intellectual powers, and everything that he now teaches under the name of philosophy is nothing but a justification of Catholicism. The authorities were also gambling on the additional advantage that the celebrated name would lure to Munich young Germans thirsting for wisdom and that the Jesuit lie in the garb of philosophy would fool them all the more easily. These young men kneel down reverently before the man whom they consider the high priest of truth and unsuspectingly receive from his hands the poisoned Host.

Mr. Joseph Görres, whom I have already mentioned several times and who likewise belongs to the Schelling School, is a kindred spirit. He is known in Germany under the name "the fourth ally." A French journalist had given him this name when, in 1814, under instructions from the Holy Alliance, he preached hatred of France. The man is still living off this compliment to the present day. As a matter of fact, however, no one was able to inflame so violently as he, by means of national memories, the hatred of the Germans toward the French, and the journal that he edited for this purpose, the *Rheinische Merkur*, is full of conjurations which, if it ever came to a war again, might still have some effect. Since then

Mr. Görres has almost been forgotten. The sovereigns did not need him any longer and dismissed him. When he began to snarl at this, they even persecuted him . . . When, thus persecuted, he had nothing more to eat, he threw himself into the arms of the Jesuits, has been serving them until this very moment, and is a mainstay of Catholic propaganda in Munich. I saw him there some years ago in the flower of his humiliation. He was giving lectures on world history to an audience consisting chiefly of Catholic seminary students and had already gotten as far as the fall of Adam and Eve.[138] What a terrible end the enemies of France come to! The fourth ally is now condemned to relate to Catholic seminary students, the *École polytechnique*[139] of obscurantism, year in, year out, the fall of Adam and Eve! In the man's lectures, as in his books, the greatest confusion prevailed, the greatest disorder in concepts and in language, and he has often been compared, not without reason, with the tower of Babel. He actually resembles an enormous tower in which a hundred thousand thoughts labor and confer with each other and call back and forth and quarrel without any one of them understanding the other. Occasionally the tumult in his head seemed to cease for a moment, and he then spoke at length and slowly and boringly,[140] and from his ill-tempered lips the monotonous words fell like doleful raindrops from a lead gutter.

Sometimes when the old demagogic savagery awoke again in him and contrasted repulsively with his monkishly pious and humble words or when he whimpered with Christian loving kindness while leaping back and

138. Görres was then professor of history at the University of Munich. South Germany was largely Catholic, and the University of Munich was of course a "Catholic" university.

139. Polytechnical School.

140. There is no way to convey in English Heine's pun on the word *lang* in the three adverbs *lang, langsam, langweilig.*

forth in blood-thirsty rage, you thought you were seeing a tonsured hyena.

Mr. Görres was born in Koblenz January 25, 1776.

I beg to be excused from giving further details of his life or those of the lives of most of his companions. In my criticism of his friends, the two Schlegels, I have perhaps overstepped the bounds permissible in the discussion of their lives . . .

While on the topic of German philosophers, I cannot refrain from correcting an error concerning German philosophy that I find all too widespread here in France. Ever since several Frenchmen have occupied themselves with Schelling's and Hegel's philosophy, communicated in French the results of their studies, and have also applied these results to conditions in France—since then the friends of clear thought and of liberty complain that the craziest fancies and sophisms are being introduced from Germany with which to confuse the minds and clothe every lie and every act of despotism with the appearance of truth and justice. In a word, these excellent people, concerned for the interests of liberalism, are complaining about the harmful influence of German philosophy in France. But this is unfair to German philosophy. In the first place, what has hitherto been presented to the French under the name of German philosophy, particularly by Mr. Victor Cousin,[141] is not German philosophy. Mr. Cousin has expounded a lot of clever twaddle, but not German philosophy. Secondly, real German philosophy is that which originated directly from Kant's *Critique of Pure Reason* and, preserving the character of its origin, paid little attention to political or religious conditions, but all the more attention to the ultimate grounds of all knowledge.

It is true that the metaphysical systems of most Ger-

141. Victor Cousin (1792–1867), founder of the so-called eclectic school of philosophy, was the first to introduce recent German philosophy to the French.

man philosophers bore very close resemblance to mere cobwebs. But what harm did that do? Jesuitism certainly couldn't use these cobwebs for its nets of lies, and despotism was certainly just as unable to use them for braiding its snares to constrain the minds. Only after Schelling did German philosophy lose this flimsy but harmless character. After him our philosophers no longer analyzed the ultimate grounds of knowledge and of being in general; they no longer hovered among idealistic abstractions; instead they sought reasons for justifying the *status quo;* they became vindicators of what exists. While our earlier philosophers squatted, poor and resigned, in wretched little attic rooms and brooded out their systems, our present-day philosophers wear the dazzling livery of power; they became state philosophers, for they invented philosophical justifications for all the interests of the state in which they were employed. Hegel, for example, professor in Protestant Berlin, took into his system the entire Lutheran Protestant dogmatics, and Mr. Schelling, professor in Catholic Munich, now justifies in his lectures even the most extravagant dogmas of the Apostolic Roman Catholic Church.

Yes, just as once the Alexandrian philosophers[142] summoned all their ingenuity to preserve, through allegorical interpretations, the declining religion of Jupiter from total downfall, so our German philosophers are attempting something similar for the religion of Christ. We care little about examining whether these philosophers have a disinterested aim, but when we see them allied with the party of priests whose material interests are connected with the preservation of Catholicism, we call them Jesuits. They should not think, however, that we are confusing them with the earlier Jesuits. They were great and powerful, full of wisdom and strength of will. Alas for the feeble dwarfs who fancy they would overcome the difficulties

142. I.e., the Neoplatonists.

which were the ruin of even those black giants! Never has the human mind invented grander dialectics than those with which the ancient Jesuits tried to preserve Catholicism. Yet they did not succeed because they were zealous only for the preservation of Catholicism and not for Catholicism itself. They really did not care much about the latter for its own sake; hence at times they profaned the Catholic principle itself in order to bring it to power; they came to an understanding with paganism, with the despots of the world, encouraged their lusts, became murderers and merchants, and when necessary, they even became atheists. But in vain did their father confessors grant the friendliest absolutions and their casuists coquette with every vice and crime. They competed in vain with laymen in art and science in order to use both as tools. Here their weakness became quite obvious. They were jealous of all great scholars and artists, yet could not discover or create anything extraordinary. They wrote pious hymns and built cathedrals, but no spirit of freedom flows through their poems, only the sighs of trembling obedience to the superiors in the Order. Even in their buildings one sees only anxious constraint, stony pliancy, sublimity on command. Barrault[143] once said quite rightly, "The Jesuits could not raise the earth up to Heaven, and they dragged Heaven down to earth." All their activities were fruitless. No life can flower from a lie, and God cannot be saved by the devil.

Mr. Schelling was born January 27, 1775, in Würtemberg.

IV

I have been able to give only a few intimations of Mr. Schelling's relationship to the Romantic School. His in-

143. Émile Barrault (1800–1869), a French journalist and an enthusiastic follower of Saint-Simon.

fluence was primarily of a personal nature. In addition, ever since Schelling made nature philosophy the fashion, nature has been interpreted much more thoughtfully by poets. Some plunged into nature with all their human emotions; others had discovered a few magic formulas for evoking from nature a human quality in appearance and language. The former were the real mystics and resembled in many respects the Indian religious, who become a part of nature and finally begin to feel at one with it. The others were more like magicians, summoning from nature at their own will even the hostile spirits; they resembled the Arabian magicians who can at will bring any stone to life and turn any life to stone. Novalis[144] belonged, *par excellence*, to the former, Hoffmann[145] to the others. Novalis saw everywhere only marvels, lovely marvels. He listened to the plants conversing with each other, he knew the secret of every young rose, in the end he identified himself with all of nature, and when autumn came and the leaves fell, he died. Hoffmann, on the other hand, saw everywhere only ghosts; they nodded at him from every Chinese teapot and every Berlin wig. He was a magician who transformed humans into beasts and the latter even into royal Prussian *Hofräte;* he could summon the dead from their graves, but life itself rejected him as a dreary phantom. This he felt; he felt that he himself had become a ghost; all of nature now was to him a poorly ground mirror, in which, distorted a thousand fold, he saw only his own death mask, and his works are nothing but a terrible cry of anguish in twenty volumes.

Hoffmann does not belong to the Romantic School. He had no contact with the Schlegels, still less with their views. I mentioned him here only as a contrast to Novalis, who is quite strictly a poet of that School. Novalis

144. Pseudonym for Friedrich von Hardenberg (1772–1801).
145. E. T. A. Hoffmann (1776–1822).

is less well-known in France than Hoffmann, who has been introduced to the French public in a most attractive form by Loeve-Veimars[146] and thus has acquired a great reputation in France. Hoffmann is now not at all *en vogue* with us in Germany, though he was at one time. In his day he was much read, but only by people whose nerves were too strong or too weak for them to be affected by soft chords. The really gifted and the poetic natures would have nothing to do with him. They much preferred Novalis. The latter, with his idealized figures, always hovered above, his head in the clouds, whereas Hoffmann, with all his bizarre caricatures, still always clung firmly to earthly reality. Just as the giant Antaeus, however, remained invincibly strong when he was touching Mother Earth with his foot and lost his strength as soon as Hercules lifted him up, a poet, too, is strong and vigorous as long as he does not leave the ground of reality, and becomes feeble the moment he soars about on the wings of fancy and loses himself in the blue.

The great similarity between the two poets probably lies in the fact that their poetry was in reality a disease. It has been said in regard to this that the judgment of their writings is not the business of the critic but of the physician. The rosy light in the works of Novalis is not the color of health but of tuberculosis, and the fiery glow in Hoffmann's *Fantastic Tales* is not the flame of genius but of fever.

But do we have a right to such remarks, we who are not all too blessed with health ourselves? Especially now, when literature looks like a huge hospital? Or is poetry perhaps a disease of mankind, as the pearl is really only the morbid substance from which the poor oyster beast is suffering?

Novalis was born on May 2, 1772. His real name was

146. M. Loève-Veimars, French translator who assisted in preparing the French edition of Heine's works.

Hardenberg. He loved a young lady who suffered from tuberculosis and died of it. This sad story pervades everything he wrote, his life was only a dreamy passing away, and he died of tuberculosis in 1801, before completing his twenty-ninth year and his novel. In its present form this novel is only a fragment of a large allegorical work which, like Dante's *Divine Comedy*, was to celebrate all earthly and heavenly things. Heinrich von Ofterdingen, the famous poet,[147] is the hero. We see him as a youth in Eisenach, the pleasant little town that lies at the foot of the ancient Wartburg, where the greatest but also the most stupid things took place, where Luther translated his Bible and some silly Teutomaniacs burned Mr. Kamptz' *Police-Code*.[148] In this fortress that contest of the Minnesingers was also once held,[149] in which, among other poets, Heinrich von Ofterdingen and Klingsohr von Ungerland[150] sang in the hazardous competition in poetry which the *Manessische Sammlung* has preserved for us.[151] The loser's head was to be forfeit to the executioner, and the landgrave of Thuringia was the arbitrator. The Wartburg, scene of his later fame, towers momentously above the hero's cradle, and the beginning of Novalis' novel shows him, as I have said, in his father's

147. This is also the title of the novel. As far as is known, he was not an historical figure.

148. Karl von Kamptz, a Prussian statesman. On October 18, 1817, the anniversary of the battle of Leipzig (1813), a national convention of the *Burschenschaften* met at the Wartburg, and as a re-enactment of Luther's burning of the papal bull, old printed paper inscribed with the names of despised reactionary authors was thrown into the fire lit to celebrate the victory of Leipzig over Napoleon.

149. It is not certain that such a contest ever took place. The ultimate source is a thirteenth-century poem about the contest, which was preserved in a fourteenth-century manuscript, but this is of course not a reliable source.

150. I.e., Hungary. Klingsor appears as an important character in the medieval epic *Parzival* by Wolfram von Eschenbach.

151. A famous manuscript from the fourteenth century containing a collection of medieval poems, among them the poem about the contest in the Wartburg.

house in Eisenach. "His parents were already in bed and asleep, the wall clock beat its monotonous rhythm, and outside the rattling windows roared the wind; intermittently the room was illuminated by the glimmer of the moon.

"The youth lay tossing on the bed, thinking of the stranger and his tales. 'It is not the treasures that have aroused such an inexpressible yearning in me,' he said to himself. 'Avarice is alien to me, but I long to see the blue flower. It is constantly in my mind, and I can think and write of nothing else. I have never felt this way before. It is as if I had been dreaming before or as if I had passed over in my sleep to another world, for in the world in which I used to live who would have cared about flowers? And I certainly never heard there about such a strange passion for a flower.' "

With these words *Heinrich von Ofterdingen* begins, and all through the novel the blue flower shines and exhales its fragrance. It is curious and significant that even the most mythical characters in this book seem as familiar to us as if in earlier times we had lived quite intimately with them. Old memories awake, even Sophia has such familiar features, and we remember whole avenues of beeches where we walked up and down with her in loving communion. But all this lies in the dim past like a half-forgotten dream.

Novalis' muse was a pale, slender girl with serious blue eyes, golden jacinth hair, smiling lips, and a little red birth-mark on the left side of her chin. For I imagine as muse of Novalis' poetry the very same girl who first made me acquainted with him when I saw in her lovely hands the red morocco volume with gilt edges, which contained *Ofterdingen.* She always wore a blue dress, and her name was Sophia . . . She was as tender as a sensitive plant, and her words were so exquisite, so pure in tone, and when you put them together, they were poetry. I have written down many things she said, and they are strange poems, quite in Novalis' manner, but even more ethereal, dying away to an almost inaudible faintness. I am especially fond of one of these poems which she spoke to me when I took my departure for Italy. In an autumn garden, which had been illuminated for a special occasion, we hear the last lamp, the last rose, and a wild swan conversing together. The morning mists now close in, the last lamp has gone out, the rose is bare of petals, and the swan spreads his white wings and flies southward . . .

When I returned from the south in the late autumn of 1828, my path led me to the neighborhood of Göttingen, and I dismounted at the home of my fat friend, the postmistress, to change horses . . . When I asked Coachman Pieper about the sister of the postmistress, he answered, "Mademoiselle Sophia will soon die and is already an angel." How admirable a person had to be when even sour Pieper said she was an angel! . . . Mademoiselle Sophia was standing upstairs at the window, reading, and when I went up, I found once more in her hands a book bound in red morocco, with gilt-edged leaves, and it was again *Ofterdingen* by Novalis. So she had gone on and on reading this book and had caught tuberculosis from the reading and looked like a transparent shadow. But she was now of a spiritual beauty the sight of which moved me most grievously. I took her two pale, thin hands and looked deep into her blue eyes and finally asked, "Mademoiselle Sophia, how are you?" "I am well," she answered, "and shall soon be even better." And she pointed out the window to the new graveyard, a small hill, not far from the house. On this bare hillside stood a single slender, withered poplar with only a few leaves still hanging on it, and it moved in the autumn wind, not like a living tree, but like the ghost of a tree.

Mademoiselle Sophia now lies beneath this poplar, and the keepsake she bequeathed to me, the book bound in red morocco with gilt-edged leaves, Novalis' *Heinrich von Ofterdingen,* now lies before me on my desk, and I used it in writing this chapter.

BOOK THREE

I

Do you know China, the homeland of winged dragons and porcelain teapots? The whole country is a cabinet of curios surrounded by a tremendous long wall and a hundred thousand Tartar sentinels. But birds and the ideas of European scholars fly over it, and when they have looked around enough there and return home again, they tell us the most delightful things about this strange country and its strange people. There nature, in its glaring colors and ornate forms, fantastic giant flowers, dwarf trees, clipped-off mountains, baroquely voluptuous fruits, crazily adorned birds, is a caricature just as incredible as the men with their pointed queues, polite bows, long nails, their prematurely wise manner, and their childish, monosyllabic language. Man and nature cannot look at each other there without inwardly longing to laugh. They do not laugh aloud, however, because both are much too civilized and polite; and in order to suppress their laughter they make the most seriously droll faces. Neither shading nor perspective exists there. From the houses, which are all colors of the rainbow and are stacked up one above the other, rise a multitude of roofs resembling open umbrellas, their edges hung full of small metal bells, so that even the wind as it passes cannot help making itself ridiculous by a foolish tinkling.

In such a house of bells there once lived a princess whose little feet were even smaller than those of other Chinese women, whose small, slanting eyes blinked even more sweetly and dreamily than those of the other ladies of the Celestial Empire, and in whose small, giggling heart the wildest caprices nested. You see, it was her most supreme delight to rip to pieces costly fabrics of silk and gold brocade. When these rustled and crackled loudly under her lacerating fingers, she rejoiced for joy. But at last, having wasted her entire fortune on this pastime and torn up all her possessions, she was locked up in a round tower, at the advice of all the mandarins, as incurably insane.

This Chinese princess, caprice personified, is also the personified muse of a German poet who must not remain unmentioned in a history of Romantic literature. She is the muse who smiles at us so insanely from the poems of Mr. Clemens Brentano. In them she tears up the smoothest satin trains and the most glittering gold lace, and her destructive amiability and her exuberant madness fill our souls with an uncanny rapture and a voluptuous terror. For fifteen years, however, Mr. Brentano has been living remote from the world, locked up, indeed walled up, in his Catholicism. There was nothing valuable left to tear up. They say he has torn the hearts that loved him, and each of his friends complains of wanton injury. He has exercised his destructiveness most against himself and his poetic talent. I refer in particular to one of his comedies, entitled *Ponce de Leon*.[152] There is nothing that is more dismembered than this work, the ideas as well as the language. But all these tatters are alive and whirl around in confused gaiety. You think you are seeing a masked ball of words and ideas. It is all a bustle of the sweetest disorder, and only the prevailing madness

152. Written about 1801, published in 1804.

produces a certain unity. The craziest puns run like harlequins through the whole piece, striking out in all directions with their smooth wooden swords. Sometimes a serious expression appears, but it stutters like the Doctor of Bologna.[153] Here a phrase saunters along like a white Pierrot with too broad, trailing sleeves and all too large vest buttons. There humpbacked jokes with short little legs leap like Pulcinella.[154] Words of love flutter about like teasing Columbines, sorrow in their hearts. And everything dances and hops and whirls and rattles, and above it all sound the trumpets of the Bacchanalian mania for destruction.

A long tragedy by the same poet, *The Founding of Prague*,[155] is also very remarkable. In it are scenes in which the most mysterious terrors of ancient sagas seize you. The gloomy forests of Bohemia rustle there; the angry Slavic gods are still alive; pagan nightingales still warble; but the soft rosy dawn of Christianity is already lighting up the treetops. Mr. Brentano has also written some good stories, especially *The Story of the Just Caspar and Fair Annie*.[156] When fair Annie was still a child and went with her grandmother to the executioner's to buy some healing medicines, as the common people in Germany used to do, all of a sudden something moved in the large cabinet in front of which fair Annie was standing, and the child cried out in fright, "A mouse! A mouse!" But the executioner was even more frightened and became as solemn as death and said to the grandmother, "My dear woman, in this cabinet hangs my executioner's sword, and it moves of its own accord whenever anyone

153. The learned *dottore* of Bologna, a pedant, and other characters mentioned here, were stock figures in the Italian *commedia dell' arte*. It was Tartaglia who was the stutterer.

154. One of the servants or men of the lower classes, who were responsible for much of the comic action.

155. Published in 1815.

156. Published in 1817.

comes near it who shall some day be beheaded with it. My sword is thirsting for this child's blood. Allow me just to graze the child's neck with it. The sword will then be satisfied with a drop of blood and will feel no further longing." But the grandmother paid no attention to this sensible counsel and later regretted it bitterly when fair Annie was actually beheaded with the same sword.

Mr. Clemens Brentano is now about fifty years old and lives in Frankfurt, in hermit-like seclusion, as a corresponding member of the organization for Catholic propaganda. His name has been almost forgotten in recent years, and only when there is discussion of the folksongs that he edited with his late friend Achim von Arnim, is his name occasionally mentioned. In collaboration with Arnim he published under the title *The Boy's Magic Horn*[157] a collection of poems, part of which they found still current among the common people, part in broadsheets and rare publications. I cannot praise this book enough. It contains the fairest flowers of the German spirit, and whoever wishes to know the lovable side of the German people should read these folksongs. The book is lying before me at this very moment, and I feel as if I were smelling the fragrance of German linden trees. For the linden plays a leading role in these songs; in its shade lovers talk in the evenings; it is their favorite tree, perhaps because the linden leaf has the shape of a human heart. This comment was once made by a German poet who is my favorite, namely myself. On the title page of that book is a boy blowing his horn, and if a German in a foreign land looks long at this picture, he fancies he hears the most familiar tones, and homesickness might steal upon him as on that Swiss mercenary who was standing guard on the bastions of Strassburg,

157. Three volumes published 1806–1808.

heard the call of the Alpine cowherds in the distance, threw away his pike, and swam the Rhine, but was soon caught again and shot as a deserter. *The Boy's Magic Horn* contains this touching song about the incident:

> In Strassburg, at the fort,
> my trouble was to start.
> I heard the alphorn calling from beyond,
> I had to swim back to my fatherland.
> But fate was hard.
>
> They caught me the same night,
> put to an end my flight.
> They dragged me from the river to the shore
> and rushed me to the captain's door.
> I am done for.
>
> Tomorrow morn at ten
> I'll face the captain's men.
> For pardon I'm to plead,
> but it will mean defeat,
> I know indeed.
>
> My friends and company,
> you've seen the last of me.
> O shepherd boy, what did you do?
> The alphorn lured me, that you blew.
> I'm blaming you.

What a beautiful poem! There is a curious magic about these folksongs. Literary poets try to imitate these products of nature in the same way that artificial water is manufactured. But even though they discover the constituents by means of a chemical process, the main thing still escapes them, the indivisible, mysterious force of nature. In these songs you feel the heartbeat of the German people. Here all its gloomy mirth, all its mad sanity are revealed. Here German anger drums, German mockery whistles, German love kisses. Here real German wine and real German tears sparkle, and the tears are sometimes even more precious than the wine; they contain much iron and salt. What naivete in loyalty! In disloyalty, what honorableness! What an honorable fellow the poor tramp is, even though he is a highwayman! Just listen to the stoical, moving story he tells about himself:

> I came upon a village inn,
> they asked me, "What's your line?"
> "I am a ragged vagabond,
> I like good food and wine."
>
> They led me to the common room,
> the drinks began to pass;
> I looked around the company
> and soon put down my glass.
>
> They sat me at the table head,
> gave me a merchant's chair,
> but when I had to pay the bill
> my money bag was bare.
>
> At night I asked where I could sleep,
> they showed me to a shed.
> Not even for a vagabond
> was this a rosy bed.
>
> And when I lay down in the barn,
> I tried to build my nest;
> the hawthorns and the thistles stung
> and did not let me rest.
>
> And when next morning I got up,
> the roof was full of frost.
> I laughed—but for the vagabond
> good luck, I felt, was lost.

So I picked up my trusty sword
and slung it on my side—
poor me, I had to go on foot,
I had no horse to ride.

And so I left and hit the road
for better or for worse;
I met a wealthy merchant's son
and took away his purse.

This poor tramp is the most German character I know.
What composure, what conscious power prevails in this
poem! But you shall also meet our Gretel. She is an hon-
est girl, and I love her very much. Hans said to Gretel:

"Dress up, dress up, my Gretel,
come with me and be mine,
the grain is safely gathered,
the grapes are off the vine."

She answered happily:

"Ah, Hansel, my dear Hansel,
with you I'll run away;
we'll work the fields on weekdays,
drink wine each holiday."

Now by the hands he took her,
and snow-white was her skin,
then down the road he led her,
until he found an inn.

"O hostess, friendly hostess,
bring wine to drink our fill;
we'll use this dress of Gretel's
to settle up the bill."

Now Gretel started weeping,
Oh, how her anger showed!
And how her tears were shining
as down her cheeks they flowed!

"Ah, Hansel, my dear Hansel,
that's not the way you talked
when you came to my father's
and out the door we walked."

Now by her hands he took her,
and snow-white was her skin,
and when he found a garden
he led his Gretel in.

"Ah, Gretel, my dear Gretel,
don't cry in such distress.
Do you regret your honor?
Repent your wantonness?"

"I care not that I'm wanton,
nor that I'm honorless;
I only fear I'll never
get back my pretty dress."

She is not Goethe's Gretchen, and her remorse would
not be a subject for Scheffer.[158] There is no German
moonlight here. There is just as little sentimentality
when a young coxcomb demands that his girl let him into
her room at night and she refuses with the words:

"Ride on to where you came from,
ride on to yonder heath
whence you have come to me.
There you will find a good-sized rock;
if you will use it as a bed,
there won't be feathers on your head."

But moonlight, moonlight in abundance, flooding the
whole soul, gleams in the lyric:

158. Ary Scheffer, Dutch painter in France who painted scenes from the
works of Goethe, Schiller, and Byron. See Heine's description of his
"Gretchen," p. 103 f. above.

Were I a little bird,
I'd spread my wings and would
fly to you, dear.
But since this cannot be
I must stay here.

Though I am far from you,
I'm in my dreams with you,
talking with you.
But when I wake at dawn,
there is but me.

At night I lie awake,
wait for the day to break,
thinking that you,
darling, a thousand times
vowed your love true.

If, charmed, we now inquire about the composers of these songs, they seem to give the answer themselves in their final words:

Whence came that beautiful song?
Three geese have brought it along,
'cross the river—two gray and one white.

Usually the writers of such songs were wanderers, vagabonds, soldiers, itinerant scholars, or traveling apprentices, particularly these last. Very often on my walking tours I joined company with these people and noticed how, at times, inspired by some unusual event, they would improvise a snatch of a folksong or whistle it into the open air. The birds sitting on the tree branches heard this, and when another had later come strolling past with knapsack and walking stick, they would whistle that little snatch of song in his ear, and he would add the missing lines, and the song was finished. The words come from out of the blue to the lips of such a lad, and he needs only to utter them, and they are then even more poetic than all the fine poetical phrases that we concoct from the depths of our hearts. The character of these traveling apprentices lives and moves in such folksongs. They are a strange sort. Without a penny in their pockets, they travel through all of Germany, harmless, happy, and free. I usually found that three set out together on such a journey. Of these three one was always the faultfinder. He found fault with everything that came along, with every gay-colored bird flying in the air, with every fine horseman that rode by, and if they came to a poor quarter with miserable huts and beggars in rags, he was likely to remark ironically, "The good Lord created the world in six days, but just look, the result shows it." The second companion interrupted only occasionally with angry comments; he couldn't say anything without cursing; he grumbled furiously about all the masters for whom he had worked; and his continual refrain was how much he regretted not having given his landlady in Halberstadt, who had served him cabbage and turnips every day, a sound thrashing to remember him by. At the word "Halberstadt" the third lad sighed from the depths of his heart. He was the youngest, was setting out into the world for the first time, still thought constantly of his sweetheart's dark brown eyes, always hung his head, and never said a word.

The Boy's Magic Horn is a much too remarkable monument of our literature and had a much too significant influence on the lyricists of the Romantic School, particularly on our excellent Mr. Uhland, for me to leave it undiscussed. This work and the *Nibelungenlied* played an important role during this period. I must also give the latter special mention here. For a long time nothing was talked about in Germany but the *Nibelungenlied,* and classical scholars were not a little annoyed when this epic was compared to the *Iliad* or when people argued about

which of the two poems was the better. And the public
looked on like a boy who is asked in all seriousness,
"Which do you like better, a horse or gingerbread?" At
any rate, the *Nibelungenlied* is possessed of great and
mighty vigor. A Frenchman can scarcely get any idea of
it. And certainly not of the language in which it is written.
It is a language of stone, and the stanzas are like rhymed
blocks of stone. Here and there, out of the crevices, red
flowers well up like drops of blood, or long sprays of ivy
trail down like green tears. Of the gigantic passions stir-
ring in this poem, well-behaved little people like you can
get even less of an idea. Imagine a bright summer night,
the stars, pale as silver but as large as suns, standing out
in the blue sky; and imagine that all the Gothic cathedrals
of Europe had arranged a rendezvous on an enormous,
broad plain, and that then the Strassburg minster, the
Cologne cathedral, the bell tower of Florence, the cathe-
dral of Rouen, etc., strode calmly up and paid court very
politely to lovely Notre Dame of Paris. To be sure, their
gait is a trifle ungainly, some of them behave very awk-
wardly, and one might laugh sometimes at their in-
fatuated waddle. But this laughter would end as soon as
you saw them fly into a rage and strangle each other and
saw Notre Dame of Paris lift both stony arms despair-
ingly toward Heaven and suddenly seize a sword and cut
off the head from the rump of the greatest of all cathe-
drals. But no, even then you cannot get any idea of the
main characters of the *Nibelungenlied;* no tower is as tall
and no stone as hard as grim Hagen and vengeful Kriem-
hilde.

Who composed this poem? We do not know the name
of the poet who wrote the *Nibelungenlied* any more than we
know the composers of the folksongs. One rarely knows
the originator of the best books, poems, buildings, and
other monuments of art. What was the name of the ar-
chitect who planned the Cologne cathedral? Who

painted the altarpieces there, in which the lovely Blessed
Virgin and the three wise men are so delightfully por-
trayed? Who wrote the book of Job, which has comforted
so many generations of suffering humanity? People for-
get only too easily the names of their benefactors. The
names of the good and noble men who spent themselves
for the welfare of their fellow citizens are seldom heard
in the mouths of the peoples, and their dull memory
preserves only the names of their oppressors and their
brutal military heroes. Mankind is a tree that forgets the
quiet gardener who cared for it in the cold season, wa-
tered it during the drought, and protected it from harm-
ful animals, but it faithfully preserves the names merci-
lessly carved in its bark with sharp steel and passes them
on in ever increasing size to the latest generations.

II

Due to their joint edition of *The Magic Horn* the names
of Brentano and Arnim are usually coupled together,
and having discussed the former, I must not overlook the
other, all the less so as he merits our attention far more.
Ludwig Achim von Arnim is a great poet and had one of
the most original minds in the Romantic School. Lovers
of the fantastic would enjoy him more than any other
German writer. In the realm of fantasy he surpasses
Hoffmann as well as Novalis. He succeeded in penetrat-
ing more intimately into nature than the latter and could
conjure up far more uncanny specters than Hoffmann. In
fact, sometimes when I watched Hoffmann himself, it
seemed to me as if Arnim had invented him. Arnim has
remained completely unknown to the general public; he
has a name only among men of letters. These, however,
while paying him the most unqualified recognition, have
never praised him publicly as he deserves. Indeed, some

writers used to speak of him disdainfully, and they were
the very ones who imitated his style. One might apply to
them Steevens'[159] jibe at Voltaire for belittling Shakes-
peare after having made use of *Othello* for his *Orosman:*
"These people are like the thieves who set fire to the
house after robbing it." Why has Mr. Tieck never spoken
suitably about Arnim, he who could pay so many brilliant
compliments to so many an insignificant piece of trash?
The Schlegel brothers also ignored Arnim. Only after his
death did he receive a kind of obituary recognition from
a member of the School.[160]

In my opinion, it was especially impossible for Arnim's
reputation to spread because he always remained too
much of a Protestant for his friends, the Catholic party,
and also because the Protestant party thought he was a
clandestine Catholic. But why did the public reject him,
the public to whom his novels and *novelle* were available
in any lending library? Hoffmann, too, was hardly dis-
cussed at all in our literary gazettes and esthetic journals,
higher criticism observed a genteel silence about him,
and yet he was read everywhere. Why, then, did the
German public neglect an author whose imagination was
of universal scope, whose nature was of the most awe-
some profundity, and whose powers of description were
so unsurpassable? One thing this poet lacked, and it is
precisely the one thing that the public looks for in books
—life. The public demands that a writer sympathize with
their everyday passions, that he excite their emotions,
either pleasantly or painfully; the public wants to be
moved. This need Arnim could not satisfy. He was not
a poet of life, but of death. In everything he wrote the

159. George Steevens, an English scholar who collaborated with Samuel
Johnson in preparing an edition of Shakespeare's plays.

160. Written in 1831 for a Berlin journal by Georg Wilhelm Häring, who
wrote historical novels in the manner of Scott under the pseudonym Willibald
Alexis.

prevailing agitation is not real; the characters bustle about in a hurry, moving their lips as if in speech, but you only see their words, you don't hear them. These figures leap, wrestle, stand on their heads, approach us secretly, and whisper softly in our ears, "We are dead." Such a spectacle would be all too uncanny and annoying were it not for Arnim's charm, which pervades each of these works like the smile of a child, but a dead child. Arnim can describe love, sometimes sensuality as well, but even then we cannot feel with him. We see beautiful bodies, heaving bosoms, delicately formed hips, but a cold, moist shroud veils all of it. Sometimes Arnim is witty, and we even have to laugh, but still it seems as if Death were tickling us with his scythe. Usually, however, he is serious, as serious as a dead German. A living German is already a sufficiently serious creature, but a *dead* German! A Frenchman has absolutely no idea how very serious we Germans are when dead; our faces then become much longer still, and the worms that dine off us become melancholy if they look at us while eating. The French think how very dreadfully serious Hoffmann can be, but this is child's play compared with Arnim. When Hoffmann conjures up his dead and they climb out of their graves and dance around them, he himself trembles for terror and dances in their midst, making the wildest, monkey-like grimaces. But when Arnim conjures up his dead, it is as if a general were reviewing his troops, and he sits so calmly on his tall ghost of a white horse and commands the horrible troops to file past him, and they look up at him fearfully and seem to be afraid of him. He, however, nods to them affably.

Ludwig Achim von Arnim was born in Brandenburg in 1784 and died in the winter of 1830.[161] He wrote plays in verse, novels, and *novelle.* His plays are full of intrinsic

161. Heine is in error here. Arnim was born in 1781 in Berlin and died in January, 1831.

poetry, especially one of them, entitled *The Mountain-Cock.*[162] The first scene would not be unworthy even of the very greatest poet. How realistically, how faithfully the most dismal boredom is pictured there! One of the three illegitimate sons of the deceased landgrave is sitting alone in the vast, deserted castle-hall, yawning as he talks to himself and complains that his legs are growing longer and longer beneath the table and that the moaning wind is whistling so icily through his teeth. His brother, good Franz, now comes shuffling in slowly, in the clothes of his late father, which are much too big for him, and he recalls sorrowfully that at this hour he was usually helping his father dress, that the latter often threw him a crust of bread which he, with his old teeth, could no longer chew, and that he also sometimes kicked him angrily. This last memory moves good Franz to tears, and he laments that his father is now dead and can no longer kick him.

The titles of Arnim's novels are *The Guardians of the Crown* and *Countess Dolores.*[163] The former also has an excellent beginning. The scene is laid in the upper part of the watch tower in Waiblingen, in a cozy little parlor of the warder and his good, fat wife, who is not, however, so fat as they say down below in the town. As a matter of fact, it is slander when they said she had become so corpulent in the tower rooms that she could no longer descend the narrow tower stairs, and after the death of her first husband, the old warder, had been obliged to marry the new warder. The poor woman up there fretted not a little at such malicious rumors; and the only reason she couldn't go down the tower stairs was that she got dizzy.

Arnim's second novel, *Countess Dolores,* also has a mag-

162. First published in 1813.

163. The first was published in 1817; the second had appeared earlier, in 1810. The full title of the latter is *Countess Dolores' Poverty, Wealth, Guilt, and Repentance.*

nificent beginning. The author describes the poetry of poverty, an aristocratic poverty at that, which he, at that time himself living in straitened circumstances, very often chose as his theme. What a master Arnim is here also in the portrayal of ruin! I still feel as though I see young Countess Dolores' desolate castle, looking all the more desolate because the old Count began the building in a gay, Italian style, but did not finish it. Now it is a modern ruin, and in the castle garden everything is dilapidated. The paths of clipped yews have gone shrubby and wild; the trees are growing together; the laurels and oleanders are creeping dismally along the ground; the beautiful tall flowers are smothered by nasty weeds; the statues of the gods have fallen from their pedestals; and a few mischievous beggar boys are crouching beside a poor Venus lying in the tall grass and are lashing her marble bottom with nettles. When the old Count returns to his castle after a long absence, the strange behavior of his household, especially of his wife, astonishes him very much. All sorts of things happen at meals, and this is probably because the poor woman had died of grief, and the other members of the household were also long since dead. Finally the Count himself seems to suspect that he is living among nothing but ghosts and, without showing that he is aware of this, departs again secretly.

Of Arnim's *novelle* his *Isabella of Egypt*[164] seems to me the best. Here we see the nomadic life of the gypsies, called in France *Bohémiens*, also *Egyptiens*. This strange fairy-tale people, with their brown faces, friendly sooth-sayer eyes, and melancholy mysteriousness, comes to life here. The chaotic, deceptive gaiety conceals a great mystic sorrow. For according to the legend, told very charm-ingly in this *novella*, the gypsies must wander for a time

164. Published in 1811.

all over the world as penance for that inhospitable harsh-
ness with which their forefathers once turned away the
Blessed Virgin with her child when she requested lodg-
ing for the night during her flight in Egypt. Thus people
felt justified in treating them cruelly. Since they did not
yet have any philosophers of the Schelling type in the
Middle Ages, literature had to undertake the extenuation
of the most shameful and brutal laws. Against no one
were these laws more barbaric than against the poor
gypsies. In many countries it was permissible to hang any
gypsy on suspicion of theft without investigation or judi-
cial sentence. Thus their chief, Michael, called Duke of
Egypt, though innocent, was hanged. Arnim's *novella* be-
gins with this sad event. In the night the gypsies took
down their dead Duke from the gallows, placed his royal
cloak of red around his shoulders, set the silver crown
upon his head, and lowered him into the Scheldt, firmly
convinced that the compassionate stream would carry
him home to his beloved Egypt. The poor gypsy princess
Isabella, his daughter, knew nothing of this sad incident.
She lived alone in a dilapidated house on the Scheldt and
heard in the night a strange murmuring in the water and
suddenly saw her pale father emerge in his crimson
death-robes, and the moon cast its sorrowful light upon
the silver crown. The heart of the beautiful child almost
broke from unutterable grief; in vain she tried to hold
fast to her dead father; he floated on toward Egypt, his
native wonderland, where people were awaiting his ar-
rival in order to bury him worthily in one of the great
pyramids. The funeral feast with which the poor child
honored her dead father is touching. She spread her
white veil over a fieldstone, and on this she set food and
drink, which she solemnly consumed. Everything the ex-
cellent Arnim tells us about the gypsies is profoundly
moving. He had already proffered his sympathy to them
in other places, for instance in his epilogue to the *Magic*

Horn, where he maintains that we owe the gypsies so many good and beneficial things, in particular most of our medicines, and says we ungratefully rejected and persecuted them. Despite all their love, he laments, they had not been able to secure a home among us. He compares them in this respect with the little dwarfs of whom legend relates that they procured everything their great and powerful enemies desired for banquets but one time were pitifully beaten and chased out of the country for having picked themselves a few peas from the field out of dire need. It was a distressing sight to see the poor little creatures pattering away over the bridge at night like a herd of sheep, and each one having to put down a small coin until they had filled a barrel with them.

A translation of the *novella* just mentioned, *Isabella of Egypt,* would give the French not merely an idea of Arnim's writings, but would also show that all the terrible, uncanny, gruesome, and ghostly stories that they have toiled so painfully to create in recent years seem to be only the rosy morning dreams of an opera danseuse in comparison with Arnim's works. In the whole lot of French thrillers not as much uncanniness has been concentrated as in that coach which Arnim causes to travel from Brake to Brussels[165] and in which the following four persons are seated:

1) An old gypsy woman who is also a witch. She looks like the fairest of the seven deadly sins, lavishly clothed in the most variegated finery of gold tinsel and silk.

2) A dead sluggard who, in order to earn a few ducats, has risen from his grave and contracted to serve as servant for seven years. He is a fat corpse, wears an overcoat of white bearskin, . . . and yet is always cold.

3) A golem, that is, a figure of clay which is shaped like a beautiful woman and behaves like a beautiful woman.

165. Heine's error. The party drove from Buik to Ghent.

On its forehead, concealed under black curls, is written in Hebrew letters the word "truth," and if the word is erased, the whole figure collapses again lifeless, as the mere clay that it is.

4) Fieldmarshal Cornelius Nepos, who is absolutely not related to the famous historian of this name, who indeed cannot even boast of a middle-class origin, being by birth really a root, a mandrake root, which the French call "mandragora." This root grows under the gallows, on the spot where the very ambiguous tears of a hanged man have flowed. It gave a horrible shriek when beautiful Isabella pulled it out of the ground there at midnight. It looked like a dwarf, except that it had no eyes, mouth, nor ears. The sweet girl planted two black juniper berries and a red rose-hip in its face, from which eyes and mouth developed. After this she strewed a little millet on its head, which grew up as hair, though somewhat shaggy. She rocked the monster in her white arms when it cried like a child; with her sweet rosy lips she kissed its rose-hip-mouth so often that it became all crooked; for sheer love she almost kissed its juniper-eyes out of its head; and the nasty manikin became so spoiled that he finally wanted to become a fieldmarshal and put on a brilliant fieldmarshal's uniform and insisted on being addressed by that title.

These are four very distinguished persons, aren't they? If you strip the morgue, the Court of Miracles,[166] and all the pest-houses of the Middle Ages, you will still not assemble such a good company as that which rode in a single coach from Brake to Brussels. You French should finally realize that the uncanny is not your forte and that France is not a suitable soil for ghosts of this sort. When you conjure up ghosts, we have to laugh. Yes,

166. The *cour des miracles* was the sanctuary for Parisian beggars and swindlers, where the blind and the lame could be cured.

we Germans, who can remain perfectly serious at your gayest jokes, we laugh all the more heartily at your ghost stories. For your ghosts are still always Frenchmen. And French ghosts—what a contradiction in terms! In the word "ghost" there is so much that is lonely, morose, German, taciturn; and in the word "French," on the other hand, there is so much that is sociable, polite, French, loquacious! How could a Frenchman be a ghost, or how could ghosts even exist in Paris! In Paris, the foyer of European society! Between twelve and one, the hour that has been allotted to ghosts from time immemorial, the full stream of life is still roaring through the streets of Paris, in the opera the thundering finale is just sounding, out of the Variétés and the Théâtre-Gymnase[167] come streaming the gayest groups, and the boulevards are thronging with rollicking, laughing, bantering crowds, and everybody goes to the soirées. How unhappy a poor walking ghost would feel amidst this animated multitude! And how could a Frenchman, even when he is dead, preserve the necessary gravity for ghost-walking when the gaiety of the people at their varied pleasures surrounds him on all sides with joyous sound! I myself, though a German, if I were dead and should go ghost-walking at night here in Paris—I could certainly not maintain my ghostly dignity if, let us say, one of those goddesses of frivolity who know how to laugh so delightfully to your face came running to meet me at a street corner. If there were really ghosts in Paris, I am convinced, sociable as the French are, that they would seek each other's friendship, even as ghosts, they would soon form ghost clubs, found a café for the dead, publish a newspaper for the dead, a Paris *Revue for the Dead,* and there would soon be soirées for the dead *ou l'on fera de la musique.*[168] I am convinced that ghosts would

167. Theaters for variety shows, comedy, farce, etc.
168. Where music would be played.

have far more fun here in Paris than the living do in Germany. As for me, if I knew that one could exist this way in Paris as a ghost, I would no longer fear death. I would just make arrangements to be buried in Père Lachaise[169] so that I could go ghost-walking in Paris between twelve and one. What an exquisite hour! You German fellow countrymen, if after my death you come to Paris and catch sight of me here at night as a ghost, don't be alarmed. I will not be spooking in the dreadfully unhappy German manner; I will be spooking for pleasure. . . .

III

The history of literature is as difficult to describe as natural history. In both cases the author must confine himself to the most salient phenomena. But as a small glass of water contains a whole world of curious little creatures which testify just as much to the omnipotence of God as the largest beasts, so the smallest literary journal[170] sometimes contains a great number of poetasters who seem to the tranquil scholar just as interesting as the largest elephants of literature. God is great!

Modern literary historians actually give us a literary history like a well-arranged menagery and show us, always in separate cages, epic mammal poets, lyric aerial poets, dramatic aquatic poets, prose amphibians who write both land and sea novels, humorous mollusks, etc. Others, in contrast, write literary history pragmatically, beginning with the primitive human emotions, following them as they developed in the various epochs and finally assumed artistic form; they begin *ab ovo* like the historian

169. A cemetery in Paris.
170. Literally "Almanac of the Muses," then a favorite title for many journals.

who begins the Trojan War with the story of Leda's egg.[171] And like him, they act foolishly. For I am convinced that if Leda's egg had been used for an omelet, Hector and Achilles would still have met in knightly combat before the Skaian Gate. Great events and great books do not originate from trifles but are inevitable; they are connected with the orbits of the sun, moon, and stars and perhaps originate from their effect on the earth. Events are only the results of ideas.—But how does it happen that at certain times certain ideas make themselves felt so powerfully that they transform in the most miraculous fashion the whole life of man, his desires and aspirations, his thoughts and writings? It is perhaps time to write a literary astrology, explaining from the constellation of the stars the appearance of certain ideas or of certain books in which these ideas are revealed.

Or does the rise of certain ideas merely correspond to certain momentary human needs? Do human beings always look for the ideas with which to justify their wishes of the moment? As a matter of fact, at bottom all men are doctrinaires; they can always find a doctrine to justify all their renunciations or desires. In bad, lean times, when enjoyment has become almost unattainable, they embrace the dogma of abstinence and maintain that earthly grapes are sour. When, however, the times become more affluent and people can reach up for the beautiful fruits of this world, a cheerful doctrine appears, which vindicates all the sweets of life and its full, inalienable right to pleasure.

Are we nearing the end of the Christian Lenten age, and is the rosy age of joy already dawning brightly? How will this cheerful doctrine shape the future?

In the hearts of a nation's writers there already lies the image of its future, and a critic who dissected a modern

171. Zeus came in the form of a swan as lover to Leda. Helen of Troy was their daughter.

poet with a knife sharp enough could very easily prophesy, as from the entrails of a sacrificial animal, how Germany will turn out in the future. With this intention in mind I would be very glad, as a literary Calchas, to slaughter with criticism some of our most recent poets if I were not afraid of seeing in their entrails many things I cannot talk about here. For you cannot discuss our most recent German literature without getting into the depths of politics. In France, where belletristic writers try to withdraw from contemporary political movements, even more than is commendable, you can now pass judgment on the literary figures of the day and leave the day itself undiscussed. On the other side of the Rhine, however, belletristic writers are now plunging ardently into current movements, from which they have held themselves remote for so long. For fifty years you Frenchmen have constantly been active, and now you are tired. But we Germans have been sitting at our desks until now, annotating the classics, and would like to get some exercise.

The same reason I indicated above prevents me from discussing with proper appreciation a writer to whom Madame de Staël made only casual reference and of whom, since then, the French public has been made particularly aware through Philaret Chasles'[172] brilliant articles. I am speaking of Jean Paul Friedrich Richter. He has been called unique. An excellent judgment which I only now comprehend fully after having pondered in vain over the proper place to discuss him in a history of literature. He appeared on the scene about the same time as the Romantic School, without participating in it to the slightest degree, and neither did he later have the slightest connection with the Goethean school of art. He stands quite isolated in his age just because, in contrast

172. Philarète Chasles (1798–1873), a French writer. The essay on Jean Paul can be found in his *Études sur l'Allemagne ancienne et moderne.*

to both schools, he devoted himself entirely to his own age, and his heart was completely filled with it. His heart and his writings were one and the same. This characteristic, this wholeness, we also find in the writers of present-day Young Germany, who likewise wish to make no distinction between life and writing, who never separate politics from science, art, and religion, and who are simultaneously artists, tribunes, and apostles.

Yes, I repeat the word "apostles," for I know no more expressive word. A new belief animates them with a passion of which writers of the preceding period had no conception. This is the belief in progress, a belief that originated from science. We have surveyed the lands, weighed the forces of nature, calculated the resources of industry, and behold, we have discovered that this earth is large enough; that it offers sufficient space for everyone to build on it the shelter for his happiness; that this earth can nourish all of us properly if we all work and no one tries to live at another's expense; and that it is not necessary for us to refer the larger and poorer class to Heaven.—To be sure, the number of enlightened persons and believers is still small. But the time has come when the peoples will no longer be counted by heads but by their hearts. And is not the great heart of a single Heinrich Laube[173] worth more than a whole zoo of Raupachs[174] and actors?

I have mentioned the name Heinrich Laube, for how could I speak about Young Germany without mentioning the great, flaming heart that shines forth most brightly from this group. Heinrich Laube, one of the writers who have come to the fore since the July Revolution, has for Germany a social significance, the complete importance of which cannot yet be measured. He has all the good

173. A German journalist, author of novels, *novelle*, and plays, director of the Vienna Burgtheater from 1849 to 1867.

174. Ernst Raupach (1784–1852), German playwright who with his 117 plays rivaled Kotzebue in popularity.

qualities we find in authors of the preceding period, combined with the apostolic zeal of Young Germany. And his intense ardor is softened and transformed by a fine feeling for art. He is just as enthusiastic about beauty as about goodness, he has a sensitive ear and a sharp eye for consummate form, and vulgar natures repel him even when they are useful to the fatherland as champions of noble views. This artistic sense, inherent in him, protected him from the great error of the political rabble which still continues to slander and revile our great master, Goethe.

In this respect another writer of recent times, Mr. Karl Gutzkow,[175] also deserves the highest praise. If I mention him only after Laube, it is not in the least because I do not give him credit for just as much talent and still less because of not being pleased with his tendencies. No, in my opinion Karl Gutzkow is also gifted in the highest degree with creative power and a discriminating artistic sense, and his works delight me by their accurate interpretation of our time and its needs. But everything Laube writes is dominated by an all-pervading serenity, a confident grandeur, and a quiet assurance which appeal to me personally more deeply than the picturesque, colorful, stingingly spicy vivacity of Gutzkow's mind.

Like Laube, Mr. Karl Gutzkow, a man of true poetic spirit, had to detach himself in no uncertain terms from those zealots who revile our great master. This is also true of L. Wienbarg[176] and Gustav Schlesier,[177] two very distinguished writers of the recent period whom I must

175. German journalist, playwright, and novelist (1811–1878). Soon after the revolution of 1830 he became a leader of progressive thought in Germany.

176. Ludolf Wienbarg (1802–1872) had presented in his *Esthetic Campaigns* some of the main ideas of these politically and socially minded writers and used here for the first time the term "Young Germany," which soon came into general use.

177. From 1832 to 1834 he worked under Laube in editing the *Zeitung für die elegante Welt*, later published a work on Wilhelm von Humboldt, but is now completely forgotten.

not leave unmentioned here in discussing Young Germany. They certainly deserve to be named among its choir leaders, and their names have won a good repute in Germany. This is not the place to enlarge on their abilities and activities. I have wandered too far from my topic; I shall just say a few more words about Jean Paul.

I have said that Jean Paul Friedrich Richter, in his main tenor, was a predecessor of Young Germany. These writers, however, directed toward the practical, were able to keep away from the abstruse confusion, the baroque manner of description, and the unbearable style of Jean Paul's writings. A clear, logical French mind can never have any idea of this style. Jean Paul's sentence structure consists of nothing but tiny rooms, often so narrow that if one idea meets another there, they bump heads; up above, on the ceilings, are nothing but hooks on which Jean Paul hangs all sorts of thoughts, and in the walls are nothing but secret drawers where he hides emotions. No German author is so rich as he in thoughts and feelings, but he never lets them ripen, and he furnishes us more amazement than pleasure with the riches of his mind and his heart. Thoughts and feelings that would develop into enormous trees if he let them take root properly and spread out with all their branches, blossoms, and leaves —he pulls them out when they have scarcely become small plants or are often even just shoots, and in this fashion whole intellectual forests are placed before us in an ordinary dish as vegetables. Now this is strange, unpalatable fare, for not every stomach can digest young oaks, cedars, palm trees, and banyans in such quantities. Jean Paul is a great poet and philosopher, but a more inartistic writer and thinker is hardly conceivable. He gave birth to genuinely poetic figures in his novels, but all these creatures drag an absurdly long umbilical cord around with them and entangle and choke themselves with it. Instead of thoughts he gives us his own process of thinking itself; we see the corporeal activity of his brain; he gives us, so to speak, more brain than thought. And at the same time his jokes are hopping in all directions, the fleas of his impassioned mind. He is the merriest and also the most sentimental of writers. Yes, sentimentality always gets the upper hand, and his laughter suddenly changes to weeping. He often disguises himself as a gross, shabby fellow, but then suddenly, like princes incognito that we see in the theater, he unbuttons his coarse overcoat, and we see the shining star.

In this, Jean Paul is just like the great Irishman with whom he is often compared. The author of *Tristram Shandy*, after losing himself in the crudest trivialities, can also remind us suddenly, by sublime transitions, of his princely dignity, of his equality in rank with Shakespeare. Like Laurence Sterne, Jean Paul, too, exposed his personality in his works and revealed himself in the most human nakedness, but yet with a certain awkward shyness, especially in sexual matters. Laurence Sterne shows himself to the public completely undressed, completely naked; Jean Paul, however, only has holes in his trousers. Some critics wrongly believe that Jean Paul possessed more genuine feeling than Sterne because Sterne, as soon as the subject he is treating reaches a tragic climax, suddenly vaults to the most jesting, laughing tone, whereas Jean Paul, when a joke becomes the least bit serious, gradually begins to blubber and calmly lets his tearglands drip until they're empty. No, Sterne perhaps felt even more deeply than Jean Paul, for he is a greater poet. As I have said before, he is William Shakespeare's equal, and the Muses reared him too, Laurence Sterne, on Parnassus. But in feminine fashion they spoiled him early, especially by their caresses. He was the pet of the pale goddess of tragedy. Once, in a fit of cruel affection, she kissed his young heart so intensely, so passionately, sucking at it so ardently, that the heart began to bleed and suddenly understood all the sorrows of this world and was filled with infinite compassion. Poor young poet's heart! But Mnemosyne's younger daughter, the rosy goddess of jest, quickly sprang toward them and took the suffering boy in her arms and tried to cheer him with laughter and song and gave him the mask of Comedy and the fool's bells as toys and kissed his lips soothingly, kissing onto them all her frivolity, all her defiant gaiety, all her witty raillery.

And after that Sterne's heart and his lips engaged in a curious conflict. Often when his heart was moved by tragedy and he wished to express the deepest feelings of his bleeding heart, then, to his own surprise, there streamed from his lips words of wild laughter and merriment.

IV

In the Middle Ages most people believed that when a building was to be erected, it was necessary to kill some living creature and lay the cornerstone on its blood; in this way the building would stand firm and indestructible. Whether it was the absurd ancient pagan idea that one could win the favor of the gods by blood sacrifices or whether it was a misunderstanding of the Christian doctrine of atonement that produced this notion about the magic power of blood, about healing by blood, about this belief in blood—suffice it to say, the belief was prevalent, and there live on in songs and sagas the gruesome particulars about how to slaughter children or animals in order to strengthen large buildings with their blood. Today mankind is more sensible. We no longer believe in the magic power of blood, either the blood of an aristocrat or a god, and the great masses believe only in money. Does present-day religion consist then in God as money incarnate or money as God incarnate? In a word, people believe only in money; they ascribe magic power only to minted metal, to the Host of silver and gold; money is the beginning and the end of all their works; and when they have a building to erect, they take great pains to see that some coins, a capsule with all kinds of coins, is placed under the cornerstone.

Yes, as in the Middle Ages everything, single buildings as well as the whole complex of state and church buildings, rested on the belief in blood, all our present-day institutions rest on the belief in money, in real money. The former was superstition, but the latter is pure egotism. Reason destroyed the former; feeling will destroy the latter. The foundation of human society will some day be a better one, and all noble hearts of Europe are agonizingly engaged in discovering this new and better basis.

Perhaps it was dissatisfaction with the present belief in money and disgust at the egotism they saw sneering out everywhere that had first moved certain poets of the Romantic School in Germany with the best of intentions to flee from the present age to the past and to promote the restoration of medievalism. This may be the case, especially with those who did not form the real coterie. To it belonged the writers I discussed in particular in the second book, after having written in the first book about the Romantic School in general. Only because of their importance for literary history, not because of their intrinsic value, did I speak first and in some detail about those coterie comrades who worked together as a group. Hence I trust I will not be misunderstood for giving a later and scantier report on Zacharias Werner, Baron de la Motte Fouqué, and Mr. Ludwig Uhland. As far as worth is concerned, these three writers would deserve to be discussed and praised far more fully. For Zacharias Werner was the only dramatist of the School whose plays were produced on the stage and applauded by the pit. Baron de la Motte Fouqué was the only narrative poet of the School whose novels appealed to the whole reading public. And Mr. Ludwig Uhland is the only lyric poet of the School whose poems entered into the hearts of the great mass of people and still remain alive on their lips.

In this respect the three poets mentioned deserve preference over Mr. Ludwig Tieck, whom I praised as one of the best writers of the School. For although the theater is his hobby and he has occupied himself with acting and its smallest details from his childhood on, yet Mr. Tieck never succeeded in producing any emotional impact on the public by his use of the stage as Zacharias Werner did. Mr. Tieck was always compelled to keep a drawing-room audience to whom he himself read his plays and whose applause he could safely count on. Whereas Mr. de la Motte Fouqué was read with equal pleasure by the duchess down to the washerwoman and blazed forth as the sun of lending libraries, Mr. Tieck was merely the astral lamp[178] of teaparties who basked in the light of his poetry and placidly swallowed their tea during the reading of his *novelle.* The strength of this poetry must have stood out all the more, the more it contrasted with the weakness of the tea, and in Berlin, where one gets the weakest tea, Mr. Tieck must have seemed to be one of the most forceful poets. While the songs of our excellent Uhland resounded in forest and valley and are still bellowed by uproarious students and whispered by tender maidens, not a single lyric by Mr. Tieck has penetrated our hearts; not a one has remained in our ears; the general public does not know a single poem by this great lyricist.

Zacharias Werner was born in Königsberg in Prussia

178. An Argand lamp so constructed that no interruption of light upon the table is made by the flattened ring-shaped reservoir containing the oil.

November 18, 1768. His connection with the Schlegels was not a personal one but only due to kindred interests. From far away he understood their aims and did his best to write in accordance with their ideas. But he could be enthusiastic about only one aspect of the medieval revival, namely, the hierarchic, Catholic aspect; the feudal aspect did not move his spirit as intensely. His fellow countryman T. A. Hoffmann has given us a bit of strange information about this in *The Serapion Brethren.*[179] He says that Werner's mother had a mental disorder and during her pregnancy had fancied that she was the Blessed Virgin and would give birth to the Saviour. Werner's spirit bore the mark of this religious insanity his whole life long. We find the most shocking religious fanaticism in all his works. A single one, *The Twenty-fourth of February,*[180] is free of it and is among the most valuable productions of our dramatic literature. In stage performances it has elicited the greatest enthusiasm, more than Werner's other plays. His other dramatic works had less appeal for the great mass of people because, with all his dynamic vigor, he was almost completely ignorant about the stage.

Hoffmann's biographer, Kriminalrat[181] Hitzig, also wrote a biography of Werner. A conscientious piece of work, just as interesting to the psychologist as to the literary historian. As I was told recently, Werner was for some time here in Paris,[182] where he took particular pleasure in the peripatetic women philosophers[183] who at that time strolled of an evening through the galleries of the Palais Royal in their most dazzling finery. They pur-

179. A collection of stories and fairy tales, first published 1819–1821.

180. A tragedy of fate, a very popular type at that time, first published in 1815.

181. Chief of police detectives.

182. In 1808.

183. The prostitutes.

sued him and teased him and laughed at his comical suit
and his even more comical manners. Those were the
good old times! Alas, like the Palais Royal, Zacharias
Werner changed greatly later on. The last lamp of joy
went out in the troubled man's spirit, he entered the
order of the Liguorians[184] in Vienna, and preached there
in the church of St. Stephen about the vanity of earthly
things. He had discovered that everything on earth was
vain. The girdle of Venus, he now maintained, was only
an ugly serpent, and majestic Juno wore under her white
robe a pair of buckskin coachman's trousers that were
not very clean. Father Zacharias now mortified his flesh
and fasted and declaimed passionately against our im-
penitent sensual pleasure. "Cursed is the flesh!" he cried
out so loudly and with such a glaring East Prussian ac-
cent that the saints' images in St. Stephen's trembled and
the Vienna grisettes smiled their sweetest smiles. Be-
sides this important novelty, he constantly told the peo-
ple that he was a great sinner. Viewed accurately, the
man always remained consistent, only that formerly he
merely wrote about what he later actually practiced. The
heroes of most of his plays are already monastically absti-
nent lovers, ascetic libertines, who have discovered in
abstinence a heightened ecstasy, who spiritualize their
epicureanism by martyrdom of the flesh, who seek the
most gruesome delights in the depths of religious mysti-
cism—saintly roués.

Shortly before his death the joy of dramatic creation
once more awakened in Werner, and he wrote another
tragedy, entitled *The Mother of the Maccabees.*[185] Here,
however, it was not a matter of festooning the serious-
ness of worldly life with romantic jests; for the sacred
subject matter he also chose a leisurely, ecclesiastical

184. Also known as the Redemptorists, a Roman Catholic order founded in
1732 by Saint Alphonsius Liguori.
185. Published in 1820.

style, the rhythms are solemnly measured like the peal-
ing of bells, moving as slowly as a procession on Good
Friday, and the play is a Palestinian legend in the form
of the Greek tragedy. It found little favor among people
here below; whether the angels in Heaven liked it better
I don't know.

But Father Zacharias died soon after, at the beginning
of the year 1823, having walked this sinful earth for more
than fifty-four years.

We shall let the deceased rest in peace and turn to the
second poet of the Romantic triumvirate. This is the
excellent Baron Friedrich de la Motte Fouqué, born in
Brandenburg in 1777 and appointed professor at the
University of Halle in 1833. Prior to this he was a major
in the Royal Prussian army and was one of the bardic
heroes or heroic bards whose lyres and swords rang out
loudest during the so-called War of Liberation. His lau-
rel wreath is genuine. He is a true poet, and the sanctifi-
cation of poetry rests upon his head. Few writers have
enjoyed as their lot such general admiration as our excel-
lent Fouqué. Now he has his readers only among the
patrons of lending libraries. But this public is always
large enough, and Mr. Fouqué can boast that he is the
only member of the Romantic School whose works even
the lower classes relish. While the esthetic tea clubs of
Berlin turned up their noses at the knight who had fallen
to such depths, I found in a small town in the Harz a very
beautiful girl who spoke of Fouqué with charming enthu-
siasm and blushingly confessed that she would gladly
give a year of her life if she could kiss the author of *Undine*
just once.—And this girl had the most beautiful lips I
have ever seen.

But what a very lovely poetical work *Undine* is! It is
itself a kiss. The spirit of poetry kissed the sleeping
Spring, who, smiling, opened her eyes, and all the roses
wafted their fragrance, and all the nightingales sang, and

what the roses sent forth as fragrance and what the night-
ingales sang, our excellent Fouqué clothed in words and
called *Undine*.

I do not know whether the story has been translated
into French. It is the tale of the beautiful nymph who has
no soul, and can acquire a soul only by falling in love with
a knight—but alas, with this soul she also acquires our
human sorrows, her knightly spouse becomes unfaithful,
and she kills him with a kiss. For in this work death, like
life, is only a kiss.

Undine may be considered the muse of Fouqué's po-
etry. Though she is beautiful beyond measure, though
she suffers just as we do, and the full burden of earthly
grief weighs upon her, she is still not a real human being.
Our age, however, repudiates all such creatures of air
and water, even the most beautiful; it demands real living
figures, and the last thing it wants is nymphs who are in
love with noble knights. The retrograde tendency, the
continual eulogy of the hereditary aristocracy, the un-
ceasing glorification of the old feudal system, the ever-
lasting playing at chivalry—these were the things that
displeased the educated middle class among the German
reading public, and it deserted the outdated minstrel. As
a matter of fact, this constant sing-song about armor,
tournament steeds, ladies of the castle, honorable guild
masters, dwarfs, squires, castle chapels, love and faith,
and whatever else this medieval rubbish is called, finally
bored us, and when the ingenious hidalgo Friedrich de
la Motte Fouqué became more and more absorbed in his
chivalric romances, and in his dream of the past lost the
understanding for the present, even his best friends had
to turn away from him, shaking their heads.

The works he wrote during this later period are un-
bearable. The defects of his earlier writings are inten-
sified to an extreme. His knights are all iron and senti-
ment, without either flesh or common sense. His women

are only images, or rather, dolls whose golden locks flow gracefully down over their charming flower-faces. Like Walter Scott's works, Fouqué's novels of chivalry are reminiscent of woven Gobelin tapestries, which by their richness of design and magnificent colors, delight our eyes more than our spirits. There are knightly festivals, pastoral games, duels, old costumes, all nicely side by side, romantic without any deeper meaning, showy superficiality. Fouqué's imitators, like Walter Scott's, perfected even more disturbingly this mannerism of portraying only the outward appearance and the costumes of persons and things instead of their inner nature. This superficial style and facile manner are now rampant in Germany as well as in England and France. Even if the works no longer glorify the period of chivalry, but deal with our modern life, it is still always the same old style which grasps only the non-essential aspects of the subject matter instead of its essence. Instead of knowledge of human nature our modern novelists manifest only knowledge of dress, perhaps relying on the saying "Clothes make the man." How different the older novelists were, especially the English! Richardson gives us an anatomy of feelings. Goldsmith treats pragmatically the love affairs of his heroes. The author of *Tristram Shandy* shows us the most secret depths of the soul; he opens a dormer window in the soul, permits us a glance into its abysses, paradises, and dirty corners, and immediately lets the curtain fall again. We have looked from the front into this strange theater, lighting and perspective did not fail to have their effect, and, by seeming to have glimpsed the infinite, we come away with a feeling of infinity, of poetry. As for Fielding, he leads us right behind the scenes, shows us the false rouge on all emotions, the coarsest motives for the most delicate actions, the rosin that will later flare up as enthusiasm, the kettle-drum, and on it, still resting peacefully, the stick that will presently drum out the mightiest thunder of passion—in short, he shows us the entire inner mechanism, the great lie, by which men appear to be other than they really are and by which all the joyous reality of life is lost. Yet why choose the English as examples when our Goethe has provided in his *Wilhelm Meister* the best model for a novel?

The number of Fouqué's novels is legion; he is one of the most prolific writers. *The Magic Circle* and *Thiodolph the Icelander*[186] deserve special praise. His verse plays, which are not meant for the stage, contain great beauties. *Sigurd the Dragon-Killer,* in particular, is a bold work in which the Scandinavian heroic saga is reflected with all its giants and fairy-tale creatures. The main character, Sigurd, is a colossal figure. He is as strong as the cliffs of Norway and as violent as the ocean that surges about them. He has as much courage as a hundred lions and as much intelligence as two donkeys.

Mr. Fouqué also wrote poems. They are charm itself. They are so airy, so colorful, so radiant, flitting along so gaily like sweet lyric hummingbirds.

The real lyric poet, however, is Mr. Ludwig Uhland, who was born in Tübingen in 1787 and now lives as a lawyer in Stuttgart. He has written one volume of poems, two tragedies, and two treatises, one on Walther von der Vogelweide,[187] the other on French troubadours. These are two brief historical investigations and testify to industrious study of the Middle Ages. The titles of the tragedies are *Ludwig the Bavarian* and *Duke Ernst of Swabia.* The former I have not read; I have been told it is not the better of the two. The second, however, contains great beauties and is pleasing because of the nobility of the

186. The complete title is *The Travels of Thiodolf the Icelander.*

187. One of the best lyric poets in German during the flowering period of medieval German literature at the end of the twelfth century and the beginning of the thirteenth.

feelings and the worthiness of its sentiments. A sweet breath of poetry wafts through it such as is no longer found in the plays that now reap so much applause in our theater. German loyalty is the theme of this play, and we see it here, strong as an oak, defying all storms; German love flowers, scarcely noticeable, in the background, but its fragrance of violets penetrates our hearts all the more movingly. This play—it should better be called a poem —contains passages that are among the most beautiful pearls of our literature. But nonetheless the theater public received the play with indifference, or rather, rejected it. I do not want to reproach the good people in the pit all too bitterly. These people have definite needs which they expect the poet to satisfy. The creations of the poet should not merely accord with the inclinations of his own heart but rather with the desire of the public. The public is just like the hungry Bedouin in the desert who, thinking he has found a sack of peas, hastily opens it, but alas, it is only pearls. The public consumes with delight Mr. Raupach's dried peas and Madame Birch-Pfeiffer's broad beans; but Uhland's pearls it cannot stomach.

Since in all probability the French do not know who Madame Birch-Pfeiffer[188] and Mr. Raupach are, I must mention here that this divine pair, standing beside each other like the brother and sister Apollo and Diana, are the most revered figures in the temples of our dramatic art. Yes, Mr. Raupach is just as comparable to Apollo as Madame Birch-Pfeiffer is to Diana. As for their actual positions, Madame Pfeiffer is employed as an imperial Austrian court actress in Vienna and Mr. Raupach as a royal Prussian dramatist in Berlin. The lady has already written a great many plays in which she herself plays a role. I cannot resist mentioning here a fact which to

188. Charlotte Birch-Pfeiffer, German actress and author of popular sentimental plays.

Frenchmen will seem almost incredible. Many of our actors are also dramatic poets and write plays for themselves. They say Mr. Ludwig Tieck brought about this misfortune by an indiscreet remark. In his reviews he noted that actors can always play better in a bad play than in a good one. On the basis of this axiom actors in droves seized their pens, wrote tragedies and comedies by the dozen, and it was sometimes hard for us to decide whether a vain actor intentionally made his play bad in order to play well in it or whether he played badly in such a homemade play in order to make us think the play was good. The actor and the poet, who had previously had a colleague-like relation with each other (approximately like the executioner and the poor sinner), now became openly hostile. The actors tried to push the poets out of the theater altogether with the excuse that they understood nothing of the demands of the stage world and nothing about drastic effects and stage tricks as only the actor learns them in practice and knows how to make use of them in his plays. Therefore the actors or, as they liked best to call themselves, the artists, preferred to act in their own plays or at least in plays written by one of their party, "an artist." These plays did indeed meet their needs completely. Here they found their favorite costumes, their poetry in flesh-colored tights, their exits accompanied by applause, their traditional grimaces, their tinsel phrases, their whole affected Bohemianism of art—a language that is spoken only on the stage, flowers that spring up only from this artificial soil, fruits that have ripened only under the footlights, a kind of nature in which not the breath of God, but of the prompter, blows, a frenzy that shakes the scenery, gentle melancholy with titillating flute accompaniment, rouged innocence with dives into vice, monthly-pay emotions, flourish of the trumpets, etc.

In this way German actors have emancipated themselves from poets and from poetry itself. Only mediocrity did they still permit to practice its art in their sphere. But they watch out carefully that no true poet penetrates their ranks under the cloak of mediocrity. How many tests Mr. Raupach had to endure before he succeeded in gaining a footing on the stage! And even now they keep a sharp eye on him, and if he occasionally writes a play that is not totally bad, he immediately has to produce a dozen more pieces of utter rubbish for fear of being ostracized by the actors. You are suprised at the expression "a dozen"? It is by no means an exaggeration. This man can actually write a dozen plays every year, and people admire his productivity. But "it is not magic," says Jantjen of Amsterdam, the famous magician, when we are amazed at his tricks, "it is not magic, but simply a matter of speed."

There is another, special reason for Mr. Raupach's success in the German theater. This writer, by birth a German, lived in Russia for a long time, received his education there, and it was the Muscovite muse who initiated him into poetry. This muse, the beauty wrapped in sables, with the charmingly turned-up nose, handed our poet her brimming brandy cup of inspiration, hung around his shoulders her quiver with Kirghiz shafts of wit, and put in his hands her tragic knout. When he first began beating our hearts with it, how he moved us! The strangeness of the whole spectacle astonished us not a little. Civilized Germans certainly did not like the man, but his stormy Sarmatian temperament, a clumsy dexterity, a certain snarling aggressiveness in his behavior, nonplused the public. At any rate it was a queer sight when Mr. Raupach raced along on his Slavic Pegasus, the little nag, over the steppes of poetry, riding his dramatic themes to death beneath the saddle, in genuine Bashkir fashion. This met with approval in Berlin where, as you know, everything Russian is well received . . . He gets thirty taler for every act he writes, and he writes nothing but plays in six acts by giving the first act the title "Prologue." He has already shoved all kinds of subjects under the saddle of his Pegasus and ridden them to death. No hero is safe from this tragic fate. He even got the best of Siegfried, the dragon killer. The muse of German history is in despair. Like a Niobe, she gazes with pale sorrow at her noble children whom Raupach-Apollo has finished off so dreadfully. O Jupiter! he even dared to lay hands on the Hohenstaufens, our beloved old Swabian emperors! It was not enough that Mr. Friedrich Raumer[189] butchered them in history; now comes Mr. Raupach as well and trims them up for the stage. He clothes Raumer's wooden figures in his leather poetry, his Russian hides, and the sight of such caricatures and their foul smell end by spoiling for us the memory of the finest and noblest emperors of our German fatherland . . .

The association of ideas by contrast is responsible for the fact that, intending to talk about Mr. Uhland, I suddenly got onto Mr. Raupach and Madame Birch-Pfeiffer. But although this divine pair does not belong to real literature, our Diana of the theater even less than our Apollo of the theater, I still felt bound to mention them because they represent the contemporary world of the stage. In any case I owed it to our true poets to state in a few words what sort of people are usurping the control of the theater in Germany.

V

At this moment I am in a strange dilemma. I must not leave undiscussed Mr. Ludwig Uhland's collection of poems, and yet I am not in the right mood for such a discussion. Silence might appear to be cowardice or even

189. A German historian who wrote a history of the Hohenstaufens and their epoch, published 1823–1825.

perfidy, and honest, frank words might be interpreted as lack of charity. In fact, I shall scarcely satisfy the kith and kin of Uhland's muse and the copyholders of his fame with the enthusiasm within my reach today. But I beg you to take into consideration the conditions under which I am writing, the time and place. Twenty years ago—I was a boy—yes, then, with what abounding enthusiasm I could have celebrated the excellent Uhland! Then I felt his excellence perhaps better than now; he was closer to me in thought and feelings. But since then so much has happened! What seemed to me so splendid, that chivalrous, Catholic world, those knights who cut and thrust at each other in aristocratic tournaments, those gentle squires and well-bred noble ladies, those Nordic heroes and Minnesingers, those monks and nuns, those ancestral vaults and awesome shudders, those pallid sentiments of renunciation to the accompaniment of bellringing, and the everlasting melancholy wailing—how bitterly it has been spoiled for me since then! Yes, things were different then. How often I sat amid the ruins of the old castle at Düsseldorf on the Rhine and recited to myself the most beautiful of all Uhland's poems:

> The handsome shepherd wandered by,
> beneath the castle of the king.
> The maiden saw him from up high,
> her heart began to sing.

> She called to him in tender words,
> "Oh, could I but come down to you!
> How white the lambs glow in your herd!
> How red the flowers' hue!"

> In turn, she heard the young man speak,
> "Oh, if you could come down to me!
> How red the glow is on your cheek,
> how white the arms I see!"

When grievingly each day he led
his flock past her, he looked above
till from the turret leaned the head
of her, his dearest love.

Then merrily the shepherd cried,
"Hail, lovely princess fair and fine!"
She sweetly from above replied,
"I thank you, shepherd mine!"

The winter went, back came the spring,
and flowers bloomed around.
The shepherd passed the castle's wing,
his love no more he found.

The shepherd cried, an anguished moan,
"Hail, lovely princess fair and fine!"
Down came a muffled, ghostly tone,
"Farewell, O shepherd mine!"

Sitting amid the ruins of the old castle and reciting this poem, I sometimes heard the nymphs in the Rhine, which flows by there, imitating my words, and from the waters came a sighing and a moaning with a comical pathos:

Down came a muffled, ghostly tone,
"Farewell, O shepherd mine!"

But I ignored the chaffing of the nymphs, even when they giggled ironically at the most beautiful passages in Uhland's poems. At that time I modestly assumed that this giggling was at me, especially toward evening as darkness approached, and I would declaim with voice somewhat raised to overcome the mysterious awe inspired in me by the ancient castle ruins. You see, there was a legend that a headless lady wandered about there at night. Sometimes I thought I heard her long silk train rustling past, and my heart pounded.—This was the time and the place for me to be enthusiastic about the *Poems* by Ludwig Uhland.

I hold this same volume in my hands once more, but twenty years have passed since then, I have heard and seen much in the meantime, a very great deal, I no longer believe there are people without heads, and the old spectral show no longer has any effect on my feelings. The house in which I am sitting and reading is on the Boulevard Montmartre; here the wildest waves of the times break; here screech the loudest voices of the modern age; there is laughing, roaring, and beating of drums; the National Guard marches past in double-quick time; and everyone is speaking French.—Is this the place to read Uhland's poems? I have once more recited to myself three times the last lines of the poem mentioned above, but I no longer feel the inexpressible grief that once seized me when the king's daughter dies and the handsome shepherd called up to her so plaintively, "Hail, lovely princess, fair and fine!"

> Down came a ghostly, muffled tone,
> "Farewell, O shepherd mine!"

Perhaps I have also become somewhat cool toward such poems since I learned that there is a far more painful love than that which never attains possession of the beloved or loses her through death. In reality it is more painful when the beloved lies in our arms day and night but ruins the day and night for us by constant perversity and silly caprices, so that we cast out of our heart what our heart loves most, and we ourselves have to take the cursed, beloved woman to the coach and send her off:

> "Farewell, my princess fair and fine!"

Yes, more painful than loss through death is loss through life, for instance, when the beloved turns away from us out of crazy frivolity, when she absolutely insists on going to a ball to which no decent person can accompany her, and when, in quite absurdly garish dress and with hair defiantly curled, she then gives her arm to the first scoundrel she meets and turns her back on us:

"Farewell, O shepherd mine!"

Possibly Mr. Uhland himself did not fare any better than we. His mood, too, must have changed somewhat since then. With few exceptions he has put no new poems on the market for twenty years. I do not believe that this fine poetic temperament was so meagerly endowed by nature that it bore within only a single springtime. No, I explain Uhland's silence by the contradiction between the inclinations of his muse and the demands of his political position. The elegiac poet who was able to celebrate the Catholic feudal past in such beautiful ballads and romances, the Ossian of medievalism, has since become an ardent representative of the rights of the people in the Würtemberg Diet, a bold speaker for civic equality and freedom of thought. Mr. Uhland proved that these democratic and Protestant views of his are genuine and pure by the great personal sacrifices that he made for them. Having once won a poet's laurels, he now also won the oak wreath of civic virtue. But precisely because his intentions toward the modern age were so honorable, he could no longer keep on singing the old song about ancient times with his old enthusiasm. And since his Pegasus was only a knight's steed that liked to trot back into the past but immediately became balky when it was supposed to go ahead into modern life, good Uhland dismounted with a smile, and calmly had the intractable beast unsaddled and led to the stable. There he has remained until the present day, and like his colleague, the steed Bayard,[190] he has all kinds of virtues and only a single defect—he is dead.

Sharper eyes than mine claim to have perceived that the tall knightly steed with the gay-colored armorial trappings and proud plumes of feathers never really suited his middle-class rider, who wore on his feet instead of boots with golden spurs only shoes and silk stockings, and on his head, instead of a helmet, only a Tübingen doctoral cap. They claim to have discovered that Mr. Ludwig Uhland never could accord completely with his subject; that he does not really reproduce in idealized veracity the naive, grimly powerful tones of the Middle Ages, but rather dissolves them into a sickly sentimental melancholy; that he soft-boiled, so to speak, in his sentimentality the robust strains of the heroic saga and the folksong to make them palatable to the modern public. And indeed, when observed closely, the women in Uhland's poems are merely lovely phantoms, moonlight personified, with milk in their veins and sweet tears in their eyes, that is, tears without salt. If we compare Uhland's knights with the knights of the ancient songs, they seem to consist of tin armor with nothing but flowers beneath it instead of flesh and bones. Uhland's knights thus have for sensitive noses a fragrance far more suitable for love than the ancient warriors, who wore very thick iron trousers, ate a lot, and swilled even more.

But this is not meant as criticism. Mr. Uhland had no intention of producing a faithful copy of the German past, he perhaps meant to delight us merely by its image, and he created a pleasant reflection of it from the dusky surface of his spirit. This may possibly lend his poems a special charm and win for them the love of many good, gentle souls. Portraits of the past exercise their magic even in the palest evocation. Even men who espouse the

190. In romances of chivalry a wonderful bay horse, remarkable for his spirit and for his unique ability to fit his size to his rider.

modern age always retain a secret fondness for the tradi-
tions of olden times; even the weakest echo of these
ghostly voices moves us strangely. And we can readily
understand that our excellent Uhland's ballads and ro-
mances found the greatest favor not simply among the
patriots of 1813,[191] among upright youths and lovely
maidens, but also among many persons endowed with
greater powers and among many modern thinkers.

I have added the year 1813 to the word "patriots" in
order to distinguish them from present-day patriots, who
no longer live off the memories of the so-called War of
Liberation. Those older patriots must derive the sweet-
est pleasure from Uhland's muse, since most of his po-
ems are completely impregnated with the spirit of their
time, a time when they themselves were reveling in
youthful emotions and proud hopes. They passed on the
preference for Uhland's poems to their disciples, and the
boys on the athletic grounds used to be given credit for
patriotism if they bought Uhland's poems. They found
among them lyrics which even Max von Schenkendorf[192]
and Mr. Ernst Moritz Arndt[193] could not have surpassed.
And indeed, what descendant of staunch Arminius and
blonde Thusnelda is not satisfied with this poem of Uh-
land's?[194]

> "Forward, forward, one and all!
> Russia sounds the valiant call:
> Forward!

191. The year of the battle of Leipzig, in which Napoleon's forces were
roundly defeated.

192. A German poet who wrote many patriotic lyrics.

193. The representative poet of the struggle against Napoleon, combining
ardent patriotism with devout Protestantism.

194. This is a poem in honor of Fieldmarshal Blücher, one of the outstand-
ing military leaders against Napoleon. During the War of Liberation he was
known as "Fieldmarshal Forward."

"Prussia hears the noble word,
likes the sound, and joins the chord:
Forward!

"Mighty Austria, arise!
Join your brethren's enterprise!
Forward!

"Forward, ancient Saxon land!
Ever forward, hand in hand!
Forward!

"Bavaria, Hesse, Swabia!
To the Rhine, Franconia!
Forward!

"Forward, Holland, Netherland!
High your sword, free in your hand!
Forward!

"Hail, Helvetia's regiment!
Alsace, Burgundy, Lorraine!
Forward!

"Forward, on, Hispania!
Join your kin, Britannia!
Forward!

"Forward! What a gallant sport!
Lucky wind and nearby port!
Forward!

"Forward is a general!
Forward, gallant fighters all!
Forward!"

I repeat—the men of 1813 find the spirit of their time splendidly preserved in Mr. Uhland's poems, and not simply the political, but also the moral and esthetic spirit. Mr. Uhland represents a whole epoch, and he now represents it almost alone, since its other representatives have been forgotten and are actually summed up in Uhland. The dominant tone in his lyrics, ballads, and romances was the tone of all his Romantic contemporaries, and many of them produced just as good things, if not even better. This is the place where I can still praise some members of the Romantic School who, as I have said, in the content and tone of their poems, manifest the most striking similarity to Mr. Uhland, are also not inferior to him in poetic worth, and differ from him perhaps only by less assurance in matters of form. What an excellent poet Baron von Eichendorff is![195] The lyrics that he wove into his novel *Foreshadowing and the Present*[196] cannot be distinguished from Uhland's, not even from the best of them. If there is a difference, it lies in the greener forest freshness and the more crystalline genuineness of Eichendorff's poems. Mr. Justinus Kerner,[197] who is almost completely unknown, also deserves honorable mention. He too wrote very fine poems in the same tone and style. He is a fellow countryman of Mr. Uhland, as is Mr. Gustav Schwab,[198] a more famous poet, who likewise burst into bloom in Swabian territory and who still regales us every year with pretty, fragrant lyrics. His forte is the ballad, and in this form he has celebrated native legends most delightfully. Wilhelm Müller, whom death snatched away from us in the very prime of youth, must also be mentioned.[199] In imitating the German folksong he is completely in harmony with Mr. Uhland; I even think he

195. Joseph Freiherr von Eichendorff (1788–1857), a much more gifted poet than Heine's description indicates. He wrote much else besides, but it is for his lyrics that he is remembered.

196. *Ahnung und Gegenwart*, published in 1815.

197. A minor German poet and writer of fiction.

198. A minor German poet and man of letters, a life-long friend of Uhland's and Kerner's.

199. He died in 1827 before his thirty-third birthday. He was a prolific writer of facile verse and, for some reason, was particularly admired by Heine.

was often more successful in this sphere and excelled him in naturalness. He understood more profoundly the spirit of the old song forms and thus did not need to imitate them in externals; we find in him a freer treatment of nuances and a sensible avoidance of all obsolete idioms and expressions. I must also call to mind here the late Wetzel,[200] now completely forgotten. He too is a kindred spirit of our excellent Uhland, and in some poems of his that I know he surpasses Uhland in sweetness and soulful fervor. These lyrics, half flowers, half butterflies, dissipated their fragrance and fluttered into oblivion in one of the older volumes of Brockhaus' annual *Urania.* It goes without saying that Mr. Clemens Brentano wrote most of his lyrics in the same style and vein as Mr. Uhland; both drew from the same source, the folksong, and offer us the same drink; but in Uhland's poetry the goblet, the form, is more polished. I really must not speak of Adalbert von Chamisso here.[201] Although a contemporary of the Romantic School, in whose activities he took part, yet this man's heart has in recent times been so wonderfully rejuvenated that he modulated to completely different keys, had an influence as one of the most original and most important modern poets, and belongs far more to young Germany than to old Germany. But in the lyrics of his earlier period stirs the same breath that flows toward us from Uhland's poems; the same sound, the same color, the same fragrance, the same melancholy, the same tear—Chamisso's tears are perhaps more moving because, like a spring gushing out of a rock, they well up from a far stouter heart.

200. Karl Friedrich Gottlob Wetzel (1779–1819), author of a collection of poems, also a collection of war-songs, and several tragedies.

201. A Franco-German lyric poet and fiction writer (1781–1838), also a botanist of some repute, serving for many years as keeper of the Royal Botanical Collection in Berlin.

The poems that Mr. Uhland wrote in Southern verse forms are also very closely related to the sonnets, assonances, and ottava rima of his schoolmates from the Romantic School and are indistinguishable from them in form or style. But as I have said, most of Uhland's contemporaries together with their poems are being forgotten . . .

Mr. Uhland is not the father of a school like Schiller or Goethe or some other such writers from whose individuality emerged a particular style that found a definite echo in the works of the contemporaries. He is not the father, but is himself only the child of a School that passed on to him a style which likewise did not originally belong to it but which it had laboriously squeezed out of earlier poetic works. As a substitute for this lack of originality, of individual novelty, Mr. Uhland offers a number of excellent qualities, as splendid as they are rare. He is the pride of fortunate Swabia, and all comrades of the German tongue rejoice in this noble minstrel. He is the epitome in the lyric of most of his comrades from the Romantic School, which the public now loves and honors in the one man. And we honor and love him now perhaps all the more because we are about to part from him forever.

Oh, not from a frivolous whim, but obeying the law of necessity, Germany is stirring.—Pious, peaceful Germany!—It casts a melancholy glance at the past it leaves behind, once more it bends tenderly over the ancient era which gazes at us, so deathly pale, from Uhland's poems, and it bids farewell with a kiss. And another kiss, even a tear, for all I care! But let us tarry no longer in idle compassion.—

Forward, forward, one and all!
France now sounds the valiant call:
Forward!

VI

"When, after many years, Emperor Otto III went to the grave where Charles' corpse lay buried,[202] he entered the cavern in the company of two bishops and the Count of Laumel (who related all this). The corpse was not lying down like others, but sat upright on a chair like a living person. On his head was a crown of gold, he held the scepter in his hands, which were covered with gauntlets, but the fingernails had pierced the leather and grown out. The arched vault was constructed very durably of marble and plaster. In order for them to enter, an opening had to be broken; as soon as they were inside, they smelled a strong odor. All immediately genuflected and did reverence to the dead. Emperor Otto clothed him in a white garment, cut his nails, and had all defects repaired. No part of the limbs was rotted except that a bit of the tip of the nose was missing; Otto had it replaced with gold. Finally he took a tooth from Charles' mouth, ordered the vault walled up again, and departed.—The following night Charles is said to have appeared to him in a dream and prophesied that Otto would not live to old age and would leave no heir."

The *German Legends*[203] give us this account, nor is it the only example of its kind. Your King Francis also had the grave of the famous Roland opened to see for himself whether the hero had been of such gigantic stature as the poets say. This took place shortly before the battle of Pavia.[204] Sebastian of Portugal had the graves of his

202. Otto III was Emperor of the Holy Roman Empire from 996 to 1002. Charles is of course Charlemagne.

203. By Jakob and Wilhelm Grimm, published 1816–1818.

204. Francis I, king of France 1515–1547. He was defeated at Pavia by Emperor Charles V.

ancestors opened and viewed the dead kings before go-
ing to Africa.[205]

Strange, gruesome curiosity that often impels people
to look down into the graves of the past! This happens
in unusual times, after the end of an epoch or shortly
before a catastrophe. In our modern age we have ex-
perienced a similar phenomenon. There was a great sov-
ereign, the French people, who suddenly felt a desire to
open the grave of the past and view by the light of day
the ages long since buried and forgotten. There was no
lack of learned grave-diggers who were right at hand
with spades and crow-bars to grub up the ancient rubble
and break open the graves. A strong scent could be no-
ticed which, as Gothic *haut-gout*,[206] tickled very pleas-
antly the noses of those who were blasé about attar of
roses. French writers knelt down reverently before the
exposed Middle Ages. One clothed it in a new garment,
another cut its nails, a third put a fresh nose on it; at last
there even came some poets who ripped the teeth out of
the Middle Ages—just as Emperor Otto had done.

I do not know whether the ghost of the Middle Ages
appeared to these teeth-extractors in a dream and pro-
phesied an early end to their whole romantic rule. In any
case, I mention this aspect of French literature only in
order to declare categorically that in criticizing rather
sharply in this volume a similar occurrence in Germany,
I have no intention of attacking the French Romantic
School either directly or indirectly. The writers who
pulled medievalism out of its grave in Germany had
other aims, as can be seen from these pages, and the
influence they were able to exercise on the general pub-
lic endangered the liberty and happiness of my country.
The French writers had only artistic interests, and the

205. King of Portugal, born 1554, died 1578. He tried to revive the Cru-
sades and died in a crusade against the Moors.

206. Seasoning.

French public sought only to satisfy its suddenly awakened curiosity. Most of the French looked into the graves of the past merely with the intention of picking out an interesting costume for the carnival. In France the Gothic fad was simply a fad, and it served only to heighten the pleasure of the present. The French let their hair flow down long in medieval fashion, and at a casual remark by the barber that it is not becoming, they have it cut off short together with the rest of their medieval ideas. Alas, in Germany it is different. Perhaps just because in Germany medievalism is not completely dead and putrefied, as it is in France. German medievalism is not lying mouldered in its grave; on the contrary, it is often animated by an evil spirit and steps into our midst in bright, broad daylight and sucks the red life from our hearts.—

Alas, don't you see how sad and wan Germany is? Especially the German youth, who just recently were shouting so joyously and enthusiastically? Don't you see how bloody is the mouth of the fully authorized vampire that resides in Frankfurt and there sucks so horribly slowly and protractedly at the heart of the German people?[207]

What I have indicated in general regarding the Middle Ages has a very special application to its religion. Honesty demands that I distinguish precisely between a group called Catholic in this country and those disgraceful fellows who bear the same name in Germany. In these pages I have spoken only of the latter, and indeed in terms that still seem to me much too lenient. They are the enemies of my country, a fawning rabble, hypocrites, liars, arrant cowards. There's a hissing in Berlin, there's a hissing in Munich, and as you are strolling on the Boulevard Montmartre, you suddenly feel the sting in

207. Heine is referring to the anti-democratic Confederate Council (*Bundestag*) in Frankfurt.

your heel. But we shall crush the old serpent's head under foot. This is the party of lies, the myrmidons of despotism, the restorers of all the misery, horror, and folly of the past. How infinitely different is the party here called Catholic, whose leaders are among the most talented writers of France. Although they are not exactly our comrades-in-arms, we nevertheless fight for the same interests, namely, for the interests of mankind. In our love for mankind we are united; we differ only in our opinions as to what benefits mankind. They believe that mankind needs only spiritual consolation, whereas we are of the opinion that it needs the opposite, material happiness. If they, the Catholic party in France, misjudging their own significance, proclaim themselves the party of the past, the restorers of faith, we must defend them against themselves. The Eighteenth Century so thoroughly crushed Catholicism in France that there is almost no living trace of it left, and anyone who tries to restore Catholicism in France is preaching, so to speak, an entirely new religion. By France I mean Paris, not the provinces, for what the provinces think is a matter of as much indifference as what our legs think; the head is the seat of our thoughts. I was told that the French in the provinces are good Catholics; I can neither confirm nor deny it. The people I saw in the provinces all looked like milestones that had written on their foreheads their greater or lesser distance from the capital. The women there may seek consolation in Christianity because they can't live in Paris. In Paris itself Christianity has not existed since the Revolution, and even before that it had lost all real importance. It lay lurking in a remote church corner like a spider and sprang out hastily now and then whenever it could seize a child in the cradle or an old man in his coffin. Yes, only at two times, when he had just come into the world or when he was just leaving it, did a Frenchman get into the power of a Catholic priest.

During the whole interval between, he was in his right mind and laughed at holy water and extreme unction. But do you call this the rule of Catholicism? Just because Catholicism had died out completely in France, it was able, under Louis XVIII and Charles X, to win over a few unselfish souls by the charm of novelty. At that time Catholicism was something unheard of, something fresh, something surprising! The religion that was dominant in France shortly before then was classical mythology, and this beautiful religion had been preached to the French people by its writers, poets, and artists with such success that at the end of the last century the French, in action as in thought, were all dressed in pagan costumes. During the French Revolution classical religion flowered in its grandest splendor. This was no Alexandrian mimicking; Paris was a natural continuation of Athens and Rome. During the Empire the classical spirit vanished again, the Greek gods ruled only in the theater, and Roman virtue still had possession only of the battlefield. A new faith had arisen, and it was summed up in the sacred name Napoleon! This faith still prevails among the masses. Thus whoever says that the French are irreligious because they no longer believe in Christ and His saints is wrong. It must rather be said that the irreligion of the French consists in the fact that they now believe in a man instead of in the immortal gods. It must be said that the irreligion of the French consists in the fact that they no longer believe in Jupiter, in Diana, in Minerva, in Venus. This last point is dubious, but so much I know —regarding the Graces, the French women still remain orthodox.

I hope these remarks will not be misunderstood, for they were meant precisely to save the reader of this book from a serious misunderstanding.

Concerning the History of Religion and Philosophy in Germany

BOOK ONE

In recent times the French believed they could attain an understanding of Germany if they made themselves acquainted with the best products of our literature. By so doing they have merely raised themselves from a state of total ignorance to the level of superficiality. The best products of our literature will remain for them only mute blossoms, the whole German mind a dreary puzzle, so long as they do not know the significance of religion and philosophy in Germany.

I believe I am undertaking a useful enterprise in trying to provide some explanatory information about both. This is not an easy task for me. It is necessary first of all to avoid technical scholarly language completely unfamiliar to the French. And yet I have not explored thoroughly enough the subtleties of theology nor those of metaphysics to be able to formulate them quite simply and briefly to suit the needs of the French. Therefore I shall deal only with the large questions which have been discussed in German theology and philosophy, I shall examine only their social significance, and I shall always bear in mind the limitations of my own resources as an expositor and the capacity of the French reader for understanding the subject.

Great German philosophers who may chance to glance at these pages will shrug their shoulders with a superior air at the inadequate treatment of everything I offer here. But I trust they will be so good as to consider that the little I say is expressed clearly and comprehensibly, while their own works are, to be sure, very thorough, infinitely thorough, very profound, stupendously profound, but equally incomprehensible. Of what help to the people are locked granaries for which they have no key? The people are hungry for knowledge and will thank me for the bit of intellectual bread which I will share fairly with them.

I do not think it is lack of talent which prevents most German scholars from discussing religion and philosophy in a manner suitable for the general public. I think it is fear of the results of their own thinking, results they do not dare to impart to the people. As for me, I do not have this fear, for I am not a scholar; I am one of the people myself. I am not a scholar; I am not among the seven hundred wise men of Germany. I stand with the great multitude before the portals of their wisdom, and if any bit of truth has slipped through, and if this truth has gotten as far as to me, then it has gone far enough: —I write it on paper in pretty lettering and give it to the compositor; he sets it in lead and gives it to the printer; the latter prints it, and then it belongs to the whole world.

The religion we have in Germany is Christianity. My task will therefore be to tell what Christianity is, how it became Roman Catholicism, how from the latter Protestantism developed, and from Protestantism German philosophy.

In beginning now with a discussion of religion, I beg in advance all pious souls for Heaven's sake not to be alarmed. Fear nothing, pious souls. No profane jests shall offend your ears. At most, these are still useful in Germany, where it is important at the moment to neutralize the power of religion. You see, we Germans are in the same situation as you were before the Revolution, when Christianity and the old regime formed an absolutely inseparable alliance. This could not be destroyed so long as Christianity still exerted its influence on the masses. Voltaire had to start up his cutting laughter before Samson[1] could let his axe fall. Yet just as nothing was proved by this axe, neither was anything really proved but simply accomplished by that laughter. Voltaire succeeded only in wounding the body of Christianity. All his jokes, derived from ecclesiastical history, all his witticisms about dogma and worship, about the Bible, that holiest book of mankind, about the Virgin Mary, that fairest flower of poetry, the whole dictionary of philosophical arrows that he let loose on the clergy, wounded only the mortal body of Christianity, not its inner essence, not its deeper spirit, not its immortal soul.

For Christianity is an idea, and as such, indestructible and immortal like every idea. But what is this idea?

It is just because this idea has not yet been clearly understood and because externals have been considered the main point that there is still no history of Christianity. Two opposing parties write ecclesiastical history and constantly contradict each other; yet neither the one nor the other will ever state definitely what the idea really is which serves Christianity as a focal point, which strives

1. The executioner in Paris who performed the most executions during the French Revolution.

to reveal itself in the symbolism of Christianity, its dogma as well as its form of worship, and in its entire history, and which has manifested itself in the actual life of Christian peoples. Neither Baronius,[2] the Catholic cardinal, nor the Protestant Hofrat Schröckh[3] reveals to us what this idea really was. And if you leaf through all the folio volumes of Mansi's collection of the Acts of the Councils,[4] of Assemani's *Code of the Liturgies*,[5] and Sacarelli's *Historia ecclesiastica*,[6] you will still not understand what the idea of Christianity really was. What do you find then in the histories of Oriental and Occidental churches? In the former, Oriental ecclesiastical history, you find nothing but dogmatic subtleties in which ancient Greek sophistry is once more displayed; in the latter, Occidental ecclesiastical history, you find nothing but quarrels about discipline as it concerned ecclesiastical interests, and here the legal casuistry and statecraft of ancient Rome again exert their influence in new formulas and constraints. In fact, just as people in Constantinople had quarreled about *logos*, so people in Rome quarreled about the relationship between temporal and spiritual power; and as people in Constantinople had attacked each other about *homousios*,[7] so the Romans at-

2. Cardinal Caesar Baronius (1538–1607) wrote an important work on ecclesiastical history.

3. Johannes Matthias Schröckh from Vienna, from 1767 on a professor at the University of Wittenberg, wrote a thirty-five-volume history of the Christian Church and a ten-volume history of the Church since the Reformation.

4. Gian Domenico Mansi, archbishop of Lucca, published this collection of thirty-one volumes beginning in 1759.

5. Josephus Aloysius Assemani, professor of Oriental languages in Rome, published this *Codex* in thirteen volumes, 1749–1766.

6. A member of an international order of priests in Rome, he published this history in twenty volumes beginning in 1770.

7. A Greek word meaning "identical." The reference is to the difference of opinion between the Orthodox (Eastern) and Roman Catholic churches as to whether God and Christ are "identical," as Western Christianity believes, or whether they are merely similar in nature.

tacked each other about investiture. But the Byzantine questions—Whether *logos* is *homousios* with God the Father? Whether Mary should be called Mother of God or Mother of man? Whether Christ suffered hunger for lack of food or was hungry only because he wanted to be hungry?—all these questions had as their background simply court intrigues, and their solution depended on what was whispered and giggled in the private apartments of the *Palatium Sacrum,* whether, for example, Eudoxia or Pulcheria should fall,[8]—for the last-named lady hated Nestorius,[9] the betrayer of her love affairs, and the former hated Cyril,[10] whom Pulcheria protected—everything went back ultimately to nothing but the gossip of women and eunuchs, and in the name of dogma it was actually the man, and in the man a party that was persecuted or supported.[11] It is the same in the Occident. Rome wanted to rule; "when its legions fell, it sent dogmas into the provinces."[12] All disputes about dogma had as their origin Roman usurpations; it was a question of consolidating the supremacy of the Bishop of Rome. The latter was always very indulgent about real articles of faith, but he spit fire and brimstone the minute the rights of the Church were attacked. He did not argue a great deal about the persons in Christ, but he did argue about the consequences of the Isidorian

8. In 395 Eudoxia, daughter of the chieftain of the Franks, became the wife of the East Roman Emperor Arcadius. After the Emperor's death his son Theodosius II succeeded to the throne, but he left most affairs of state in the hands of his sister Pulcheria. Eudoxia opposed her daughter's influence.

9. Patriarch of Constantinople from 428 to 431.

10. Patriarch of Constantinople from 412 to 444.

11. This is not, of course, to be taken at face value as an objective historical account. In dealing with history Heine had no qualms about using only facts that serve his purpose. The facts he gives here are only part of the total picture, as Heine no doubt knew.

12. Heine quotes here from an earlier work of his own, *The North Sea, Part III.*

Decretals.[13] He centralized his power by canonical law, by the investiture of bishops, by reducing the power of the princes, by establishing monastic orders, by celibacy of the priesthood, and so on. But was this Christianity? Is the idea of Christianity revealed to us by reading such histories? What is this idea?

It would probably be possible to discover already in the first centuries after Christ's birth how this idea was shaped historically and how it manifested itself in the physical world by examining, without prejudice, the history of the Manicheans and the Gnostics. Although the former were accused of heresy and the latter were in ill repute, and both groups were condemned by the Church, their influence on the dogma still remained; Catholic art developed out of their symbolism, and their mode of thought permeated the whole life of Christian peoples. In their fundamental principles the Manicheans are not very different from the Gnostics. The doctrine of the two principles, good and evil, opposing each other, is common to both. The one sect, the Manicheans, acquired this doctrine from the ancient Persian religion, in which Ormuzd, light, is opposed to Ahriman, darkness, as his enemy. The other sect, the real Gnostics, believed, on the contrary, in the pre-existence of the principle of good and explained the origin of the principle of evil by emanation, by generations of eons which deteriorate all the more, the further they are removed from their origin. According to Cerinthus,[14] the creator of our world was by no means the supreme god, but only an emanation from him, one of those eons, the real Demiurge, who has

13. A collection of partly falsified papal decrees and instructions composed by a man who called himself Isidore Mercator. Since they contributed to the increase in papal power, they were used by the popes from the ninth century on in spite of their dubious origin, and for the most part incorporated into the *Corpus juris canonici.*

14. One of the first Christian Gnostics, who lived at the beginning of the second century.

gradually degenerated and now, as the evil principle, stands hostilely opposed to the *logos*, the good principle, emanating directly from the supreme god. This gnostic cosmogony is of Indian origin and brought with it the doctrine of the incarnation of God, of the mortification of the flesh, and of the contemplative life of the spirit; it gave birth to ascetically contemplative monasticism, the purest flower of the Christian idea. This idea manifested itself only very confusedly in dogma, and only very vaguely in worship. Yet everywhere we see the doctrine of the two principles appear; the evil Satan stands opposed to the good Christ; the world of the spirit is represented by Christ, the material world by Satan; our soul belongs to the former, our body to the latter. The whole world of phenomena, Nature, is therefore evil in its origin, and Satan, Prince of Darkness, tries, by means of it, to lure us to destruction, and it is necessary to renounce all the sensuous pleasures of life, to torture our body, Satan's fief, so that the soul may soar upward all the more gloriously into the bright Heaven, into the radiant kingdom of Christ.

This cosmogony, the real idea of Christianity, had spread over the entire Roman Empire with incredible rapidity, like a contagious disease, at times a raging fever, at times exhaustion, lasted all through the Middle Ages, and we moderns still feel spasms and lassitude in all our limbs. Though many of us have already recovered, we cannot escape the all-pervading hospital atmosphere and feel unhappy in being the only healthy persons among all the diseased. Sometime, when mankind regains its complete health, when peace is restored between body and soul, and they blend again in their original harmony, we will scarcely be able to comprehend the unnatural discord that Christianity has sown between the two. The happier and finer generations who, begotten in an embrace of free choice, come to flower in a religion of joy, will smile sadly at their poor ancestors, who gloomily refrained from all the pleasures of this beautiful earth and by deadening warm, colorful sensuousness almost faded away into bloodless ghosts! Yes, I say it with conviction—our descendants will be finer and happier than we. For I believe in progress, I believe mankind is destined to happiness, and I therefore cherish a grander conception of the Divinity than those pious people who fancy that man was created only to suffer. Even here on earth I would like to establish, through the blessings of free political and industrial institutions, that bliss which, in the opinion of the pious, is to be granted only on the Day of Judgment, in Heaven. The one hope is perhaps as foolish as the other, and there may be no resurrection of humanity either in a political, moral sense, or in an apostolic, Catholic sense.

Perhaps mankind is destined for eternal misery, the peoples are perhaps doomed in perpetuity to be trodden underfoot by despots, exploited by their accomplices, and scorned by their lackeys.

Alas, in this case we would have to try to preserve Christianity even if we know it is a mistake; we would have to journey through Europe barefoot and in monk's cowl, preaching renunciation and the vanity of all earthly possessions, holding up the comforting crucifix before the eyes of the scourged and derided people, and promising them up above, after death, all the joys of Heaven.

It is perhaps just because the great men on this earth are so sure of their superior power and have decided in their hearts to abuse it forever to our misfortune that they are convinced of the necessity of Christianity for their peoples, and it is really a tender, humane impulse that prompts them to take such pains to preserve this religion!

The ultimate fate of Christianity thus depends on whether we still need it. For eighteen centuries this religion was a blessing for suffering humanity; it was providential, divine, holy. Every contribution it has made to civilization by curbing the strong and strengthening the weak, by uniting the peoples through a common sentiment and a common language, and all else that its apologists have urged in its praise—all this is as nothing compared with that great consolation which it has bestowed on human beings by its very nature. Everlasting praise is due the symbol of that suffering God, the Saviour with the crown of thorns, the crucified Christ whose blood was as a soothing balm flowing down into the wounds of mankind. The poet in particular will acknowledge with reverence the awesome sublimity of this symbol. The whole system of symbols expressed in the art and life of the Middle Ages will always arouse the admiration of poets. What colossal consistency there really is in Christian art, especially in its architecture! The Gothic cathedrals—how they harmonize with the ceremonies of worship, and how the idea of the Church itself is revealed in them! Everything about them strives upward, everything is transubstantiated; the stone buds forth into branches and foliage and becomes a tree; the fruit of the vine and the ear of corn become blood and flesh; man becomes God; God becomes pure spirit! Christian life in the Middle Ages is a fertile and inexhaustibly precious material for poets. Only through Christianity could there develop in this world conditions which include such bold contrasts, such motley sorrows, and such marvelous beauty that one would think the like could never have existed in the real world and that it was all a vast hallucination, the hallucination of a delirious deity. In those times Nature itself seems to have assumed fantastic disguises; yet though man, absorbed in abstract subtleties, turned away from her with annoyance, she nonetheless often roused him with a voice so uncannily sweet, so terrifyingly tender, so powerfully enchanting that he listened instinctively and smiled and was frightened and even fell sick unto death. The story of the nightingale of Basle comes to my mind here, and as you probably do not know it, I will relate it.

In May, 1433, at the time of the Council of Basle, a group of clerics composed of prelates, doctors, and monks of all orders, were walking in a woods near the city, debating about points of theological controversy, differentiating and arguing, or quarreling about annates, prospects of obtaining a certain office, and provisos, or inquiring whether Thomas Aquinas was a greater philosopher than Bonaventura, and Heaven knows what else. But suddenly, in the midst of their dogmatic and abstract discussions, they fell silent and stopped as if rooted to the spot before a blossoming linden tree, in which sat a nightingale exulting and sobbing in its most melodious and tenderest melodies. The learned gentlemen began to feel strangely blissful as the warm tones of spring penetrated their scholastic hearts so limited by provisos; their emotions awoke from their torpid hibernation, and they looked at each other in marveling ecstasy. At last one of them remarked shrewdly that there was something queer about this, that the nightingale might well be a devil, trying with his sweet strains to divert them from their Christian converse and to entice them into lust and other alluring sins, and he proceeded to exorcize the evil spirit, probably with the customary formula of that time: *Adjuro te per eum, qui venturus est, judicare vivas et mortuos,*[15] etc., etc. To this exorcism, they say, the bird replied, "Yes, I am an evil spirit," and flew away laughing. Those, however, who had heard its song are said to have fallen ill that very same day and died shortly thereafter.

This story needs no commentary. It bears the dreadful

15. I command you in the name of Him who will come to judge the quick and the dead.

impress of a time when all that was sweet and lovely was
decried as the work of the devil. Even the nightingale was
slandered, and people crossed themselves when it sang.
The true Christian walked about amidst verdant nature
like an abstract ghost, with senses apprehensively sealed.
I shall perhaps deal in more detail with this relationship
of the Christian to nature in a later work, where, in order
to further the understanding of modern romantic litera-
ture, I must discuss thoroughly German folk supersti-
tions. For the present I can only remark that French
writers, misled by German authorities, are greatly mis-
taken in assuming that popular superstitions during the
Middle Ages were the same everywhere in Europe. It was
only with regard to the principle of good, the Kingdom
of Christ, that the same views were entertained in all of
Europe. The Church of Rome saw to this, and anyone
who deviated on this point from the prescribed opinion
was a heretic. But with regard to the principle of evil, the
realm of Satan, different opinions prevailed in the vari-
ous countries. In the Teutonic North people had entirely
different conceptions of it from those in the Latin coun-
tries of the South. This difference arose from the fact
that the Christian priesthood did not reject the old na-
tional gods it met with there as idle phantoms, but
conceded to them a real existence, maintaining, how-
ever, at the same time, that all these gods were merely
male or female devils who, because of Christ's triumph,
had lost their power over men and were now trying to
lure them into sin through lust and deceit. All Olympus
now became an aerial hell, and no matter how finely a
poet of the Middle Ages celebrated in song the Greek
tales of the gods, the devout Christian still saw in them
only spooks and devils. This gloomy illusion of the
monks hit poor Venus hardest; she, most especially, was
considered to be a daughter of Beelzebub, and the good
knight Tannhäuser tells her right to her face:

O Venus, lovely lady mine,
You're nothing but a devil![16]

You see, she had enticed Tannhäuser into that marvelous cavern called the Mountain of Venus, in which, so the legend went, amidst pastime and dancing, the beautiful goddess, with her maidens and lovers, led a very dissolute life. Even poor Diana, despite her chastity, was not exempt from a similar fate, and was described passing through the woods by night with her nymphs—hence the legend of the fierce host of hunters and the wild chase.[17] Here we still see intact the gnostic concept of the deterioration of what was previously divine, and in this transformation of an earlier national religion the idea of Christianity manifests itself most profoundly.

National religion in Europe, much more markedly in the North than in the South, was pantheistic. Its mysteries and symbols were related to a worship of nature; in every element the people worshipped marvelous beings; a divinity breathed in every tree; all the phenomena of the universe were permeated by a divine spirit. Christianity reversed this view, and a diabolized nature took the place of a nature permeated by divinity. But the serene figures of Greek mythology that reigned in the South together with Roman civilization, their beauty enhanced by art, could not be transformed into ugly, gruesome, satanic ghouls so easily as the Teutonic gods, whom, to be sure, no particular feeling for art had helped to fashion and who were already as depressed and dreary as the North itself. Thus in France you could produce no such gloomy and terrible realm of Satan as we did in

16. My translation.
17. The legend of the host of spirits, souls of the dead, led by "the wild huntsman," which rides through the air at night. Any traveler who encounters them must throw himself on the ground and give no greeting; otherwise he is doomed to join the spirits in their hunt until Judgment Day.

Germany, and the world of apparitions and sorcery itself assumed with you a cheerful aspect. How beautiful, clear, and colorful your folk legends are in comparison with ours, these monstrosities of blood and mist that sneer at us so somberly and cruelly. Our medieval poets, usually selecting materials that you, in Brittany and Normandy, had either invented or treated first, gave their works, perhaps intentionally, as much as possible of the serene spirit of ancient France. But in our national literature and in our folk legends of oral tradition the gloomy northern spirit remained, a spirit of which you can scarcely conceive. Like us, you have various types of nature-spirits, but ours are as different from yours as a German from a Frenchman. How brightly colored and especially how cleanly are the demons in your *fabliaux* and romances of sorcery in comparison with our dismal and very often filthy rabble of spirits! Your fairies and nature-spirits, wherever you took them from, whether from Cornwall or from Arabia,[18] are completely at home with you, and a French spirit differs from a German much as a dandy wearing yellow kid gloves and sauntering along the Coblence Boulevard differs from a clumsy German porter. Your water sprites, such as Melusine,[19] are just as different from ours as a princess from a washerwoman. How frightened Morgan le Fay[20] would be if she chanced to meet a German witch, naked, smeared with ointment, riding to the Brocken on a broomstick! This mountain is no fair Avalon, but a rendezvous for everything abominable and hideous. On the summit of the mountain sits Satan in the form of a black billy goat. Each of the witches approaches him with a candle in her hand and kisses him behind where his back ends. After that the

18. The ultimate source of Arthurian legends is probably Wales, and Oriental legends became popular and more familiar through the Crusades.

19. The story of the nymph who fell in love with a mortal.

20. Sister of King Arthur and pupil of Merlin, the magician.

infamous sisterhood dances around him singing, *"Don-deremus, donderemus!"* The billy goat bleats, the infernal cancan[21] triumphs. It is a bad omen for a witch to lose a shoe in this dance; it means she will be burned that very same year. Yet the mad sabbat-music,[22] pure Berlioz, overpowers all foreboding anxiety, and when the poor witch awakens in the morning from her intoxication, she finds herself lying naked and exhausted in the ashes by the dying hearth fire.

The best information concerning these witches is found in the *Demonology* of the honorable and most learned Doctor Nicholas Remigius,[23] criminal judge to His Serene Highness, the Duke of Lorraine. This keen-witted man certainly had the best opportunity to become acquainted with the doings of witches, since he prepared the cases against them, and at his time eight hundred women ascended the funeral pyre in Lorraine alone after having been convicted of witchcraft. The proof of their guilt usually consisted in tying their hands and feet together and throwing them into the water. If they sank and drowned, they were innocent; if they stayed above water and swam, they were declared guilty and were burned. Such was the logic of those times.

We see as the main trait in the character of German demons that they are stripped of any ideal features and that they are a mixture of the vulgar and the monstrous. The more crudely familiar the form in which they appear to us, the more horrible is the effect they have. Nothing is more uncanny than our hobgoblins, cobolds, and pix-

21. Heine uses here a Germanized form of the French word *chahut,* meaning "din" or "uproar," but both Elster and Walzel state that the word means "cancan," the French dance. I have accepted their explanation, hesitating to question the accuracy of two such serious scholars.

22. Sabbat is a term for the midnight assembly of witches and sorcerers held in medieval times on certain occasions such as Walpurgis Night or Halloween, hence the expression witches' sabbath.

23. Remigius published a book on demonolatry in 1598.

ies. In his *Anthropodemus* Praetorius has a passage on this subject which I quote here from Dobeneck.[24]

"The ancients could not conceive of hobgoblins as other than real human beings, in stature like small children, wearing gay-colored coats or dresses. Some add that a number of them are said to have knives sticking in their backs; others appeared in different and very frightful forms, depending on what instrument they had formerly been murdered with. For the superstitious believe them to be the souls of former occupants of their houses, murdered there long ago. And they tell many stories about how the cobolds had done the maids and cooks good service for a time in the house and had won their favor, how many a wench had thus been seized with such affection for the cobolds that they also ardently wished to see the little servants and demanded this of them, which longing, however, the spirits would never willingly gratify, making the excuse that no one could see them without being terrified. If the lustful maids still would not yield, the cobolds are said to have told them one place in the house where they would present themselves in the flesh, but the maids were to bring with them a pail of cold water. Whereupon it happened that one of the cobolds would lie down naked, perhaps on the floor, on a cushion, with a huge butcher knife sticking in his back. Many a maid was so frightened by this that she fell into a faint. Thereupon the creature immediately sprang up, took the water, and doused the wench with it thoroughly in order to bring her to her senses. After this the maids lost their desire and never asked to see dear Chimgen[25] again. To wit, all the cobolds are said to have individual

24. Ferdinand von Dobeneck's *German Popular Superstitions and Heroic Legends of the Middle Ages (Des deutschen Mittelalters Volksglauben und Heroensagen)*, published in 1815, was Heine's main source for all the material on folk superstitions that he gives in this work. Praetorius' book appeared in 1666–1667.

25. A dialectal diminutive form of *Joachimchen* (little Joachim).

names too, although generally called Chim. It is also said that they do all the housework for the men and maid servants to whom they are devoted, currying and feeding the horses, cleaning the stable, scrubbing up everything, keeping the kitchen clean, and taking great pains to do whatever else is necessary in the house, and the cattle are said to grow fat and thrive under their care. In return the cobolds must be toadied to; the domestics must never give them the slightest offence, either by laughing at them or neglecting to feed them well. If, for instance, a cook has once accepted such a creature as her secret helper in the house, she must put out every day at a certain time and at a definite place in the house a little dish she has prepared for him full of good food and then go away again; afterward she can be idle if she likes and go to bed betimes; yet early in the morning she will find her work done. But if she once forgets her duty, perhaps neglecting to put out the food, she has to do her work again by herself and has all sorts of mishaps, either burning herself with hot water, breaking pots and dishes, spilling food or letting it drop, and so on, so that as punishment she has to be scolded by the mistress or master of the house, at which, they say, the cobold is often heard giggling or laughing. And such a cobold is said always to remain in the same house even though the servants are changed. Indeed, a maid, when leaving a house, had to recommend the cobold most highly to her successor in order that the latter might wait on it in the same fashion. If the new servant happened not to want to, she had no lack of perpetual misfortune and very soon had to leave."

The following anecdote[26] is perhaps one of the most dreadful of such stories:

26. Also from Dobeneck, who had taken it from Luther's *Tischreden* (*Table Talks*).

A maid servant had for many years an invisible family spirit sitting beside her by the hearth, where she had given him his own little place and where she conversed with him during the long winter evenings. Now once the maid asked Heinzchen (for this was the name she gave him) to let her see him in his natural form just once, but Heinzchen refused. Finally, however, he consented and told her to go down into the cellar and there she would see him. Taking a candle, the maid goes down into the cellar, and there in an open cask she sees a dead infant swimming in its blood. Now many years before, this maid had given birth to an illegitimate child and had secretly murdered it and concealed it in a cask.

Such is the nature of the Germans, however, that they frequently seek in the horrible itself their best jokes, and the folk legends about cobolds are often full of delightful touches. The stories about Hüdeken are particularly amusing. He was a cobold who played his pranks in Hildesheim in the twelfth century and of whom there is so much talk by the women in the spinning rooms and in our ghost stories. A passage from an old chronicle,[27] already often printed, gives the following information about him:

"About the year 1132 there appeared over quite a long time to many persons in the bishopric of Hildesheim an evil spirit in the form of a peasant with a hat on his head, for which reason the peasants called him in the Saxon language Hüdeken.[28] This spirit took pleasure in associating with people, sometimes being visible to them, sometimes invisible, asking and answering questions. He offended no one without cause. If, however, anyone laughed at him or otherwise insulted him, he amply repaid the injury done him. When Count Burchard of Luka

27. Heine's source is again Dobeneck.
28. Little hat.

was killed by Count Hermann of Wiesenburg and the
latter's land was in danger of becoming the booty of the
victim's avengers, Hüdeken woke Bishop Bernhard of
Hildesheim out of his sleep and addressed him as fol-
lows: 'Get up, bald head. The county of Wiesenburg has
been abandoned and is in abeyance because of murder,
and so can easily be occupied by you.' The bishop
speedily assembled his warriors, fell upon the land of the
guilty count, and united it, with the Emperor's consent,
to his bishopric. The spirit frequently warned the said
bishop voluntarily of impending dangers and appeared
particularly often in the court kitchen, where he con-
versed with the cooks and rendered them all manner of
services. The servants having gradually become familiar
with Hüdeken, one kitchen-boy was daring enough to
tease him and even to douse him with dirty water every
time he appeared. The spirit requested the chief cook or
steward of the kitchen to forbid the naughty lad his mis-
chief. The chief cook responded, 'You are a spirit and are
afraid of a mere boy!' whereupon Hüdeken replied
menacingly, 'Since you won't punish the boy, I will show
you in a few days how much I fear him.' Soon afterward
the boy who had insulted the spirit sat sleeping all alone
in the kitchen. In this condition the spirit seized him,
strangled him, tore the body into pieces, and put these
in pots on the fire. When the cook discovered this prank,
he cursed the spirit, so the next day Hüdeken spoiled all
the roasts that were on the spit by pouring the venom
and blood of toads over them. Desire for revenge called
forth new insults from the cook, after which the spirit
finally led him onto a non-existent phantom bridge and
plunged him into a deep moat. All the while Hüdeken
industriously made the rounds of the walls and towers of
the town the whole night long, compelling the sentinels
to constant watchfulness. A man who had an unfaithful
wife once said as a jest when he was about to take a trip,

'Hüdeken, good friend, I commend my wife to your care. Guard her carefully.' As soon as her husband was gone, the adulterous woman allowed one lover after another to visit her. But Hüdeken would not permit any of them to join her, throwing them all out of the bed onto the floor. When the husband returned from his journey, the spirit went a long distance to meet him and said to the returning traveler, 'I am very glad you are here, so that I shall be free of the burdensome duty you imposed on me. I have with indescribable difficulty preserved your wife from actual faithlessness. But I beg you never to entrust her to me again. I would rather keep watch over all the pigs in the whole of Saxony than over a woman who tries by trickery to get to the arms of her lovers.' "

For the sake of accuracy I must note that Hüdeken's head covering differs from the ordinary costume of the cobolds. They are usually dressed in gray and wear a little red cap. At least this is the way they look in Denmark, where they are said to be most numerous nowadays. I used to think the cobolds liked so much to live in Denmark because red groats were their favorite dish. But a young Danish poet, Mr. Andersen,[29] whom I had the pleasure of seeing here in Paris this summer, assured me very definitely that the *nissen,* as the cobolds are called in Denmark, like best porridge with butter. Once these cobolds have settled in a house, they are not readily inclined to leave it. They never come unannounced, however, and when they wish to live somewhere, they notify the master of the house of their intention in the following manner:—They carry into the house by night a large quantity of wood chips and scatter cattle dung in the milk cans. If the master of the house does not throw out the wood chips or if he and his family drink the befouled milk, then the cobolds remain permanently in his house.

29. Hans Christian Andersen, the well-known author of fairy tales.

For many a person this has become extremely unpleasant. A poor Jutlander at last became so annoyed at the companionship of such a cobold that he was even willing to give up his house. Loading all his possessions on a cart, he drove to the nearest village in order to settle there. On the way, however, when he happened to look back, he saw, peering out of one of the empty tubs, the little red-capped head of the cobold, who called to him affably, *"Wi flütten!"*[30]

I have perhaps lingered too long over these small demons, and it is time to return to the big ones. But all these stories illustrate the beliefs and the character of the German people. In past centuries these beliefs were just as powerful as the creed of the Church. When the learned Dr. Remigius had completed his large work on witchcraft, he believed himself to be so well informed on his subject that he fancied he could now practice sorcery himself; and, conscientious man that he was, he did not fail to denounce himself to the tribunals as a sorcerer, and in consequence of this denunciation he was burned for the crime.

These atrocities did not originate directly from the Christian Church, but indirectly they did, for the Church had so cunningly perverted the old Teutonic religion that it transformed the pantheistic cosmogony of the Germans into a pandemonic cosmogony and changed things previously held sacred by the people into hideous demonism. Yet human beings do not willingly relinquish what was precious and dear to them and their forefathers, and their affections secretly cling to it firmly even if it has been corrupted and distorted. Hence these perverted folk beliefs in Germany may perhaps outlive Christianity, which, unlike them, is not rooted in national tradition. At the time of the Reformation the belief in

30. Low German dialect meaning "We're moving,"

Catholic legends of saints disappeared very rapidly, but not so the belief in magic and sorcery.

Luther no longer believed in Catholic miracles, but he still believed in devils. His *Table Talks* are full of curious anecdotes about Satanic arts, cobolds, and witches. In periods of distress he himself often thought he was struggling with the devil in person. At the Wartburg, where he translated the New Testament, he was so much disturbed by the devil that he threw the inkstand at his head. Ever since then the devil has had a great dread of ink, but a still greater dread of printers' ink. In the *Table Talks* just mentioned many delightful anecdotes are told about the devil's cunning, and I can't resist giving one of them.

"Doctor Martin Luther related that one day some good comrades were sitting together in a tavern. Now among them was a wild, dissolute fellow who had said that if anyone were to offer him enough wine for a good drinking bout, he would sell him his soul for it.

"Not long afterward a man came into the room and, going to him, seated himself beside him, drank with him, and, among other things, said to him who had been so rash,

" 'Listen, didn't you say just now that if anyone gave you wine for a drinking bout you would sell him your soul for it?'

"Then the other said once more, 'Yes, and I'll do it. Just let me drink and carouse today to the limit and be happy.'

"The man, who was the devil, said, 'Yes,' and soon afterward stole away again. Now when the carouser had been merry all day and finally also became drunk, the above-mentioned man, the devil, returned, sat down beside him, and asked the other topers, 'Good gentlemen, what is your opinion? When someone buys a horse, don't the saddle and bridle belong to him too?' They were all frightened. At last the man said, 'Well, answer me straightway.' Then they admitted it was so and said, 'Yes, saddle and bridle belong to him too.' At this the devil seized the wild, rough fellow and carried him off through the roof so that no one knew where he had disappeared to."

Although I entertain the highest respect for our great master, Martin Luther, still I can't help thinking that he completely misunderstood the nature of Satan, who certainly does not look on the body with such contempt as is here indicated. Whatever evil one can say about the devil, no one could ever accuse him of being a spiritualist.

But Martin Luther misjudged the attitude of the pope and the Catholic Church even more than the attitude of the devil. In my strict impartiality I must defend the two, as well as the devil, against the far too zealous man. Indeed, if I were asked in all conscience, I would admit that Pope Leo X was actually much more sensible than Luther, and that Luther had absolutely no understanding of the fundamental principles of the Catholic Church. For Luther had not understood that the idea of Christianity, the annihilation of sensuality, was far too great a contradiction of human nature for it ever to have been completely realized in actual life. He had not understood that Catholicism was, so to speak, a concordat between God and the devil, that is, between spirit and matter, whereby the autocracy of the spirit is pronounced in theory but matter is enabled to exercise in practice all its nullified rights. Hence a clever system of concessions which the Church made for the benefit of the senses, though always in such a form as to stigmatize every act of sensuality and to preserve for the spirit its scornful usurpation of power. You may obey the tender affections of your heart and embrace a pretty girl, but you must confess that it was a disgraceful sin, and you must do penance for this sin. That this penance could be done with money was as advantageous for humanity as it was profitable for the Church. The Church permitted weregild to be paid, so to speak, for any pleasure of the flesh, and a tariff developed for every kind of sin. There were religious pedlars who offered throughout the land, in the name of the Roman Catholic Church, indulgence for every taxable sin, and one such was that Tetzel against whom Luther made his first attack. Our historians are of the opinion that this protest against the traffic in indulgences was an insignificant event and that only through Romish stubbornness had Luther, who at first merely objected passionately to an abuse within the Church, been driven to attack the entire authority of the Church at the very top of the hierarchy. This is simply an error; traffic in indulgences was not an abuse, it was a consequence of the whole ecclesiastical system, and in attacking it, Luther had attacked the Church itself, and the Church was forced to condemn him as a heretic. Leo X, the cultivated Florentine, the disciple of Politian,[31] the friend of Raphael, the Greek philosopher with the Pope's tiara conferred on him by the conclave, possibly because he was suffering from a disease by no means caused by Christian abstinence and at that time still very dangerous—how must this Leo de Medici have smiled at the poor, chaste, simple monk who imagined the Gospel to be the charter of Christendom and this charter to be a truth! He may not even have noticed what Luther wanted, being at that time much too occupied with the construction of St. Peter's, the cost of which was to be met by this very sale of indulgences, sin thus actually providing the money for the building of this church, which thereby became, as it were, a monument to sensual pleasure like that pyramid built by an Egyptian courtesan

31. Angelo Poliziano, Italian poet and scholar, friend of Lorenzo de Medici.

with the money she had earned from prostitution.[32] One could perhaps assert more truthfully of this house of God than of the cathedral of Cologne that it was built by the devil. This triumph of spiritualism, that sensualism itself was compelled to construct for it its most beautiful temple; that the means for glorifying the spirit were obtained from the many concessions to the flesh—this triumph was incomprehensible in the German North. For here, far more easily than beneath Italy's glowing sky, it was possible to practice a Christianity that makes as few concessions as possible to sensuality. We Northerners are more cold-blooded, and we didn't need as many indulgences for carnal sins as Leo, with fatherly concern, had sent to us. The climate makes the practice of Christian virtues easier for us, and on October 31, 1516,[33] when Luther nailed his theses against indulgences on the door of the Augustine Church, the moat around the city of Wittenberg was perhaps already frozen over, and one could go skating there, a very chilly pleasure and consequently not a sin.

In the above I have already used the words spiritualism and sensualism several times. These words, however, do not refer here, as they do with the French philosophers, to the two different sources of our knowledge; on the contrary, I use them, as is always clear of itself just from the sense of my argument, to designate those two different modes of thought of which the one attempts to glorify the spirit by striving to destroy matter, whereas the other seeks to vindicate the natural rights of matter against the domination of the spirit.

I must also call your particular attention to the above-mentioned beginnings of the Lutheran Reformation—beginnings that already reveal the whole spirit of it—

32. The pyramid of Rhodope.
33. The incorrect date is Heine's mistake.

since here in France people entertain the old misconceptions about the Reformation which Bossuet propagated in his *Histoire des variations*[34] and which make their influence felt even among present-day writers. The French understood only the negative side of the Reformation. They saw in it merely a battle against Catholicism and often believed that this battle had always been conducted on the other side of the Rhine for the same reasons as a similar struggle on this side, in France. But the motives were totally different and contradictory. The struggle against Catholicism in Germany was nothing but a war which spiritualism began when it realized that it possessed only the title of authority and ruled only *de jure*, while sensualism, by means of a fraud of long tradition, was exercising actual sovereignty and governing *de facto*. The dealers in indulgences were driven off, the pretty concubines of the priests were exchanged for frigid wives, the charming images of the Madonna were dashed to pieces, and here and there a Puritanism developed that was utterly hostile to all sensuous pleasures. The struggle against Catholicism in France in the seventeenth and eighteenth centuries, on the other hand, was a war which sensualism began when it saw that it ruled *de facto* and yet that every act of its sovereign authority was derided as illegitimate and denounced in the most cruel manner by a spiritualism which maintained that it reigned *de jure*. Instead of battling with chaste seriousness, as in Germany, in France they fought with obscene jokes, and instead of carrying on a theological discussion, as in Germany, they wrote funny satires. The object of these satires was usually to demonstrate the conflict that arises in a human being when he tries to be completely spiritual; hence the flowering of the most price-

34. Jacques Bénigne Bossuet (1627–1704) wrote a *Histoire des variations des Églises protestantes* (*History of the Variations of the Protestant Churches*) and other works in the hope of bringing Protestants back to the Catholic Church.

less stories of pious men involuntarily succumbing to their animal natures or even trying to preserve the appearance of sanctity and taking refuge in hypocrisy. The Queen of Navarre[35] had already portrayed such abuses in her *novelle*. The relationship between monks and women is her customary theme, and her aim is not merely to convulse with laughter but to shake monasticism to its foundations. Molière's *Tartuffe* is undoubtedly the most malicious gem of such comical polemic, for it is not directed simply against the Jesuitism of its age, but against Christianity itself, indeed, against the idea of Christianity, against spiritualism. Tartuffe's ostentatious display of fear of Dorine's naked bosom, the words:[36]

> *Le ciel défend, de vrai, certains contentements,*
> *Mais on trouve avec lui des accomodements—*

These things ridicule not only ordinary hypocrisy, but also the universal falsehood that necessarily arises from the impossibility of putting the Christian idea into practice, as well as the whole system of concessions that spiritualism was forced to make to sensualism. In fact, Jansenism[37] had far more reason than Jesuitism to feel insulted at the performance of *Tartuffe,* and Molière may still be as offensive to the Methodists of our day as he was to the Catholic devotees of his own time. It is just this which makes Molière so great, that, like Aristophanes and Cervantes, he ridicules not merely contemporary incidents, but the eternal absurdities, the original weak-

35. Margaret of Navarre (1492–1549) wrote a number of *novelle,* which were published under the title *Heptaméron des nouvelles.* Both title and content are reminiscent of Boccaccio's *Decameron.*

36. Tartuffe speaking to Elmire, Act IV, Scene 5: "Heaven forbids certain pleasures, it is true,/But you can come to some sort of compromise with it."

37. A Roman Catholic movement originating from the work of the Dutch theologian, Cornelius Jansen. Its purpose was a reform of Christian life by a return to greater personal holiness, hence the characteristic mystical trend in Jansenist writings.

nesses of mankind. Voltaire, who always attacked only things temporary and unessential, is in this respect inferior to Molière.

This kind of ridicule, however, especially the Voltairean, has fulfilled its mission in France, and any attempt to continue it would be both untimely and unwise. For if the last visible remains of Catholicism were to be destroyed, it might easily happen that the idea of Catholicism would take refuge in a new form, assume, so to speak, a new body, and, laying aside the very name of Christianity, might in this transformation harass us far more vexatiously than in its present shattered, ruined, and universally discredited form. Yes, there is a certain advantage in the fact that spiritualism is represented by a religion that has already lost the better part of its strength and by a priesthood that stands in direct opposition to all the enthusiasm for freedom that is characteristic of our time.

But why then is spiritualism so very repugnant to us? Is it something so bad? Not at all. Attar of roses is a precious thing, and a small flask of it is refreshing for those who must pass their days mournfully in the locked chambers of a harem. But nonetheless we don't want all the roses of this life to be crushed and trampled in order to obtain a few drops of attar of roses, however comforting their effect. We resemble rather the nightingales that delight in the roses themselves and are enraptured by their blushing blossoms as by their invisible fragrance.

I have stated above that it was actually spiritualism which attacked Catholicism in Germany. But this applies only to the beginning of the Reformation. As soon as spiritualism had made a breach in the ancient structure of the Church, sensualism rushed forth with all its long restrained passion, and Germany became the most tumultuous arena for the intoxication with liberty and sensual pleasures. The oppressed peasants had found in the new doctrine spiritual weapons with which to wage war against the aristocracy; the desire for such a war had existed for a century and a half. In Münster sensualism, in the person of John of Leiden,[38] ran naked through the streets and lay down with its twelve wives on that huge bedstead still to be seen today in the town hall there. Everywhere the portals of cloisters flew open, and nuns and monks rushed billing and cooing into each other's arms. Yes, the external history of that period consists almost entirely of sensual mutinies. We shall see later how few results remained; how spiritualism again suppressed those rioters; how it gradually made its authority secure in the North, but was mortally wounded by an enemy it had nurtured in its own bosom, namely, by philosophy. It is a very complicated history, difficult to unravel. For the Catholic party it is easy to stress at will the worst motives, and to hear them talk one might think the only motives were to legitimize the most brazen sensuality and to plunder Church property. To be sure, in order to gain the victory, spiritual interests must always form an alliance with material interests. But the devil had shuffled the cards so strangely that it is now impossible to state with certainty anything about the intentions.

The illustrious personages assembled in the Diet Hall at Worms in the year 1521 may well have borne in their hearts thoughts that were at odds with the words on their lips. There sat a young Emperor,[39] wrapping himself in his new crimson mantel with youthful delight in power and secretly rejoicing that the proud Roman who had so

38. A Dutch Anabaptist leader (c. 1509–1536). He moved to Münster, where in 1534 the Anabaptists took up arms and deposed the civil and religious authorities.

39. As an ardent Spanish Catholic, Charles V was strongly opposed to Luther and used his influence to have him condemned as a heretic.

often mistreated his imperial predecessors and had still not abandoned his arrogant pretensions had now received a very effectual reprimand. The representative of that Roman, on his part, felt a secret joy that dissension was arising among those Germans who, like drunken barbarians, had so often invaded and plundered beautiful Italy and were still threatening it with fresh invasions and plunderings. The secular princes were glad that they could appropriate the new doctrine and at the same time the old Church domains. The high prelates were already considering whether they might not marry their cooks and bequeath their electoral dominions, bishoprics, and abbeys to their male offspring. The deputies of the towns rejoiced at a further extension of their independence. Everyone had something to gain here and was secretly thinking of earthly advantages.

Yet there was *one* man there who, I am convinced, was not thinking of himself but only of the divine interests which he was to represent. This man was Martin Luther, the poor monk chosen by Providence to destroy the world empire of Rome, against which even the most powerful emperors and the boldest sages had struggled in vain. But Providence is well aware upon what shoulders it lays its burdens; here not only spiritual, but also physical strength was necessary. There was need of a body steeled from youth by monastic rigor and chastity to endure the hardships of such a duty. At that time our dear master was still thin and looked very pale, so that the ruddy, well-fed lords of the Imperial Diet gazed down almost with compassion at the wretched man in the black cowl. But he was nonetheless quite healthy, and his nerves were so steady that the glittering throng did not intimidate him in the least. Even his lungs must have been strong, for after having delivered his long defense, he had to repeat it in Latin because the Emperor did not understand High German.[40] I get angry whenever I think of it, for our dear master was standing beside an open window, exposed to the draft, while sweat dripped from his forehead. He was probably exhausted from speaking so long, and his mouth had probably gotten a little dry. The Duke of Brunswick certainly must have thought, "The man must be very thirsty"; at any rate, we read that he sent Martin Luther in his inn three jugs of the best Eimbeck beer. I shall never forget this noble deed of the House of Brunswick.

Just as people in France have very wrong ideas about the Reformation, so also about its heroes. The immediate cause of this lack of understanding is probably that Luther is not merely the greatest, but also the most *German,* man in our history, that in his character are united most magnificently all the virtues and the defects of the Germans, and that he represents in his own person the wonderful country of Germany. He also possessed qualities that we seldom find combined but usually encounter as hostile antitheses. He was both a dreamy mystic and a practical man of action. His thought not only had wings but also hands; he spoke and he acted. He was not merely the tongue but also the sword of his time. He was both a cold, scholastic quibbler and an inspired prophet intoxicated by the Divinity. After working laboriously all day at his dogmatic distinctions, in the evening he would take his flute and go out to watch the stars, and he would dissolve in melody and worship. The same man who could scold like a fishwife could also be as gentle as a tender girl. He was often as fierce as the storm that uproots the oak, and then again he was as mild as the

40. Not High German in the modern use of the phrase, meaning the standard German spoken by educated Germans. At that time there was as yet no standard German language used and understood by all German-speaking people. Latin was still the lingua franca in Germany and between European countries.

breeze that caresses the violets. He was full of the most awesome piety, full of self-sacrificing devotion to the Holy Spirit; he could lose himself completely in pure spirituality. And yet he was well acquainted with the glories of this earth and knew how to appreciate them, and from his lips came the famous saying: "Who loves not woman, wine, and song, remains a fool his whole life long." He was a complete man, I might say an absolute man, in whom matter and spirit are not separate. To call him a spiritualist, therefore, would be just as wrong as to call him a sensualist. How shall I say it?—he had something primordial, incomprehensible, miraculous in him such as we find in all men sent by Providence, something terrifyingly naive, something boorishly wise, something sublimely provincial, something invincibly demonic.

Luther's father was a miner in Mansfeld, and the boy was often with him in his subterranean workshop, where the mighty metals grow and the lively parent springs ripple, and his young heart had perhaps unconsciously absorbed the most mysterious forces of Nature or was even protected from harm by the magic powers of the mountain spirits. This may also be the reason why so much earthiness, so much of the dross of passion still clung to him, a reproach often enough made against him. But the reproach is unjust, for without that admixture of earthiness he could not have been a man of action. Pure spirits cannot act. Don't we learn from Jung Stilling's[41] *Theory of Ghosts* that spirits can in fact make themselves visible in color and distinct form, and can walk, run, dance, and bear themselves otherwise just like living human beings, but that they cannot move any material object, not even the smallest nightstand, from its place?

Praise be to Luther! Eternal praise for the dear man to

41. Johann Heinrich Jung, known as Jung-Stilling (1740–1817), a well-known Pietist and mystic who wrote a number of widely read works on ghosts.

whom we owe the salvation of our noblest possessions
and from whose benefactions we still live today! It little
becomes us to complain of the narrowness of his views.
The dwarf standing on the shoulders of the giant can of
course see farther than the giant himself, especially if he
puts on glasses, but the elevated perspective lacks the
noble emotion, the giant heart that we cannot lay claim
to. It becomes us still less to pronounce harsh judgment
on his failings; these failings have benefited us more than
the virtues of a thousand others. Neither the subtlety of
Erasmus nor the gentleness of Melancthon would ever
have gotten us as far as, occasionally, the godly brutality
of Brother Martin. Yes, the error in regard to the begin-
ning, as I mentioned before, has borne very precious
fruits, fruits from which all mankind derives strength.
From the day of the Diet, when Luther denied the au-
thority of the Pope and openly declared "that his doc-
trine could be refuted only by the word of the Bible itself
or on rational grounds," a new era began in Germany.
The chain with which Saint Boniface had bound the Ger-
man church to Rome was cut asunder. This church,
which had hitherto formed an integral part of the great
hierarchy, split into religious democracies. Religion it-
self underwent a change; the Indo-Gnostic element dis-
appeared, and we see the Judaic-Deistic element again
becoming prominent. Evangelical Christianity emerged.
Because the most essential claims of matter were not
merely respected but also legitimized, religion once
more became a truth. The priest became a human being
and took a wife and begot children, as God has ordained.
On the other hand, God himself became once more a
celestial bachelor without a family; the legitimacy of His
Son was disputed; the saints were deposed; the angels'
wings were clipped; the Blessed Virgin lost all claims to
the crown of heaven and was forbidden to perform mira-
cles. From this time on, especially once the natural

sciences began making such great progress, miracles
ceased altogether. Whether it be that the dear Lord is
annoyed when the physicists view His activities with such
distrust, or that He doesn't like to compete with Bosco,[42]
certain it is that even in most recent times, when religion
is in such very great danger, He has disdained to support
it by any sort of dazzling miracle. Perhaps from now on,
with all the new religions that He introduces on this
earth, He will have nothing more to do with any holy
tricks and will always demonstrate the truths of the new
doctrines by means of reason, which is indeed the most
sensible thing. At any rate, in the case of Saint-Simo-
nism,[43] the newest religion, not a single miracle has oc-
curred, except possibly that an old tailor's bill Saint-
Simon still owed when he died was paid in cash by his
disciples ten years after his death. I can still see the
worthy Père Olinde[44] rise enthusiastically in the Tait-
bout Hall, holding up before the astonished congrega-
tion the receipted tailor's bill. Young grocers were taken
aback at such evidence of the supernatural. The tailors,
however, immediately began to have faith!

Yet though we in Germany lost the old miracles be-
cause of Protestantism and much else that was poetic, we
gained various compensations. People became nobler
and more virtuous. Protestantism had the most benefi-
cial influence on that purity of manners and that strict-
ness in the performance of duties which we usually call
morality; indeed, in many communities Protestantism

42. Bartolommeo Bosco, a famous Italian magician who caused quite a stir
in Europe after 1814.

43. Count Claude Henri Saint-Simon (1760–1825) was a French social
philosopher whose ideas were taken up by his followers after his death and
developed into the movement known as Saint-Simonism. It aimed at social,
economic, and religious reform, and some aspects were to influence later
sociologists, e.g., Comte. What appealed to Heine was not so much social
reform as the so-called "emancipation of the senses."

44. One of the leaders among the Saint-Simonists.

took a direction that ultimately caused it to become completely identical with this morality, and the Gospel remains valid only as a beautiful parable. We now notice especially a refreshing change in the life of the clergy. The debauchery and vices of the monks vanished together with celibacy. Among the Protestant clergy it is not unusual to find extremely virtuous men, men for whom even the ancient Stoics would have had respect. One has to travel on foot, as a poor student, through North Germany[45] to discover how much virtue and, to give this word "virtue" a beautiful epithet, how much evangelical virtue is often to be found in a modest parsonage. How often, of a winter evening, I found there a hospitable welcome, I, a stranger bringing no recommendation other than that I was hungry and tired. When I had then eaten well and slept soundly and was about to go on my way the next morning, the old pastor would appear in his dressing gown to bestow his blessing on my journey—a thing that never brought me misfortune. And his kindly, garrulous wife would put into my pocket some slices of buttered bread, which were no less comforting to me. And at a distance, silent, stood the pastor's lovely daughters with their blushing cheeks and violet eyes; their shy ardor, remaining in my memory, kept my heart warm the whole winter day.

When Luther declared that his doctrine could be refuted only by the Bible itself or on grounds of reason, human reason was granted the right to explain the Scriptures, and reason was acknowledged as the supreme judge in all religious controversies. Thus there arose in Germany so-called spiritual freedom or, as it is also called, freedom of thought. Thought became a right, and the authority of reason became legitimate. To be sure,

45. North Germany was then predominantly Protestant, South Germany predominantly Catholic.

for several centuries already one had been able to think and speak with considerable freedom, and the scholastics disputed about matters which we can scarcely conceive even being mentioned in the Middle Ages. But this came about through the distinction made between theological and philosophical truth, a distinction whereby one explicitly protected himself against heresy; and such controversies took place only in the lecture rooms of the universities and in a Latin Gothically abstruse, which the people could not understand a word of, so that little harm to the Church was to be feared. Nevertheless, the Church had never really sanctioned such proceedings, and now and then it actually did burn a poor scholastic at the stake. Since Luther, however, no distinction was any longer made between theological and philosophical truth, and people disputed in the public marketplace and in the German language, without hesitation or fear. The princes who accepted the Reformation made this freedom of thought legitimate, and an important, internationally important result is German philosophy.

In fact, from the middle of the last century until the French invasion, nowhere, not even in Greece, could the human mind express itself so freely as in Germany. In Prussia especially an unrestrained freedom of thought prevailed. The Marquis of Brandenburg had understood that he, who could be a legitimate king of Prussia only because of Protestant principles, also had to preserve Protestant freedom of thought.

Since then, to be sure, things have changed, and the natural protector of our Protestant freedom of thought has come to an understanding with the Ultramontane party to suppress that liberty, and for this purpose he often uses the weapon first invented and directed against us by the Papacy: censorship.

Strange! We Germans are the strongest and cleverest of peoples. Princes of our race sit on all the thrones of

Europe, our Rothschilds dominate all the exchanges in the world, our scholars reign supreme in all the sciences, we invented gunpowder and the printing-press—and yet anyone who fires a pistol in our country pays a fine of three taler, and if we want to announce in the *Hamburger Korrespondent:* "My dear spouse has given birth to a daughter as beautiful as Liberty!," Dr. Hoffmann[46] immediately seizes his red pencil and crosses out "Liberty."

Can this continue much longer? I do not know. But I know that the question of the freedom of the press, at present so vehemently discussed in Germany, is significantly connected with the reflections outlined above, and I believe its solution is not difficult if one considers that freedom of the press is nothing other than a consequence of freedom of thought and hence a Protestant right. The Germans have already given their best blood for rights of this kind, and they may well be brought to the point of entering the lists once more.

The same remarks apply to the question of academic freedom, now so passionately rousing people in Germany. Since the supposed discovery that political agitation, that is, love of liberty, is most rampant in the universities, intimations come from all sides to the rulers that these institutions should be suppressed or at least converted into ordinary instructional institutions. Plans are now being concocted, and pros and cons discussed. But the avowed opponents of the universities do not seem to understand the fundamental principles of the question any better than the avowed defenders whom we have heard from so far. The former do not understand that youth everywhere and under all forms of disciplines will be enthusiastic about liberty and that, if the universities are suppressed, these enthusiastic young people will

46. The censor in Hamburg. Needless to say, this paragraph, the one before it, and the one following, did not appear in the early German editions of this work.

find expression all the more energetically elsewhere, perhaps in an alliance with the youth of the commercial and industrial classes. The defenders seek only to prove that with the closing of the universities the flower of German scholarship would be destroyed, that it is precisely academic freedom that is so valuable for these studies, providing the youth with such a fine opportunity to develop in many and varied ways, etc. As if a few Greek phrases or a few crude actions, more or less, had anything to do with the matter!

And what use would all science, study, or culture be to the princes if the sacred security of their thrones were endangered! They were heroic enough to sacrifice all those relative benefits for the one absolute good, their absolute sovereignty. For this has been entrusted to them by God, and where Heaven commands, all earthly considerations must yield.

There is also misunderstanding of the question on the part of the poor professors who appear publicly as representatives of the universities as well as on the part of the government officials who appear as opponents of them. It is only Catholic propaganda in Germany that comprehends the significance of the universities. These pious obscurantists are the most dangerous enemies of our university system, treacherously working against it with lies and deception, and whenever one of them makes a kindly pretence of saying a good word for the universities, some Jesuit intrigue is revealed. These cowardly hypocrites know very well what gains are at stake here. For with the destruction of the universities the Protestant Church will also fall, a Church that since the Reformation has had its roots so exclusively in the universities that the whole history of the Protestant Church for the last centuries consists almost entirely of theological disputes among the university scholars of Wittenberg, Leipzig, Tübingen, and Halle. The consistories are only a feeble reflection of the theological faculty; if the latter should disappear, they will lose all support and character and will sink into a desolate dependence on the ministries of the government or even on the police.

But let us not give these melancholy reflections too much space, especially since we still have to speak of the providential man who did such great things for the German people. I have shown above how through him we achieved the broadest freedom of thought. But this Martin Luther gave us not merely freedom of movement, but also the means to move, that is, he gave the spirit a body. He put the thought into words. He created the German language.

This he did by translating the Bible.

As a matter of fact, the Divine Author of this book seems to have known as well as anyone else that it is by no means unimportant who the translator is, and He himself chose His translator and bestowed on him the marvelous power to translate a dead language which was already buried, so to speak, into another language which had not yet come into existence.

We had the Vulgate, of course, which people understood, as well as the Septuagint, which by that time could also be understood. But the knowledge of Hebrew had completely died out in the Christian world. Only the Jews, who kept themselves hidden here and there in some corner or other of the earth, still preserved the traditions of this language. Like a ghost that watches over a treasure once entrusted to it, this massacred people, this ghost of a people, sat in their ghettos and guarded the Hebrew Bible. And into these hiding places of ill repute German scholars could be seen stealthily creeping down to unearth the treasure in order to acquire a knowledge of Hebrew. When the Catholic clergy noticed the danger thus threatening them, that the people might by this bypath arrive at the true Word of God and discover the Romish falsifications, they would have liked to suppress the Jewish tradition as well. They set to work to destroy all Hebrew books, and on the Rhine there began that book-persecution against which our admirable Dr. Reuchlin fought so gloriously.[47] The Cologne theologians who were active at that time, especially Hochstraaten, were by no means so stupid as Reuchlin's valiant fellow-combatant, the knight Ulrich von Hutten, portrays them in his *Litterae Obscurorum Virorum*.[48] Their aim was the suppression of the Hebrew language. When Reuchlin gained the victory, Luther was able to begin his work. In a letter he wrote to Reuchlin at this time, he seems already to sense the importance of the victory Reuchlin had won—a victory won by a man in a dependent and difficult position—whereas he, as an Augustinian monk, was completely independent. Very naively Luther says in this letter, *"Ego nihil timeo, quia nihil habeo."*[49]

But how Luther arrived at the language into which he translated the Bible is a mystery to me even now. The old Swabian dialect had totally disappeared with the chivalric literature of the Hohenstaufen imperial era. The old Saxon dialect, so-called Low German, was in use only in one portion of North Germany and, despite all attempts that were made, never proved to be suitable for literary

47. Johann Reuchlin (1455–1522), a German humanist, scholar of Greek and the best Hebrew scholar among the Christians of his day. Johann Pfefferkorn, a converted Jew, advocated the destruction of all Hebrew books. Emperor Maximilian requested Reuchlin's opinion on the matter, and when Reuchlin suggested that only Hebrew books calumniating Christianity should be suppressed, he was violently attacked by bigots and obscurantists.

48. The first word of the Latin title was *Epistolae*. *Letters of Obscure Men*, published anonymously, the first series in 1515–1517, was a witty and satirical defense of Reuchlin's liberal attitude and a humanistic attack upon the Church party. Hutten contributed a few letters, but Johann Jäger (Crotus Rubianus) seems to have had the chief share in the book.

49. "I fear nothing because I possess nothing." Heine's quotation is not quite accurate, but the sense is the same.

purposes. If Luther had taken for his translation of the Bible the language then spoken in present-day Saxony, Adelung[50] would have been right in maintaining that the Saxon dialect, particularly that of Meissen, was our actual High German, that is, our literary language. But this error has long since been refuted, and I must call attention to it here all the more pointedly because it is still current in France. Present-day Saxon was never a dialect of the German people, any more than Silesian was, for the latter, like the former, was in its origins strongly tinged with Slavic.[51] I therefore frankly confess that I do not know how the language we find in the Lutheran Bible originated. But I know that through this Bible, of which the newly invented press, the black art, hurled thousands of copies among the people, the Lutheran language spread in a few years over all of Germany and was elevated to the rank of the common written language. This written language still prevails in Germany and gives that politically and religiously dismembered country a literary unity. Such a priceless gain may well make amends to us for the fact that this language in its modern development lacks something of that inner warmth which we usually find in languages originating from a single dialect. The language in Luther's Bible, however, is far from lacking such inner warmth, and this ancient book is a perennial source of rejuvenation for our language. Every expression and every turn of phrase in the Lutheran Bible is German; an author can still use them without hesitation; and since this book is in the hands of the poorest people, they need no special scholarly instruction in order to be able to express themselves in a literary fashion.

50. Johann Adelung (1732–1806), well-known German grammarian.

51. Heine's comments on the origin of High German and of these dialects are wrong, but the history of their origins is too complicated to be summarized adequately in a footnote.

This circumstance will have most remarkable consequences when political revolution breaks out in Germany. Liberty will be able to speak everywhere, and its language will be Biblical.

Luther's original writings have also contributed to standardizing the German language. Owing to their polemical passionateness they penetrated deeply into the heart of his time. Their tone is not always delicate, but you can't make even a religious revolution out of orange blossoms. Coarseness must often be countered with coarseness. In the Bible Luther's language is always restrained within the bounds of a certain dignity out of reverence for the ever-present spirit of God. In his polemical writings, on the other hand, he abandons himself to a plebeian vulgarity that is often as repulsive as it is magnificent. His expressions and his images then resemble those gigantic stone figures which we find in Hindu or Egyptian temple grottos and whose gaudy coloring and fantastic ugliness both repel and attract us. Because of this baroque granite style the bold monk sometimes seems to us like a religious Danton, a preacher of the mountain, who, from its peak, hurls down his motley word-boulders onto the heads of his adversaries.

More remarkable and more significant than these prose works are Luther's poems, the songs that sprang from his heart in the midst of conflict and distress. Often they resemble a flower growing on a rocky cliff, often a moonbeam quivering across a tossing sea. Luther loved music; he even wrote a treatise on this art; and his lyrics are therefore unusually melodious. In this respect also he deserves the name: the Swan of Eisleben.[52] He was, however, anything but a gentle swan in many songs in which he rouses the courage of his followers and inspires himself with wildest ardor for the combat. That defiant

52. Luther was born in Eisleben, and he gave himself this name.

song with which he and his companions entered Worms[53] was a battle song. The old cathedral trembled at these novel tones, and the ravens started up in terror in their obscure nests in the towers. This song, the Marseillaise Hymn of the Reformation, has retained its power of inspiration right up to the present time.[54]

> A mighty fortress is our God,
> A bulwark never failing;
> Our helper He amid the flood
> Of mortal ills prevailing.
> For still our ancient foe
> Doth seek to work us woe;
> His craft and and power are great,
> And, armed with cruel hate,
> On earth is not his equal.
>
> Did we in our own strength confide,
> Our striving would be losing,
> Were not the right Man on our side,
> The Man of God's own choosing.
> Dost ask Who that may be?
> Christ Jesus, it is He,
> Lord Sabaoth His name,
> From age to age the same,
> And He must win the battle.
>
> And though this world, with devils filled,
> Should threaten to undo us,
> We will not fear, for God hath willed
> His truth to triumph through us.
> The Prince of Darkness grim,
> We tremble not for him;
> His rage we can endure,
> For lo! his doom is sure,
> One little word shall fell him.

53. It is doubtful that this song was written so early.
54. I use here the widely known translation by Frederick H. Hedge.

That word above all earthly powers,
No thanks to them, abideth;
The spirit and the gifts are ours
Through Him Who with us sideth.
Let goods and kindred go,
This mortal life also;
The body they may kill;
God's truth abideth still,
His kingdom is forever.

I have shown that we owe our beloved Doctor Martin Luther the intellectual freedom that modern literature needed for its development. I have shown how he also created for us the word, the language, in which this new literature could express itself. I have now only to add that he is himself the originator of this literature; that our belles-lettres in the real sense begin with Luther; that his religious songs prove to be the first significant manifestations of our modern literature and already reveal its distinctive character. Anyone wishing to speak about modern German literature must therefore commence with Luther and not, for instance, with a certain Nürnberg philistine by the name of Hans Sachs,[55] as has been done with deceitful malice by some writers of the Romantic School. Hans Sachs, the troubadour of the honorable guild of shoemakers, whose Meistergesang was only a silly parody of the earlier Minnelieder[56] and whose plays were mere clumsy travesties of the old mystery plays,— this pedantic buffoon who painfully imitates the natural naivete of the Middle Ages can perhaps be regarded as

55. See above, p. 206, note 135. Heine is rather hard on Sachs here.

56. The German Minnesang, cultivated from about the middle of the twelfth century until into the fourteenth century, was, broadly speaking, the lyric of courtly love belonging to the feudal tradition. Hans Sachs' poems may have followed the form of the Minnesang, but the content derives from a different world. His poetry is not chivalric love poetry, but religious, didactic, and, as Heine said, philistine or middle-class.

the last poet of the older period but certainly not as the first poet of the modern age. No further proof will be needed for this than to discuss in specific terms the contrast between our modern literature and earlier literature.

If we examine the German literature that flourished before Luther, we find:

1) Its material, its content, is, like the life of the Middle Ages itself, a combination of two heterogeneous elements which wrestled so mightily with each other in a long duel that they finally blended together, namely, Germanic national character and Hindu-Gnostic, so-called Catholic, Christianity.

2) The treatment of the subject matter, or rather the spirit of the treatment, in this earlier literature is romantic. The same term, "romantic," is also applied incorrectly to the content of that literature and to all the aspects of the Middle Ages that originated through the blending of the two elements just mentioned, Germanic national character and Catholic Christianity. For just as certain poets of the Middle Ages treated Greek history and mythology in a fashion truly romantic, so also medieval customs and legends can be presented in classical form. The terms "classical" and "romantic" thus apply only to the spirit of the treatment.[57] The treatment is classical when the form of what is represented is completely identical with the idea of what is to be represented, as is the case in the art works of the Greeks, in which therefore the greatest harmony between form and idea can be found in this identity. The treatment is romantic when the form does not reveal the idea by means of identity but makes it possible by means of a parable to divine this idea. I prefer to use here the word "para-

57. The following ideas can also be found in *The Romantic School*, pp. 138 f.

ble" rather than the word "symbol." Greek mythology possessed an array of deities, each one of which, despite all identity of form and idea, could nevertheless be given a symbolic meaning. But in this Greek religion only the form of the gods was fixed; everything else, their lives and their activities, was left to the fancy of the poets to treat as they pleased. In the Christian religion, however, there are no such definite figures but rather definite facts, definite sacred events and deeds to which the creative spirit of man could lend a parabolic significance. It has been said that Homer invented the Greek gods. This is not true; they already existed in definite outlines, but he invented their biographies. The artists of the Middle Ages, however, never dared to invent the slightest detail in the historical portion of their religion; the fall of man, the incarnation, the baptism, the crucifixion, and the like, were unimpeachable facts which could not be reshaped, but to which the creative spirit of man could lend a parabolic significance. All the arts of the Middle Ages were actually treated in this parabolic spirit, and their treatment is romantic. Hence the mystical universality in the poetry of the Middle Ages; the figures are so shadowy, what they do is so vague, everything about them has a twilight air as if illuminated only fitfully by moonlight. The idea is hinted at in the form only as a puzzle, and we see here a vague form such as was quite appropriate for a spiritualistic literature. There is no obvious harmony between form and idea as with the Greeks; on the contrary, the idea often transcends the given form, which strives despairingly to attain the same level, and we see then bizarre, fantastic sublimity. Sometimes the form completely outgrows the idea, a trivial little thought is dragged along in a colossal form, and we see grotesque farce. Almost always we find deformity.

3) The universal character of this literature was that in all its productions there was manifested the firm, secure

faith which then prevailed in all secular and spiritual matters. All opinions of the period were based on authorities; the poet walked with the confidence of a mule along the abysses of doubt, and in his works prevail an intrepid serenity, a blissful trust, such as was impossible later when the chief of those authorities, namely the authority of the Pope, was overthrown and all other authorities fell in its wake. All literary works of the Middle Ages thus have the same character, as if not an individual person but the whole people had created them; they are objective, epic, and naive.

In the literature, however, which burst into flower under Luther's influence we find just the opposite:

1) Its material, the content that is to be dealt with, is the struggle between the interests and views of the Reformation and the old order of things. To the new spirit of the age the mongrel creed that originated, as mentioned, from two elements, Germanic national character and Hindu-Gnostic Christianity, was completely repugnant. The latter almost seemed to it to be heathen idolatry, which must be replaced by the true religion of the Judaic-Deistic gospel. A new order of things takes shape; the intellect makes inventions that further the success of material things; through the prospering of industry and through philosophy, spiritualism is discredited in public opinion; the third estate emerges; the Revolution is already rumbling in hearts and heads; and what the age feels and thinks and needs and wants is expressed, and this is the content of modern literature.

2) The spirit of the treatment is no longer romantic, but classical. Due to the revival of ancient literature, a joyful enthusiasm for Greek and Roman writers spread over all of Europe, and scholars, the only people then writing, tried to appropriate the spirit of classical antiquity or at least to imitate classical art forms in their writings. Though, unlike the Greeks, they failed to

achieve harmony between form and idea, they clung all the more rigidly to the externals of the Greek treatment. They distinguished, according to Greek precepts, among the various genres, refrained from any romantic extravagance, and in this respect we call them classical.

3) The universal characteristic of modern literature is the predominance of individuality and scepticism. The authorities have collapsed; reason alone is now the only lamp man has, and his conscience is his only staff in the dark labyrinths of this life. Man now stands alone face to face with his Creator and sings his song to Him. Hence this literature begins with religious songs. But even later, when literature becomes secular, there prevails in it the most intense self-awareness, the sense of personality. Poetry is now no longer objective, epic, and naive, but subjective, lyric, and reflective.

BOOK TWO

In the previous book we dealt with the great religious revolution represented in Germany by Martin Luther. Now we must speak of the philosophical revolution that arose out of it and indeed is nothing else but the last consequence of Protestantism.

But before relating how the outbreak of this revolution was caused by Immanuel Kant, it is necessary to mention the philosophical developments in other countries, the significance of Spinoza, the fate of Leibnitz's philosophy, the mutual relations, discords, and dissensions between this philosophy and religion, and the like. We shall, however, constantly keep in view those philosophical questions to which we attribute a social significance and towards whose solution philosophy competes with religion.

We shall deal first with the question of the nature of God. "God is the beginning and the end of all wisdom" say the believers in their humility, and the philosopher, in all the pride of his knowledge, is compelled to agree with this pious axiom.

Not Bacon,[58] as we are usually taught, but René Descartes[59] is the father of modern philosophy, and we shall demonstrate very clearly to what degree German philosophy is derived from him.

René Descartes is a Frenchman, and here too the glory of the initiative belongs to great France. But great France, the noisy, lively, loquacious land of the French, has never been a suitable soil for philosophy, which perhaps will never flourish there, and René Descartes felt this and went to Holland, the peaceful, silent land of *trekschuiten*[60] and Dutchmen, and there he wrote his philosophical works. Only there could he free his spirit from traditional formalism and construct a complete system of philosophy from pure thought that is borrowed neither from faith nor from empiricism—a method since then required of any genuine philosophy. Only there could he plunge so deeply into the abysses of thought that he chanced upon it in the ultimate grounds of self-awareness and was able to substantiate self-awareness by means of thought itself in the world-famed axiom, *Cogito, ergo sum.*[61]

But also perhaps nowhere else than in Holland could Descartes have dared to teach a philosophy that conflicted quite obviously with all traditions of the past. To him is due the honor of having established the autonomy of philosophy; it no longer needed to beg from theology

58. Francis Bacon (1561–1626), founder of empiricism.
59. French philosopher of the seventeenth century (1596–1650) who took issue with the belief in traditionally accepted knowledge and developed a philosophical system based on the cognitive process, thus breaking with religious tradition.
60. The small boats on canals in Holland pulled along by men or horses.
61. I think, therefore I exist.

permission to think; it could now take its place beside the latter as an independent science. I do not say in opposition to the latter, for at that time it was an acknowledged principle that the truths at which we arrive through philosophy are ultimately the same as those transmitted by religion. The scholastics, as I have already remarked, had, on the contrary, not only conceded to religion the supremacy over philosophy, but had also declared philosophy to be a worthless pastime, a vain haggling, the instant it came into conflict with the dogmas of religion. The scholastics were concerned only with expressing their thoughts, no matter under what conditions. They said, "One times one is one," and proved it; but they added with a smile, "This is another error of human reason, which always errs when it comes into conflict with the decisions of the Ecumenical Councils; 'One times one is three,' and this is the real truth, long since revealed to us in the name of the Father, the Son, and the Holy Ghost!" In private the scholastics formed a philosophical opposition to the Church. But publicly they feigned the greatest submissiveness, in many instances they even fought for the Church, and during processions they paraded among its followers, somewhat as the French deputies of the opposition paraded at the ceremonies of the Restoration. The comedy of the scholastics lasted more than six centuries and became more and more trivial. In destroying scholasticism Descartes likewise destroyed the superannuated opposition of the Middle Ages. The old brooms had worn out from long sweeping, too much rubbish was sticking to them, and the new age required new brooms. After every revolution the former opposition must abdicate; otherwise great follies are committed. We have seen this ourselves. In the times I am writing about, it was not so much the Catholic Church as her old adversaries, the rear-guard of the scholastics, who first took up arms against the Cartesian philosophy. Not until 1663 did the Pope ban this philosophy.

I can assume that Frenchmen have an adequate and sufficient acquaintance with the philosophy of their great countryman, and it is not necessary for me to show here how the most contradictory doctrines could borrow from it material they needed. I refer to Idealism and Materialism.

Since these two doctrines, especially in France, are called Spiritualism and Sensualism, and since I use these latter terms in a different fashion, I shall have to discuss in more detail the above-mentioned expressions to avoid confusion of ideas.

From the earliest times there have been two opposing views regarding the nature of human thought, that is, regarding the ultimate sources of intellectual cognition, regarding the origin of ideas. Some maintain that we acquire ideas only from without, that our mind is only an empty receptacle in which the impressions gulped down by the senses are digested, much as the foods we eat are digested in the stomach. To use a better image, these persons view our mind as a *tabula rasa,* on which experience subsequently writes something new every day according to definite principles of composition.

Others, holding the opposite view, maintain that ideas are innate in man, that the human mind is the original seat of ideas, and that the external world, experience, and the mediating senses only lead us to the knowledge of what was already present in the mind, only awaken there the dormant ideas.

The first view has been called sensualism, sometimes also empiricism; the other was called spiritualism, sometimes also rationalism. From these terms, however, misunderstandings can easily result, since we have for some time been using these names, as I mentioned in the previous book, to designate those two social systems which make themselves felt in every manifestation of existence. Hence we shall assign the name spiritualism to that outrageous arrogance of the human spirit which, striving for exclusive self-glorification, attempts to trample matter under foot, or at least to vilify it. And we give the name sensualism to that opposition which, in passionate revolt, aims at rehabilitating matter and vindicates the rights of the senses without denying the rights of the spirit or even its supremacy. To the philosophical opinions concerning the nature of knowledge, however, I prefer to give the names idealism and materialism; and I shall designate with the former the theory of innate ideas, of ideas *a priori,* and with the second term I shall designate the theory of cognition through experience, through the senses, the theory of ideas *a posteriori.*

It is significant that the idealistic side of Cartesian philosophy was never a success in France. Several famous Jansenists pursued this direction for a time, but they soon went astray into Christian spiritualism. It may have been this circumstance that brought discredit on idealism in France. Nations have an instinctive presentiment of what they need in order to fulfill their mission. The French were already on the way toward that political revolution which did not break out until the end of the eighteenth century and for which they needed an axe and a philosophy equally cold and sharp and materialistic. Christian spiritualism stood as a fellow-combatant in the ranks of their enemies; hence sensualism became their natural ally. French sensualists being ordinarily materialists, the erroneous idea arose that sensualism was but a product of materialism. No, sensualism can just as well claim to be the result of pantheism, and as such it appears beautiful and splendid. It is by no means our intention, however, to deny French materialism its merits. French materialism was a good antidote against the evil of the past, a desperate remedy for a desperate disease, mercury[62] for an infected people. French philosophers chose John Locke as their master. He was the saviour they needed. His *Essay Concerning Human Understanding* became their gospel, and they swore by it. John Locke had gone to school to Descartes and from him had learned everything that an Englishman can learn—mechanics, the analytical method, deduction, synthesizing, and arithmetic. There was only one thing he could not comprehend, namely, innate ideas. He therefore perfected the doctrine that we acquire our knowledge from without, by means of experience. He turned the human mind into a kind of calculating machine; the whole human being became an English machine. The same thing applies to man as constructed by Locke's disciples, though they tried to distinguish themselves from one another by the use of different terminology. They were all afraid of the ultimate inferences of their leading principle, and the disciple of Condillac[63] was horrified at being put into the same category with a Helvetius,[64] or, worse, with a Holbach,[65] or perhaps, worst of all, with a La Metrie.[66] Yet such a classification is inevitable, and I can therefore characterize the French philosophers of the eighteenth century and their present-day successors, one and all, as materialists. *L'homme machine* is the most

62. Heine is probably referring to mercury chloride, one form of which was and is used as an anti-syphilitic.

63. Particularly in his *Traité des sensations*, Étienne Bonnot de Condillac (1715–1780) demonstrated that sensuous perception is the only source of knowledge and that thinking is only the result of perceptions derived from sensory experience.

64. Claude Adrien Helvétius (1715–1771) dealt primarily with ethical questions. Self-interest was for him the only reliable guide for action, though a certain training was necessary to bring it into conformity with the common good.

65. Paul Henri Thiry, baron d'Holbach (1723–1789), was a materialistic philosopher whose main work was his *Système de la nature*.

66. Julien Offray de La Mettrie (1709–1751) was a radical materialist and atheist. His best-known work was *L'homme machine*.

consistent product of French philosophy; even the title reveals it as the last word on the subject of this whole concept of the universe.

Most of these materialists were also adherents of deism, for a machine presupposes a mechanic, and it is part of the highest perfection of such a machine to recognize and appreciate the technical skills of such an artificer, as seen in its own construction or in his other works.

Materialism has fulfilled its mission in France. It is perhaps now completing the same task in England, and the revolutionary factions there, especially the Benthamites,[67] the preachers of utility, are based on Locke. These latter are men of powerful intellect who have grasped the right lever for setting John Bull in motion. John Bull is a born materialist, and his Christian spiritualism is for the most part traditional hypocrisy or even just material dullness—his flesh is resigned because the spirit does not come to its aid. In Germany it is different, and the German revolutionaries are mistaken if they think that a materialistic philosophy is advantageous for their aims. Indeed, no general revolution is possible there at all unless its principles have been deduced from a more rational, more religious, and more German philosophy which has come to prevail through their power. What philosophy is this? We shall discuss it later with all candor. I say "with all candor," for I am counting on Germans reading these pages too.

Germany has always shown a dislike for materialism and hence became for a century and a half the true arena of idealism. The Germans also went to the school of Descartes, and the name of his great disciple was Gottfried Wilhelm Leibnitz. As Locke followed the materialistic direction of his master, Leibnitz followed the idealistic direction. In Leibnitz we find the doctrine of innate

67. Jeremy Bentham (1748–1832) was the founder of Utilitarianism.

ideas in its most decisive form. In his *Nouveaux essays sur l'entendement humain*[68] he opposed Locke. With Leibnitz there sprang up among the Germans a great passion for philosophical studies. He awakened their minds and directed them into new paths. Because of the inherent kindliness, the religious feeling that animated his writings, even his opponents became reconciled in some measure to their boldness, and their effect was enormous. The boldness of this thinker is shown particularly in his theory of monads, one of the most remarkable hypotheses that ever originated from the mind of a philosopher. It is also the best thing he produced, for in it there already dawns the perception of the most important laws that have been accepted by modern philosophy. The theory of monads was perhaps only a crude formulation of these laws, which have now been expressed in better formulas by the philosophers of nature. Actually, instead of the word "law," I ought to say here simply "formula," for Newton is quite right when he remarks that what we call laws of nature does not really exist, that these are only formulas which help our power of comprehension to explain a succession of phenomena in nature. Of all the writings of Leibnitz', the *Theodicy* is the one that has been most discussed in Germany. Yet it is his weakest work. This book, like several other writings in which Leibnitz' religious spirit finds expression, exposed him to many a malicious rumor and much cruel misunderstanding. His enemies accused him of maudlin silliness; his friends, defending him, made him out to be a sly hypocrite. Leibnitz' character remained a subject of controversy among us for a long time. The fairest critics could not absolve him from the accusation of duplicity. The freethinkers and men of enlightenment reviled him most. How could they forgive a philosopher for having

68. *New Essays Concerning Human Understanding.*

defended the Trinity, eternal punishment in Hell, and, worst of all, the divinity of Christ! Their tolerance did not go as far as that. But Leibnitz was neither a fool nor a knave, and from his serene heights he could very well defend the whole of Christianity. I say the whole of Christianity, for he defended it against semi-Christianity. He demonstrated the consistency of the orthodox as opposed to the halfheartedness of their adversaries. More than this he never intended. And thus he stood at that neutral point of equilibrium where the most diverse systems seem to be merely different sides of the same truth. Mr. Schelling later also recognized this neutral point, and Hegel established it scientifically as a system of systems. In the same manner Leibnitz tried to reconcile Plato and Aristotle. Even in subsequent times this attempt has been made often enough in Germany. Has the problem been solved?

No, certainly not! For this problem is nothing less than a settlement of the struggle between idealism and materialism. Plato is an idealist through and through and recognizes only inborn or rather co-born ideas; man brings ideas with him into the world, and when he becomes conscious of them, they seem to him like recollections of a former state of existence. Hence the vagueness and mysticism of Plato; his recollections are sometimes more clear, sometimes less. With Aristotle, however, everything is clear, intelligible, certain; for his perceptions are not revelations connected with any preexistence; he draws everything from experience and can classify everything with the utmost precision. He therefore remains a model for all empiricists, and they cannot thank God enough that He made him Alexander's teacher, that due to his lord's conquests Aristotle found so many opportunities for the advancement of science, and that his victorious pupil gave him so many thousand talents of gold for zoological research.[69] The old master used this money conscientiously, and with it was able to dissect a respectable number of mammals and to stuff a like number of birds, and in so doing made very important observations. But the great beast which he had right before his eyes, which he had reared himself, and which was far more remarkable than the whole world-menagerie of that time, he overlooked, alas, and failed to investigate. He has indeed left us totally without information about the nature of that youthful king whose life and deeds we still marvel at as wonder and enigma. Who was Alexander? What did he want? Was he a madman or a god? To this day we do not know. But Aristotle gives us all the more complete information about Babylonian monkeys, Indian parrots, and Greek tragedies, the last of which he also dissected.[70]

Plato and Aristotle! These are not merely the two systems but also the representatives of two different types of human beings who have opposed each other more or less hostilely in many different guises since time immemorial. Especially throughout the entire Middle Ages and right up to the present day this conflict raged, and it is the most essential part of the history of the Christian church. The discussion is always about Plato and Aristotle, though under other names. Visionary, mystical, Platonic natures reveal from the depths of their being Christian ideas and the corresponding symbols. Practical, orderly, Aristotelian natures construct out of these ideas and symbols a solid system, a dogma, and a cult. The Church ultimately embraces both natures, the one group usually entrenching itself within the clergy, the other within monasticism, yet feuding with each other incessantly. The same struggle is evident in the Protes-

69. Aristotle wrote a *History of Animals.*
70. In his *Poetics.*

tant church, the conflict between Pietists and Orthodox, who correspond after a fashion to the Catholic mystics and dogmatists. The Protestant Pietists are mystics without imagination, and the orthodox Protestants are dogmatists without intelligence.

We find these two Protestant groups engaged in bitter combat at the time of Leibnitz, whose philosophy intervened later when Christian Wolff made himself master of it, adapted it to contemporary needs, and, most important of all, lectured on it in German.[71] Before giving more information about this pupil of Leibnitz, however, about the effects of his endeavors, and about the subsequent fate of Lutheranism, we must mention the providential man who, at the same time as Locke and Leibnitz, had educated himself in the school of Descartes, had for a long time been viewed only with scorn and hatred, and who nevertheless today is rising to exclusive supremacy in the world of intellect.

I am speaking about Benedict Spinoza.

One great genius shapes himself by means of another, less through assimilation than through friction. One diamond polishes the other. Thus Descartes' philosophy did not originate, but merely furthered, Spinoza's. Hence we find in the pupil, first of all, the method of the master; this is a great gain. We also find in Spinoza, as in Descartes, a method of demonstration borrowed from mathematics. This is a great defect. The mathematical form gives Spinoza's work a harsh exterior. But this is like the hard shell of the almond; the kernel is all the more delightful. On reading Spinoza we are seized by an emotion similar to that which we feel at the sight of great Nature in her most animated composure. A forest of heaven-aspiring thoughts whose blossoming treetops are tossing like waves, while the immovable trunks are

71. Until 1688 all professors at German universities lectured in Latin.

rooted in the eternal earth. There is a certain mysterious aura about Spinoza's writings. The air of the future seems to flow over us. Perhaps the spirit of the Hebrew prophets still hovered over their late-born descendant. There is, withal, a seriousness in him, a confident pride, a solemn dignity of thought, which also seem to be a part of his inheritance; for Spinoza belonged to one of those martyr families exiled from Spain by the most Catholic of kings. Added to this is the patience of the Hollander, which was always revealed in the life of the man as well as in his writings.

It is a fact that Spinoza's life was beyond reproach and pure and spotless as the life of his divine cousin, Jesus Christ. Like Him, he too suffered for his teachings; like Him he wore the crown of thorns. Wherever a great mind expresses its thought, *there* is Golgotha.

Dear reader, if you go to Amsterdam sometime, have a guide show you the Spanish synagogue. It is a beautiful building. The roof rests on four colossal pillars, and in the center stands the pulpit from which excommunication was pronounced on the man who despised the Mosaic law, the hidalgo Don Benedict de Spinoza. On such an occasion a ram's horn called the shophar was blown. There must be something very frightening about this horn. For, as I once read in the life of Salomon Maimon,[72] when the rabbi of Altona once tried to lead him, the pupil of Kant, back again to the old faith, and when he stubbornly persisted in his philosophical heresies, the rabbi resorted to threats, showed him the shophar, and asked sinisterly, "Do you know what this is?" But when Kant's pupil replied with calm indifference, "It is a ram's horn," the rabbi fell flat on his back from horror.

72. A Jewish philosopher (1754-1800) and pupil of Kant, who, however, differed with his teacher on some important issues.

The excommunication of Spinoza was accompanied by the sound of this horn; he was solemnly expelled from the communion of Israel and declared unworthy henceforth of bearing the name of Jew. His Christian enemies were magnanimous enough to leave him the name. The Jews, however, the Swiss guard of deism, were inexorable, and the place is still pointed out in front of the Spanish synagogue in Amsterdam where they once tried to stab Spinoza with their long daggers.

I could not refrain from calling particular attention to these personal misfortunes of the man. It was not merely schooling that shaped him, but life as well. In this he is different from most philosophers, and in his writings we recognize the indirect influence of his own life. Theology was for him not simply a branch of knowledge. Nor was politics. This too he became acquainted with through experience. His fiancée's father was hung in the Netherlands for political offences. And nowhere in the world are people so badly hung as in the Netherlands. You have no idea what innumerable preparations and ceremonies are connected with the procedure. The delinquent dies of boredom while these are going on, and the spectator has plenty of time for reflection. So I am convinced that Benedict Spinoza reflected a great deal on the execution of old Van Ende, and just as he had previously learned to understand religion by its daggers, so now he learned to understand politics by its ropes. His *Tractatus politicus* gives evidence of this.

My aim is merely to point out how the philosophers are related to each other, and whether more or less closely, and I shall show only the degrees of relationship and the genealogy. The philosophy of Spinoza, the third son of René Descartes, as he teaches it in his main work, the *Ethics,* is as remote from the materialism of his brother Locke as from the idealism of his brother Leibnitz. Spinoza does not torment himself with analytical inquiry into the ultimate grounds of our knowledge. He gives us his grand synthesis, his explanation of the Deity.

Benedict Spinoza teaches: there is only one substance, and that is God. This one substance is infinite; it is absolute. All finite substances originate from it, are contained in it, arise out of it, are immersed in it; they have only a relative, transient, accidental existence. The absolute substance is revealed to us both in the form of infinite thought and in the form of infinite dimension. These two, infinite thought and infinite dimension, are the two attributes of the absolute substance. We recognize only these two attributes, but it is possible that God, the absolute substance, has other attributes that we do not know. *"Non dico, me deum omnino cognoscere, sed me quaedam ejus attributa, non autem omnia, neque maximam intelligere partem."*[73]

Only stupidity and malice could attach to this doctrine the epithet "atheistic." No one has ever spoken more sublimely of the Deity than Spinoza. Instead of saying that he denied God, one might say that he denied man. All finite things are to him only *modi*[74] of the infinite substance. All finite things are contained in God; the human mind is but a light-ray of infinite thought; the human body is but a particle of the infinite dimension. God is the infinite cause of both, of spirits and of bodies, *natura naturans.*[75]

In a letter to Madame du Devant[76] Voltaire professes himself quite delighted at a sally of this lady's, who had said that everything man can know absolutely nothing about is certainly of such a nature that knowledge about it would be of no use to him. I would like to apply this

73. I do not say that I know God completely, but that I understand certain of his attributes, though not all and certainly not the greatest part of them.

74. Manifestations.

75. As Spinoza uses the phrase, it means nature in its unity, as the creative principle which determines the multiplicity of its modes or manifestations.

76. Marquise du Deffand, a French woman of letters whose salon was frequented by many important writers and scholars.

remark to the passage from Spinoza just quoted in his own words, according to which not only the two knowable attributes, thought and dimension, pertain to the Deity, but also possibly other attributes that we cannot know. What we cannot know has no value for us, at least no value from a social point of view, where the important thing is to bring to realization as a corporeal phenomenon what the intellect perceives. In our explanation of the nature of God, therefore, we refer only to these two knowable attributes. And besides, everything we call an attribute of God is ultimately but a different form of our intuition, and these different forms are identical in the absolute substance. Thought is, after all, only invisible dimension, and dimension is only visible thought. Here we come to the main point of the German Philosophy of Identity,[77] which in essence differs in no way from the doctrine of Spinoza. No matter how violently Mr. Schelling may protest that his philosophy is different from Spinozism, that it is rather "a living amalgam of the ideal and the real," that it differs from Spinozism "as the perfection of Greek sculpture differs from the rigid Egyptian originals," nevertheless I must declare most emphatically that in his earlier period, when he was still a philosopher, Mr. Schelling did not differ in the slightest from Spinoza. He merely arrived at the same philosophy by a different path. I shall illustrate this later when I tell how Kant entered on a new path, how Fichte followed him, how Mr. Schelling in turn continued in Fichte's footsteps and, wandering lost in the forest darkness of nature philosophy, finally found himself face to face with the great figure of Spinoza.

The only merit of modern nature philosophy is that it demonstrated most ingeniously the eternal parallelism

77. According to this philosophy, represented here by Schelling, spiritual and corporeal phenomena are identical, two aspects of the entity of being. Spinoza calls this entity "the substance," Schelling calls it "the absolute."

between spirit and matter. I say spirit and matter, and I use these terms as equivalents for what Spinoza calls thought and dimension. These terms are also, to some extent, synonymous with what our nature philosophers call spirit and nature or the ideal and the real.

In what follows I shall designate by the name Pantheism not so much Spinoza's system as his way of viewing things. Pantheism, like Deism, assumes the unity of God. But the god of the pantheist is in the world itself, not by permeating it with his divinity in the manner which St. Augustine tried to illustrate by comparing God to a large lake and the world to a large sponge lying in the middle of it and absorbing the Deity—no, the world is not merely God-imbued, God-impregnated; it is identical with God. "God," called by Spinoza the one and only substance, and by German philosophers the absolute, "is everything that exists"; he is matter as well as spirit, both are equally divine, and whoever insults the sanctity of matter is just as sinful as he who sins against the Holy Ghost.

The god of the pantheist is thus distinguished from the god of the deist by the fact that he is in the world itself, whereas the latter is completely outside of it or, what is the same thing, is above it. The god of the deist rules the world from above as an establishment separate from him. The deists differ among themselves only with regard to the type of rule. The Hebrews conceive of God as a thundering tyrant; the Christians, as a loving father; the disciples of Rousseau, the whole Geneva school, conceive of him as a knowledgeable artist, who constructed the world somewhat as their fathers constructed watches, and as connoisseurs they admire the work and praise the master high above.

To the deist, who assumes an extra-mundane or supra-mundane god, only the spirit is holy, since he views it, so to speak, as the divine breath which the creator breathed into the human body, the work of his hands kneaded out of clay. Hence the Jews looked on the body as something inferior, as a wretched cloak for the *ruach hakodasch*, the holy breath, the spirit, and only to the latter did they award their attention, their reverence, their worship. They therefore became in a very special sense *the* people of the spirit, chaste, temperate, serious, abstract, obstinate, capable of martyrdom; and their sublimest flower is Jesus Christ. He is, in the true sense of the word, spirit incarnate, and it is a beautiful legend and profoundly significant, that He was brought into the world by an immaculate virgin, conceived only by the spirit.

But if the Jews regarded the body merely with contempt, the Christians went much farther on this road and regarded it as something objectionable, something bad, as evil itself. Thus, several centuries after the birth of Christ, we see a religion arise that will forever amaze mankind and will cow the latest generations into the most terrified admiration. Yes, it is a great, a holy religion, full of infinite bliss, a religion that sought to conquer for the spirit the most absolute domination on earth. But this religion was all too sublime, all too pure, all too good for this earth, where the idea of it could only be proclaimed in theory, but could never be realized in practice. The attempt to realize this idea has produced countless manifestations in history, and poets of all times will celebrate them in song and tale for ages to come. As we shall see in the end, however, the attempt to realize the idea of Christianity failed miserably, and this unfortunate attempt has cost mankind incalculable sacrifices, one distressing result of them being the present social disorder in all of Europe. If, as many believe, humanity is still in its adolescence, then Christianity was, so to speak, among its most extravagant illusions of youth, which do far more credit to its heart than to its intelligence. Christianity relinquished temporal things to the hands of Caesar and his Jewish chamberlains[78] and contented itself with denying the supremacy of the former and with stigmatizing the latter in the opinion of the public—but behold! the sword they hated and the money they despised gained supreme power in the end, and the representatives of the spirit had to come to an understanding with them. Indeed, out of this understanding there has even developed a joint alliance. Not just the Roman priests, but also the English, the Prussian, in short, all privileged clergy, have allied themselves with Caesar and his confederates for the oppression of the peoples. But due to this alliance the religion of spiritualism will perish all the more speedily. Certain priests already understand this, and in order to save religion, they pretend to renounce this ruinous alliance, and they come over to our side, put on red caps, swear death and hatred for all kings, the seven bloodsuckers, they demand equality of wealth on this earth, and they curse even more than Marat and Robespierre.—Just between us, if you observe them closely, you will see that they read the mass in the language of Jacobinism, and just as they once gave Caesar poison concealed in the Host, they try now to give the people their consecrated wafers by concealing them in the poison of Revolution; for they know we love this poison.

But all your efforts are in vain! Mankind is weary of all Eucharistic wafers and longs for more nourishing food, for real bread and good meat. Mankind smiles pityingly at those youthful ideals which it could not realize despite all efforts and is becoming manfully practical. Mankind now worships a worldly system of utilitarianism and is considering seriously the establishment of middle-class prosperity, sensible management of funds, and comfort

78. The term *Kammerknechte* derives from German medieval history and refers to Jews under the protection of the Emperor and paying tribute to him.

in its old age. There is certainly no more talk about leaving the sword in Caesar's hands and certainly not of leaving the money bag in the hands of his servants. Service to royalty is stripped of privilege and honor, and industry is freed from its ancient lack of respectability. The primary task is to become healthy, for our limbs still feel very weak. The holy vampires of the Middle Ages have sucked so much life-blood out of us. And after this, great sacrifices must be offered upon the altar of matter to atone for old offenses against it. It might even be advisable to institute festivals and to bestow on matter still more extraordinary honors as compensation. For Christianity, unable to annihilate matter, has always denounced it. Christianity has degraded the noblest pleasures, the senses were forced to play the hypocrite, and the result was deceit and sin. We must clothe our women in new garments and in new ideas, and we must fumigate all our emotions, as if we had survived a plague.

Thus the immediate aim of all our new institutions is the rehabilitation of matter, its restoration to dignity, its moral recognition, its religious sanctification, its reconciliation with the spirit. Purusa is re-wedded to Prakriti.[79] Due to their enforced separation, as the Indian myth relates so ingeniously, the great rupture of the world, evil, originated.

Do you know what evil is? The spiritualists have always reproached us because in the pantheistic view there is no distinction between good and evil. But evil is in part only an illusory concept of their own philosophy of life, and in part it is an actual result of their own world-order. According to their philosophy of life, matter is evil in and of itself, which is surely nothing less than calumny and dreadful blasphemy. Matter becomes evil only when it is forced to conspire secretly against the domination of the

79. In Indian philosophy *purusha* is pure consciousness, or in Heine's terms, spirit; *prakriti* is nature, or in Heine's terms, matter.

spirit, when the spirit has stigmatized it and it prostitutes itself out of self-contempt, or when matter goes so far as to take revenge on the spirit with the hatred born of despair. Hence evil becomes only a result of the spiritualistic world-order.

God is identical with the world. He manifests himself in plants, which unconsciously lead a cosmic-magnetic life. He manifests himself in animals, which, in their sensuous, dreamlike life, have a feeling of their more or less vague existence. But he manifests himself most magnificently in man, who both feels and thinks, who is able to distinguish himself as an individual from objective nature and already possesses in his intellect the ideas that present themselves to him in the world of phenomena. In man the deity attains self-awareness and reveals this self-awareness again through man. This process does not take place in and through the individual human being, but in and through collective humanity, the result being that every human being comprehends and represents only one portion of the divine universe, whereas collective humanity will comprehend and represent the totality of the divine universe in idea and in reality. Perhaps each nation has the mission of recognizing and making known a certain part of this divine universe, of comprehending a series of phenomena and bringing to realization a series of ideas, and of transmitting the result to succeeding races on whom a similar mission is imposed. God is therefore the real hero of universal history, which is but his never-ending thought, his never-ending action, his word, his deed; and we can rightly say of all mankind that it is an incarnation of God.

It is wrong to think that this religion, Pantheism, leads men to indifference. On the contrary, the consciousness of his divinity will inspire man to bear witness to it, and only then will the really noble achievements of true heroism glorify this earth.

The political revolution that is based on the principles

of French materialism will find in the pantheists not opponents, but allies, allies, however, who have drawn their convictions from a deeper source, from a religious synthesis. We promote the welfare of matter, the material happiness of the peoples, not, like the materialists, because we despise the spirit, but because we know that the divinity of man is also revealed in his corporeal form, that misery destroys or debases the body, God's image, and that as a result the spirit likewise perishes. The great maxim of the Revolution pronounced by St. Just,[80] *"Le pain est le droit du peuple,"*[81] is translated by us, *"Le pain est le droit divin de l'homme."*[82] We are fighting not for the human rights of the people, but for the divine rights of mankind. In this and in many other things we differ from the men of the Revolution. We do not want to be sansculottes, nor simple citizens, nor venal presidents; we want to found a democracy of gods, equal in majesty, in sanctity, and in bliss. You demand simple dress, austere morals, and unspiced pleasures, but we demand nectar and ambrosia, crimson robes, costly perfumes, luxury and splendor, the dancing of laughing nymphs, music and comedies. Don't be angry with us because of this, you virtuous Republicans. To your censorious reproaches we will respond in the words of one of Shakespeare's fools: "Dost thou think because thou art virtuous, there shall be no more nice cakes and sweet champagne in this world?"[83]

The Saint-Simonists understood and desired something of the sort, but the soil they stood on was unfavorable, and the surrounding materialism repressed them,

80. Louis Antoine Saint-Just was a French revolutionist, a friend of Robespierre, and was executed at the same time.

81. Bread is the right of the people.

82. Bread is the divine right of man.

83. From *Twelfth Night*, Act II, Scene 3, speech by Sir Toby. Heine adapts Shakespeare's text to German taste. The last part of the quotation reads in the original, "there shall be no more cakes and ale."

for the time at least. In Germany they were more highly regarded. For Germany is the most fertile soil for pantheism. This is the religion of our greatest thinkers, of our best artists, and in Germany deism, as I shall presently explain, was long ago overthrown in theory. Like many other things, it still maintains its position only among the mindless masses, a position without rational justification. No one says it, but everyone knows that pantheism is an open secret in Germany. We have, in fact, outgrown deism. We are free and don't want any thundering tyrant. We are of age and need no paternal care. Nor are we the botches of any great mechanic. Deism is a religion for servants, for children, for the Genevese, for watchmakers.

Pantheism is the clandestine religion of Germany, and those German writers who fifty years ago railed against Spinoza foresaw that this would happen. The most furious of these opponents of Spinoza was F. H. Jacobi,[84] who is occasionally honored by being classed among German philosophers. He was nothing but a quarrelsome sneak, who disguised himself in the cloak of philosophy and insinuated himself among the philosophers, first whimpering to them ever so much about his affection and softheartedness, then letting loose a tirade against reason. His perpetual refrain was that philosophy, knowledge acquired by reason, was a vain illusion; that reason itself did not know where it was going; that it led mankind into a dark labyrinth of error and contradiction; and that faith alone could guide man safely. Mole that he was, he could not see that reason resembles the eternal sun which, pursuing its appointed course through the heavens above, illumines its path with its

84. Friedrich Heinrich Jacobi (1743-1819), a religious philosopher who recognized the logic of Spinoza's philosophy but opposed it on religious grounds.

own light. Nothing resembles the pious, unrestrained hatred of the little Jacobi toward the great Spinoza.

It is a curious thing, how the most diverse parties battled against Spinoza. They form an army whose motley composition is a very amusing sight. Next to a swarm of black and white Capuchins with crosses and smoking censers marches the phalanx of the Encyclopedists, who also rail at this *penseur téméraire.*[85] Beside the rabbi of the Amsterdam synagogue, who sounds the attack with the ram's horn of faith, walks Arouet de Voltaire playing the piccolo of irony for the benefit of Deism. In between whines the old milksop Jacobi, the camp follower of this army of the faith.

Let us escape as quickly as possible from this caterwauling. Returning from our pantheistic excursion, we shall go back to Leibnitz' philosophy and relate its subsequent fortunes.

Leibnitz had written his works, which are familiar to you, partly in Latin, partly in French. Christian Wolf is the name of the excellent man who not merely systematized Leibnitz' ideas, but also lectured on them in German. His real merit consists not in having fitted Leibnitz' ideas into a firm system, still less in having made them accessible to a wider public by the use of the German language; his merit lies in having stimulated us to philosophizing in our mother tongue. Until Luther's time we could treat theology only in Latin; until the time of Wolf we were able to deal with philosophy only in that language. The example of a very few scholars who had previously lectured on such subjects in German had no effect, but the literary historian must call them to mind with special praise. We therefore mention here particularly Johannes Tauler,[86] a Dominican monk who was

85. Daring thinker.
86. One of the most important German mystics (1290-1361).

born on the Rhine at the beginning of the fourteenth century and who died there, I believe in Strassburg, in 1361. He was a devout man, one of those mystics whom I have named the Platonic party of the Middle Ages. In the last years of his life this man, renouncing all scholarly arrogance, was not ashamed to preach in the humble language of the people, and these sermons, which he wrote down, together with German translations of some of his earlier Latin sermons, are among the most remarkable documents in the German language. For here German already shows that it is not merely adequate for metaphysical investigations but is far more suitable than Latin. The latter, the language of the Romans, can never belie its origin. It is a language for generals' orders, a language for administrators' decrees, a legal language for usurers, a lapidary language for the stone-hard Roman people. It became the appropriate language for materialism. Though Christianity, with truly Christian patience, struggled for more than a thousand years to spiritualize this language, it did not succeed; when Johannes Tauler sought to fathom the most terrifying abysses of thought, and when his heart was overflowing with the holiest emotions, he was compelled to speak German. His speech is like a mountain spring with strange aromatic fragrance and mysterious metallic virtues. Not until recent times, however, did the usefulness of the German language for philosophy become fully apparent. In no other language than in our beloved German mother tongue could Nature have revealed her most secret workings. Only on the sturdy oak could the sacred mistletoe thrive.

This would probably be the fitting place to discuss Paracelsus, or, as he called himself, Theophrastus Paracelsus Bombastus of Hohenheim.[87] For he too usually

87. Paracelsus (1493-1541) was a well-known physician, chemist, and alchemist, of great influence on his own and succeeding centuries.

wrote in German. But I shall have occasion to speak of him later in an even more significant context. His philosophy was what today we call nature philosophy, and such a doctrine of nature animated by ideas, so mysteriously appealing to the German mind, would have developed among us already at that time had not, through a chance influence, the inanimate, mechanistic physics of the Cartesians become universally dominant. Paracelsus was a great charlatan, always wore a scarlet coat and breeches, red stockings and a red hat, and claimed to be able to create *homunculi*, little men; at any rate he was on familiar footing with invisible beings that dwell in the various elements. Yet he was also one of those very profound naturalists who, with truly German ardor for scholarly investigation, understood pre-Christian popular beliefs, German pantheism, and what they did not know they very accurately divined.

I really ought to say something here about Jakob Böhme as well.[88] He too used German for philosophical expositions for which he has been much praised. But I have never yet been able to bring myself to read him. I don't like to be made a fool of. You see, I suspect the eulogists of this mystic of trying to mystify the public. As to the content of his works, Saint-Martin[89] has given you a sample in French. His works have also been translated into English. Charles I had so high an opinion of this theosophical shoemaker that he sent a learned man to him in Görlitz for the express purpose of studying him. This scholar was more fortunate than his royal master. For while the latter lost his head at Whitehall under Cromwell's axe, the former merely lost his mind at Görlitz through Jakob Böhme's theosophy.

88. A religious mystic of the early seventeenth century whose influence was felt not only in Germany but also in Holland and England.
89. Louis Claude St.-Martin (1743-1804), French author and mystic. He was influenced by Böhme and translated several of his works.

As I have already said, Christian Wolf first successfully established the German language in the field of philosophy. His least merit was his systematizing and popularizing of Leibnitz' ideas. Both undertakings have incurred the gravest censure, and we must speak of this at least in passing. His systematizing was merely empty illusion, and the most important aspect of Leibnitz' philosophy was sacrificed to this illusion, for instance, the best part of the theory of monads. To be sure, Leibnitz had left behind him no systematic body of theory, only the ideas necessary for its construction. A giant was needed to fit together the colossal blocks and columns that a giant had raised from the depths of the marble quarries and delicately chiseled out. It might have become a beautiful temple. Christian Wolf, however, was of very short stature and was able to master only a portion of these materials, which he worked up into a wretched tabernacle of deism. Wolf had a mind more encyclopedic than systematic, and he could not comprehend the unity of a doctrine except as a complete whole. He was satisfied with a certain framework in which the compartments are arranged in perfect order, filled to the brim, and provided with unambiguous labels. Hence he gave us an "encyclopedia of the philosophical sciences." Naturally, as the grandson of Descartes, he inherited his grandfather's form of mathematical demonstration of proof. I have already criticized this mathematical form in Spinoza's works, and due to Wolf it caused a great deal of trouble. In his disciples it degenerated into the most insufferable schematicism and a ridiculous mania for demonstrating everything in mathematical form. Thus arose the so-called Wolfian dogmatism. Any investigation of a more profound character ceased, and a tedious zeal for obviousness took its place. Wolf's philosophy became more and more watery and finally flooded all Germany. Traces of this deluge are still visible today, and here and there, at our greatest universities, old fossils from the Wolf school are still found.

Christian Wolf was born in Breslau in 1678 and died in Halle in 1754. His intellectual domination of Germany lasted more than half a century. We must mention particularly his relationship with the theologians of his time, and in so doing we will supplement our remarks about the fate of Lutheranism.

In the whole history of the Church there is no portion more complicated than the quarrels of Protestant theologians since the Thirty Years' War. Only the sophistical wrangling of the Byzantines can be compared with them, but it was not so boring, for behind it were concealed major court intrigues of concern to the state, whereas Protestant polemics usually had their origin in the pedantry of provincial scholars and academicians. The universities, especially Tübingen, Wittenberg, Leipzig, and Halle, were the arenas for these theological struggles. The two parties which we saw fighting in Catholic garb during the entire Middle Ages merely changed costumes and continued to feud with each other just as before. They were the Pietists and the Orthodox, whom I mentioned earlier and defined as mystics without imagination and dogmatists without intelligence. Johannes Spener[90] was the Scotus Erigena[91] of Protestantism, and as the latter, by his translation of the legendary Dionysus the Areopagite, founded Catholic mysticism, the former founded Protestant mysticism by his Assemblies for Worship, *colloquia pietatis*,[92] from which, perhaps, the

90. Philipp Jakob Spener (1635-1705), founder of Pietism.

91. John Scotus Erigena (c. 810-880), scholastic philosopher. He translated the writings of Pseudo-Dionysus and developed a religious philosophy which contained the origins of both Catholic scholasticism and mysticism.

92. A misprint in all Heine editions for *collegia pietatis*, due either to the carelessness of the printers or to an oversight on Heine's part. (A similar mistake is the name "Johannes," found in all editions as Spener's first name.) These meetings for fellowship and Bible study led to a religious revival in Germany.

name "Pietists" fell to his disciples. He was a devout man
—all honor to his memory. A Berlin Pietist, Mr. Franz
Horn, has produced a good biography of him. Spener's
life was an incessant martyrdom for the Christian idea.
In this respect he was superior to his contemporaries. He
demanded good works and piety and was a preacher of
the spirit rather than of the letter. His homiletic nature
was laudable, considering the times. For all theology, as
taught at the universities just mentioned, consisted only
in strait-laced dogmatism and hair-splitting polemics.
Exegesis and church history were completely neglected.

A pupil of Spener's, Hermann Francke,[93] began to
lecture at Leipzig, following his teacher's example and
ideas. He lectured in German, a merit we are always glad
to mention with appreciation. The approbation these
lectures received aroused the envy of his colleagues, who
accordingly made our poor Pietist's life miserable. He
was forced to quit the field and went to Halle, where he
taught Christianity by word and deed. His memory is
imperishable there, for he was the founder of the Halle
Orphanage. The University of Halle now became popu-
lated with Pietists, who were called "the Orphanage
Party." Incidentally, this group has been preserved there
until the present day; Halle is as yet still the *taupinière*[94]
of the Pietists, and just a few years ago their quarrels with
the Protestant rationalists created a scandal that spread
its stench through all of Germany. You fortunate French-
men, who have heard nothing about this! You have re-
mained ignorant of even the existence of those Evangeli-
cal scandal sheets in which the pious fishwives of the
Protestant Church insulted each other roundly. Fortu-
nate Frenchmen, who have no idea how maliciously, pet-
tily, and disgustingly our Evangelical clergy can slander
one another. You know that I am no partisan of Catho-

93. August Hermann Francke (1663-1727) was the founder of the well-
known home for orphans in Halle.
94. Mole-hill.

licism. Among my present religious convictions there
still survives not indeed the dogma, but nevertheless the
spirit of Protestantism. Thus I am still partial to the
Protestant Church. And yet I must in all honesty confess
that nowhere in the annals of the Papacy have I found
anything so contemptible as appeared in *The Berlin Evan-
gelical Church Journal* during the scandal just mentioned.
The most dastardly knavery of the monks, the meanest
intrigues of the cloister are still noble and generous in
comparison with the Christian heroics of our pietist and
orthodox Protestants in combating the hated rational-
ists. You French have no conception of the hatred that
is displayed on such occasions. The Germans are in gen-
eral more vindictive than the Latin peoples.

The reason is that they are idealists even in their ha-
tred. We do not hate each other, as you French do,
because of external things, perhaps because of wounded
vanity, perhaps on account of an epigram or a visiting-
card to which there was no response,—no, we hate in our
enemies the most profound, most basic characteristic
they have, their thought. You French are frivolous and
superficial in hatred as well as in love. We Germans hate
thoroughly, permanently; too honest and also too inept
to avenge ourselves with speedy perfidy, we hate until
our dying breath.

"I know this German calmness, sir," a lady said re-
cently, looking at me with wide-eyed incredulity and anx-
iety; "I know that you Germans use the same word for
forgiving and for poisoning." And as a matter of fact, she
is right; the word *vergeben* has this double meaning.

If I am not mistaken, it was the orthodox of Halle who,
in their struggle against the pietist settlers, called to their
assistance Wolf's philosophy. For religion, when it can
no longer burn us, comes to beg us for alms. Yet all our
donations profit it little. The garment of mathematical
demonstration in which Wolf had affectionately clothed

poor Religion fitted her so badly that she felt even more constrained, and in this constraint made herself very ridiculous. Weak seams burst open everywhere. Especially the organ of shame, original sin, appeared in its most glaring nakedness. Here a logical fig-leaf was of no avail. Christian-Lutheran original sin and Leibnitz-Wolfian optimism are incompatible. The French raillery at optimism was thus least displeasing to our theologians. Voltaire's wit came to the aid of naked original sin, but the German Pangloss[95] lost much by the destruction of optimism and searched long for a similar doctrine that would be consoling, until the Hegelian statement, "Everything that is is reasonable!," offered him a partial equivalent.

From the moment when a religion requires the aid of philosophy, its downfall is inevitable. Attempting a defense, it chatters itself more and more deeply into destruction. Religion, like any absolutism, must not try to justify itself. Prometheus is chained to the rock by silent force. Indeed, Aeschylus does not allow personified Force to utter a single word.[96] It must remain mute. As soon as religion prints a catechism supported by arguments, as soon as political absolutism publishes an official newspaper, both are done for. But this is precisely our triumph; we have forced our adversaries to speak, and they must justify themselves.

It certainly cannot be denied that religious, as well as political, absolutism has found very powerful organs of expression. Still, let us not be alarmed by this. If the word is alive, it may be carried by dwarfs; if the word is dead, not even giants can support it.

Now, as I said above, since Religion looked to Philoso-

95. Voltaire's *Candide, ou l'optimisme* was a satire directed against Leibnitz' optimistic belief that this world is the best of all conceivable worlds. Pangloss is young Candide's tutor.

96. In *Prometheus Bound* Force does not speak.

phy for aid, German scholars, besides providing new clothing, made innumerable experiments with her. They wanted to furnish her a new youth, and in doing this they acted somewhat like Medea at the rejuvenation of King Aeson.[97] First she was bled, and all superstitious blood was slowly drained out of her. To express myself without metaphors, the attempt was made to remove from Christianity all historical content and to retain only the moral portion. By this process Christianity was transformed into pure deism. Christ ceased to be God's co-regent; He was mediatized, so to speak, and only as a private person did He still receive appreciative recognition. His moral character was extolled beyond measure. There was no end to the eulogies describing what a splendid man He had been. As for the miracles He performed, they were either explained according to the laws of nature or were given as little attention as possible. Miracles, said some, were necessary in those superstitious times, and a sensible man having a truth of any kind to proclaim made use of them about as one would use an advertisement. Those theologians who eliminated the historical element from Christianity are called Rationalists, and against them was directed the wrath of both Pietists and Orthodox, who since then have quarreled with each other less violently and not infrequently joined forces as allies. A common hatred of the Rationalists succeeded in doing what love could not.

This tendency in Protestant theology began with the peaceful Semler,[98] whom you do not know, rose to a disquieting height with the lucid Teller,[99] whom you don't know either, and reached its peak with the shallow

97. Heine refers here to Ovid's description in his *Metamorphoses*, Book 7. By means of her magic powers Medea transformed Jason's aged father, Aeson, into a man of forty.

98. Johann Salomo Semler, professor of theology in Halle from 1752 until his death in 1791.

99. Wilhelm Abraham Teller, from 1767 on a pastor and member of the high consistorial court in Berlin.

Bahrdt,[100] by the lack of whose acquaintance you have lost nothing. The strongest stimulus came from Berlin, where Frederick the Great and the book dealer Nicolai[101] ruled.

About the first, crowned Materialism, you are sufficiently informed. You know that he wrote poetry in French, played the flute very well, won the battle of Rossbach, took quantities of snuff, and believed in nothing but cannons. Some of you have doubtless also visited Sans Souci, and the old disabled veteran who is the warden there has pointed out to you in the library the French novels which Frederick, when crown prince, used to read in church and which he had bound in black morocco so that his stern father would think he was reading the Lutheran hymnal. You know him, that royal philosopher whom you have called the Solomon of the North. France was the Ophir of this northern Solomon, and from there he obtained his poets and philosophers, for whom he cherished a great partiality, like the Solomon of the South, who, as you can read in the first book of Kings, chapter ten, ordered through his friend Hiram whole shiploads of gold, ivory, poets, and philosophers from Ophir. To be sure, this preference for foreign talent prevented Frederick the Great from gaining any considerable influence over the German mind. On the contrary, he insulted and wounded German national feeling. The contempt he displayed for our literature cannot but offend even us today, the descendants of those writers. Except for old Gellert[102] not one of them enjoyed any

100. Karl Friedrich Bahrdt, professor of theology at various universities, but always shocking people by his aggressiveness and his dissolute life. He later became an innkeeper in the vicinity of Halle and was a notorious representative of Rationalism.

101. See above, p. 146 and note 35 on that page, also pp. 200 f.

102. Christian Fürchtegott Gellert (1715-1769), from 1751 professor of philosophy at the University of Leipzig, popular with students and with the large public that knew and applauded his writings. To a later generation, like Heine's, he must have seemed very naive and old-fashioned in his approach to literature and scholarship.

sign of his most gracious favor. The interview he had with Gellert is remarkable.[103]

But if Frederick the Great jeered at us without supporting us, the book dealer Nicolai supported us all the more, without our having on that account any scruples about jeering at him. His whole life long he was unceasingly active for the welfare of his country, he spared neither pains nor money when he hoped to further a good cause, and yet never has anyone in Germany been so brutally, so relentlessly, so devastatingly ridiculed as this very man. Although we, a later generation, know very well that old Nicolai, the friend of Enlightenment, was definitely not in error about essentials, though we know that it was chiefly our own enemies, the obscurantists, who wrecked him with their abuse, still we cannot think of him with a perfectly straight face. Old Nicolai tried to do in Germany the same thing that the French philosophers had done in France; he tried to destroy the past in the mind of the people, a laudable preliminary, without which no radical revolution can take place. But in vain—he was not equal to such a task. The ancient ruins still stood too securely, and the ghosts arose from them and mocked him, whereat he became very cross and struck out at them blindly, and the spectators laughed when the bats whizzed about his ears and got entangled in his well-powdered wig. At times it also happened that he mistook windmills for giants and fought them. But he fared still worse when he occasionally mistook real giants for mere windmills, for instance, a Wolfgang Goethe. He wrote a satire on Goethe's *Werther*[104] in which he displayed the grossest misunderstanding of all the author's intentions. Yet about essentials he was always right. Even though he did not understand what

103. This took place in Leipzig on December 18, 1760.
104. *The Sorrows of Young Werther*, 1773, Goethe's first novel.

Goethe really meant with his *Werther,* he nonetheless understood very well its effect—the effeminate dreaminess, the barren sentimentality which came into vogue because of this novel and which were in hostile contradiction to every sensible attitude that we needed. In this, Nicolai was in complete agreement with Lessing, who wrote to a friend the following opinion about *Werther:*

"If such a fervent production is not to do more harm than good, don't you think it should have appended to it a brief, dispassionate epilogue, a few hints as to how Werther came to have such a strange character, and how some other young man on whom nature had bestowed a similar tendency could protect himself against it? Do you think that a Greek or Roman youth would ever have killed himself in such a manner and for the same reason? Certainly not. They knew how to protect themselves from the extravagancies of love in quite a different way; and at Socrates' time even a *girl* would scarcely have been forgiven for such transports of love as drive a man to venture something so unnatural. It was reserved for Christian training, which understands so wonderfully how to transform a physical need into a spiritual perfection, to produce eccentrics at once so mean and so great, so contemptible and so estimable. So, dear Goethe, give us another chapter as a brief conclusion, and the more cynical, the better."

In accordance with this suggestion friend Nicolai actually did publish a different *Werther.* In his version the hero did not shoot himself, but merely befouled himself with chicken blood, for the pistol was loaded with it instead of lead. Werther makes himself ridiculous, keeps on living, marries Charlotte—in short, he ends even more tragically than in Goethe's original.

The *Allgemeine deutsche Bibliothek* is the name of the journal Nicolai founded and in which he and his friends fought against superstition, Jesuits, court lackeys, and the like. It cannot be denied that many a blow directed against superstition unfortunately struck poetry itself. Nicolai fought, for instance, against the rising partiality for old German folksongs. But essentially he was once more in the right. Despite all their excellence, the songs did contain many recollections that were anything but up-to-date; these ancient strains of the Alpine cowherds of the Middle Ages could not lure the hearts of the people back into the stables of a bygone faith. Like Ulysses, Nicolai tried to stop the ears of his companions so that they would not hear the songs of the sirens, not caring that they then also became deaf to the innocent tones of the nightingale. In order to clear the field of the present completely of all weeds, this practical man hardly scrupled at pulling up the flowers as well. But the party of the flowers and the nightingales, with all that belonged to it, beauty, grace, wit, and playfulness, rose up in arms against this, and poor Nicolai was defeated.

In present-day Germany circumstances have changed, and the party of the flowers and the nightingales is closely allied with the Revolution. To us belongs the future, and already the morning glow of victory is dawning. When in time this beautiful day sheds its light on our whole fatherland, then we will also remember the dead. We will then certainly remember you, old Nicolai, poor martyr of reason; we will bear your ashes to the German Pantheon, the sarcophagus surrounded by an exultant triumphal procession and accompanied by a band of players among whose wind instruments there shall certainly not be a flute; we will place on your bier a most befitting laurel wreath, and while so doing we will try very hard not to laugh.

Since I would like to give an idea of the philosophical and religious conditions of that time, I must also mention here those thinkers who, in more or less intimate association with Nicolai, were active in Berlin and formed, as it were, a *juste milieu* between philosophers and belles-lettres. They had no definite system, merely a definite tendency. In style and in basic principles they resembled the English moralists.[105] They used no strict scientific form in their writing; moral awareness was the sole source of their knowledge. Their tendency was the same as that of the French Philanthropists.[106] In religion they were rationalists. In politics they were cosmopolitans. In morals they were human beings, noble, virtuous human beings, strict in regard to themselves, tolerant toward others. As for talent, Mendelssohn,[107] Sulzer,[108] Abbt,[109] Moritz,[110] Garve,[111] Engel,[112] and Biester[113] might be named as the most distinguished. I like Moritz best. He accomplished a great deal in experimental psychology. He had a delightful ingenuousness little appreciated by his friends. His autobiography is one of the most important documents of that time. Mendelssohn, however, has great social significance beyond all the others. He was the reformer of the German Israelites, his

105. A reference to the didactic element in much English literature of the eighteenth century, but most particularly to newspapers such as Addison's and Steele's, which had great influence in Germany and were widely imitated.

106. French writers and thinkers such as Voltaire, Montesquieu, Diderot, Rousseau, and others, liberals who condemned all forms of despotism and believed in the best ideals of the eighteenth century, tolerance, social justice and equality, and political freedom.

107. Moses Mendelssohn (1729–1786), the well-known Jewish philosopher, one of Lessing's best friends.

108. Johann Georg Sulzer (1720–1779), prominent esthetician of the time, for many years a professor at the University of Berlin.

109. Thomas Abbt (1738–1766), journalist and writer, of considerable influence on the young Herder.

110. Karl Philipp Moritz (1757–1793), author of an autobiographical novel *Anton Reiser, a Psychological Novel,* and of two books on his travels in England and Italy. The novel is the autobiography referred to by Heine in what follows.

111. Christian Garve (1742–1798), popular moral philosopher.

112. Johann Jakob Engel (1741–1802), writer, editor, and theater director in Berlin.

113. Johann Erich Biester (1749–1816), librarian at the Royal Library in Berlin, editor of various journals.

co-religionists; he destroyed the authority of Talmudism and founded pure Mosaism. This man, whom his contemporaries called the German Socrates and whom they admired so reverently for his nobility of spirit and vigor of intellect, was the son of a poor sexton at the synagogue in Dessau. In addition to this misfortune of birth, Providence had also afflicted him with a hunchback, as if to teach the common people in a very vivid way that one should judge a person not by his outward appearance but by his intrinsic worth. Or did Providence assign him a hunchback with benevolent foresight, so that he could attribute many an insult of the masses to a misfortune for which a wise man can readily console himself?

As Luther had overthrown the Papacy, so Mendelssohn overthrew the Talmud, and in the very same way, namely, by repudiating tradition, by declaring the Bible to be the source of religion, and by translating the most important part of it. By so doing he destroyed Judaic catholicism, as Luther had destroyed Christian catholicism. The Talmud is, in fact, the catholicism of the Jews. It is a Gothic cathedral, which, to be sure, is overloaded with childish and superfluous ornament, yet nevertheless astounds us with its heaven-aspiring, gigantic proportions. It is a hierarchy of religious laws, often dealing with the quaintest, most absurd subtleties, but so ingeniously superimposed and subordinated, each part supporting and sustaining another, and so formidably consistent in their collective effect as to form an awesomely bold, colossal whole.

After the downfall of Christian catholicism, Jewish catholicism, the Talmud, also had perforce to decline. For the Talmud had now lost its significance. It served simply as a bulwark against Rome, and the Jews owe it to the Talmud that they were able to resist Christian Rome just as heroically as they had formerly resisted pagan Rome. And they did not merely resist; they were victorious. The poor Rabbi of Nazareth, over whose dying head the pagan Roman wrote the sardonic words "King of the Jews"—it was precisely this thorn-crowned mock-king of the Jews, decked out in ironic scarlet, who finally became the God of the Romans, and they had to kneel down before Him! Like heathen Rome, Christian Rome was also defeated and even had to pay tribute. If you, dear reader, during the first days of the trimester, will betake yourself to Lafitte Street, to the hotel at no. 15, you will see there in front of a tall gate a lumbering carriage from which a stout man will descend. He will go upstairs to a small room where a blond young man is sitting, actually older than he probably looks, in whose elegant, grand-seignorial nonchalance there is yet something as solid, something as positive, something as absolute as if he had all the money in this world in his pocket. And indeed he *has* all the money in this world in his pocket, and his name is Mr. James Rothschild, and the stout man is Monsignor Grimbaldi, legate of His Holiness the Pope, and he is bringing in the latter's name the interest on the Roman loan, the tribute from Rome.

But of what use is the Talmud now?

Moses Mendelssohn thus deserves great praise for having overthrown this Jewish catholicism, at least in Germany. For anything superfluous is harmful. Rejecting tradition, he nonetheless tried to preserve the Mosaic ceremonial law as religious obligation. Was this cowardice or prudence? Was it a melancholy nostalgia that kept him from laying a destructive hand on objects that were most sacred to his forefathers and for which so much martyrs' blood and tears had flowed? I think not. Like the sovereigns of material kingdoms, the sovereigns of the spirit must also harden their hearts against family affections; even on the throne of thought one must not give way to tender sentiments. Therefore I am rather of the opinion that Moses Mendelssohn saw in pure Mos-

aism an institution that could serve as a last entrench-
ment for deism, so to speak. Deism was his innermost
faith and his deepest conviction. When his friend Lessing
died and was accused of being a follower of Spinoza, he
defended him with the most anxious fervor and worried
himself to death over the incident.

I have already mentioned for the second time the
name no German can utter without rousing in his bosom
an echo more or less loud. Since Luther, Germany has
produced no greater nor better man than Gotthold
Ephraim Lessing. These two are our pride and our de-
light. In the gloom of the present we look up to their
comforting figures, and they nod in affirmation of a bril-
liant promise. Yes, the third man will also come, who will
complete what Luther began, what Lessing continued,
and what the German fatherland needs so much—the
third emancipator!—I can already see his golden armor
shining through his imperial crimson cloak "like the sun
through the rosy dawn"!

Like Luther, Lessing was influential not only because
he did something definite but because he roused the
German people to its very depths and because he
brought about a beneficial intellectual movement by his
criticism and by his polemics. He was the living criticism
of his time, and his whole life was a polemic. His criticism
made itself felt throughout the whole range of thought
and of feeling, in religion, in science, in art. His polemics
overcame every adversary and grew more vigorous with
every victory. Lessing, as he himself admitted, simply
had to have conflict for his own intellectual develop-
ment. He was just like that legendary Norman who inher-
ited the talents, knowledge, and powers of the men he
slew in combat and thus was ultimately endowed with all
possible merits and excellencies. It is understandable
that such a pugnacious warrior caused no small stir in

Germany, in peaceful Germany, where in those days an even greater Sabbath-like peace reigned than today. The majority were dumfounded at his literary boldness. But it was this very quality that came to his aid, for *oser*[114] is the secret of success in literature as in revolution—and in love. Everyone trembled before Lessing's sword. No head was safe from it. Indeed, he even struck off many a skull out of sheer high spirits, and then was malicious enough to lift it up from the ground and show the public that it was empty inside. The man whom his sword could not reach he slew with the arrows of his wit. His friends admired the gay-colored feathers of these arrows; his enemies felt the points in their breasts. Lessing's wit bears no resemblance to that *enjouement*,[115] that *gaieté*,[116] those bounding *saillies*[117] so familiar here in France. His wit was not a little French lapdog[118] chasing its own shadow; it was more like a big German tomcat playing with a mouse before strangling it.

Yes, polemic was Lessing's delight, and for this reason he never thought very much about whether his opponent was worthy of him. With his polemic he snatched many a name from well-deserved oblivion. He wove a web, as it were, of the wittiest mockery, the most delightful humor, about not a few paltry scribblers, who are now preserved for all time in Lessing's works like insects embedded in a piece of amber. While slaying his adversaries, he made them immortal. Who among us would ever

114. To dare.
115. Sprightliness.
116. Gaiety.
117. Sallies.
118. In German the word is *Windhündchen*, the diminutive of *Windhund*, which means "greyhound." According to Grimm's *Wörterbuch*, after the introduction of dogs as luxury articles, the word was also used to represent weakness. As far as I know, the English word has no such connotation, hence my use of an equivalent rather than a literal translation.

have heard anything about that Klotz[119] on whom Lessing lavished so much derision and ingenuity! The boulders which he hurled at this wretched antiquarian and with which he crushed him are now an indestructible monument to his victim.

It is remarkable that this man, the wittiest in Germany, was also the most honest man. There is nothing comparable to his love of truth. Lessing made not the slightest concession to a lie, even if by doing so, in the usual manner of the worldly-wise, he might promote the triumph of truth. He could do anything for the truth except lie. Anyone, he once said, who plans to display truth with all sorts of make-up and disguises might well be the pander, but has never been the lover, of truth.

The nice saying of Buffon's, "The style is the man himself," can be applied to no one better than to Lessing. His style of writing is just like his character, genuine, stable, unadorned, beautiful, and imposing by virtue of its inherent vigor. His style is altogether like that of Roman architecture: the greatest solidity and at the same time the greatest simplicity; the sentences rest one upon the other like square-hewn blocks of stone, and just as with the latter the law of gravity, so with the former logical reasoning is the invisible cement. For this reason we find in Lessing's prose so few of those expletives and rhetorical arts which we employ as mortar, so to speak, in constructing our sentences. Still less do we find in it those caryatides of thought which you French call *la belle phrase*.[120]

You will readily understand that a man like Lessing could never be happy. Even if he had not loved truth, even if he had not defended it obstinately on every occa-

119. Christian Adolf Klotz (1738–1771), professor of classical literature at Halle. Lessing attacked him violently in his *Briefe antiquarischen Inhalts* (*Letters Concerning Antiquarian Questions*).

120. A fine phrase.

sion, he would still perforce have been unhappy, for he was a genius. "People will forgive you anything," said a poet recently, with a sigh, "they will forgive you your wealth, they will forgive you your noble birth, they will forgive you your fine figure, they won't even mind if you are talented, but they are pitiless toward a genius." And alas! even though he may not encounter ill will from without, a genius would still find within himself the enemy preparing misery for him. Thus the history of great men is always a martyrology; even when they did not suffer for the great human race, they suffered for their own greatness, for the grand mold of their existence, for their antipathy to philistinism, for their discomfort in the presence of vulgarity, of grinning baseness of their surroundings, a discomfort that naturally leads them to extravagances, to the theater, for example, or even to the casino, as happened to poor Lessing.

But malicious rumor has not been able to charge him with anything worse than this, and from his biography we learn only that pretty actresses seemed to him more amusing than Hamburg clergymen and that speechless cards afforded him better entertainment than babbling Wolfian philosophers.

It is heartrending to read in this biography how fate denied him any joy whatsoever and would not even permit him to relax from his daily conflicts in the peace of the family circle. Only once did fortune seem to wish to smile on him; it gave him a beloved wife and a child—but this happiness was like the sunbeam that gilds the wing of a bird flying past, for it vanished just as quickly. His wife died as a result of childbirth, and the child very soon after birth. To a friend he wrote about his child the bitterly witty words:

"My joy was but brief. And I lost him with such regret, this son! For he possessed so much intelligence—so much intelligence! Don't think that my few hours of paternity made me such an ape of a father. I know what I am saying. Didn't it show intelligence on his part that he had to be brought into the world with iron forceps, and that he smelled a rat so soon? Wasn't it intelligence that he seized the first opportunity to take to his heels again? I wanted for once to have things as good as other people, but it cost me dearly."

There was one misfortune which Lessing never spoke to his friends about; this was his terrible loneliness, his intellectual solitariness. Some of his contemporaries loved him; none understood him. Mendelssohn, his best friend, defended him zealously against the charge of Spinozism. Defense and zeal were as absurd as they were superfluous. Rest easy in your grave, old Moses. Your Lessing was, to be sure, on the way to that dreadful error, that wretched misfortune, namely, to Spinozism—but the Almighty, our Father in heaven, saved him by death just at the right moment. Rest easy, your Lessing was not a Spinozist, as slander maintained; he died a good deist like you and Nicolai and Teller and the *Allgemeine deutsche Bibliothek!*

Lessing was merely the prophet who pointed out the way from the second to the third Testament.[121] I have called him Luther's continuator, and it is actually in this relation that I must discuss him here. I can speak only later of his significance for German art. In this he brought about a salutary reform, not merely by his criticism but also by his example, and this side of his activity is usually the one most emphasized and analyzed. We, however, are considering him from a different standpoint, and his philosophical and theological battles are more important for us than his dramaturgy and his plays. Yet the latter, like all his writings, have a social significance, and *Nathan the Wise* is not only a good comedy, but

---

121. As, for instance, in his late work *The Education of the Human Race.*

also a philosophical-theological treatise on behalf of pure deism. For Lessing art was also a rostrum, and when he was pushed down from the pulpit or driven from the lecture room, he leaped to the theater and spoke there even more plainly and gained an even more numerous audience.

I say that Lessing continued Luther's work. After Luther had liberated us from tradition and had set up the Bible as the one and only source of Christianity, there arose, as I have already related previously, a rigid literalism, and the letter of the Bible ruled just as tyrannically as tradition had once ruled. Lessing contributed the most to liberation from this tyrannical letter. Just as Luther was not the only one who battled tradition, so, to be sure, Lessing was not the only, but still the most valiant, warrior against the letter. Here his battle cry resounds loudest. Here he wields his sword most joyfully, and it flashes and slays. But it is here also that Lessing is most sorely beset by the black legion, and in such straits he once cried out:

"O sancta simplicitas! But I am not yet at the place where the good man who cried out thus could still utter only these words. (Huss cried out thus when burned at the stake.) We must first be heard; we must first be judged by those who can and wish to hear and judge.

"O, if *he* could only do so, he whom I would most like to have as my judge! You, Luther! Great, misunderstood man! And misunderstood by no one more than by those obstinate persons who, your slippers in their hands, dawdle along the path you made for them, clamorous but indifferent. You saved us from the yoke of tradition. Who will save us from the more intolerable yoke of the letter? Who will at last bring us a Christianity such as you would teach today, such as Christ Himself would teach?"

Yes, the letter, said Lessing, is the last veil enveloping Christianity, and only after its destruction will the spirit of Christianity stand revealed. This spirit, however, is none other than what the Wolfian philosophers meant to demonstrate, what the Philanthropists felt in their hearts, what Mendelssohn found in Mosaism, what Freemasons chanted, what poets sang, what at that time was making itself felt in Germany in all manner of ways —pure Deism.

Lessing died in Brunswick in 1781, misunderstood, hated, and denounced. In the same year Immanuel Kant's *Critique of Pure Reason* appeared in Königsberg. With this book, which due to a strange delay did not become generally known until the end of the decade, there began in Germany an intellectual revolution which presents the most striking analogies to the material revolution in France and which must seem to more profound thinkers just as important. It went through the same phases of development, and the most remarkable parallelism exists between both revolutions. On both sides of the Rhine we see the same break with the past; all respect for tradition has been renounced. Just as here in France every privilege must be justified, so, in Germany, must every thought be justified, and just as here the monarchy, the keystone of the old social order, so there deism, the keystone of the old intellectual regime, has fallen.

Of this catastrophe, deism's 21st of January,[122] we shall speak in the following section. A peculiar awe, a mysterious piety, prevents our writing more today. Our heart is filled with shuddering compassion—it is ancient Jehovah himself who is preparing for death. We knew him so well, from his cradle in Egypt, where he was reared among divine calves and crocodiles, sacred onions, ibis, and cats. We saw him as he bade farewell to these playmates of his childhood and to the obelisks and sphinxes of his native Nile valley and became a little

122. Louis XVI was beheaded on January 21, 1793.

god-king in Palestine among a poor shepherd people
and lived in his own temple-palace. We saw him later
when he came in contact with Assyrian-Babylonian civili-
zation and put aside his all too human passions, no
longer spitting nothing but wrath and vengeance, at least
no longer thundering at every trifle. We saw him emi-
grate to Rome, the capital, where he renounced all na-
tional prejudices and proclaimed the divine equality of
all nations, and with such fine phrases established an
opposition to old Jupiter, and intrigued until he gained
supreme authority and from the Capitol ruled the city
and the world, *urbem et orbem*. We saw how he became
even more spiritual, how he whimpered in bland bliss,
becoming a loving father, a universal friend of man, a
world benefactor, a philanthropist—but all this could
avail him nothing—

Do you hear the little bell ringing? Kneel down. They
are bringing the sacraments to a dying god.

BOOK THREE

The tale goes that an English inventor, who had al-
ready invented the most ingenious machines, finally hit
on the idea of constructing a human being. In the end he
succeeded; the work of his hands could behave and act
just like a man; it even bore within its leathern breast a
sort of human feeling differing not too greatly from the
usual feelings of the English; it could communicate its
emotions by articulate sounds, and it was precisely the
noise of the wheels inside, of springs and screws, which
was then audible, that lent these sounds a genuinely
English pronunciation. In short, this automaton was a
perfect gentleman, and nothing was wanting to make it

a real human being except a soul. This, however, the English inventor could not give him, and the poor creature, aware of its deficiency, tormented its creator day and night with the plea to give it a soul. This request, repeated day after day with growing urgency, at last became so unendurable to the poor artist that he ran away to escape from his own masterpiece. But the automaton immediately took a special coach, followed him to the continent, traveled incessantly at his heels, sometimes caught up with him, and then rattled and grunted at him, "Give me a soul." These two figures may now be met in every country, and only he who knows their particular relationship understands their strange haste and their anxious discontent. But as soon as we know about this particular relationship, we recognize in it something of a general nature; we see how one part of the English people is weary of its mechanical existence and demands a soul, whereas the other part, out of anxiety at such a desire, is driven about in all directions, and neither can endure things at home any longer.

This is a dreadful story. It is terrifying when the bodies we have created demand from us a soul. It is far more dreadful, terrifying, uncanny, however, when we have created a soul and it demands from us its body and pursues us with this demand. The thought we have conceived is such a soul, and it leaves us no peace until we have given it its body, until we have helped it to become a material phenomenon. Thought strives to become action, the word to become flesh. And marvelous to relate, man, like God in the Bible, needs only to express his thought, and the world takes shape, there is light or there is darkness, the waters separate from the dry land, or it may even be that wild beasts appear. The world is the symbol of the word.

Take note of this, you proud men of action. You are nothing but unconscious handymen for the men of thought who, often in the humblest quiet, have pre-scribed with the utmost precision all your actions. Max-imilian Robespierre was nothing but the hand of Jean Jacques Rousseau, the bloody hand that drew forth from the womb of time the body whose soul Rousseau had created. Did not, perhaps, the restless anxiety that em-bittered the life of Jean Jacques stem from a premonition in his spirit as to what sort of accoucheur his thoughts would need in order to enter the world in corporal form?

Old Fontenelle[123] may have been right when he said, "If I held all the ideas of this world in my hand, I would be very careful not to open it." For my part, I think differently. If I held all the ideas of this world in my hand, I would perhaps beg you to cut off my hand immediately; under no circumstances would I keep it closed so long. I was not made to be a gaoler of ideas. By God, I would set them free. Even though they should materialize into the most hazardous realities, though they should storm through all lands like a mad bacchanalian procession, though they should crush our most innocent flowers with their thyrsi, though they should break into our hospitals and chase the sick old world from its bed—my heart would sorrow, to be sure, and I myself would come to grief! For alas, I too am part of this sick old world, and the poet says rightly, even though you make fun of your crutches, you can't walk any better for it. I am the sickest of you all, and am the more to be pitied since I know what health is. But you—you don't know, you enviable ones! You are capable of dying without even noticing it. Yes, many of you are long since dead and maintain that your real life is only now beginning. When I contradict such a delusion, you get mad at me and revile me—and—a horrible thing!—the corpses rush at me and insult me,

123. Bernard Le Bovier de Fontenelle (1657–1757), a writer, nephew of Corneille.

and still more annoying than their insults is the smell of
their putrefaction. Away, you ghosts! I shall now speak
of a man whose very name has the power of an exorcism.
I shall speak of Immanuel Kant.

It is said that nocturnal spirits are terrified at sight of
the executioner's sword. How terrified they must then be
when someone holds up to them Kant's *Critique of Pure
Reason*! This book is the sword with which deism was
executed in Germany.

To speak frankly, you French are tame and moderate
compared with us Germans. The most you could do was
kill a king, and he had already lost his head before you
beheaded him. And in doing this you had to drum and
shriek so much and stamp your feet till the whole uni-
verse trembled. Truly, it does Maximilian Robespierre
too much honor to compare him with Immanuel Kant.
Maximilian Robespierre, the great bourgeois of the Rue
Saint Honoré, did indeed have his attacks of destructive
rage when it was a question of the monarchy, and his
convulsions were frightful enough in his regicidal epi-
lepsy; but as soon as there was any mention of the Su-
preme Being, he washed the white froth from his mouth
and the blood from his hands, put on his blue Sunday
coat with the shiny buttons, and, what's more, stuck a
nosegay in the front of his broad vest.

The history of Immanuel Kant's life is difficult to por-
tray, for he had neither life nor history. He led a me-
chanically ordered, almost abstract bachelor existence in
a quiet, remote little street in Königsberg, an old town
on the northeastern border of Germany. I do not believe
that the great clock of the cathedral there performed
more dispassionately and methodically its outward rou-
tine of the day than did its fellow countryman Immanuel
Kant. Getting up in the morning, drinking coffee, writ-
ing, giving lectures, eating, walking, everything had its
appointed time, and the neighbors knew for certain that

it was half-past three when Immanuel Kant, in his gray frock-coat, his Spanish cane in his hand, stepped out of his house and strolled to the little linden avenue called after him to this day the "Philosopher's Path." Eight times he walked up and down it, in every season of the year, and when the sky was overcast, or gray clouds announced a rain coming, old Lampe, his servant, was seen walking anxiously behind him with a big umbrella under his arm, like an image of Providence.

What a strange contrast between the outward life of the man and his destructive, world-crushing thoughts! Truly, if the citizens of Königsberg had had any premonition of the full significance of his ideas, they would have felt a far more terrifying dread at the presence of this man than at the sight of an executioner, an executioner who merely executes people. But the good folk saw in him nothing but a professor of philosophy, and as he passed by at his customary hour, they gave him a friendly greeting and perhaps set their watches by him.

If, however, Immanuel Kant, the arch-destroyer in the realm of ideas, far surpassed Maximilian Robespierre in terrorism, yet he possessed many similarities with the latter which invite comparison of the two men. In the first place, we find in both the same stubborn, keen, unpoetic, sober integrity. We also find in both the same talent for suspicion, only that the one directs his suspicion toward ideas and calls it criticism, while the other applies it to people and entitles it republican virtue. But both represented in the highest degree the type of the provincial bourgeois. Nature had destined them to weigh coffee and sugar, but Fate determined that they should weigh other things and placed on the scales of the one a king, on the scales of the other a god.

And they gave the correct weight!

The *Critique of Pure Reason* is Kant's chief work, and we must give preference to it in our discussion. None of all his other works has greater significance. This book, as already mentioned, appeared in 1781 but did not become generally known until 1789.[124] In the beginning it was completely overlooked, only two insignificant reviews of it appeared at that time, and only late, with articles by Schütz, Schulz, and Reinhold, was the attention of the public directed to this great work. The reason for the tardy recognition probably lies in the unusual form and bad style in which the book is written. As to his style, Kant deserves more severe censure than any other philosopher, all the more when we consider the better style of his earlier writing. The recently published collection of his minor works contains his first attempts, and we are surprised at the fine and often very witty style. While Kant was working out in his mind his great work, he hummed to himself these little essays. In them he is smiling like a soldier calmly arming himself for a battle he feels certain of winning. Especially remarkable among them are the *General Natural History and Theory of the Heavens*, written as early as 1755; *Observations on the Emotions of the Beautiful and the Sublime*, written ten years later; and *Dreams of a Spirit-Seer*, full of fine wit after the manner of the French essay. The wit of a Kant, as displayed in these lesser works, is something extremely individual. The wit clings to the thought, and despite its weakness is thus able to achieve a refreshing height. Without such support, to be sure, not even the most fertile wit can succeed; like the grapevine that lacks a stake, it must then creep wretchedly along on the ground and rot together with all its most precious fruits.

But why did Kant write his *Critique of Pure Reason* in such a colorless, dry, wrapping-paper style? I think he feared that because he had rejected the mathematical form of the Cartesian-Leibnitzian-Wolfian philosophers,

124. It was the second edition, in 1787, that caused a stir in Germany.

science might lose something of its dignity if it were expressed in a light, pleasantly cheerful tone. Hence he gave it a stiff, abstract form which coldly repelled any familiarity on the part of intellects of the lower order. He wanted to separate himself superciliously from the contemporary popular philosophers, who strove for the plainest clarity, and he clothed his ideas in a courtly, frigid, bureaucratic language. In this he shows himself to be a true philistine. Possibly, however, Kant also needed for his carefully calculated sequence of ideas a language that was similarly calculated, and he was not capable of creating a better one. Only a genius possesses for a new idea a new word as well. But Immanuel Kant was not a genius. Conscious of this deficiency, like the worthy Maximilian, Kant was all the more suspicious of genius, and in his *Critique of Judgment* he even maintained that a genius had no function in the pursuit of scientific knowledge, that his effectiveness belonged to the realm of art.

Due to the ponderous, pedantic style of his main work, Kant did an enormous amount of damage. For his brainless imitators aped him in this external characteristic, and hence there arose among the Germans the superstition that you can't be a philosopher if you write well. After Kant, however, the mathematical form could no longer prevail in philosophy. In his *Critique of Pure Reason* he quite mercilessly pronounced the sentence of death on this form. The mathematical form in philosophy, he said, produced nothing but houses of cards, just as the philosophical form in mathematics produces only vain prattle. For in philosophy there can be no definitions such as in mathematics, where definitions are not discursive but intuitive, that is, they can be demonstrated by perception; what are called definitions in philosophy are put forth only experimentally and hypothetically, the truly correct definition appearing only at the end, as result.

Why is it that philosophers show such a great preference for the mathematical form? This preference begins as early as Pythagoras, who designated the principles of things by numbers. This was a brilliant idea. In a number the material and the finite are cast aside, and yet the number designates something definite and also the relationship of this definite thing to another definite thing, which last, if it is likewise designated by a number, has assumed the same dematerialized and infinite character. In this respect a number resembles ideas that have the same character and the same relationship to each other. Ideas, as they appear in our minds and in nature, can be designated very precisely by numbers; but the number nonetheless always remains a symbol for the idea, not the idea itself. The master is always aware of this difference, but the pupil forgets it and passes on to future pupils only a hieroglyphic of numbers, mere ciphers whose living significance no one knows any longer and which are repeated parrot-fashion with schoolboy-pride. This also applies to the other principles of mathematical demonstration. The intellectual process in its perpetual activity does not permit any fixity; it cannot be fixed by line, triangle, square, or circle any more than by numbers. Thought can neither be calculated nor measured.

Since I am chiefly interested in facilitating the study of German philosophy in France, I always discuss principally those external characteristics that can easily discourage a foreigner if he has not been informed about them in advance. I want particularly to call the attention of men of letters who wish to adapt Kant for the French public to the fact that they can omit that part of his philosophy which serves merely to combat the absurdities of Wolfian philosophy. This polemic, constantly reappearing, can create only confusion in the minds of the French and can be of no benefit to them . . .

As I have already said, the *Critique of Pure Reason* is

Kant's chief work, and his other writings can to some extent be viewed as superfluous or at any rate as commentaries. The social significance contained in that chief work will become clear from what follows.

Philosophers before Kant did, to be sure, ponder the origin of our cognitions and, as we have already shown, followed two different paths, depending on whether they assumed ideas as *a priori* or as *a posteriori*. There has been less reflection on the faculty of knowing itself, on the scope or on the limits of this faculty. This now became Kant's task; he subjected our faculty of knowing to a ruthless examination; he sounded all the depths of this faculty and established all its limits. He found, to be sure, that about a great many things which previously we believed ourselves to have the most intimate acquaintance with, we can know nothing at all. This was extremely annoying. But it has always been useful to know what things we cannot know anything about. He who warns us about useless roads does us just as good a service as he who shows us the right road. Kant proved to us that we can know nothing about things as they are in and of themselves, but that we know something about them only in so far as they are reflected in our minds. Thus we are just like the prisoners of whom Plato paints such a depressing picture in the seventh book of his *Republic*. These unfortunate beings, fettered at their necks and thighs so that they cannot turn their heads, are seated in a dungeon open at the top, and they get some light from above. This light, however, comes from a fire burning on a height behind them, and indeed is separated from them by a low wall. Along this wall walk people carrying all sorts of statues, images made of wood or stone, and talking with one another. Now the poor prisoners can see nothing at all of these people, who are not so tall as the wall, and of the statues carried past, which tower above the wall, they see only the shadows which move along on the wall opposite them. They take these shadows to be the real objects, and, deceived by the echo of their dungeon, they think it is the shadows that are talking with one another.

Earlier philosophy, which ran about sniffing at things and collecting and classifying their characteristics, came to an end when Kant appeared. He directed investigation back to the human mind and examined what was to be found there. Hence he compared his philosophy, and not without reason, with Copernicus' procedure. Previously, when the world was made to stand still and the sun to revolve around it, astronomical calculations did not agree very well. Then Copernicus made the sun stand still and the earth revolve around it, and behold, everything now functioned splendidly. Previously reason, like the sun, moved around the physical world and tried to illumine it, but Kant made reason, the sun, stand still, and the physical world revolves around it and is illumined wherever it comes within the realm of this sun.

After these few words, with which I have indicated Kant's mission, everyone will understand why I consider that section of his book in which he deals with the so-called phenomena and noumena the most important part, the center, of his philosophy. For Kant distinguishes between the appearances of things and things themselves. Since we can know nothing about things except in so far as they manifest themselves to us through their appearance, and since, therefore, things, as they are in and of themselves, are not revealed to us, Kant called things as they appear to be, phenomena, and things in and of themselves, noumena. We can know something only about things as phenomena, but we can know nothing about things as noumena. The latter are purely problematic. We can neither say that they exist nor that they do not exist. Indeed, the word noumenon is paired with the word phenomenon only so that one can speak about things, in as far as they are accessible to our knowledge, without touching, in our judgment, upon things not accessible to our knowledge.

Thus Kant did not, as do many teachers whom I do not care to name, divide things into phenomena and noumena, into things that for us exist and things that for us do not exist. This would be an Irish bull in philosophy. His intention was simply to give a concept of limitation.

According to Kant, God is a noumenon. As a result of his argument, this transcendental ideal being which we have hitherto called God is nothing but a fiction. It arose from a natural illusion. Yes, Kant shows that we can know nothing at all about this noumenon, about God, and that even any future proof of his existence will be impossible. We shall write Dante's words, "Leave hope behind,"[125] at the head of this section of the *Critique of Pure Reason*.

I believe you will gladly exempt me from attempting a discussion for the general public of this section which deals with "the arguments of speculative reason in favor of the existence of a supreme being." Although the actual refutation of these arguments does not occupy much space and does not appear until the second half of the book, it is quite deliberately prepared for from the very beginning and is one of the main points of the work. Upon this follows the "Critique of All Speculative Theology," in which the remaining phantoms of the deists are destroyed. I cannot help remarking that in attacking the three principal types of proof for the existence of God, namely, the ontological, the cosmological, and the physicotheological, Kant succeeded, in my opinion, in destroying the last two but not the first. I do not know whether the above terms are understood here in France,

125. A reference to the inscription above the gate of Hell in Dante's *Divine Comedy*. It begins: "All hope abandon, ye who enter here."

and I therefore quote the passage from the *Critique of Pure Reason* in which Kant formulates the differences:

"Only three kinds of proof of the existence of God are possible on the basis of speculative reason. All the paths that may be taken with this aim in view start either from definite experience and the particular nature of the material world as revealed by experience and ascend from this world according to the laws of causality up to the supreme first cause beyond the world; or they are based merely on an indefinite experience, on some sort of existence or being; or, lastly, they make an abstraction from all experience and arrive at the conclusion, entirely *a priori* from pure ideas, of the existence of a supreme first cause. The first proof is the physicotheological, the second the cosmological, and the third the ontological. There are no other proofs, nor can others exist."

After repeated and thorough study of Kant's chief work I fancied I perceived everywhere visible his polemic against the existent proofs of the existence of God, and I would discuss it at greater length were I not restrained by religious sentiment. The mere fact that I see someone discussing the existence of God arouses in me a strange anxiety, a dismal dejection, such as I once experienced at New Bedlam[126] in London when I lost sight of my guide and found myself surrounded by nothing but madmen. "God is all that is," and doubt of His existence is doubt of life itself, is death.

As objectionable as any dispute about the existence of God may be, all the more praiseworthy is reflection on the nature of God. This reflection is true worship of God; the spirit is thereby diverted from the transitory and finite and attains to consciousness of innate love and of eternal harmony. In prayer or in the contemplation of spiritual symbols this consciousness thrills the man of

126. An insane asylum.

feeling; the thinker finds this holy fervor in the exercise
of that sublime faculty of the mind called reason, whose
highest function is to inquire into the nature of God.
People of specially religious bent occupy themselves
with this task from childhood on; as early as the first
stirring of reason they are mysteriously obsessed by it.
The author of these pages is most thankfully aware of
having possessed this early primitive religiosity, and it
has never deserted him. God was always the beginning
and the end of all my thoughts. I now ask: what is God?
what is His nature?, but even as a small child I used to
ask: what is God like? how does He look? And at that
time I could gaze up into the sky for days on end and in
the evening was very sad that I had not once caught sight
of God's most holy countenance but had seen only silly,
grotesque faces in the gray clouds. Information about
astronomy, which then, in the Age of Enlightenment, not
even the youngest children were spared, confused me
completely, and I was no end astonished that all those
thousands of millions of stars were spheres just as large
and beautiful as ours and that over all this sparkling
throng of worlds a single god ruled. Once in a dream, I
remember, I saw God, far above in the remotest distance.
He was looking contentedly out of a little window in the
sky, a pious old man's face with a little Jewish beard, and
scattering quantities of seeds which, as they fell down
from heaven, sprouted, as it were, in infinite space and
expanded to vast dimensions until they became gleam-
ing, blossoming, populated worlds, each as large as our
own earth. I have never been able to forget that face;
afterwards in dreams I often saw the cheerful old man
pouring down from his little window in the sky the seeds
of the universe; once I even saw him clucking like our
servant girl when she threw the hens their barley feed.
I could see only how the falling seeds always expanded
into huge, sparkling globes, but the huge hens that were

perhaps waiting somewhere impatiently with beaks wide open in order to be fed with the scattered globes I could not see.

You smile, dear reader, at the huge hens. But this childish notion is not so very far removed from the view of the most advanced deists. Orient and Occident have exhausted themselves with childish hyperboles in order to provide a conception of an extramundane god. The imagination of the deists, however, has exerted itself to no purpose in dealing with the infinity of space and time. It is here that their impotence, the emptiness of their world view, of their conception of the nature of God, becomes fully apparent. Hence we are not greatly disturbed when this conception is destroyed. Kant did indeed inflict this injury on them by refuting their proofs of the existence of God.

A vindication of the ontological proof would not particularly benefit deism, for this proof can also be used for pantheism. To make this easier to understand, let me note that the ontological proof is the one which Descartes put forward and which long before that, in the Middle Ages, had been expressed in the form of a moving[127] prayer by Anselm of Canterbury. Indeed, one might say that St. Augustine already established the ontological proof in the second book of *De libro arbitrio*.[128]

I shall refrain, as I have said, from any discussion for the benefit of the general public of Kant's polemic against these proofs. I shall content myself with assuring you that since then deism has vanished from the realm of speculative reason. It may perhaps take several centuries before this sad death notice gets into general circulation—we, however, have long since put on mourning. *De profundis!*

127. I follow here Strodtmann's reading of *rührenden* instead of *ruhenden* ("resting" or "peaceful"), as in the editions by Elster and Walzel.
128. *On Free Will.*

You think we can go home now? Not on your life! There is another piece still to be performed. After the tragedy comes the farce. Up to this point Immanuel Kant presents the picture of the relentless philosopher; he stormed heaven, put the whole garrison to the sword, the sovereign of the world swam unproven in his own blood, there was now no all-mercifulness, no paternal kindness, no reward in the other world for renunciation in this, the immortality of the soul lay in its last throes—you could hear its groans and death rattle; and old Lampe stood there, a mournful spectator, his unbrella under his arm, cold sweat and tears pouring from his face. Then Immanuel Kant relented and showed that he was not simply a great philosopher but also a good man, and he deliberated and said, half good-naturedly and half ironically, "Old Lampe must have a God, otherwise the poor fellow can't be happy. But man ought to be happy in this world —practical reason says so—that's certainly all right with me—then let practical reason also guarantee the existence of God." As a result of this argument Kant distinguished between theoretical reason and practical reason, and by means of the latter, as with a magician's wand, he revived the corpse of Deism, which theoretical reason had killed.

But did Kant perhaps undertake this resurrection, not simply for old Lampe's sake, but also because of the police? Or did he really act out of conviction? Did he perhaps, just by destroying all the proofs for the existence of God, intend to show us clearly how awkward it is not to be able to know anything about the existence of God? In this matter he acted almost as wisely as a Westphalian friend of mine who had smashed all the lamps in Grohnder Street and then, standing in the dark, delivered a long lecture to us on the practical necessity of lamps, which he had broken scientifically only in order to show us that we could see nothing without them.

I have already mentioned that when it appeared, the *Critique of Pure Reason* did not create the slightest sensation. Not until several years later, when certain perceptive philosophers had written commentaries on it, did it arouse public attention, and in 1789 nothing was talked of in Germany but Kant's philosophy, and it received an abundance of commentaries, chrestomathies, interpretations, criticisms, apologies, etc. One needs only to glance at the first philosophic catalogue at hand, and the legion of works about Kant published at that time testifies adequately to the intellectual stimulus that originated with this single man. Some showed a bubbling enthusiasm, others bitter annoyance, many a gaping curiosity about the result of this intellectual revolution. We had riots in the intellectual world just as you had in the material world, and we became just as excited over the demolition of ancient dogmatism as you did over the storming of the Bastille. There was also but a handful of the totally disabled, all old, left for the defense of dogmatism, that is, the philosophy of Wolf. It was a revolution, and there was no lack of atrocities. In the party of tradition the really good Christians were the least indignant at these atrocities. In fact, they desired still worse ones so that patience might be exhausted and the counterrevolution take place more speedily as an inevitable reaction. We had pessimists in philosophy as you had in politics. Many of our pessimists went so far in their self-deception as to believe that Kant was in secret alliance with them and that he had detroyed the previous proofs of the existence of God merely in order that the world might realize that one can never arrive at a knowledge of God by the use of reason and must therefore, in this matter, adhere to revealed religion.

Kant brought about this great intellectual movement less by the content of his writings than by the critical spirit that pervaded them and now made its way into all branches of knowledge. All disciplines were affected by it. Yes, even poetry did not escape its influence. Schiller, for instance, was a strong Kantian, and his views on art are impregnated with the spirit of Kantian philosophy. Because of its dry, abstract character this philosophy was extremely harmful to belles-lettres and fine arts. Fortunately it did not interfere with the art of cooking.

The German people is not easily set in motion; but once it has been directed to a certain path, it will follow this path with the most dogged perseverance to the very end. We showed this trait in matters of religion. We also showed it in philosophy. Will we continue to advance as consistently in politics?

Germany had been drawn by Kant onto the path of philosophy, and philosophy became a national cause. A sizeable troop of great thinkers suddenly emerged from German soil as if conjured up by magic. If some day German philosophy finds, as the French Revolution found, its Thiers and its Mignet,[129] its history will provide just as remarkable reading, and Germans will read it with pride and Frenchmen with admiration.

Among Kant's followers Johann Gottlieb Fichte rose to prominence at an early stage.

I almost despair of being able to convey an accurate idea of the importance of this man. In the case of Kant we had only a book to examine. But here, besides the book we have to examine the man. In this man thought and conviction were one, and in this magnificent unity they influenced the contemporary world. Thus we have not only a philosophy to discuss but a personality by which that philosophy is conditioned, so to speak, and in order to understand the influence of both, a description of the contemporary state of affairs would be necessary.

129. François Mignet, French historian and journalist. He and his friend Thiers played an important part in the liberal opposition to the government of Charles X.

What an extensive task! We shall surely be fully ex-
onerated for offering here only meager information.

It is extremely difficult to give an account even of
Fichte's ideas. We encounter peculiar difficulties, diffi-
culties connected not merely with the subject matter but
also with the form and method of presentation, two
things with which we would like to make the foreigner
acquainted at the very outset. First, then, concerning
Fichte's method. Originally it was borrowed entirely
from Kant, but it soon underwent a change because of
the nature of the subject. Kant had only to put forward
a critique, that is, something negative, whereas Fichte
had, later on, to set up a system, consequently, some-
thing positive. Because of the lack of a definite system
Kant's philosophy was sometimes denied the name "phi-
losophy." As regards Immanuel Kant himself, this was
correct, but certainly not as regards the Kantians, who
constructed from Kant's propositions a quite sufficient
number of definite systems. In his earlier writings Fichte
remained, as I have said, entirely faithful to Kant's
method, so much so that his first treatise, published
anonymously, was understandably thought to be a work
of Kant's. But when Fichte later set up a system, he was
seized with an ardent and headstrong passion for con-
struction, and after constructing the whole universe, he
began, just as ardently and obstinately, to prove every
detail of these constructions. In this constructing and
proving Fichte manifests, so to speak, a passion for the
abstract. As in his system itself, subjectivity also soon
prevailed in his exposition. Kant, on the other hand, laid
a thought before him, and dissected it, and analyzed it
down to its most minute fibers, and his *Critique of Pure
Reason* is a kind of anatomical theater of the intellect.
During the dissection he himself remained cold and un-
feeling, like a true surgeon.

The form of Fichte's works resembles the method. It

is full of life, but it also has all the defects of life: it is unbalanced and confusing. In order to remain lively Fichte rejected the usual terminology of philosophers, which he felt to be dead, but this makes him still more difficult to understand. He had, after all, quite peculiar ideas about intelligibility. When Reinhold[130] shared an opinion with him, Fichte declared that no one understood him better than Reinhold. But when afterward the latter differed with him, Fichte declared that Reinhold had never understood him. When Fichte disagreed with Kant, he published the statement that Kant did not understand himself. I am here touching only on the comical aspect of our philosophers. They are forever complaining about not being understood. When Hegel was lying on his deathbed, he said, "Only one person has understood me," but immediately afterward he added crossly, "and even he didn't understand me."

As far as content alone is concerned, Fichte's philosophy is not of great importance. It provided no fruits for society. Only insofar as it is one of the most remarkable phases of all German philosophy, only insofar as it attests to the sterility of idealistic philosophy in its final consequences, and only insofar as it forms the necessary transition to present-day nature philosophy, is the content of Fichte's doctrine of some interest. Since this content is thus more important historically and scientifically than socially, I shall sketch it only very brieflly.

The task that Fichte set himself was: what reasons do we have for assuming that there are objects external to us which correspond to our ideas of them? And to this question he gave the answer: all things have reality only in our minds.

Just as the *Critique of Pure Reason* is Kant's chief work,

130. Karl Leonhard Reinhold (1758-1823), for a long time professor at the University of Jena, was the first to call the attention of a wider public to Kant's philosophy.

the *Science of Knowledge* is Fichte's. The latter work is a kind of continuation of the former. The *Science of Knowledge* likewise directs the mind back to itself. But where Kant analyzes, Fichte constructs. The *Science of Knowledge* begins with an abstract equation (I = I); it creates the world out of the depths of the mind; it reunites the fragmented parts; it retraces its course along the road of abstraction until it reaches the world of phenomena. The mind can then declare the phenomenal world to be a necessary operation of the intelligence.

With Fichte there is also the special difficulty that he attributes to the mind the ability to observe itself while it is active. The ego is supposed to reflect on its intellectual activities while performing them. Thought is to spy upon itself while it thinks, while it gradually becomes warm, then warmer, and is finally cooked to a turn. This operation reminds us of the monkey sitting on the hearth in front of a copper kettle, cooking his own tail. For it was his opinion that true culinary art does not consist merely in the objective act of cooking but also in becoming subjectively aware of the process of cooking.

It is a singular circumstance that Fichte's philosophy always had to endure a great deal of satire. I once saw a caricature representing a Fichtean goose. It had such a large liver that it no longer knew whether it was a goose or a liver. On its stomach was written: I = I . . . To the general public the fact that idealistic philosophy, pursued consistently to its ultimate conclusions, should end by denying even the reality of matter seemed to be carrying the joke too far. We rather enjoyed making fun of the Fichtean Ego, which created by mere thought the whole physical world. The mockers among us were aided by a misunderstanding that had become too popular to permit me to leave it unmentioned. The great mass of people really thought that the Fichtean Ego was the ego of Johann Gottlieb Fichte, and that this individual ego de-

nied all other existences. "What impudence!" exclaimed
the good people, "this fellow doesn't believe that we
exist, we who are far more corpulent than he is and, as
mayors and magistrates, are actually his superiors!" The
ladies asked, "Doesn't he at least believe in the existence
of his wife? No? And Madame Fichte doesn't mind?"

The Fichtean Ego, however, is not an individual ego,
but the universal world-Ego awakened to self-awareness.
The Fichtean process of thought is not the thinking of an
individual, of a certain person called Johann Gottlieb
Fichte; quite the contrary—it is the universal thought
manifesting itself in an individual. Just as we say, "It is
raining," "It is lightening," and so on, so Fichte ought
not to say, "I think," but "It thinks," "Universal world-
thought is thinking in me."

In a comparison between the French Revolution and
German philosophy I once, more in jest than in earnest,
compared Fichte with Napoleon. But there are, in fact,
remarkable similarities between them. After the Kant-
ians had completed their terroristic work of destruction,
Fichte appeared, just as Napoleon appeared after the
Convention had demolished the whole past, and like the
Kantians by using a critique of pure reason. Napoleon
and Fichte represent the great inexorable Ego in which
thought and action are one, and the colossal structures
successfully created by both testify to a colossal will. But
due to the boundlessness of this will their structures
soon collapsed, and both the *Science of Knowledge* and the
Empire disintegrated and vanished as quickly as they
arose.

The Empire is now nothing but history, but the agita-
tion which the Emperor produced in the world has not
yet subsided, and from this agitation our times still draw
their vitality. So it is also with Fichte's philosophy. It has
completely perished, but men's minds are still excited by

the thoughts that found a voice in Fichte, and the after-effect of his words is incalculable. Even supposing all transcendental idealism was an error, yet Fichte's writings were animated by a proud independence, a love of liberty, a manly dignity that have had a wholesome influence, especially on the young. The Ego of Fichte was in complete accord with his inflexible, stubborn, austere character. The theory of such an all-powerful Ego could perhaps originate only from such a character, and such a character, rooted in such a theory, could not but become still more inflexible, more stubborn, more austere.

How unscrupulous sceptics, frivolous eclectics, and moderates of all shades must have loathed this man! His whole life was a constant battle. The story of his youth, like that of almost all our distinguished men, is a series of afflictions. Poverty sits by their cradles and rocks them to manhood, and this scrawny nurse remains their faithful companion through life.

Nothing is more touching than the sight of the proud-willed Fichte struggling to make his way in the world by being a private tutor. He could not find even this wretched servant's wage in his own country and had to go to Warsaw. There it was the old story. The tutor fails to please the gracious lady of the house, or perhaps even the ungracious lady's maid. His bows are not genteel enough, not French enough, and he is no longer judged worthy of directing the education of a young Polish nobleman. Johann Gottlieb Fichte was dismissed like a lackey, received from his dissatisfied employers scarcely a meager sum for traveling expenses, left Warsaw, and, with youthful enthusiasm, went to Königsberg to make the acquaintance of Kant. The meeting of these two men is interesting in every respect, and I do not think I can illustrate their ways and their circumstances better than by citing a fragment from Fichte's diary, to be found in a biography of him recently published by his son.[131]

"On the 25th of June I set out for Königsberg with a coachman from there and arrived without any particular hazards on the first of July.—On the fourth I visited Kant, who did not, however, receive me with any special attention. I attended a lecture of his at his invitation and again found my expectations disappointed. His delivery is dull. Meantime I have begun this journal.—

"I have long wished for a more serious interview with Kant, but found no way of bringing this about. At last I hit upon the plan of writing a 'Critique of All Revelation' and of presenting it to him instead of a letter of introduction. I began about the thirteenth and since then have been working at it continuously.—On the eighteenth of August I finally sent the completed work to Kant, and on the twenty-fifth went to call on him to hear his opinion of it. He received me with the most marked kindness and seemed very well satisfied with my essay. We did not get into any detailed scholarly discussion; in regard to my philosophical doubts he referred me to his *Critique of Pure Reason* and to the court chaplain, Schulz, whom I shall look up immediately. On the twenty-sixth I dined with Kant in the company of Professor Sommer, and I found Kant to be a very pleasant and clever man. I now for the first time perceived in him traits worthy of the great intellect that reposes in his writings.

"On the twenty-seventh I brought this journal entry to a close, after having completed the excerpts from Kant's lectures on anthropology, lent me by Mr. von S. At the same time I resolve from now on to continue this journal regularly every evening before going to bed and to record everything of interest that happens to me, but especially traits of character and observations.

131. *Johann Gottlieb Fichte's Life and Literary Correspondence* by Immanuel Hermann Fichte, published 1830-1831.

"The twenty-eighth, evening. Yesterday I began to revise my 'Critique,' and many good and profound ideas occurred to me which, however, unfortunately convinced me that the first version is completely superficial. Today I wanted to continue my new investigations, but found myself so carried away by my imagination that I have not been able to do anything all day. Alas, in my present position this is not surprising. I have calculated that, counting from today, I can subsist here only fourteen more days.—To be sure, I have been in such straits before, but it was in my own country, and besides, with advancing years and a stronger sense of honor, such circumstances become harder and harder to endure.—I have made no decision, cannot make one.—I don't want to confide in Pastor Borowski, to whom Kant sent me; if I must confide in someone, it will be to no one but Kant himself.

"On the twenty-ninth I visited Borowski and found him to be a truly good and honorable man. He suggested a position for me, but it is not yet absolutely definite and besides, I don't like it. At the same time, by the frankness of his manner, he extorted from me the admission that I was in dire need of finding a position. He advised me to go to Professor W. It has been impossible for me to work.—The following day I did in fact call on W. and afterwards visited the court chaplain, Schulz. The prospects held out by the former are very uncertain; still he mentioned positions as house tutor in Kurland, which certainly nothing but the most extreme necessity will induce me to accept! . . .

"By the first of September I had made a firm decision which I wanted to tell Kant about. A position as private tutor, however reluctantly I might have accepted it, is not to be found, and the uncertainty of my situation prevents me from working here with freedom of mind and benefiting from the instructive association with my friends. So off, and back to my own country! The small loan that I need for this purpose will perhaps be obtained through Kant's good offices. But as I was about to go to him and make my proposal, my courage failed me. I decided to write. For the evening I was invited to the court chaplain's, where I spent a very pleasant evening. On the second I finished the letter to Kant and sent it off."

Despite the remarkableness of this letter, I cannot bring myself to give it here in French. I fancy a red blush mounting to my cheeks, and I feel as if I were relating in the presence of strangers the most humiliating troubles of my own family. In spite of my striving for French urbanity, in spite of the cosmopolitanism of my philosophy, old Germany, with all its petty bourgeois sentiments, still holds its place in my heart.—Enough, I cannot transmit this letter and shall simply relate: Immanuel Kant was so poor that, notwithstanding the pathetic, heartrending tone of the letter, he could not lend Johann Gottlieb Fichte any money. The latter was not in the least annoyed by this, as we can see from the words in his journal which I shall add here:

"On the third of September I was invited to Kant's. He received me with his usual candor, telling me, however, that he had not yet come to a decision about my proposal, that he would not be able to do so for two weeks. What kind frankness! For the rest, he raised objections to my plans which revealed that he is not sufficiently familiar with our situation in Saxony.—During all these days I have done nothing, but I want to set to work again and simply leave the rest to God.—The sixth.—I was invited to Kant's, and he suggested that I sell my manuscript on 'The Critique of All Revelation' to the publisher Hartung, through the intervention of Pastor Borowski. 'It is well written,' he said, when I spoke of revising it.—Is this true? And yet Kant says so!—I might add that he refused my first request.—On the tenth I had lunch at Kant's. Nothing said about our affair; Magister Gensichen was present, and only general conversation, in part very interesting. And Kant remains the same toward me, completely unchanged.—On the thirteenth, today, I wanted to work, and I get nothing done. I am overcome by depression. How will this end? How will things be a week from now? By that time my money will be all gone!''

After much wandering about and after a long stay in Switzerland, Fichte finally found a permanent position at Jena, and his most brilliant period dates from this time. Jena and Weimar, two little Saxon towns only a few hours distant fom each other,[132] were then the center of German intellectual life. At Weimar were the court and poetry; at Jena, the university and philosophy. *There* we saw the greatest poets, *here* the greatest scholars of Germany. In 1794 Fichte began his lectures at Jena. The date is significant and explains the spirit of his writings at this period as well as the tribulations to which he was exposed from then on and to which, four years later, he finally succumbed. For in 1798 there were raised against him the accusations of atheism which brought insufferable persecutions upon him and were also the cause of his departure from Jena. This event, the most noteworthy in Fichte's life, has a general significance too, and we must not pass over it in silence. This is also the natural place to speak of Fichte's views concerning the nature of God.

In the periodical *The Philosophical Journal*, of which Fichte was then the editor, he published an article called "The Development of the Concept of Religion," sent to him by a certain Forberg, a schoolteacher in Saalfeld. To this article he appended a short explanatory essay with the title "Concerning the Basis of Our Belief in a Divine Government of the Universe."[133]

132. Hours by coach or on horseback, of course.

133. In this article Fichte declared that God and the moral order of the universe were synonymous.

Both articles were suppressed by the government of the Electorate of Saxony under the pretext that they contained atheistic doctrine, and at the same time a requisition was sent from Dresden to the court of Weimar demanding that it punish Professor Fichte severely. The court of Weimar had of course not let itself be misled by such a demand, but since Fichte on this occasion committed the gravest blunders, for instance, writing an appeal to the public[134] without consulting official authorities, the Weimar government, annoyed at this action and under pressure from outside, had no alternative but to goad with a mild reproof the professor who had been so indiscreet in expressing his views. Fichte, however, believing himself to be in the right, had no intention of submitting humbly to such reproof and left Jena. To judge from his letters written at this time, he was particularly annoyed at the behavior of two men who, due to their official positions, had an especially weighty voice in his affair; these persons were His Reverence the President of the Consistorial Council, von Herder, and His Excellency the Privy Councillor, von Goethe. But there is sufficient excuse for both. It is touching to read in Herder's posthumous letters how much difficulty the poor man had with the candidates in theology who, after studying at Jena, came to him in Weimar to undergo examination as Protestant ministers. He no longer dared to ask them anything about Christ the Son; he was only glad if they merely acknowledged the existence of the Father. As for Goethe, he expressed himself about this occurrence in his memoirs as follows:

"After Reinhold's departure from Jena, which quite rightly appeared to be a great loss for the University, Fichte had rashly, even audaciously, been appointed as his successor, a man who had expressed himself in his

134. "Appeal to the Public. A Work the Public is Requested to Read before It is Suppressed," published in Jena and Leipzig, 1799.

writings with grandeur, but perhaps not quite properly concerning the most important topics of morality and politics. He was one of the most able men ever seen, and, considered in their broader aspects, there was nothing to find fault with in his views, but how could he conform to a world which he regarded as his own created possession?

"Objections having been raised to the hours he wanted to use on weekdays for public lectures, he undertook to give on Sundays the lectures that had met obstacles. The annoyances arising fom this, some petty, others of more importance, had scarcely been smoothed over and adjusted, not without inconvenience for the higher authorities, when his remarks about God and things divine, about which, to be sure, it would have been better to maintain profound silence, brought us protests from outside circles.

"In his *Philosophical Journal* Fichte had ventured to express himself about God and things divine in a way that seemed to contradict the traditional language used in dealing with such mysteries. He was called to account for this; his defense did not improve matters because he set to work passionately, without any idea of how well disposed people here were towards him, how well they understood how to interpret his ideas, his language,—a thing that couldn't just be explained to him bluntly—and with just as little idea of how people were intending to help him out of the affair with as much lenience as possible. Innumerable discussions, surmises and assertions, corroborations and resolutions, surged confusedly through the university in frequent indecisive deliberations; there was talk of a reproach from the Ministry, of nothing less than a kind of reprimand which Fichte might have to expect. Distraught at hearing this, Fichte considered himself justified in presenting to the Ministry a violent document in which, assuming the certainty of this action against him, he declared vehemently and defiantly that he would never submit to such treatment, that he would rather quit the university without further ado, in which case he wuld not go alone, as several influential teachers, in agreement with him, were intending to leave the place.

"Because of this all the benevolent intentions that had been entertained in his behalf were now suddenly curbed, indeed paralyzed. No solution, no compromise was possible, and the kindest thing was to dismiss him without delay. Only then, after the affair was beyond remedy, did Fichte hear of the turn his friends had meant to give the matter, and he of course regretted his precipitate action, as we also regret it."

Isn't this the very essence of the ministerial Goethe, smoothing things over and hushing them up? In reality he censures Fichte only for having said what he thought and for not having said it with the customary euphemistic expressions. He finds fault not with the thought, but with the word. That deism, since Kant, had been annihilated in the German intellectual world was, as I have already said, a secret everyone knew, a secret, however, that was not to be shouted from the housetops. Goethe was as little of a deist as Fichte; he was a pantheist. But his very position on the heights of pantheism enabled Goethe, with his sharp eyes, to see through perfectly the untenableness of Fichtean philosophy, and his charitable lips could not but smile at it. To the Jews (and every deist is, after all, a Jew) Fichte's philosophy was necessarily an abomination; to the great pagan it was simply a folly. "The great pagan" is the name bestowed on Goethe in Germany, But this name is not entirely appropriate. Goethe's paganism is strangely modernized. His vigorous pagan nature shows itself in his clear, penetrating interpretation of all external phenomena, of all forms and colors. But at the same time Christianity endowed him with a more profound understanding; in spite of his rebellious antipathy toward it, Christianity initiated him into the mysteries of the spiritual world; he drank of the blood of Christ and thus came to understand the most secret voices of nature, like Siegfried, the hero of the *Nibelungen*, who suddenly understood the language of the birds when a drop of blood from the slain dragon moistened his lips. It is a remarkable thing that Goethe's pagan nature was permeated by our most modern sentimentality, that the antique marble pulsated in such a modern fashion, and that he sympathized just as deeply with the sorrows of a young Werther as with the joys of an ancient Greek god. Goethe's pantheism is therefore very different from pagan pantheism. To express myself briefly, Goethe was the Spinoza of poetry. The whole of Goethe's poetry is filled with the same spirit that is wafted toward us from the writings of Spinoza. There is no doubt whatsoever that Goethe paid undivided allegiance to Spinoza's doctrine. At any rate, he occupied himself with it throughout his entire life; in the first part of his memoirs as well as in the last volume, recently published, he frankly acknowledged this. I don't remember now where I read that Herder once exploded peevishly at the constant preoccupation with Spinoza, "If Goethe would only for once pick up some other Latin book than Spinoza!" But this applies not only to Goethe; quite a number of his friends, who later became more or less well-known as poets, paid homage to pantheism in their youth, and this doctrine flourished actively in German art before it attained supremacy among us as a philosophic theory. Just at Fichte's time, when idealism celebrated its most sublime flowering period in the realm of philosophy, it was being violently destroyed in the realm of art, and there began that famous revolution in art which even now is not at an end and which started with the struggle of the Romanticists, the mutinies of the Schlegel brothers, against the ancient classical regime.

As a matter of fact, our first Romanticists acted out of

a pantheistic instinct which they did not themselves understand. The feeling which they took to be nostalgia for the Catholic mother church was of deeper origin than they themselves suspected, and their veneration and partiality for the traditions of the Middle Ages, for the popular beliefs, the Satanism, the sorcery, and the witchcraft of those times—all this was a suddenly awakened, though uncomprehended desire to return to the pantheism of the old Teutons, and what they really loved about it in its despicably befouled and maliciously mutilated form, was the pre-Christian religion of their ancestors. I must remind you here of the first section of this book, where I showed how Christianity absorbed the elements of the old Germanic religion, how these elements, after undergoing the most outrageous transformations, were preserved in the popular beliefs of the Middle Ages in such a way that the old worship of nature came to be regarded as nothing but wicked sorcery, the old gods as nothing but ugly demons, and their chaste priestesses as nothing but profligate witches. From this point of view the aberrations of our first Romanticists can be judged more leniently than is usually the case. They wanted to restore the Catholicism of the Middle Ages because they felt that in it were preserved many of the sacred relics of their earliest ancestors and many of the glories of their earliest national culture. It was these mutilated and desecrated relics that were so sympathetically attractive to their temperaments, and they detested Protestantism and Liberalism, which strove to destroy these relics together with the whole Catholic past.

But I shall return to this subject later. At present it is sufficient merely to mention that even in Fichte's time pantheism was penetrating German art, that even the Catholic Romanticists unconsciously followed this tendency, and that Goethe gave the movement its most definite expression. This is true already in *Werther*, where he yearns for a blissful identification with nature. In *Faust* he tries to establish a relationship with nature by a method boldly mystical and direct: he conjures up the mysterious forces of the earth by the spells from his book of magic. But it is in his lyrics that Goethe's pantheism reveals itself with greatest purity and charm. Spinoza's doctrine has burst out of its mathematical cocoon and flutters about us as Goethean song. Hence the rage of our orthodox believers and pietists against Goethe's lyric. With their pious bears' paws they grope clumsily for this butterfly that constantly eludes them. It is so delicately ethereal, so airily winged. You French can have no idea of it if you do not know the language. These lyrics of Goethe's have a tantalizing charm that is indescribable. The melodious lines cling to your heart like a dearly beloved; the word embraces you as the thought kisses you.

Thus we do not see in Goethe's behavior toward Fichte any of the base motives characterized in even baser language by many contemporaries. They had not understood the different natures of the two men. The most moderate among them misinterpreted Goethe's passivity when, later, Fichte was sorely pressed and persecuted. They did not take into consideration Goethe's situation. This giant was minister in a lilliputian German state. He could never act naturally. It was said of the seated Jupiter of Phidias at Olympia that he would shatter the dome of the temple if he were suddenly to stand up. This was precisely Goethe's position at Weimar; if he had suddenly jumped to his feet from the tranquility of his sitting posture, he would have shattered the housetop of the state, or, what is more probable, he would have broken his head against it. And was he to risk this for a doctrine that was not merely wrong, but also absurd? The German Jupiter remained calmly seated and allowed himself to be worshipped in peace and perfumed with incense.

It would lead me too far from my subject if I tried, from the standpoint of the artistic interests of that time, to justify even more thoroughly Goethe's conduct on the occasion of the accusation against Fichte. In Fichte's favor there is only the fact that the accusation was in reality a pretext behind which political persecution was concealed. A theologian can certainly be accused of atheism because he has obligated himself to teach certain doctrines. A philosopher, however, has not entered into any such obligation, cannot do so, and his thought remains as free as a bird in the air. It is perhaps unfair of me that, partly to spare my own feelings, partly to spare those of others, I do not state here all the circumstances on which that accusation was founded and justified. I shall quote only one of the dubious passages from the censured essay: "--The living and active moral order is itself God; we need no other God, nor can we comprehend any other. There is no basis in human reason for going beyond this moral order of the universe and for assuming, as a conclusion from effect to cause, some special being as the source of this effect. Consequently, the natural intelligence of man certainly does not come to this conclusion; only a philosophy that fails to understand itself deduces it. --"

As is characteristic of stubborn people, Fichte, in his "Appeal to the Public" and in his judicial vindication, spoke out even more sharply and harshly and in language that offends our deepest feelings. We who believe in a real God, a God who reveals Himself to our senses in infinite space and to our spirit in infinite thought; we who worship in nature a visible God and hear His invisible voice in our own souls; we are repelled by the harsh words with which Fichte declares our God to be a mere chimera and even treats Him with irony. It is doubtful, in fact, whether it is irony or simple madness when Fichte frees the dear Lord so absolutely from any sentient attribute that he even denies His existence, since existence is a sentient concept and is only possible as such! "The science of knowledge," he says, "knows no other mode of existence but the sentient, and since existence can be attributed only to the phenomena of experience, this predicate cannot be used to apply to God." Accordingly, Fichte's God has no existence; he does not exist; he manifests himself only as pure action, as a sequence of events, as *ordo ordinans*,[135] as the law of the universe.

It is in such a way that idealism filtered deity through every possible abstraction until in the end not a vestige of it remained. From then on, instead of a king, as with you, instead of a god, as with us, law was sovereign.

But which is more absurd, a *loix athée*,[136] a law that has no god, or a *Dieu-loix*,[137] a god who is only a law?

Fichtean idealism is one of the most colossal errors ever contrived by the human mind. It is more godless and more detestable than the grossest materialism. What is called here in France the atheism of the materialists would be, as I could easily demonstrate, an edifying and devout doctrine in comparison with the consequences of Fichte's transcendental idealism. This much I know: both are repugnant to me. Both views are also anti-poetic. The French materialists have written just as bad verses as the German transcendental idealists. But Fichte's doctrine was not at all dangerous to the State and deserved still less to be persecuted as such. In order to be capable of being led astray by this heresy, one had need of a speculative acumen to be found only in very few people. This false doctrine was completely inaccessible to the great masses with their thousands of thick heads. Fichte's views about God should have been refuted, therefore, by the use of reason, but not by the use of the police. The accusation of atheism in philoso-

135. Regulating order.
136. Law of atheism.
137. A God-law.

phy was something so strange even in Germany that at first Fichte really did not understand what it meant. He said, and quite rightly, that the question as to whether a certain philosophy was atheistic or not sounded to a philosopher just as peculiar as the question whether a triangle was green or red would sound to a mathematician.

This accusation thus had its secret motives, and Fichte soon understood them. Since he was the most honorable person in the world, we can put absolute trust in a letter to Reinhold in which he discusses these secret motives, and since this letter, dated May 22, 1799, describes the entire period and succeeds in giving a clear picture of the man's whole distressing predicament, we shall quote a part of it:

"Weariness and disgust determine[138] my decision, which I have already told you about, to disappear completely for a few years. From the view I took of the matter at that time, I was even convinced that duty required this decision, for in the midst of the present turmoil I would not be listened to anyway and would only make the turmoil worse; but after a few years when the first reaction of astonishment had calmed down, I would speak with all the greater force.—I now think differently. I dare not hold my tongue; if I keep silent now, I might very likely never again have a chance to speak out. Since the alliance between Russia and Austria, I have long thought probable what is now for me a complete certainty after the most recent events and especially since the shocking murder of the ambassadors,[139] about which people here

138. In the original the past tense was used here, as is necessary to fit properly with what follows. Heine's occasional deviations from Fichte's text are usually not significant, but this one is.

139. On April 28, 1799, the French ambassadors Roberjot, Bonnier, and Jean Debry were attacked by Austrian hussars. Debry escaped; the others were murdered.

are jubilant, and about which S. and G.[140] exclaimed, 'That's right, these dogs must be killed!', namely, that from now on despotism will defend itself desperately, that with the aid of Paul and Pitt[141] it will become consistent, that the basis of its plan is to wipe out freedom of thought, and that the Germans will not hinder the attainment of this object.

"Don't imagine, for example, that the court of Weimar believed that attendance at the university would be adversely affected by my presence; it knows the opposite only too well. It was *forced* to remove me as the result of a general plan, strongly supported by the Electorate of Saxony. Burscher[142] in Leipzig, privy to these secrets, bet a considerable sum as early as the end of last year that I would be an exile by the end of this year. Voigt[143] was long ago won over to the opposition through Burgsdorf. The department of science at Dresden has announced that no one who specializes in modern philosophy will be promoted or, if already promoted, will not be allowed to advance further. In the Free School at Leipzig even Rosenmüller's enlightened views were thought suspicious.[144] Luther's Cathechism has recently been reintroduced there, and the teachers have once more been confirmed according to the symbolical books.[145] This sort of thing will keep on and will spread.—In short, nothing is more certain[146] than the absolute certainty that unless the French gain the most tremendous ascend-

140. Schiller and Goethe.

141. Paul, the czar of Russia from 1796 to 1801, and William Pitt (1759–1806), the famous English statesman.

142. A theologian and philosopher, professor at the University of Leipzig.

143. Secretary of state in Weimar.

144. Johann Georg Rosenmüller (1736–1815), from 1785 on professor of theology in Leipzig, established a modern Lutheran liturgy.

145. I.e., the officially recognized Protestant doctrines.

146. Here Heine again changed Fichte's wording. The original reads *es ist mir gewisser als* (it is more certain than).

ancy and unless they accomplish a change in Germany, at least in a considerable portion of it, in a few years no one in Germany who is known to have thought a free thought in the course of his life will any longer find a resting-place.—So for me it is more certain than absolute certainty that even if I now find a modest niche somewhere, within a year or in two years at the most, I would be chased out of it again, and it is dangerous to let oneself be chased from place to place. Rousseau's case is an historical example.

"Suppose I should remain completely silent and never write another word—will I be left in peace on this condition? I think not. And suppose I could hope for this peace from the courts, won't the *clergy,* wherever I go, stir up the masses against me and incite them to stone me and then—request the governments to banish me as a person who disturbs the peace? But *can* I be silent? No, I really can't, for I have reason to believe that if anything of the German spirit can still be saved, it can be saved by my speaking, and by my silence philosophy would be totally and prematurely ruined. Those I do not trust to allow me to exist in silence, I trust even less to permit me to speak.

"But I shall convince them of the harmlessness of my doctrine.—Dear Reinhold, how can you think so well of these people! The more my reputation is cleared, the more innocent I appear, the blacker do these people become and the more enormous does my real crime become. I never did believe they were persecuting my so-called *atheism;* what they are persecuting in me is a free-thinker who is beginning to make himself *intelligible* (Kant's obscurity was his good fortune) and a disreputable *democrat;* they are frightened as by a ghost at the *independence* which, as they vaguely suspect, my philosophy is arousing."

I call attention once more to the fact that this letter was

not written yesterday, but bears the date of May 22, 1799. The political conditions of that time possess a very sad resemblance to present-day conditions in Germany, except that then the spirit of liberty flourished more among scholars, poets, and other men of letters, while today this spirit finds expression much less among such men, but rather among the great active mass of people, among artisans and tradespeople. At the time of the first revolution, while a leaden, most Teutonic lethargy oppressed the people and a brutal calm prevailed in all of Germany, our literary life revealed the wildest seething and ferment. The most isolated author, living in some remote little corner of Germany, participated in this movement; though not being accurately informed about political events, he sensed their social importance with an almost intuitive affinity and expressed it in his writings. This phenomenon reminds me of the big sea shells which are sometimes placed as ornaments on our fireplace mantels and which, however distant they may be from the sea, nonetheless suddenly begin to roar as soon as the hour of flood tide arrives and the waves break against the coast. When the tide of the Revolution began to rise here in Paris, that great human ocean, when its waves surged and roared here, German hearts across the Rhine also roared and raged.—But they were so isolated, surrounded as they were by nothing but unfeeling porcelain, tea cups and coffee pots and Chinese pagodas that nodded their heads mechanically as if they understood what it was all about. Alas, our poor predecessors in Germany had to atone very bitterly for their revolutionary sympathies. Junkers and clerics played their coarsest and meanest tricks on them. Some of them fled to Paris and disappeared or died here in poverty and misery. I recently saw a blind fellow countryman who has been in Paris since that time. I saw him at the Palais Royal, where he had been warming himself a bit in the sun. It was painful to see how pale and thin he was and how he groped his way along the sides of the houses. They told me he was the old Danish poet Heiberg.[147] I also saw not long ago the attic in which citizen Georg Forster died.[148] The friends of liberty who remained in Germany would have had a far worse fate if Napoleon and his Frenchmen had not soon conquered us. Napoleon certainly never had any idea that he himself had been the saviour of ideology. Without him our philosophers along with their ideas would have been exterminated by the gallows and the wheel. But the German friends of liberty, too republican in their sentiments to do homage to Napoleon, and too honorable to ally themselves with a foreign rule, from this time on veiled themselves in profound silence. They went about sorrowfully with broken hearts and sealed lips. When Napoleon fell, they smiled, though sadly, and were silent; they took scarcely any part in the patriotic enthusiasm which then, with the sanction of the highest authorities, burst forth jubilantly in Germany. They knew what they knew, and were silent. As these Republicans lead a very chaste and simple life, they usually live to be very old, and when the July Revolution broke out, many of them were still alive, and we were not a little surprised when the old fellows, whom we had always used to see walking around bent over and in almost imbecile silence, suddenly raised their heads, smiled affably at us young ones, shook hands with us, and told funny stories. I even heard one of them singing; he sang the Marseillaise for us in a café, and we

147. Peter Andreas Heiberg (1758–1841), known chiefly for his comedies. Due to his liberal political opinions he was exiled from Denmark in 1799, and in 1800 he went to Paris, where he spent the rest of his life.

148. Johann Georg Forster (1754–1794) followed in the footsteps of his father to become a traveler and naturalist. His sympathy with the French Revolution led to his going to Paris in 1792 as deputy of the Jacobin Club in Mainz with the mission of effecting a union between France and the Rhineland left of the Rhine. He died in Paris two years later.

learned the melody, and it wasn't long until we sang it better than the old man himself, for sometimes in the middle of the best stanza he would laugh like a fool or cry like a child. It is always a good thing when such old people remain alive to teach young ones the songs. We youngsters shall not forget them, and some of us will one day teach them to grandchildren not yet born. Many of us, however, will have rotted by that time, in prison at home or in an attic in a foreign country.

Let us talk about philosophy again. I have showed above how Fichte's philosophy, constructed of extremely tenuous abstractions, nonetheless manifested an iron inflexibility in its deductions, which ascended to the most audacious heights. But one fine morning we perceived a great change in this philosophy. It began to be florid, and it sniveled; it became gentle and modest. The idealistic Titan who had climbed to heaven on the ladder of ideas and had rummaged around with daring hand in its empty chambers became a creature bowed down with Christian humility who sighed a great deal about love. Such is Fichte's second period, which concerns us little here. His whole system of philosophy underwent the oddest modifications. During this time he wrote a book that you[149] recently translated, *The Destiny of Man.* A similar work, *The Way towards the Blessed Life,* also belongs to this period.

Naturally Fichte, obstinate man that he was, was never willing to admit his own great transformation. He maintained that his philosophy was still the same, except that the terminology had changed and improved; people had never understood him. He also maintained that nature philosophy, which was becoming fashionable in Germany at that time and was supplanting idealism, was, all of it, in principle his own system, and that his pupil, Mr.

149. I.e., the French.

Joseph Schelling, who had renounced him and introduced this new philosophy, had merely revised the terminology and had amplified his, Fichte's, old theory with uninspiring additions.

We arrive here at a new phase of German thought. We have mentioned the names Joseph Schelling and nature philosophy, but as the former is almost completely unknown here and even the term nature philosophy is not generally understood, I must explain the significance of both. It is, of course, impossible to do so exhaustively in this work; we shall devote a later book to this task. At present we shall simply refute certain errors that have crept in and devote some attention only to the social importance of this philosophy.

First of all I must mention that Fichte was not very far wrong in arguing that Mr. Joseph Schelling's doctrine was in reality his own, merely formulated differently and amplified. Just as did Mr. Joseph Schelling, Fichte also taught that there exists only one being, the Ego, the absolute, and he taught the identity of the ideal and the real. In the *Science of Knowledge,* as I have shown, Fichte attempted by means of an intellectual system of ideas to construct the real from the ideal. Mr. Joseph Schelling reversed the procedure; he tried to explain the ideal by the real. To express my meaning more clearly: proceeding from the axiom that thought and nature are one and the same, Fichte, by an operation of the intellect, arrived at the external world; from thought he created nature, from the ideal the real. For Mr. Schelling, however, though he started from the same axiom, the external world became pure ideas; for him nature became thought; the real became the ideal. The two tendencies, Fichte's and Schelling's, thus supplement each other to some extent. For according to the main axiom just referred to, philosophy can be divided into two parts, one of which would show how from the idea nature takes on phenomenal substance, and the other would show how nature resolves itself into pure ideas. Philosophy can therefore be divided into transcendental idealism and nature philosophy. Mr. Schelling actually acknowledged the validity of both tendencies; the latter he followed in his *Ideas towards a Philosophy of Nature,* and the former in his *System of Transcendental Idealism.*

I mention these works, one of which appeared in 1797 and the other in 1800, only because those reciprocally complementary tendencies are expressed in their very titles and not, for instance, because they contain a complete system. No, such a system is not to be found in any of Mr. Schelling's works. Unlike Kant and Fichte, there is no main work of his that may be considered the focal point of his philosophy. It would be unjust to judge Mr. Schelling by the scope of one book or by a strict interpretation of the letter. On the contrary, one must read his books in chronological order, follow in them the gradual development of his thought, and then take firm grasp of his fundamental idea. Indeed, it also often seems to me necessary, in reading his works, to distinguish where thought ceases and poetry begins. For Mr. Schelling is one of those beings on whom nature bestowed more inclination to poetry than poetic power and who, incapable of satisfying the daughters of Parnassus, fled to the forests of philosophy, where he entered into an utterly barren union with abstract hamadryads. The feeling of such persons is poetic, but the instrument, the word, is feeble; they strive in vain for an art form in which to communicate their ideas and their knowledge. Poetry is Mr. Schelling's strength and his weakness. This is what distinguishes him from Fichte, both to his advantage and to his disadvantage. Fichte is merely a philosopher; his power consists in dialectic, and his strength lies in demonstration. This, however, is Schelling's weak side; he lives among intuitive perceptions; he does not feel at home on the cold heights of logic; he likes to slip over into the flowery valleys of symbolism, and his philosophical strength lies in the art of synthesis. But this is an intellectual aptitude found as frequently among second-rate poets as among the best philosophers.

From this last indication it becomes clear that Mr. Schelling, in that part of philosophy which is purely transcendental idealism, remained, and had to remain, only a parrot of Fichte, but that in the philosophy of nature, where he had to do with flowers and stars, he could not help but blossom and shine brilliantly. Not only he himself, but also like-minded friends, pursued this direction by preference, and the tumult that accompanied it was, so to speak, only the reaction of poetasters against the former abstract philosophy of the intellect. Like schoolboys set free after groaning all day in classrooms under the burden of memorizing vocabulary and doing arithmetic, Mr. Schelling's pupils stormed out into nature, into the fragrant, sunny world of the real, shouting with joy, turning somersaults, and making a tremendous uproar.

The expression "Mr. Schelling's pupils" must not be taken in its usual sense. Mr. Schelling himself said he had intended to found a school only after the fashion of the ancient poets, a school of poets in which no one is bound to a specific doctrine nor by a specific discipline, but one in which each member obeys the spirit and reveals it in his own way. He might also have said that he was founding a school of prophets in which the inspired begin to prophesy according to their own desire and fancy and in whatever tongue they pleased. This, in fact, was actually done by the disciples whom the master's spirit had moved, the most shallow-brained began to prophesy, each in a different tongue, and a great day of Pentecost in philosophy ensued.

We see here in the case of philosophy how the most

significant and sublime things can be used for pure masquerade and tomfoolery and how a rabble of cowardly knaves and melancholy clowns is capable of compromising a great idea. But this philosophy really does not deserve the ridicule brought upon it by Schelling's school of pupils or school of poets. For the fundamental idea of nature philosophy is indeed basically nothing but the idea of Spinoza, pantheism.

Spinoza's doctrine and nature philosophy, as set forth by Schelling during his better period, are essentially one and the same. After scornfully rejecting Locke's materialism and carrying Leibnitz' idealism to extremes and then finding it equally unfruitful, the Germans finally arrived at the third son of Descartes, Spinoza. Philosophy had once more completed a great circle, the same, it may be said, that it had already traversed in Greece two thousand years before. But a closer comparison of these two circles reveals an essential difference. The Greeks had just as daring sceptics as do we; the Eleatics denied the reality of the external world just as positively as our modern transcendental idealists. Plato rediscovered the world of thought in the world of phenomena just as did Mr. Schelling. But we have an advantage over the Greeks as well as over the Cartesian schools, namely, that we began our philosophical orbit with an investigation of the sources of human knowledge, with our Immanuel Kant's *Critique of Pure Reason*.

On mentioning Kant I might add to the above observations that the proof for the existence of God which Kant allowed to stand, namely, the so-called moral proof, was overthrown with great éclat by Mr. Schelling. I have already remarked, however, that this proof was not very sound and that Kant had perhaps let it stand just from sheer good nature. Mr. Schelling's God is the God-universe of Spinoza—at any rate, this is what he was in 1801, in the second volume of the *Journal of Speculative*

Physics. Here God is the absolute identity of nature and thought, of matter and mind, and this absolute identity is not the cause of the universe, but is the universe itself, consequently the God-universe. In it there exist neither opposites nor divisions. Absolute identity is also absolute totality. A year later Mr. Schelling developed his God still further in a work entitled *Bruno, or Concerning the Divine or Natural Principle of Things.* This title recalls the noblest martyr of our doctrine, Giordano Bruno of Nola,[150] of glorious memory. The Italians maintain that Mr. Schelling borrowed his best ideas from old Bruno and accuse him of plagiarism. They are wrong, for there is no such thing as plagiarism in philosophy. In 1804 Mr. Schelling's God appeared at last in his complete form in a work called *Philosophy and Religion.* Here we find the doctrine of the absolute in its entirety, expressed in three formulas. The first is the categorical: The absolute is neither the ideal nor the real (neither mind nor matter), but is the identity of both. The second formula is the hypothetical: When a subject and an object are present, the absolute is the essential equality of both. The third formula is the disjunctive: There is only *one* being, but this unity of being can be regarded, at one and the same time, or alternately, as wholly ideal or as wholly real. The first formula is strictly negative, the second posits a condition even more difficult to understand than the hypothesis itself, and the third formula is exactly the same as Spinoza's: Absolute substance is cognizable either as thought or as spatial dimension. On the path of philosophy, therefore, Mr. Schelling could go no further than Spinoza, since the absolute can be comprehended only under the form of these two attributes, thought and spatial dimension. But at this point Mr. Schelling abandons

150. Bruno (1548–1600) believed in a kind of pantheism, in opposition to the Catholic Church. He was imprisoned as a heretic for several years and was finally burned at the stake.

the philosophical route and seeks by a kind of mystical intuition to arrive at the contemplation of the absolute itself; he seeks to contemplate it in its very center, in its essence, where it is neither ideal nor real, neither thought nor spatial dimension, neither subject nor object, neither mind nor matter, but—Heaven knows what!

Here philosophy stops with Schelling, and poetry—I mean folly—begins. But it is here that he finds the greatest support from a lot of scatterbrains whom it suits admirably to abandon calm reflection and to imitate, as it were, those dancing dervishes who, as our friend Jules David tells,[151] spin around in a circle until both objective and subjective worlds vanish and the two worlds blend into a colorless nothing that is neither real nor ideal, until they see things that are invisible, hear what is inaudible, until they hear colors and see tones, until the absolute reveals itself to them.

It is my opinion that with the attempt to perceive the absolute intellectually Mr. Schelling's philosophical career came to a close. A greater thinker now appeared who developed nature philosophy into a complete system, explained from its synthetic basis the whole world of phenomena, supplemented the great ideas of his predecessors by greater ones, subjected these ideas to all disciplines, and thus established them on a scientific basis. He was a pupil of Mr. Schelling's, but a pupil who gradually seized possession of all his master's influence in the realm of philosophy, and, eager for power, outstripped him, and finally thrust him into obscurity. This is the great Hegel, the greatest philosopher Germany has produced since Leibnitz. There is no doubt that he far surpasses Kant and Fichte. He is as penetrating as the former and as forceful as the latter, and possesses in

151. Probably Félicien César David, composer and Saint-Simonist, who lived in the Orient in 1833–34.

addition a fundamental tranquility of mind, a harmony of thought, not to be found in Kant and Fichte, in both of whom a revolutionary spirit prevails. To compare this man with Mr. Joseph Schelling is simply impossible, for Hegel was a man of character. And though, like Schelling, he bestowed on the existing order in state and church some all too dubious vindications, he did so for a state which, in theory at least, does homage to the principle of progress, and for a church which regards the principle of free inquiry as its vital element. And he made no secret of this; he openly admitted all his intentions. Mr. Schelling, on the other hand, goes cringing about in the antechambers of practical and theoretical absolutism, and he lends a hand in the Jesuits' den, where fetters for the mind are forged; and all the while he wants to fool us into believing that he is still unalterably the same man of enlightenment he once was; he disavows his disavowal, and to the disgrace of apostasy he adds the cowardice of lying!

We must not conceal, either out of loyalty or prudence, and we do not wish to keep it a secret, that the man who proclaimed the religion of pantheism most daringly in Germany, who announced most loudly the sanctification of nature and the reinstatement of man in his God-given rights—this man has become apostate to his own doctrine; he has forsaken the altar which he himself consecrated; he has slunk back into the religious kennels of the past; he is now a good Catholic and preaches an extramundane, personal God "who committed the folly of creating the world." Let the orthodox ring their bells and sing *Kyrie eleison* over such a conversion—it still is no proof for their opinion; it proves only that man inclines toward Catholicism when he grows old and weary, when he has lost his physical and intellectual powers, when he can no longer either enjoy or reason. So many freethinkers have been converted on their deathbeds—but just don't boast about it. Such tales of conversion belong at best to pathology and would provide only poor testimony for your cause. After all, they prove only that it was impossible for you to convert those freethinkers as long as they were walking about with healthy senses under God's open heavens and were in complete possession of their reasoning faculty.

I believe it is Ballanche[152] who said it was a law of nature that initiators had to die as soon as they had completed the task of initiation. Alas, worthy Ballanche, this is only partly true, and I would prefer to maintain that when the task of initiation has been completed, the initiator dies—or becomes apostate. And so we can perhaps soften somewhat the severe judgment which thoughtful Germans pronounced on Mr. Schelling; we can perhaps transform into silent commiseration the grave and onerous contempt that is his burden and explain his desertion of his own doctrine merely as a consequence of the natural law that he who has devoted all his powers to the expression or the execution of an idea afterward collapses exhausted when he has expressed or executed this idea, collapses either into the arms of death or into the arms of his former opponents.

After such an explanation we understand perhaps even more lurid phenomena of today which grieve us so profoundly. We understand perhaps why men who have sacrificed everything for their opinion, who have fought and suffered for it, finally, when it has won the victory, abandon that opinion and go over to the enemy camp. After such an explanation I might also point out that not only Mr. Joseph Schelling, but, to a certain extent, also Fichte and Kant, can be accused of desertion. Fichte died early enough, before his desertion of his own philosophy

152. Pierre Simon Ballanche (1776–1847), a philosopher of history who tended toward a mystical type of socialism.

could become all too notorious. And Kant immediately became unfaithful to the *Critique of Pure Reason* by writing the *Critique of Practical Reason.* The initiator dies—or becomes apostate.

I don't know why this last sentence has such a depressingly paralyzing effect on my feelings that I am simply unable to communicate here the remaining bitter truths about Mr. Schelling as he is today. Instead let us praise that earlier Schelling, whose memory blooms unforgettably in the annals of German thought, for the earlier Schelling, like Kant and Fichte, represents one of the great phases of our philosophical revolution, which I have compared in these pages with the phases of the political revolution in France. Indeed, if one sees in Kant the terrorist Convention and in Fichte the Napoleonic Empire, in Mr. Schelling one sees the reaction of the Restoration which followed. But at first it was a restoration in the better sense. Mr. Schelling reinstated nature in its legitimate rights; he strove for a reconciliation between mind and nature; he tried to reunite them in the eternal world-soul. He restored that great nature philosophy which we find in the ancient Greek philosophers, which was first directed by Socrates more toward the human spirit itself, and which later blended with idealism. He restored that great nature philosophy which, sprouting up unobtrusively from the old pantheistic religion of the Germans, produced its fairest flowers during the age of Paracelsus, but was stifled by the introduction of Cartesianism. And, alas, he ended by restoring things which make it possible to compare him with the French Restoration in the bad sense. But then rational public opinion could no longer endure him, he was ignominiously driven from the throne of thought. Hegel, his major-domo, seized his crown and shaved his head, and since then the deposed Schelling has been living like a wretched monk in Munich, a city that shows even in its

name its monkish character, and in Latin is called *mona-
cho monachorum.*[153] I saw him there with his large, pale
eyes and his dejected, stupefied face, wandering about
irresolutely like a ghost, a pitiable picture of fallen gran-
deur. Hegel, however, had himself crowned in Berlin,
unfortunately also anointed a little, and has ever since
ruled supreme over German philosophy.

Our philosophical revolution is over. Hegel closed its
great circle. Since then there has been only development
and perfection of the doctrine of nature philosophy. As
I have already said, this philosophy has penetrated into
all branches of knowledge and has produced the most
extraordinary and grandiose results. As I have also in-
dicated, many undesirable effects inevitably appeared.
The effects are so numerous that a whole book would be
needed even to enumerate them. This is the really inter-
esting and colorful part of our philosophical history. I
am convinced, however, that it will be more beneficial for
the French to learn nothing at all about this part, for such
information could only contribute greater confusion in
French minds; many propositions of nature philosophy,
taken out of context, could cause considerable trouble
among you. So much I know—if you had been familiar
with German nature philosophy four years ago, you
could never have carried out the July Revolution. For
this act a concentration of ideas and of forces was neces-
sary, a high-minded partiality, a complacent reckless-
ness, such as only your old school of philosophy per-
mitted. Preposterous philosophical ideas with which, in
case of need, legitimacy and the Catholic doctrine of
incarnation could be justified, would have dampened
your enthusiasm and paralyzed your courage. Hence
I regard it as significant for world history that your great

153. "Munich of the monks." The German *München* is related to *der Mönch*
(monk) and to an old parallel form *der Münch,* and all these words are derived
from the Latin word for monk, *monachus.*

eclectic,[154] who at that time wanted to teach you German philosophy, did not have the slightest understanding of it. His providential ignorance was salutary for France and for all mankind.

Alas, nature philosophy, which in many areas of knowledge, especially in the natural sciences, in the strict sense, produced the most glorious fruits, in other areas brought forth the most pernicious weeds. While Oken,[155] a very brilliant thinker and one of Germany's greatest citizens, was discovering his new worlds of ideas and inspiring the youth of Germany with enthusiasm for the natural rights of man, for liberty and equality,—alas, at that very time Adam Müller[156] was lecturing on the stable-feeding[157] of nations according to the principles of nature philosophy; at that very time Mr. Görres[158] was preaching the obscurantism of the Middle Ages from the point of view of the natural sciences, maintaining that the state was only a tree and had to have in its organic structure a trunk, branches and leaves as well, all of which could be found so nicely in the corporate hierarchy of the Middle Ages; at that very time Mr. Steffens[159] was proclaiming the law of philosophy according to which the peasantry is distinguished from the nobility by the fact that the peasant is destined by nature to work without enjoying, whereas the nobleman is entitled to enjoy with-

154. Victor Cousin. See above, p. 211, note 141.

155. Lorenz Oken (1779–1851), a nature philosopher, professor in Jena from 1807 on, for many years the editor of *Isis*, a liberal journal primarily devoted to the natural sciences.

156. A writer with a decidedly reactionary tendency (1779–1829). He presented the first extensive application of Romantic ideas to concrete political problems.

157. A note in the edition of Heine's works edited by Oskar Walzel (vol. VII, 498) suggests that Heine uses this unusual expression as an allusion to Müller's *Letters on Agronomy (Agronomische Briefe)*.

158. See above, p. 152, note 55.

159. Henrich Steffens (1773–1845), born in Norway, a professor in Halle, Breslau, and Berlin, a disciple of Schelling's, conservative in his views.

out working;—indeed, as I am told, a few months ago a dolt of a country squire in Westphalia, a fool by the name of Haxthausen, I believe, published a pamphlet in which he asked the Government of the King of Prussia to pay some attention to the consistent parallelism demonstrated by philosophy as existing in the organization of the world and to differentiate more strictly among the political estates; for just as there are in nature four elements, fire, air, water, and earth, so there are in society four analogous elements, namely, the nobility, the clergy, the middle class, and the peasants.

When such grievous follies were seen to sprout from philosophy and to grow into the most noxious flowers; when it was observed especially that German young people, absorbed in metaphysical abstractions, were oblivious to the most urgent questions of the time and became unfit for practical life, then indeed patriots and friends of liberty naturally felt a righteous indignation at philosophy, and some went so far as to condemn it completely as an idle and useless tilting at windmills.

We shall not be so foolish as to refute these malcontents seriously. German philosophy is an important matter which concerns the whole human race, and only our latest descendants will be able to decide whether we should be blamed or praised for first developing our philosophy and afterward our revolution. In my opinion, a methodical people like us had to begin with the Reformation, only after that could it occupy itself with philosophy, and only after completion of the latter could it go on to political revolution. I find this sequence very rational. The heads that philosophy used for speculation can be cut off afterward by the revolution for any purpose it likes. But philosophy could never have used the heads cut off by a preceding revolution. Don't be uneasy, though, you German Republicans; the German revolution will not turn out to be any milder or gentler because it was preceded by Kant's *Critique,* Fichte's transcendental idealism, or even nature philosophy. Because of these doctrines revolutionary forces have developed that are only waiting for the day when they can break out and fill the world with terror and with admiration. Kantians will appear who have no more use for piety in the physical world than in the world of ideas, who with sword and axe will mercilessly rummage around in the soil of our European culture in order to eradicate the last roots of the past. Armed Fichteans will enter on the scene who, in their fanaticism of will, can be restrained neither by fear nor by self-interest, for they live in the spirit and defy matter like the first Christians, who likewise could be subdued neither by bodily torture nor by bodily delights. In fact, in a time of social revolution such transcendental idealists would be even more obstinate than the early Christians, since the latter endured earthly martyrdom in order to attain salvation in heaven, while the transcendental idealist regards martyrdom itself as a vain show and is inaccessible within the entrenchment of his own thought. But nature philosophers would be more terrifying than anyone else, since they would actively take part in a German revolution and would identify themselves with the work of destruction. If the hand of the Kantian strikes a strong, unerring blow because his heart is not moved by any traditional reverence, if the Fichtean courageously defies every danger because for him danger simply doesn't exist in reality,—the nature philosopher will be terrible because he allies himself with the primitive powers of nature, can conjure up the demonic forces of ancient German pantheism, and there awakens in him that lust for battle which we find among the ancient Germans and which fights not in order to destroy, nor in order to win, but simply in order to fight. Christianity—and this is its finest merit—subdued to a certain extent that brutal Germanic lust for battle, but could not

destroy it, and if some day that restraining talisman, the
Cross, falls to pieces, then the savagery of the old warri-
ors will explode again, the mad berserker rage about
which the Nordic poets have told so much. This talisman
is decaying, and the day will come when it will sorrily
disintegrate. The old stone gods will then arise from the
forgotten ruins and wipe the dust of centuries from their
eyes, and Thor will at last leap up with his giant hammer
and smash the Gothic cathedrals. When you hear the
crash and the clashing of arms, watch out, you neighbor
children, you French, and don't meddle in what we are
doing at home in Germany. It might cost you dearly.
Take care not to fan the fire; take care not to put it out.
You could easily burn your fingers in the flames. Don't
smile at my advice, the advice of a dreamer who warns
you against Kantians, Fichteans, and nature philoso-
phers. Don't smile at the visionary who expects in the
realm of reality the same revolution that has taken place
in the realm of the intellect. The thought precedes the
deed as lightning precedes thunder. German thunder is
of course truly German; it is not very nimble but rumbles
along rather slowly. It will come, though, and if some day
you hear a crash such as has never been heard before in
world history, you will know the German thunder has
finally reached its mark. At this commotion the eagles
will drop down dead from the skies, and the lions in the
farthest desert of Africa will put their tails between their
legs and hide themselves in their royal lairs. A play will
be performed in Germany compared with which the
French Revolution might seem merely an innocent idyll.
Just now, to be sure, everything is rather quiet, and
though here and there a few people create a little stir,
don't think they are going to appear as the real actors in
the piece. They are only the little curs running around
in the empty arena, barking and snapping at each other,
until the hour arrives when the troop of gladiators ap-

pear who are destined to fight in the struggle for life or death.

And the hour will come. As on the steps of an amphitheater, the nations will gather around Germany to witness the great contests. I advise you, you French, keep very quiet, and for Heaven's sake, *don't* applaud. We might easily misunderstand you and, in our rude fashion, might somewhat roughly shut you up. If in times past, in our servile, discontented state, we could sometimes overpower you, we could do so far more easily in the elation of our intoxication with liberty. You know yourselves what one is capable of in such a state—and you are no longer in that state. Beware then. I have your welfare at heart, and for this reason I tell you the bitter truth. You have more to fear from a free Germany than from the entire Holy Alliance together with all its Croats and Cossacks. For, in the first place, you are not loved in Germany, a thing which is almost incomprehensible, since you are really so kind, and during your stay among us took such pains to please at least the better and more beautiful half of the German people. And even if this half loved you, it is just the half that does not bear arms and whose friendship is thus of little benefit to you. What you are actually accused of I could never understand. Once in a beer parlor in Göttingen a young German chauvinist[160] remarked that we ought to take revenge on the French for Konradin von Staufen whom they beheaded in Naples. You have probably forgotten that long since. But we forget nothing. So you see that if some day we take a notion to pick a quarrel with you, we won't lack for valid reasons. In any case, I advise you to be on your guard. Whatever happens in Germany, whether the Crown Prince of Prussia or Dr. Wirth[161] should come to

160. *Ein junger Altdeutscher.*

161. Johann Wirth, editor of the *Deutsche Tribüne,* a liberal journal, and active in political affairs.

power, keep yourselves armed; stay quietly at your posts, guns in your hands. I have your welfare at heart, and I was almost frightened when I heard recently that your Ministry intended to disarm France.

Since, despite your present romantic movement, you are born classicists, you are familiar with Olympus. Among the nude gods and goddesses amusing themselves while feasting on nectar and ambrosia, you may see one goddess who, though surrounded by such gaiety and pastime, nonetheless always wears a coat of mail, a helmet on her head, and keeps her spear in her hand. She is the goddess of wisdom.

PART IV

Selected Poems

Selected Poems

A spruce is standing lonely
in the North on a barren height.
He drowses; ice and snowflakes
wrap him in a blanket of white.

He dreams about a palm tree
in a distant, eastern land,
that languishes lonely and silent
upon the scorching sand.

A young lad loves a maiden,
she likes another one;
that other marries another
whose heart and hand he won.

The maiden weds in anger
the first man she can snare
who comes across her pathway.
The lad is in despair.

It is an old, old story,
yet new with every start,
and every time it happens
it breaks a loving heart.

They made me painfully suffer,
they hurt me, early and late,
some did it with their loving
and others with their hate.

In my glass they poured their poison,
they poisoned the bread on my plate,
some did it with their loving
and others with their hate.

But she who caused most suffering,
torture, and misery,
she spoke no word of hatred,
no word of love, to me.

They sat and sipped from their teacups,
and love they discussed, without end.
The men had esthetical hiccups,
the ladies had sentiment.

"Ah, love has to be platonic,"
says the councillor, gaunt and dry.
The smile of his wife is ironic,
and yet she sighs, "Oh my!"

The canon gives this allocution,
"Love must not be rough, you know,
it may harm your constitution."
The maiden lisps, "How so?"

The countess says sentiment'lly,
"Great love is sheer ecstasy!"
And to the baron, gently,
she hands a cup of tea.

One empty chair at the table
was waiting for you, my dove.
My precious, you would have been able
to tell them about your love.

A star is softly falling
from glittering space up high.
This is the shining love star
that's falling from the sky.

The apple leaves and blossoms
are falling from the stem;
the playful winds are blowing
and having sport with them.

The swan sings on the water,
floats up and down the wave,
and singing ever softer
dives to his watery grave.

All is so dark and quiet—
the leaves and blossoms gone,
the star has burst asunder,
and silent is the swan.

My heart, my heart is saddened,
but May glows joyously,
I lean at the high old bastion
against a linden tree.

Below me the blue waters
flow gently in the moat.
A boy is fishing and whistling,
leisurely rowing his boat.

And colorful in the distance,
friendly and small, one sees
cottages, gardens, and people,
and oxen, and meadows, and trees.

In the grass some maids bleach laundry
joyful and frolicsome.
The mill wheel sprays clear diamonds,
I hear its distant hum.

There's a sentry box by the tower
that's gray and of old renown;
a lad with a scarlet tunic
is pacing up and down.

He's playing with his rifle,
it shines in the sun so red,
he shoulders and presents it—
I wish he would shoot me dead.

You fair maid on the ocean,
turn your fishing boat to land;
come hither, sit beside me,
and let me hold your hand.

Don't be afraid to trust me
and lean your head on me,
as every day you have been
trusting the stormy sea.

My heart is like the ocean,
with storms and time and tide,
where many a pearl within it
lies buried, deep inside.

It happens every morning
when past your house I stroll:
To see you at the window,
my darling, cheers my soul.

Your dark brown eyes observe me
as up and down they scan:
"Who are you and what ails you,
you strange and suffering man?"

"I am a German poet,
well-known where Germans dwell.
When the best of names are mentioned,
they mention mine as well.

"What ails me, little maiden,
ails many where Germans dwell.
When the worst of pains are mentioned,
they mention mine as well."

Heart, my heart, do not be shaken,
bear what fate has placed on you.
Spring comes back and will renew
what the winter may have taken.

There is so much to admire,
so much left for you on earth!
Love, my heart, what you find worth,
everything that you desire.

Summer twilight, dim and tender,
lies upon the woods and meadows;
comfortingly in the evening
shines the moon in golden splendor.

At the freshet chirps a cricket,
and a stirring breaks the silence,
and a wanderer hears a splashing
and some breathing near the thicket.

In the brook, among the boulders,
all alone, a nymph is bathing;
Lovely in the paling moonlight
shine her snowy arms and shoulders.

Summer Twilight

On the pale ocean beach
I sat with troubled thoughts, and lonely.
The sun sank lower and threw
flame-red bands upon the water,
and the white, wide waves,
pushed by the tide,
foamed and rushed closer and closer—
a strange sound, a whispering and whistling,
a laughing and murmuring, a sighing and swishing,
and, with it all, a mysterious singsong lullaby.
I thought I was hearing long-forgotten legends,
ancient, lovely fairy tales
that once, as a boy,
I had heard from neighbor children
when, on a summer's evening,

we squatted down to quiet story-telling
on the stone steps before the front door,
with little listening hearts
and alert, curious eyes,
while the bigger girls
sat next to the fragrant flower pots
at windows across the street,
faces like roses,
smiling, and lit by the moon.

Epilogue

Like stalks of wheat in country fields,
human thoughts grow and sway
in our minds.
But the tender thoughts of love
are like happy red and blue flowers
that bloom in between.

Red and blue flowers!
The surly reaper discards you as useless,
knotty flails crush you scornfully;
even the penniless wanderer,
who is pleased and refreshed by your sight,
shakes his head
and calls you pretty weeds.
But the country maiden,
making her wreaths,
admires and picks you,
and adorns her pretty locks with you,

and thus decked out hurries to the dance,
where flutes and violins sound delightful,
or to the quiet beech tree
where the voice of her sweetheart sounds still more
  delightful
than flutes and violins.

There was an agèd monarch,
sad was his heart, gray was his hair.
The poor old monarch married
a woman young and fair.

There was a handsome page boy,
blond was his hair, bright was his mien.
The silken train he carried
behind the youthful queen.

You know the ancient story,
so sweet, so painful to relate.
They had to die together,
their love was much too great.

The lady by the ocean
sighed long and woebegone.
She felt such deep emotion
about the setting sun.

Young lady, stop your fretting,
it's still the same old tack.
Up front the sun is setting
but it rises from the back.

Above the sea, on the ancient rock,
I sit, my daydreams roaming.
Winds howl like mad, the seagulls mock,
the waves are flowing and foaming.

My heart loved many a splendid lad
and maidens young and glowing.
Where are they now? Winds howl like mad,
the waves are foaming and flowing.

Adam the First

You sent to me, with flaming sword,
your guard from the heavenly city,
and chased me out of Paradise
neither with right nor pity.

I'll take my wife and we'll move on,
to other lands be ranging;
but that I ate from the wisdom tree
is now beyond your changing.

You cannot change my knowing of
your pettiness and blunders,
no matter how you try to bluff
us men by death and thunders.

O God! How pitiful is this
decision of ejection!
How worthy of heaven's governor!
How brilliant his perfection!

Your Garden of Eden, your Paradise,
I'll never miss a minute;
that was no real paradise,
with a tree forbidden in it.

I ask full freedom as my right,
for freedom's banner has risen!
The slightest limitation would turn
your Eden to hell and to prison.

The Asra

Daily came the very lovely
sultan's daughter promenading
in the evening by the fountain
where the sparkling water splashes.

Daily the young slave stood waiting
in the evening by the fountain
where the sparkling water splashes;
daily he grew pale and paler.

Then, one evening, the young princess
came to him with rapid questions,
"Tell me by what name they call you,
what's your country, who your kinsmen?"

And the slave replied, "My name is
Mohamet, I come from Yemen,
and my kinsmen are the Asra
who when seized by love must perish."

Which Way Now?

Which way now? My stupid foot
steers me toward Germany;
but my reason shakes its head,
wisely seems to say to me:

True, the war has ended now,
but the war tribunals stay,
and you wrote some lines for which
you could be lined up, they say.

It would be discomforting,
to be sure, if I were shot.
I have no dramatic skill,
and a hero I am not.

I might go to England, but
coal fumes make the air too thick;
and the English—just their smell
gives me cramps and makes me sick.

There are times I'd like to think
that America's for me
(freedom's stable filled with herds
seeking mob equality),

but I'm fearful of a land
where tobacco leaves they chew,
where they bowl without a king,
where without spittoon they spew.

For a pleasant land to live,
Russia may be the way out.
But I know in wintertime
I could not endure the knout.

Gloomily I lift my eyes—
stars galore are greeting me,
many thousands fill the skies
but my own star I can't see.

In that golden labyrinth
it perhaps has gone astray,
just as in the turmoil here
on this earth I've lost my way.

Burned Out

And once you die, you will stay dead
for quite a while, I am afraid.
Yes, I'm afraid the resurrecting
won't be as fast as you're expecting.

Once more, before my life has passed,
before my heart has beat its last—
once more I'd like to be befriended
in love before my days are ended.

A blonde is what I most desire,
with eyes like moonlight's paling fire.
Brunettes, with their vitality,
at my age don't agree with me.

The young ones, vigorously alive,
are full of passion and of drive,
there is much raving, fuss, and bother,
and constant torturing of each other.

Not young, my health no longer prime,
the way I'm feeling at this time,
I'd like once more the happy notion
of being loved—without commotion.

Course of the World

If a man's already rich,
more and more he will amass.
Who has little, will be robbed
of the little that he has.

If you don't have anything,
better dig yourself a ditch—
for the right to live, you scum,
is restricted to the rich.

Memorial Day

No high mass will they be chanting,
and no *kaddish** will they say.
Nothing will be said nor chanted
on my own memorial day.

*Jewish prayer for the dead.

But perhaps on such a morning,
if the air is fresh and clean,
there may stroll on the Montmartre
my Mathilde with Pauline.*

With a wreath of everlastings
she will come, my grave adorning,
sighing softly, "Poor old fellow,"
moist her eye in tearful mourning.

My new home is much too high now;
I can't offer to my dearie
so much as a chair to sit on.
Oh, she sways, her feet are weary.

Walking home, my dear plump darling,
would be much too aggravating.
Look, outside the cemetery,
by the gate, some cabs are waiting.

*Companion to Heine's wife, Mathilde.

Dame Care

When fortune's sunshine fell on me,
the swarm of gnats danced happily.
My dear old friends were good and true
and shared with me, as brothers do,
my best roast, at their pleasure,
the last sou of my treasure.

The fortune gone, the pantry bare,
I have no friends now anywhere;
the sun has set upon my day,
the swarm of gnats has flown away.
With my good fortune banished,
all friends, all gnats have vanished.

Each wintry night, next to my lair,
there sits a watchful nurse: Dame Care.
She wears a blouse of some white stuff,
a black chapeau, and uses snuff.
The snuff box creaks so eerily,
the old girl nods so drearily.

I dream I am recovering
my fortune and my youthful spring;
my friends, the swarm of gnats, are back,
the snuff box creaks—and then, alack!
the bubble pops and goes,
the old girl blows her nose.

Talking! Talking! And no actions!
Never, dear, a steak to eat,
steady diet of abstractions,
soups need dumplings, you need meat.

But perhaps the manly fire
ready daily to pursue
on the white horse of desire,
may not quite agree with you.

Oh, I almost fear such racing
of wild love, my gentle friend,
Cupid's furious steeplechasing,
may exhaust you in the end.

Healthier for you might be
one who's ailing—favor him
as a lover who, like me,
can but barely raise a limb.

Thus, I say, to our affair
of the heart devote your love;
it's your health for which I care,
love me for your health, my dove.

Miserere

I do not envy lucky men
the happy lives they spend;
I only envy them their death,
their quick and painless end.

In splendor, laurels on their heads,
with mirth and spirits blithe,
they sit with joy at the banquet of life—
'til suddenly falls the scythe.

In festive clothes, with roses decked,
these favored sons of fate
arrive, the fragment blooms still fresh,
at Hades' shadowy gate.

No sickness has disfigured them,
their death mask is serene,
and at her court they're welcomed by
Proserpina, the queen.

Oh, how I envy them their fate!
For seven years I lie
and toss in painful agony
in bed, and cannot die.

O God, cut short my agony,
my grave waits, let me go;
for martyrdom I do not have
much talent, as you know.

Your inconsistency, O Lord,
astounds me, I confess:
you made the merriest poet, and now
destroy his joyfulness.

My pain benumbs my happiness,
and sadness holds me fast.
I may, if this sad joke goes on,
turn Catholic at the last.

Then I shall cry into your ears,
as Christians all insist.
O *miserere!* Here we lose
the greatest humorist.

Oh, forget those holy fables,
sanctimonious allegories—
try to answer those damned questions
without telling silly stories.

Why must just men bear the crosses,
stumbling wretchedly and bleeding,
while the bad man, high on horseback,
is victoriously succeeding?

Why so? Could the reason be that
God Almighty has restrictions?
Or that He Himself does mischief?
Ah, what sordid contradictions!

These are our eternal questions
till they stuff, when we lie pallid,
earth clods down our mouths by handfuls—
do you think such answer valid?

I am not lured by Eden's fields,
the promised land in Paradise.
No fairer women there than those
on whom on earth I laid my eyes.

No angel with the finest wings
could substitute there for my wife.
Sitting on clouds and singing psalms
is not my dream of afterlife.

O Lord! I think it would be best
to leave me here on earth to stay.
Just cure my ailing body first
and then provide some money, pray!

I know the earth is full of sin
and vice; but I, in many years,
got used to walking up and down
the pavement in this vale of tears.

The earthly bustle I don't mind
because I rarely leave the house.
In slippers and in dressing gown
I stay home, happy with my spouse.

Leave me with her. My soul imbibes
the music of her voice. I do
delight when she is chattering.
Her look is loyal and so true.

Just better health and some more cash
I ask of you, O Lord. Bestow
more happy days of bliss on me
beside my wife *in statu quo*.

Morphine

Great is the semblance of those two exquisite
figures of youths, although the one appears
much paler than the other, and more serious.
I'm almost tempted to describe as nobler
the first one than the other one who kindly
took me into his arms; how gently mild
his smile was then—his look, how full of bliss!
Then it could happen that the wreath of poppies
he wore upon his head would touch my forehead
and with its magic scent chase all the pain
out of my soul. However, such relief
would last but short a time; complete recovery
will not be mine before the second brother,
so serious and pale, shall lower his torch.
How good it is to sleep, but death is better—
the best of all is never to be born.

Epilogue

Glory warms our grave, they say.
This is foolish, stupid! Nay!
A much better warmth there is
in a cow maid's loving kiss,
when delivered, fresh and young,
by two lips that smell of dung.
Warmth is also better when
mulled wine fills the guts of men
or when, to their heart's desire,
punch and grog set them afire
in some lowly drinking dive
where the thieves and villains thrive,
each of whom escaped the gallows,
yet he lives, draws breath, and swallows,
to be envied, everyone,
more than Thetis' famous son.
Here's the word Achilles gave:
"Living as the poorest slave
in the upper world counts more
than along the Stygian shore
being one of the shadows' kings
about whom old Homer sings."

About the Editor and Translators

HELEN M. MUSTARD is Professor Emeritus of German at Columbia University in New York. She is author of *The Lyric Cycle in German Literature*, co-translator (with Charles E. Passage) of *Parzival* by Wolfram von Eschenbach (Vintage Books), and translator of *The Nibelungenlied* in the Modern Library edition of *Medieval Epics*. She lives in Roxbury, Connecticut.

MAX KNIGHT and JOSEPH FABRY, a team of Viennese-born editors and writers at the University of California in Berkeley, have translated Christian Morgenstern, Johann Nestroy, and Bertolt Brecht; Knight has also published a mountain book, *Return to the Alps*, and Fabry a book on logotherapy, *The Pursuit of Meaning*.